It is as if, from moment to moment, he withdrew and retired, swifter than lightning, known in one mode and another mode and always new. The new life might still be sequential (in the order of time) but every instant was united to the Origin, and complete and absolute in itself. “Behold I come quickly” — the coming and the going one. The going and the coming one, and all is joy.

Charles Williams, *The Descent of the Dove*

Jesus and His Own

A Commentary on John 13–17

Daniel B. Stevick

William B. Eerdmans Publishing Company
Grand Rapids, Michigan / Cambridge, U.K.

Published 2011 by
Wm. B. Eerdmans Publishing Co.
2140 Oak Industrial Drive N.E., Grand Rapids, Michigan 49505 /
P.O. Box 163, Cambridge CB3 9PU U.K.

Printed in the United States of America

17 16 15 14 13 12 11 7 6 5 4 3 2 1

Library of Congress Cataloging-in-Publication Data

Stevick, Daniel B.
Jesus and his own: a commentary on John 13-17 / Daniel B. Stevick.
p. cm.
Includes index.
ISBN 978-0-8028-4865-9 (pbk.: alk. paper)
1. Bible. N.T. John XIII–XVII — Commentaries. I. Title.

BS2615.53.S74 2011
226.5′07 — dc22

2010045208

www.eerdmans.com

To my parents

Harlie George Stevick, 1892-1987

and

Lois Daniels Stevick, 1893-1985

who knew and loved the Bible

Contents

Preface

This study offers a close reading of the five chapters of the Fourth Gospel in which Jesus tells his disciples that he will soon leave them. He seeks to prepare them for the changed situation that will prevail when he is gone. These chapters have a distinctive tone, and they show characteristic traits of thought and style. They comprise a central, identifiable unit in the johannine presentation of Jesus and his people.

A number of book-length works on Jesus' Farewell were published in the late nineteenth and early twentieth centuries. The passage attracted interpreters, and they wrote on it, often eloquently. But these older works (as far as I am aware of them) were innocent of biblical criticism. Chapters 13-17 of the Fourth Gospel were taken to be as spoken by Jesus and were especially valued because they gave the reader the christology of Christ himself. When one looks at these books today, it is difficult to sort out their often valuable literary and theological insights from their critical naïveté.

In more recent years, when more critical sophistication might be expected, only a few full studies have been devoted to the Farewell chapters of John. The old literature on Jesus' Farewell is virtually unusable, and a newer literature is slow in coming into being.

In this biblical material — which combines simplicity and complexity — I find three levels: A basic level is clearly the acts and words of the Jesus of the Gospel narrative — how he interacts with others, what he says about himself, his followers and his mission, about the past and the future. Yet the story of Jesus everywhere overlies the subtext of the history and the faith of the first-century church, a second level. In the Farewell, as throughout the Fourth Gospel, the story of Jesus is layered with the situation, the conflicts, the needs, and the insights of the community from which the writing emerged. As the writer of the Gospel tells what Jesus said to his disciples, he is indirectly giving counsel to his first-century Christian readers. A careful reading of the Farewell material will see it as it was written, from a dual angle of vision.

Implicit in the text, however, is a third level: the engagement between the Gospel and its present-day readers. The author writes from a "we" position (1:14) and for a "you" (20:31). As historically minded modern readers, we ask what this ancient text meant to the persons for whom it was written. However, as we undertake this descriptive inquiry, the text initiates a conversation with us in our modernity. Any exploration we may undertake of past consciousness invites a dialogue with present-day consciousness. This Gospel speaks to matters that are not locked away in a past moment. In reading the Fourth Gospel sympathetically, one is perforce engaged with its witness, its claim, and its offer.

Modern experience is shaped by intellectual currents that the first-century Evangelist could not have imagined. In a few places I have sought to build bridges between the text in its original writing/reading situation and readers who approach the text carrying the burden and enjoying the advantages of modernity. However, such bridge-building tends to be heavy-handed and I have generally tried to let the relevance of this Gospel be established by describing what I see as its presentation of itself.

If the past and the present are to speak to one another through an ancient document, they can converse especially well through its use of symbols. The symbol-system of the Fourth Gospel is independent of the other great symbol-systems of the New Testament — those of the Synoptic Gospels, of Paul, and of Hebrews. Symbols have a way of escaping from the historical situations that gave rise to them. They are bells that toll for those who think they do. In working through the text, I have sought to give attention to the writer's appeal to the imagination.

In looking now at this literary/theological reading of John 13–17 as a whole, it strikes me that I have written as much a discussion of the *communio sanctorum* as I have an examination of five chapters of the Gospel. If that is so, it is because to my mind John 13–17 form the most sustained and the richest presentation of the *communio sanctorum* that is to be found anywhere in the New Testament.

I write for readers who are prepared for serious inquiry into an important source of the common faith — general readers more than scholars. But I have sought to keep preachers especially in mind. To say so should not suggest that persons with the joys and demands of Sunday morning pressing on them will find here ready-made sermon material. Rather, I seek to share the biblical homework that precedes and informs preaching — or that would, except for the distractions that bedevil the life of every conscientious pastor.

It is intimidating to write on the Fourth Gospel today. Has any generation of the church since the rise of historical criticism been better served by commentators and commentaries? By serious articles and essays? The "John industry" produces material too rapidly for anyone but specialists to follow. The vitality of this secondary literature, old and new, witnesses at the same time both to the competence of its writers and to the inexhaustibleness and fascination of their source.

Informed scholars differ on such basic matters as the origin, the structure, and the organization of the Farewell Discourses. Just on this relatively small body of text, scores of critical and exegetical issues, large and small, can be and have been argued learnedly and responsibly. In going through the text, I simply decided many things in a way that I found satisfactory. One has to get on, and my manuscript risked growing unpublishably long and unreadably dull. I hope that readers who are familiar with the literature and the range of well-defended opinions in johannine studies, when they come upon the matters that I have decided but left undiscussed, will not think too quickly of all the things I might have written about but did not.

Following Godfrey Nicholson, I refer in this study to "the Fourth Gospel," while I freely use the adjective "johannine" (lower case). Nicholson remarks that "The only *John* in the Fourth Gospel is the Baptist."[1] Yet one needs a term to designate the style of thought of this Gospel, the literature associated with it, and the community from which it came. There being "no other adjective in current use," I, like Nicholson, write "johannine."

Although in my own text I do not use generic "man" or "anyone — he," I do quote some older writers who used gender-specific language, which they understood to be inclusive. As I quote these authors I usually have ventured to edit them. (I persuade myself that they would not disapprove.) Occasionally, however, I have let their words stand as they were written.

When speaking in my own voice, I have not used masculine pronouns for God. Yet the imagery of the Fourth Gospel (and especially of the Farewell chapters) is dominated by talk of Father and Son, and in com-

1. *Death As Departure: The Johannine Descent-Ascent Schema* (Chico: Scholars, 1983), p. 169, n. 3.

menting I have sustained in my remarks the masculine imagery and the associated pronouns that are used in the biblical text. To compensate, at least in some measure, when in chapters 6 and 7 I speak of the Holy Spirit, I have used feminine pronouns. (There are some thoughts on this subject in the essay "The Father and the Son," pp. 177-83.)

Unless otherwise indicated, Scripture quotations are from the New Revised Standard Version. However, I have altered these quotations to use feminine pronouns for the Holy Spirit.

This inquiry has occupied me at intervals for a number of years, during which time I have retired and moved away from research-depth libraries and informed colleagues. My principal collaborators have come to be a small shelf of books and articles I have been able to keep with me. I have grown to know and trust several of them like old friends. While this study has been a preoccupation, many people have given me help who did not know that they were doing so. I am grateful for all the bits of clarification, suggestion, and encouragement, direct and indirect, that I have received — from works of scholarship, from responses to inquiries, and even from fragments of chance conversations.

DANIEL B. STEVICK
Cathedral Village
Philadelphia, Pennsylvania
2011

Abbreviations

CBQ	*Catholic Biblical Quarterly*
JBL	*Journal of Biblical Literature*
KJV	King James Version
NAB	New American Bible
NEB	New English Bible
NIV	New International Version
NovT	*Novum Testamentum*
NRSV	New Revised Standard Version
NTS	*New Testament Studies*
RSV	Revised Standard Version
TEV	Today's English Version

1. Jesus' Farewell and Its Interpretation

Jesus and his disciples are at a meal preparatory to the Passover. His public claims have stirred powerful opponents in Jerusalem, and he is in danger. At this time of uncertainty, Jesus tells his followers that he will soon be leaving: *I am with you only a little longer* (13:33). As they grasp what he is saying, they are dismayed. Their association with him has lifted their lives out of ordinariness and set them within the purpose of God. His leaving will bring to an end the most rewarding relationship they have ever known. Their minds are full of questions. Where is Jesus going? What will happen to him? To them? Will they ever see him again? What will come of the events he has set in motion?

In the account in the Fourth Gospel, Jesus meets his disturbed followers with a lengthy "Farewell." Knowing that when he is gone the former mode of relation cannot be brought back, he describes a new condition which will emerge for his followers from the disappearance of the old, and he helps them to move into it. He assures them that they will find sources of divine presence and leading when they no longer have him with them.

The moment that the Evangelist depicts was critical. The Christian movement began in a particular foundational event and finally in the initiative of a single life. The passage from the specific, local historical event — the world of the itinerant Galilean rabbi and his handful of friends — to the dispersed early Christian community and its vigorous faith was a rapid but crucial transition. The meaning and potency of the Jesus event were carried into new and unanticipated conditions. As the community of believers moved from its pre-Easter situation to its radically different life in the risen Christ and the Spirit, Jesus' immediate followers were the one group which knew life before as well as after this transition. The Fourth

Gospel describes, in the form of Jesus' parting counsel, their passage from the old condition into the new.

Perhaps Jesus' words *you will seek me* (13:33) preserve a memory that for a brief time his disciples tried to hold on to the old way of relating to him. In Jesus' death and resurrection and in the new conditions that emerged, the disciples went through a process of desolating loss and confusion, then of stunning reversal of perception, access of new comprehension, and ultimately of regained meaning. For a time, the future must have seemed to hold only by a thread. This transformation in the consciousness of Jesus' followers was a significant episode in the redemptive saga.

All of the New Testament was written from the church's after-Easter vantage. It comes from the age that was inaugurated by the resurrection. But does any other part of the New Testament recognize or give as much attention as these Farewell Discourses do to the reconceiving that was required as Jesus' followers passed from their life before Easter to their life after Easter?

But a second event interacts with the johannine account of Jesus' Farewell. As the Evangelist tells what Jesus said at his final meal with his disciples, he refers indirectly to the first-century readers of his Gospel, who are believers in Jesus and who, like Jesus' disciples at the Supper, are facing painful discontinuity.

The community for which the Evangelist wrote was a group of believers whose origins and even whose location are uncertain. It had been brought into being through missionary witness. The now unknown persons who had evangelized and sustained the young community evidently represented a line of testimony to Jesus which traced to the figure who in the Fourth Gospel is known as the Beloved Disciple (see 13:23; 19:35; and 21:24 and pp. 53-55). The Community of the Beloved Disciple had its traditions (see 21:23-25; 1 John 1:1-3, 5; 2:7, 24; 3:11; 2 John passim), and "Jesus was sent by the Father" may have been its basic confession of faith (see 17:3, 8, 18, 21, 23, 25; 1 John 4:9-10). There is little evidence that this community may have had links with other first-century groups that also confessed Jesus as Messiah. Virtually nothing indicates that the Evangelist or his readers knew the Synoptic Gospels or Paul. They owed what they knew of Jesus and the faith that centered in him to first-hand witnesses (1 John 1:1-3). But evidently at the time of the writing of the Fourth Gospel, these essential testimony-bearers were passing from the scene. The believers in Jesus had made a sharp break with past social solidarities and had cast their lot with a new movement which in the judgment of outsiders had doubtful legitimacy, a short past, and an uncertain future.

For the first-century believers in Jesus, the loss of their original witnesses was traumatic. What rootage would their faith have without them? Indeed, could the community endure? What might it still claim that traced to Jesus? Could it keep its sense of divine immediacy, or would it decline into a strained, derivative recalling of past events which these Christians of the second generation had not seen? In these speeches of Farewell, the Evangelist seeks to establish these suddenly leaderless first-century Christians in the sources of their own existence as believers.

This passing of the first generation was, at the time the Evangelist began to write the Farewell material, the urgent internal question in the johannine community. The writer tells what Jesus said to his immediate followers in a way that will at the same time illuminate the situation of the newly "orphaned" believers of the late first century. The Evangelist supports the unsettled believers of his own time by means of the parting counsel by which Jesus carries his followers, despite their incomprehension, from the pre–Good Friday condition to the post-Easter condition. The Farewell Discourses subtly mingle the particularity and uniqueness of Jesus' words to his disciples at the Last Supper with the crisis facing the Evangelist's late-first-century readers. Jesus tells his followers that although his work in history is ending, he is not distant — neither in the past nor in the future — but is vitally present.

Although the Evangelist is addressing a first-century community, his presentation illuminates the experience of Christians of every age for whom Jesus is powerfully real but not physically present. Written at the unique critical moment when the Community of the Beloved Disciple was passing beyond its dependence on living eyewitnesses, these Farewell Discourses can speak to the self-understanding of the church and the Christian in every generation.

The transition from the unextendable, unrepeatable experience of Jesus' disciples into the indefinitely continued next generations involved the detachment of Jesus' followers from a known life-supporting, meaning-imparting relationship and their movement into unguessed possibilities. There were no preexisting terms by which they could name what was happening. As new events were encountered and unprecedented interior demands met, new vocabulary and new categories were forged to give shape and communicability to intense experience. Through it all, the grasp of what was coming to be was imparted, as the Fourth Evangelist saw it, through the Spirit-led self-understanding of the church. The voice of Jesus himself was present to his people, being his own interpreter.

The Farewell in the Structure of the Fourth Gospel

Jesus' Farewell occupies a strategic place in the design of the Fourth Gospel. Many commentators identify the first large unit of the Gospel (chs. 1–12, approximately one half of the work) as "The Book of Signs."[1] The title comes from the unique vocabulary of the Fourth Gospel. When the Synoptic Gospels speak of Jesus' miracles, they use the term *dynameis,* acts of power. Jesus' "mighty works" — principally of healing — were demonstrations of the inbreaking reign of God. In the Fourth Gospel, however, Jesus' miracles are referred to as "signs," *sēmeia* — a term that identifies their revelatory significance. This opening "Book of Signs" consists largely of narrative in which Jesus presents himself through actions, several of which are followed by related "discourses" — extended units of speech, often built around a central image. The discourses present Jesus as the one who comes from God, bringing an offer of light and life to those who are in darkness and death.

As Jesus' ministry opens, he calls a few men to follow him; thereafter, however, these followers are hardly more than "extras" on the scene. Throughout the Book of Signs, the disciples do little, and nothing is spoken to them privately. (By contrast, in the Synoptic Gospels, Jesus sends his followers out to extend his mission, and substantial units of teaching are directed specifically to them.)

In the opening half of the Fourth Gospel, Jesus appeals to his hearers to believe in him, and he warns of the peril of failing to do so. His signs and the claims he makes for himself provoke opposition. Although some persons do believe in him, many do not. As opposition rises, the rhetoric of the exchanges between Jesus and his opponents becomes bitterly polemical. After the raising of Lazarus (ch. 11), Jesus' public mission ends, largely in rejection. The Book of Signs closes with a lament that draws on the experience of Israel's prophets, principally Isaiah:

1. Since C. H. Dodd's landmark work, *The Interpretation of the Fourth Gospel* (Cambridge: Cambridge University Press, 1953), it has become common to speak of the first twelve chapters of the Fourth Gospel as "The Book of Signs," although some commentators express misgivings about this designation.

After Jesus had said this, he departed and hid from them.
Although he had performed so many signs in their presence,
they did not believe in him.
This was to fulfill the word spoken by the prophet Isaiah:
"Lord, who has believed our message,
and to whom has the arm of the Lord been revealed?"
And so they could not believe, because Isaiah also said,
"He has blinded their eyes
and hardened their heart."
(John 12:36b-40a, quoting Isa. 53:1 and 6:10)

The second large portion of the Fourth Gospel, comprising chapters 13–21, begins with Jesus at supper with his disciples, where he washes the feet of his friends, delivers his long "Farewell" (chs. 13–16), and concludes his mission with a lengthy prayer (ch. 17). After the meal (about which almost nothing is said) and Jesus' parting words, he and his friends leave the room. The narrative of his arrest and trial follows, leading to his crucifixion and resurrection (chs. 18–21). Some commentators refer to this second part of the Fourth Gospel as "The Book of Glory."[2] This title may seem a poor choice for the portion of the story of Jesus that centers on his crucifixion, but it derives from the vocabulary of the Fourth Gospel itself. The writer does not see Jesus' trial and death in terms of suffering and loss; rather, Jesus meets cruelty as a commanding figure; his dying is the climactic act of his mission; it is his passage to the Father, his "glorification." In the johannine view, Jesus' glory does not follow after his crucifixion and, in effect, overturn it; rather, paradoxically, his glory is exhibited in his death. "The Book of Glory" as a title for the second half of the Fourth Gospel is in keeping with the author's understanding of Jesus and his cross.

Jesus' meal with his disciples is marked by two incidents: Jesus washes his disciples' feet (13:1-20), and he dismisses Judas (13:21-30). Then, as though the departure of Judas released a flow of speech, Jesus speaks

2. Dodd called the second large portion of this Gospel "The Book of the Passion." Yet of its nine chapters, five (13–17) are the "Farewell" events, discourses and prayer; and two (20–21) tell of the resurrection. Only two (18–19) are devoted specifically to the Passion. Moreover, the term "passion" (or "suffering") seems more appropriate to the story of Jesus' trial and crucifixion as it is told in the Synoptic Gospels. Raymond Brown, in his influential Anchor Bible commentary (New York: Doubleday, 1970), has called chapters 13–21 "The Book of Glory." The designation is widely followed.

virtually continuously from 13:31 through chapter 16. The disciples ask questions at the opening and they comment again toward the close, but Jesus is in command of the flow of ideas throughout. His speech concludes with his extended prayer in chapter 17.

After this lengthy passage of speech by Jesus, events resume with his arrest, trial, and crucifixion (chs. 18–19). Chapter 20 narrates appearances of the risen Jesus to his followers. Chapter 21 (which seems to be an addition by someone other than the principal author) tells of further post-resurrection encounters.

On the surface, this sequence supports the common designation of chapters 13–17 as "farewell." Jesus, before his departure, out of his confidence and understanding, prepares and reassures his anxious disciples. He tells them that a different and better condition, though not an easy one, will prevail when he is gone, and he provides an interpretation in advance of the event.

The usual pattern of the Fourth Gospel is for Jesus' explanatory discourses to follow and arise from events: after he meets the Samaritan woman at the well he speaks at length about Living Water (ch. 4); following the miraculous feeding he speaks of the Bread from Heaven (ch. 6). Jesus' discourses interpret and universalize events — usually developing a central image by which each event is turned from a wonder or a particular act into a christological disclosure.

However, the climactic event in the Fourth Gospel's narrative, Jesus' death and resurrection (chs. 18–21), is *preceded* by the fullest body of discourse anywhere in the book (chs. 13–17). Quite probably these speeches are placed before the event for literary reasons. Were they to follow the account of the passion and resurrection, they would read as a prolonged anticlimax. (Moreover, in the johannine time-scheme, where, after the resurrection, could they be placed?) However, in these discourses, spoken on the night of his arrest, Jesus explains the new situation, the new age, the Spirit, the changed relation to himself, prayer in his name, conflict with the world — he speaks of the conditions that will be created for his people by his "going to the Father." *In idea,* the Farewell units, no less than the other discourses of this Gospel, arise from the event with which they are associated. Although in the literal sequence of the Evangelist's story they are located before Jesus' death and resurrection, in the myth-scheme of the book, they refer to and interpret the new condition that is inaugurated by those epoch-ending and epoch-opening events.

In some other historical and literary accounts, later interpretive significance is written into the narrative of earlier events in the form of anticipation.

A conspicuous instance in the Bible itself is the book of Deuteronomy, which presents itself as a leave-taking by Moses before Israel's entry into Canaan. It seems to give directions in advance for life and covenant loyalty in the land under settled agricultural conditions and with a central sanctuary. Yet scores of touches indicate that Deuteronomy was written out of and for those later conditions.

An instance from Shakespeare would be the final long speech of Archbishop Cranmer in *Henry the Eighth* (V.v.15-63). The infant Princess Elizabeth is brought into court for baptism, and the Archbishop, prompted by the bidding of heaven, foretells the peace, prosperity, and glory that will mark the coming reign of this royal child: "Upon this land a thousand thousand blessings" (l. 18). When the play was written and performed, everyone who saw it knew — and everyone who has read or seen it since has known — that the speech was written by Shakespeare, putting into the mouth of Cranmer (Shakespeare's Cranmer), as prophecy, a celebration of the Elizabethan era, which had ended before the play was written. The speech is not meant to deceive. It is significant, however, not as a record of Archbishop Cranmer's prescience, but as an expression of the aura that already in Shakespeare's time had come to surround Elizabeth. (The then reigning King James gets a few flattering lines as well.)

While the level of import in the johannine "Farewell" material is deeper, the literary forces are comparable.

Although in the text of the Farewell, Jesus speaks of a time to come, we overhear in his words the first-century church interpreting its post-resurrection theological situation, but doing so in the voice of the departing Jesus.

The post-Easter or church reference of Jesus' Farewell speeches is suggested by significant links between chapters 13–17 and the resurrection account in chapter 20. After the Passion events, Jesus' private disclosure to his disciples continues, and in chapters 20–21 the risen Jesus is seen by and speaks to his followers and no one else. In these appearances, Jesus says and does things which have ties with the Farewell chapters:

- Jesus says *You will see me,* and *You will rejoice to see me* (14:19; 16:16-19, 22).

  In chapter 20 the disciples see Jesus (thirteen instances of "see" in thirty verses) with joy (20:20).
- Jesus says *My peace I leave with you* (14:27; 16:33).

The risen Jesus bestows his gift of peace (20:20-21).

- Jesus promises the Spirit (14:16-17, 26; 15:26-27; 16:7-15).

  The Spirit is expressly given by the risen Jesus (20:22).
- Jesus' people are sent into the world (13:16, 20; 15:16a; 17:18).

  The risen Jesus says to his disciples, *As the Father has sent me, so I send you* (20:21).

Such ties indicate that, although in the Gospel narrative chapters 13–17 are placed before the Passion, they speak of the situation of believers following Jesus' resurrection. The Farewell Discourses should be read as an interpretation of the age of Christ, the Spirit, and the church, which begins with chapter 20 and in which the Evangelist and his readers live.

As the Book of Glory opens, there is a change in the character of the narrative. Jesus is no longer making his public case; events and contention drop away. He speaks to his followers, whose love and loyalty he takes for granted. New terms such as "love," "abiding," "friends," "in me," "peace," and "joy" enter his speech. He speaks now of the community of his followers who are living in himself in God. The rabbi from Nazareth, soon to be crucified, speaks among his friends (knowingly, albeit somewhat indirectly) of the agenda of the new era of the church and the Spirit.

Although Jesus speaks of his departure, he says that he will return to take his followers to the place to which he is now going (14:2-3). Moreover, although he is gone, his followers remain in vital union with him (14:18-24; 15:1-7; 17:20-23). His community lives in the world where it matures and bears witness (14:12; 15:8, 16, 27; 17:18). Jesus' people form a community of prayer that may use his name as they ask the Father what they will (14:13; 15:16; 16:23). Jesus promises that the Advocate, who is sent to his people from the Father, will teach them the truth and will deal with the perverse world (14:16-17, 26; 15:26-27; 16:7-15). The thought of Jesus' departure is complex. If he says that he is going, he also says that he is coming. He and the Father will make their homes with and in his followers. Paradoxically, if he will be absent, he will at the same time be present (14:18-23). Jesus urges his followers to love one another (13:12-17, 34; 15:12-13, 17); division threatens, and he prays for their unity (17:12-13). Speaking realistically, Jesus tells the community that it lives and serves in a hostile and unbelieving world, just as he has (15:18–16:4a; 16:33; 17:14-25). Clearly, Jesus' Farewell is written with the inner life and outer conflicts of the first-century community of believers in mind.

As to the "tense" of chapters 13–17, Jesus usually speaks of the future. However, the departure setting is sometimes relaxed, and Jesus speaks as though his death and resurrection have already taken place: *I glorified you on earth by finishing the work that you gave me to do* (17:4; see also 13:31; 14:31; 15:12; 16:4, 33). These expressions set the earthly mission of Jesus in the past and indicate that his Farewell, although it is expressed as anticipation, is uttered as from within the accomplishment of his "finished work." C. H. Dodd says: "In a real sense it is the risen and glorified Christ who speaks."[3] Jesus speaks to those who are bound with (are "in") himself — who share the life and mutual indwelling that persist between himself and the Father.

Although these discourses are situated dramatistically before the Friday of the crucifixion, they speak from and about the church's "eighth-day" post-Easter situation.

The Farewell in the Church's Self-Understanding

These discourses and the prayer that follows them present themselves as the words of Jesus. Nevertheless, they are in the Evangelist's style. They quite clearly arise from and give voice to the faith and experience of a first-century community of persons who confessed Jesus. They incorporate insights which the earliest believers could not have grasped without developed communal life, taught by the Spirit (14:26; 16:13-16). These chapters seem to have been written by an author (whose work was supplemented by at least one editor) in a community of shared faith at a critical point when its leadership was passing over to a second generation.

Chapters 13–17 carry evidence of some features of the life of the community in which they were written. The believers in Jesus were being expelled from the synagogue (16:2), and the break (which, as they tell it, was not by their own wish) must have followed a period of tension. More broadly, the world rejects the adherents of this strange new faith. Persecution is a near threat, and martyrdom is a possibility (15:17–16:4a). It seems that some believers have lapsed (15:6, and see 1 John 2:19). The unity of the believers in Jesus is precarious, especially as the first generation of the church is passing to the second (17:20-21). This was not an easy period for the community of Jesus.

3. Dodd, *Interpretation*, 403.

Historical critics look at the johannine Farewell chapters and see evidence of a Christian community caught up in the conflicts and tensions of the later first century. They trace stages and influences, evidencing the story of the johannine Christians. Such historical inquiry into what may lie "behind the Fourth Gospel" is vigorous and fascinating in our time. Substantial agreement has emerged as to the general outline of the development of the first-century johannine community.[4] This present study will draw on this productive line of inquiry.

But in addition to attempting to describe the tensions and growth of the johannine community, interpreters of the Book of Glory have the task of reading, as from the inside, the Evangelist's portrayal of the new faith in Christ as it had taken on form and articulateness in a few intense years of testing and maturation. Interpretation calls for theological as well as historical construction.

The johannine Book of Glory is woven through with terms and understandings by which a body of believers might name and communicate a powerful, sharable experience of life in the risen Jesus. The writer has (no doubt with others in a community of common insight) seen things. He writes so that others may see what he has seen.

This fresh original seeing accounts for the depth and vitality of this book. The task of looking "behind the Fourth Gospel" does involve documentary analysis and historical reconstruction, but, in addition and perhaps more fundamentally, it invites one to attempt a sympathetic re-creation of a Christian imagination at work. This writer did something with existing sources that brought into being a new whole, imparting a novel but coherent grasp of reality.

The johannine Farewell describes (indirectly, to be sure) the new order of reality in which the johannine Christians understood themselves to live: Jesus has departed to a hidden glory with the Father. Yet an exchange of knowing and loving continues between him and his people. He lives in them and they in him. (A reader may remark that these discourses express

4. The Fourth Gospel, with its complexity and its concealment of its own origins, invites historical detective work. Some of the works of inquiry are John Ashton, *Understanding the Fourth Gospel* (Oxford: Oxford University Press, 1991); Raymond Brown, *The Community of the Beloved Disciple* (New York: Paulist, 1979); R. Alan Culpepper, *The Gospel and Letters of John* (Nashville: Abingdon, 1998); Barnabas Lindars, *Behind the Fourth Gospel* (London: SPCK, 1971); Wayne Meeks, "The Man from Heaven in Johannine Sectarianism," *JBL* 91 (1972), 44-72; J. Louis Martyn, *The Gospel of John in Christian History* (New York: Paulist, 1979); John Painter, *The Quest for the Messiah* (Nashville: Abingdon, 1993).

no wish for a return to the old, pre-Easter mode of association. Nostalgia has no place in them.) These Farewell passages are written as though they were spoken by Jesus, yet they express profound discoveries that believers had made of a new mode of existence in the risen Christ. The love and companionship of Jesus and of the Father through Jesus are unbroken and indeed have become more inward, even though Jesus is not present as he had been.

The fact that these discourses are expressed in the voice of Jesus gives this Farewell material a unique first-person sound. Jesus is speaking for himself and to his people. The discourses address Christian readers immediately, as though believers were hearing deeply informing things from the voice they would most wish to hear. The words do not present themselves as an apostle saying "We are a people in Christ." Rather, it is Jesus saying "You are a people in me" (15:4-10).

However, it is clear to a discriminating reader that the manner in which Jesus speaks and the manner of the writer who tells the story are indistinguishable.[5] The fact that Jesus and the Evangelist talk in the same way indicates that the "I" of the Farewell is the distinctively johannine Jesus, who is, in turn, a construction of the Evangelist and of the line of christological interpretation which he brings to expression.

A powerful re-creative process lies behind this material. On historical grounds it seems highly improbable that Jesus said these things at his final meal with his disciples and that his words were recorded and transmitted. Yet in the Fourth Gospel's presentation of Christ, these chapters, in which Jesus speaks for and about himself and his people, occupy a central place. A gifted writer in the first-century church felt competent, under the Spirit, to re-create the words of Jesus, someone who revered Jesus and his sayings yet felt no need to be literal or reportorial. Intending loyalty to the Jesus who, according to the Synoptic record, told stories of the reign of God, shrank from death, and acknowledged his ignorance of the future, the Evangelist, under some mode of divine leading, gives a Jesus who knows himself to be from God, who speaks in discourses of himself as bearer of eternal life, and who is always knowing and in command of events. And strangely, the subsequent church has held that despite their

5. Perhaps the most conspicuous instance of this passage between voices occurs in Jesus' conversation with Nicodemus in 3:1-21. At around verse 13, Nicodemus fades out, and by verses 16-21 one is not sure whether Jesus is still talking to Nicodemus, nor even whether it is Jesus or the narrator who is speaking.

obvious differences, both the Synoptic and the johannine depictions fill an indispensable place in the New Testament presentation of Christ. Believers at the time of writing and ever since have found both portraits of Christ to be authoritative and convincing, although they cannot both be read in the same way.

Can one gather from the Fourth Gospel how its author would have accounted for its existence and its character? He would certainly not satisfy modern curiosity by referring to prior written and oral sources. Rather, if he were to explain himself, he would be more likely to describe inward processes — perhaps not fully understood even by the persons for whom they held self-evidencing authority. It might come down to something like this: When Jesus was no longer with his followers in the way he had been, the divine presence (the "tabernacled" Word, 1:14) was in one sense withdrawn. Jesus had gone to the dwelling-place of his Father. Yet in another sense the divine presence, still mediated by Jesus, was closer than ever. By the Paraclete, Jesus was among and within his people, sustaining, correcting, and teaching. The one who had spoken continued to speak, albeit the mode of his speech was new. The present teaching was so fresh and so unexpected in its grace and judgment that it could not be thought of as *contrived by* the church, but as teaching that *came to* the church. It conveyed things that would have been incomprehensible during Jesus' lifetime, for they depended on the completion of his earthly mission and on his new relation to his people.

New insight could come with such undeniable authority that in the light of it the gospel events themselves were seen differently; both they and the terms in which they had been told could be recast. The story of what Jesus had said and done could be made a vehicle for expressing what Jesus was now understood to be saying and doing. The Jesus who was now known in the first-century church's faith could be portrayed as acting and speaking in a systemically retold gospel narrative. For the two figures were one. The Jesus who was now known to the church's faith was the Jesus who had walked in Galilee and Judea. The contemporaneous teaching of the Spirit, for all its newness, only showed meanings in Jesus and the interpreting Scriptures which had latently been present all along.

In the new age, believers were drawn into an intimate relation with God — loving and being loved, obeying, listening, speaking and being heard, seeing, dwelling in and being indwelt by God. As sharers in one divine-human life, in the same acts, the actors were themselves-in-God and God-in-them. What they saw and understood was God's own self-disclosure in and to them. What they knew they knew by a mysterious participation in the divine knowing.

Out of some such mingling and coinherence came this literary work which is like no other. And from these creative forces came Jesus' self-presentation in his Farewell speeches and prayer.

There is great audacity in the Fourth Gospel and in the shared experience from which it came. Out of the birth pangs through which it was living, the johannine church retold the story of Jesus, "layering" that story with an understanding of its own experience. The result is an integrated account, full of subtleties and multiple references. Surely there is no external way of verifying the truth claim of this literary product. But none was expected and none was sought on its behalf. Rather, the work appeals to inward consent — consent not to the book and its story-telling skill but to the message and the central figure that it presents, *"Come and see."*

The Farewell and the Interpreter

A passage that extends such an appeal obviously invites interpretation, but it asks for interpretation appropriate to itself.

Why do these chapters of Farewell occupy the important place they do in the mind of the church?

To propose a thesis: in these Farewell Discourses and in this prayer, spoken in the idiom of the johannine christological "I," the church explores and articulates the secrets of its own life, a life that Paul described as *hid with Christ in God* (Col. 3:3). The wonder and scandal of the church, as the New Testament sets it forth, is that even while the believing community lives in history, it is the result of, indeed, it is the correlative of, the risen Jesus, who is with the Father. Each is known in relation to the other.

The Fourth Gospel imparts a sense of original vision. It is of lasting significance for the theological imagination by which the community's self-understanding grew. Struggle drove these Christians to explore their own faith. Their hard-won insights moved beyond the situations that gave rise to them. The Fourth Gospel is a work of affirmation and discovery, representing insight that probably grew organically, perhaps quite rapidly, and (as is the way of the imagination) by all-at-once leaps.

If the Fourth Gospel is informed by a fresh grasp of reality, what specifically is grasped? To focus the question on the Farewell portions of this

Gospel, what do the Christ-and-his-own images, affirmations and claims in chapters 13–17 speak of?

To venture their central thrust, the Farewell chapters are about *the distinctive interiority of the church.* Doubtless the phrase requires explanation. The church's life may be thought of as two-sided, even though the two sides belong to a single collective, divine-human life, and they are inseparable.

The church clearly has an outwardness. It is a human community, with a distinctive history. It is embedded in a cultural context, related to the world — turned toward the world. The church is a participant in society and culture. Through institutions, communal life, artistic forms, leaders, actions, ideas, story, discourse, ritual, and characteristic behavior, the church interacts with the society in which it lives — using the common language and current concepts, giving and borrowing, challenging and conceding, judging and being judged, rising in creativity and declining into decadence. The Farewell chapters speak, albeit indirectly, of this life in history. They indicate that by the time the Fourth Gospel reached its final form, the church's doctrine and its internal organization were in an early, intense, but largely fluid stage of development. Within a short time, the world had become hostile, and the johannine church was responding by separating itself from its surrounding society and directing its care largely to its own members. This outward life of the church (in the first century or in the twenty-first) is open to description by social historians.

However, according to its own understanding, the faith community also has a hidden, inward life. It lives in relation to God. It is open to God. It traces its existence to a story of acts which it takes to have come about by divine initiative. It is a people which, by its own account, is called and given its identity and destiny by God. It is bonded to God, living in the very life of Christ, and sharing in the koinonia of the Spirit. This hidden life comes to expression in elemental actions such as celebration, praise, prayer, confession of faith, repentance, and significant ritual acts. These God-ward actions are articulated in an image-laden vocabulary, for no univocal speech can convey this hidden life. The church's characteristic forms of expression are powerful but elusive. The reality of this interior life of the church and of the Christian in relation to God has no unambiguous evidence accessible to common investigation. Its expressive forms — creed, liturgy, hymnody, catechesis, preaching, architecture — are parts of culture and can be described, but its claim to truth is open to no verification other than of the faith it presupposes. Its message is consented to in faith, spoken by faith, and known (as all important things are known) by participation — from the inside or not at all. It is expressible in language, but only in language that is strange, problematic, and multivalent. It may coin new vocabulary, or, if it uses common words, it will often give them an uncommon weight of meaning. Since these interior realities merge and overlap, the terms by which the church expresses its inner life may not be sharply distinguished, and connections among them may not always be clear.

There are perils and pathologies in this interiority. Since it is subtle, elusive, and difficult to express and communicate, one can easily reduce it to formulas and clichés, making it banal and unconvincing. Since it is exacting and demanding, it can be tamed into something sentimental, bourgeois and manageable. Since it is known only by inner exploration, it can become privatized and elude the burden of society and history. Yet, pitfalls and all, this interiority is essential. The church only knows itself as it knows itself in relation to God in Jesus Christ. It can identify redemptively with the world only when it has a firm grasp on that which distinguishes it from the world.

The Farewell chapters of the Fourth Gospel are about the church's veiled interiority. They speak of the church in relation to the final truths of its own existence. Perhaps in this matter no body of material of comparable length is more central.

How should this unusual material be interpreted?

For more than two centuries, biblical studies has been formed by historicism, which has brought the differentiating, distancing intellect into the interpretive process. The canons of historicism tell us that a body of writing must be heard as far as possible in its own situation and on its own terms. Taking care with words and grammar and with what is known of the cultural context, a modern investigator seeks the meaning that a writing had for readers in its original setting, even though approximation is all that even diligent inquiry can achieve. What did the writer intend to say to those to whom the writing was initially directed?

Yet it is almost a commonplace today to say that a purely historical approach to the biblical writings is inadequate. A rigorously scientific interpreter stays outside the text under investigation — in the present case, a confessional text whose very manner of speech would seem to plead that its meaning is not accessible to detached inquiry. Grammatical and lexical analysis pursues exactitude with material that tends to speak indirectly, allusively, and out of inward commitment. To the extent that historical interpretation leaves out the interpreter, it is unsuited for the biblical material

— material that specifically comes before a reader as witness to God and to life in relation to God. Speaking from faith, it appeals for faith and is addressed to faith.

The New Testament writings (John 13–17 in particular) are of importance to serious investigators today principally because these writings are now and have been for many centuries read in a community of faith — read not as ancient record but as life-imparting good news. The New Testament was written from and is directed to the *ecclesia.*

The Farewell Discourses of the Fourth Gospel are not confined to the time and situation from which they originated. They are not to be explained (at least not fully explained) by their sources — by what lies prior to them. Like many creative turns in art, thought, or social order, they do something with their antecedent sources so original that they cannot be fully accounted for through those sources. Their significance is apparent in what comes from them as much as in what they came from. They are to be understood partly by what came before them, of course. But their context lies also in what becomes possible because of them that would have been inconceivable had they not extended the horizons of the mind and the imagination as they did.

These Farewell chapters, written at the vital, originating moments of the Christian movement, illuminate the life of the faith community in every generation. They speak revealingly of the normal, the only situation of Christ, the Christian, and the church.

These chapters of Jesus' Farewell have a strangeness and audacity — now, and perhaps when they were written and first circulated. They are a powerful depiction, from the inside, of Christ in relation to the believing community. If they convince, it will be largely because the reader has come to stand within the order of reality which the Evangelist portrays.

A reader who seeks a sympathetic grasp of the Fourth Gospel must approach it, not as a curious examiner of the critical puzzles of a complex ancient text, but as Christian in Bunyan's allegory, who "put his fingers in his ears, and ran on, crying Life! life! eternal life!"[6] To speak more specifically of the text in hand, the johannine Farewell Discourses and Prayer are best understood by one who brings to the study of them a passionate concern for the thing they are passionately concerned about: the interiority of the church.

6. John Bunyan, *The Pilgrim's Progress* (1678). The incident is in virtually the opening scene.

As one investigates and reflects, one may become persuaded that the mystery of the Fourth Gospel is the mystery of God and ourselves.

The Farewell in Preaching and Historical Criticism

These Farewell discourses form a central presentation of Jesus and the church. Where will believers hear these words of Jesus speaking to his own?

Most Christians derive an early and basic orientation to the Bible from the way they hear it used and referred to in the public discourse of the pulpit. Preachers who have learned to read the Bible alert to its variety of thought and expression realize that the Fourth Gospel tells the story of Jesus in a way that is in important respects different from the story as it is told in the Synoptic Gospels. It is another sort of work, presenting its central figure in a different way. Conscientious preachers do not want to gloss over difficulties in the text, but neither do they want to lecture about them. The interpretive complexities of this uniquely complex Gospel make preaching from John uniquely difficult.

The New Testament scholar D. Moody Smith has described preaching from the Fourth Gospel as "interpreting an interpretation."[7] Of course, the phrase does not apply only to the Fourth Gospel. There is no uninterpreted Christ in the Christian Scriptures. Indeed, the preacher's charter rests in the fact that in all the strata of the New Testament literature, Jesus is the subject of a gospel — a gospel whose first form was the preached form. Bible readers are always caught up in a faith-informed account of Christ as a redemptive figure. However, partly because we have the Synoptic narratives for comparison, the fact that a preacher's source is itself an interpretation is particularly apparent in the Fourth Gospel.

Jesus' Farewell raises hermeneutical issues acutely. One can, as a believer, be persuaded that these discourses and this prayer of Jesus hold the utmost importance and authority for Christian faith and community; and yet also, as a historian, one can think it highly improbable that, in the form in which we have them, Jesus said these things. These Farewell passages should be considered a presentation of Jesus, expressed in the Evangelist's characteristic style of thought, worked out in the teaching and preaching

7. D. Moody Smith, *John* (Proclamation Commentaries; Philadelphia: Fortress, 1976), title and theme of the first part of section 9, pp. 90-97.

life of one otherwise poorly documented part of the first-century church, and written as before-the-event farewell, even though they are informed by after-the-event insights.

The "voice" of this Farewell material is not the now irrecoverable voice of the historical Jesus but that of the living post-Easter Jesus as it was heard in one part of the first-century church. The insights concerning life in relation to Jesus arise from within the relation itself. Forces mingle: the living Jesus speaks to and of the church in relation to himself, and the church speaks of itself in relation to the living Jesus. It was the early Christians speaking, yet it was not they, but Christ in them. From the vantage of its post-Easter condition, the johannine church repossessed the past. Both the life of Jesus and the saga of Israel were seen by the first Christians as they had not been seen (indeed, could not have been seen) before the completion of Jesus' mission and the coming into being of the new community of faith.

The Fourth Gospel is a creative reconceiving of the life of Jesus. In a complex act of the imagination, the johannine church grasped the meaning of Jesus' historic mission, the reality of the living Christ, and the truth of its own hidden life. It was unable to speak of Jesus without at the same time speaking about itself. The Evangelist set down the insights to which he and his community had come in the daring form of a significantly retold gospel narrative.

Although the Fourth Gospel was written when it was and for its own purposes, it is and has long been living Scripture, related deeply to the perennial hungers, questionings, and self-understandings of persons of faith. "The Spiritual Gospel" is read and preached (as it has been since the first years of the Christian era) among Christians gathered for word and sacrament. A primary place of a churchgoer's hearing of the Scriptures is the Lord's Day gathering of the community of faith.

Every organized program of Bible reading is implicitly an act of biblical interpretation. "The Revised Common Lectionary" — the three-year cycle of Sunday readings whose use has now spread, with some differences, through the worship practices of many churches — correlates the reading and preaching of the Scriptures with the passage of liturgical time. The appointed lections interpret the days and seasons of the Church Year, and the Scriptures in turn are interpreted by the liturgy. The structure of this lectionary represents informed, sophisticated biblical interpretation, while at the same time it taps some very old Bible-reading traditions.

In all three years of the lectionary, the Farewell units of John 13–17 are appointed to be read in the Easter-to-Pentecost season. In each year, on Easter and the Sundays immediately following, the churches that follow the lectionary read the narratives of Jesus' resurrection appearances from the Synoptic Gospels and John. Then for the remaining Sundays of the "Great Fifty Days," the Gospel readings explore the johannine Farewell chapters. (In addition, John 10, the "I am the Good Shepherd" passage, which is also about Jesus and the church, is used in all three years on the Fourth Sunday of Easter.) Grasping the idea-structure of the Fourth Gospel, the lectionary-makers have placed this Farewell, which tells of the church's relation to the living Jesus, informed by the Paraclete, not in the time prior to Good Friday, but on the Sundays of Easter. The church's ordered program of Bible reading brings these Jesus-and-his-people discourses before Christian congregations as at the table, among his own, Jesus describes the vital post-Easter relation with himself.

The weeks from Easter to Pentecost are — in today's church as in the early centuries — a time of sustained celebration. For the church, living by its Easter faith, Christ is not past but deeply present in and to his people — loving, teaching, judging, forgiving, caring, leading. And Christ, living in and with his people by the Paraclete, is the central theme of the discourses in John 13–17. As this evangelical record is read and proclaimed, Christ stands in the midst of his people declaring words that are not just descriptive but performative. His words bring his people into his own life. In the days of Easter, the church speaks the deepest mystery of its own existence.

In the church's early centuries, Easter was the time of baptism. The church carried catechumens through months or years of instruction and formation in the discipline and joy of the life of faith. At daybreak on Easter, candidates judged to be ready entered the water, confessed their faith, were baptized, and came out of the water, passing from darkness to light and from death to life. Then they shared for the first time in significant actions of the Christian people — the Prayers of the Faithful, the Greeting of Peace, and receiving the body and blood of Christ. This simple but powerful sequence of gestures brought them out of an old way of life, an old social solidarity and an old order of reality, into a new. Their baptism was a ritualization of conversion.

Then, in the days after Easter (the period known as *mystagogia*), the bishop explained to the newly born Christians what had happened in the compressed, dramatic events of Easter morning; he gave them guidance in their new life as faithful, serving, witnessing, communicating Christians.

For those present-day churches for which the Paschal season is again suffused with baptismal meaning, the period following Easter is a time in which the newly baptized persons experience and reflect on their new life in the risen Christ, and persons who are already baptized repossess the gift and renew the commitments of their once-for-all beginning place in the life of Christ and the church.

During these weeks after Easter, the liturgical Gospel readings place the Christian community at Jesus' final Supper with his followers, where it hears freshly the deepest realities that inform and support all believers in their life in relation with Christ in a new people, living by the Spirit in a new age.

2. Two Opening Incidents (13:1-30)

The Evangelist has no interest in scene-setting. He tells nothing of securing an upper room; only the incidental phrases "during supper" and "at the table" (13:2, 4, 28) place chapters 13–17 at a meal, and, except for the piece of bread dipped in wine and given to Judas, nothing is eaten or drunk. Not until chapter 18 is it clear that the Farewell events take place in Jerusalem. Some commentators and preachers work Synoptic scenery into this johannine narrative or re-create the state of mind of Jesus and his friends on this fateful night. Yet the Evangelist himself has no novelistic or psychological interests. He goes directly to what Jesus knows and does and says, concentrating on themes, ideas, and meanings.

Before Jesus' spoken Farewell begins, the author gives a brief "prologue" to the Book of Glory (13:1), followed by two incidents: (1) Jesus washes the disciples' feet, and explains what he has done (13:2-20); then (2) he dismisses Judas (13:21-30). These incidents are to some extent interwoven; in the account of the foot-washing and the subsequent explanation, Judas is mentioned three times (vv. 2, 10b-11, 18). Until he leaves the room, readers are not allowed to forget that he is there.

In these incidents things happen and people interact. The dialogue between Jesus and Peter that is part of the foot-washing account (13:6-10) is continued in a subsequent brief exchange (13:36-38), and other voices enter in the first part of chapter 14. But Jesus controls the flow of ideas throughout. His actions (13:1-30), followed by his farewell speeches (13:31–16:33) and the concluding prayer (ch. 17), form his final sustained presentation of himself.

Prologue to the Book of Glory (13:1-2a)

> Now before the festival of the Passover,
> Jesus knew that his hour had come
> to depart from this world
> and go to the Father. 13:1a

John 13:1 (which is a single sentence in Greek and is often printed as an independent paragraph) introduces the second large part of this Gospel. Although this introduction is short, its rhythmic phrases, its serious tone, and its christological emphasis may remind a reader of the much fuller prologue which had opened the Book of Signs (1:1-18). It sets the scene, not in circumstance, but through the spiritual realities that mark this turn in the narrative: the setting in ritual time, Jesus' *hour,* what he knows, his passage to the Father, and his love for *his own.*

Although the Book of Glory begins with no notice of place or situation, an opening time reference, *before the festival of the Passover,* relates the events which are about to be explained (chs. 13–17) and then narrated (chs. 18–21) to the Jewish feast of Passover. The author mentioned earlier that Jesus was going to Jerusalem for the feast (see 11:55 and 12:1). Now the festival has come, and Jesus is in Jerusalem. The mention of the Passover, beyond being a time notice, provides an interpretive background for the events that follow. Again, as they have at earlier points in the Gospel, incidents and sayings of Jesus' ministry take on meaning as they overlie Jewish holy days (2:13, 23; 4:45; 5:1 [an unnamed festival]; 6:4; 7:1-14, 37 [Booths]; 10:22 [Dedication]; and 11:55; 12:1, 12, 20; 13:1, 29 [Passover]).

This occasion sets the climactic events of Jesus' mission against the backdrop of the Jews' yearly recalling of the exodus from Egypt. (Mark and Matthew say that this coincidence was brought about by Jesus' initiative; see Mark 14:2 and Matt. 26:5.) The Passover, an eight-day festival, was and is a ritual re-creation of an exciting escape — a people's passage, by God's power, from bondage in Egypt to freedom and ultimately to possession of their own land. It was a yearly reminder of Israel's calling to special identity and destiny in covenant with the one God and a renewal in the reality of that calling. The Farewell chapters do little to develop this exodus setting, but the author evidently expects that his readers will keep it in mind and interpret the crisis of Jesus' mission — his passage from this world and to the Father — against the background of God's deliverance of Israel on the night that was different from all other nights.

In the chronology of the Fourth Gospel, the meal, the foot-washing, Jesus' discourses, and his prayer (chs. 13–17) do not take place on the Passover itself, but on the final preparatory day. This johannine time-scheme, as is often observed, differs from that of the Synoptics. Both the johannine and the Synoptic chronologies locate the meal and the arrest on Thursday, the crucifixion on Friday, and the discovery of the empty tomb on the first day of the week. But they differ as to whether or not the Last Supper was a Passover seder.

The date of the Passover was not set by a day of the week, but by a day of the month in a lunar calendar, on 15 Nisan. The Synoptic Gospels expressly identify Jesus' last meal with his disciples as a Passover meal (Mark 14:1-2, 12-16 and parallels). The Fourth Gospel, however, repeatedly says that Jesus' trial and crucifixion took place before the "high day," that is, on a Day of Preparation (14 Nisan; see 13:29; 18:28; 19:14). Officials have Jesus' body taken down and buried on the day of the crucifixion lest by remaining on the cross after sundown it defile thc Passover (19:31, 42).

By this johannine time-scheme, Jesus' death coincided with the ritual slaying of the Passover lambs which the priests began at midday on the Day of Preparation. The Evangelist makes no point of the coincidence of these two acts. (Two of the Synoptists do mention the time of the slaying of the lambs: Mark 14:12; Luke 22:7.) However, when in 19:32-37 the Evangelist tells that Jesus' legs were not broken on the cross, he cites Exod. 12:46 and Num. 9:12 from the Mosaic regulations on the Paschal lamb, identifying Jesus' death with the Passover sacrifice. Jesus is buried before sundown on that day — before the beginning of the Sabbath.

The Evangelist goes at once to the interior life of Jesus, saying that *Jesus knew.* Always in the Fourth Gospel Jesus knows (cf. v. 3). He is not taken by surprise; he is never the victim of events. Moreover, the "omniscient narrator" knows that Jesus knew. *He knew that his hour had come:* Jesus does not read the rush of events and conclude that the moment was critical. Rather, at the outset, Jesus knows.

The narrator has noted several times that Jesus' *hour* had not yet come (see 2:4; 7:30; 8:20). Now it has come. In johannine vocabulary Jesus' *hour* refers to the final crisis of his mission, culminating in his death and resurrection (2:4; 7:30; 8:20; 12:23, 27; 17:1). (The Synoptic Gospels also speak of "the hour," albeit infrequently; see Mark 14:35, 41 and parallels.) The New Testament does not think in terms of clock-time — objective bits of mechanically measured succession. It does not see time as a featureless, characterless background for human action. Rather, actions and purposes, divine and human, give character and significance to lived time. Time gathers to a saving and judging *hour* — a moment of appointment that holds off. But then it comes.

Jesus' *hour* was his time *to depart from this world and go to the Father.* Jesus' leaving the world and going to the Father is the way in which his destiny is spoken of in the Fourth Gospel. The climax of Jesus' mission is his passage from the world and to the Father. *This world* (for the term, see 8:23; 9:39; 11:9; 12:25, 31; 16:11; 18:36) is the realm of darkness, blindness, and alienation in which Jesus has manifested the light and done the works commissioned by the Father; and it is the place in which he has been rejected and is about to be put to death. What it means that he goes to the Father — the central christological emphasis in this second half of the Gospel — will be developed in the discourses that lie ahead. Here at the start of the second large part of this Gospel, the author introduces Jesus' movement to the Father as a central factor in what Jesus knows about himself and about the meaning of his *hour.* The Fourth Gospel regards the passage which will carry Jesus from the world and to the Father as a unity. The cross is subsumed in this movement; it is Jesus' "glorification," his "lifting up." There is, in the johannine narrative, no "ascension" event, and no royal or priestly imagery describes Jesus' destination. The Fourth Gospel's idiom is modest, interpersonal, and familial; Jesus is going to the Father.

> Having loved his own
> who were in the world,
> he loved them to the end. 13:1b

The prologue turns from Jesus' relation to the Father (which is the primary relation of his life) to his relation to his followers: *his own.* Jesus is now spoken of as engaged not with the uncomprehending, hostile world, but with his closest followers. He is among those who *received him, who believed in his name* (1:11-12). They are *his own (tous idious)* — his by choosing, calling, gathering (cf. 13:18; 15:16). But here, centrally, they are his by the claim of love.

These persons who are *his own,* have responded to his call, his teaching, his leadership, his love. They are what they are in relation to him. They are *his own,* but they are *his own who were in the world.* Their relation to him does not remove them from the world which he is leaving and in which he has been rejected. It does, however, set them in tension with the world (of which more will be said in the Second and Third Discourses and the Prayer: see 15:18–16:4a and 17:14-17; the case of the church is as the case of Jesus himself: see 8:23; 15:18; 1 John 3:1b). Jesus' followers are a sign in the world — a witness against the world for the world.

Having loved . . . he loved them to the end: what he had been to them he still was and always would be. As he has remained in the Father's love (15:10), they would remain in his. The Evangelist's phrase *to the end (eis telos)* can be read in two ways, and, as often in the Fourth Gospel, the ambiguity may be deliberate. It can mean love to the uttermost — unreserved, complete love, the love of one who gives himself un-self-regardingly for others (15:13). Love "to the end" is love that holds nothing back, love without limit. But the phrase can also speak of endings, finalities. Mark 13:13 uses *eis telos* to speak of enduring "to the end" (and see also Rev. 2:26). Thus the phrase can also mean love "to the final moment." Jesus loves enduringly, persistingly, through all — to his death and beyond it. Ceslaus Spicq remarks: "This love is unchanging and definitive. He who loves with *agape* is never unfaithful to his commitments. Once he has given his heart, he loves forever. . . . Although its modes of expression vary, *agape* is permanent and unchangeable."[1] The idiom of completeness (how great) and the idiom of duration (how lastingly) speak in their different ways of love that is total.

Jesus' love for his disciples is spoken of in this passage perhaps more emphatically than it is anywhere else in the Gospels. Over the generations, Christians have universalized this feature of the Gospel story, believing firmly that, as Jesus loved his disciples, he loves the church and each believer. Much devotion arises from the Christian certainty that one is known and loved, personally and particularly, by Jesus. Yet the New Testament itself says little to support this conviction, and most of what it says appears here in Jesus' Farewell.

The New Testament scholar John Knox emphasized that Jesus' love for his people is one of the things the church *knows* about the inner life of Jesus beyond any record or development of the theme in the Gospels. Knox said that in addition to Jesus' recorded words, Christians hear his voice "in the common life of the Church." He remarks that in the matter of Jesus'

> intimate relation with those who responded to him and formed the company of his disciples, . . . the "memory" of the Church goes far beyond anything a critical reading of the Gospels alone would justify. Undoubtedly one reason the Church has always cherished the Fourth Gospel and has been unable to believe that it does not contain authentic historical truth about Jesus is that

1. C. Spicq, *Agape in the New Testament* (St. Louis: Herder, 1966), 3.33.

> one can read there, and there only, such words as "Having loved his own . . . he loved them to the end" and "This is my commandment, that you love one another as I have loved you" (John 13:1; 15:12) — words which express a love of Jesus for his own which has a deep, sure place in the memory of the Church.

Knox says that this love, which is *reflected* in some language of Paul, "existed already in the body of the Church and exists there still, deeply indebted to the Gospels and Epistles, but not created by them, not exhausted by them, and never entirely to be displaced by them."[2]

This brief prologue sets the events that are to follow within Jesus' *hour* — the climax of his work. The themes of Jesus' relation to the Father and to his followers — themes which the Evangelist introduces here — will be developed in the following Discourses, as Jesus speaks for himself.

The Evangelist turns to incident. Jesus, in an unannounced act, washes the feet of his disciples. But as the Evangelist develops the story, the presence of Judas in the company is noted three times, like a persistent tragic factor. The first of these notices comes immediately after the Evangelist's "prologue," where it follows without transition, almost shockingly after the statement of Jesus' love for his disciples.

> The devil had already put it into the heart of Judas
> son of Simon Iscariot to betray him. 13:2a

The author gives this early notice that the traitor is present in the circle of Jesus' intimate friends and is already controlled by an impulse that traces beyond himself to the Adversary, the power that has access to the human heart and that opposes God. Beyond and within the local, particular conflict in Jerusalem, a cosmic spiritual conflict is taking shape. Karl Barth comments, "From above, there is the approach of His death, but also the ascent to the Father which corresponds to His departure. From beneath, the actualization of the satanic possibility of Judas has already begun."[3] Judas had not yielded to a passing idea; he had given the devil the consent of his heart, the unshared, determining place of the self.

The Evangelist describes Judas's act of betrayal with the verb *paradidōmi,* "hand over." Judas would lead Jesus' enemies to the place where he

2. John Knox, *The Church and the Reality of Christ* (New York: Harper and Row, 1962), 56.

3. Karl Barth, *Church Dogmatics* 2/2 (Edinburgh: Clark, 1957), 473.

could be apprehended away from public attention. (Judas, when he enters the narrative here, is identified as "son of Simon Iscariot." The patronymic probably is to distinguish him from another Judas who will appear later and who is identified only as "Judas, not Iscariot": see 14:22.)

1. The Master Serves (13:2b-20)

The incident with which the Farewell passage opens — Jesus washing the feet of his disciples — serves as something of a frontispiece, not only to the discourses that follow but to the entire Book of Glory. Jesus, with no prior explanation and prompted by no specific happening, gets up from the table, prepares himself, and goes from one of his followers to the next, washing their feet (vv. 3-11) — an incident unique to the Fourth Gospel. As he performs this act of serving (vv. 3-5), there is an exchange with Peter, who objects (vv. 6-11). Then Jesus explains (vv. 12-20).

Jesus Washes the Disciples' Feet (13:2b-5)

The act of courtesy Jesus performs — washing the feet of diners — would ordinarily have preceded the meal and would have been performed by a servant or by a group member with little status. Nothing indicates why it had not been done earlier, and nothing that is said at the supper suggests an occasion for the act.

The historical and literary character of this incident is a puzzle with few clues. Since none of the Synoptics tells that Jesus washed the disciples' feet at the Last Supper, a reader may ask: Where did this incident come from? Did it actually happen? (The next incident, the identification, but not the dismissal, of Judas, does appear in the Synoptic traditions. The Fourth Gospel Passion narrative is a mixture of independent and common material.)

Perhaps this incident did take place as narrated here and for some reason was omitted from the Passion accounts of the Synoptic Gospels but was included in the tradition passed to the johannine community by the Beloved Disciple. This possibility cannot be demonstrated to be true or untrue.

Yet it is difficult to guess why in a story as central to Christian memory and as circumstantially told as the Passion narratives, this vivid, revelatory episode, if it is historical, would have been left out by the Synoptists. Some exegetes have conjectured that this incident is connected with the story told in Luke 22:24-27 of a dispute among the disciples at the Supper over who would be greatest — a dispute that Jesus rebukes by saying, *I am among you as him that serves.* If this incident reported in Luke has influenced the story in the Fourth Gospel, the connection goes unremarked in the text.

The account of Jesus' act is johannine in the manner of telling. C. K. Barrett may seem to sweep all the pieces from the board when he conjectures that "the foot-washing is probably to be regarded as a Johannine construction based on the Synoptic tradition that Jesus was in the midst of his disciples as *ho diakonōn* (Luke 22:27)."[4] Exegetes who may think such a judgment too rash have little evidence on which to mount a counterproposal.

And during supper 13:2b

Words that place Jesus' act at a meal are quite incidental: "during supper" (v. 2), "rose from supper" (v. 4), and "at the table" (v. 28). The author was evidently working from a tradition of a final meal prior to Jesus' arrest that may have been familiar to his readers, but it was not part of his purpose to recount it.

The Evangelist gives Jesus' action a setting and, as he has in 13:1, he sets it in the redemptive myth of the Fourth Gospel:

Jesus, knowing
that the Father had given all things into his hands,
and that he had come from God
and was going to God, 13:3

At the outset, *Jesus, knows.* In this Gospel, he does not observe events, weigh them and then come to know. He knows (see vv. 7, 12, 17, 28), and events are shaped by his informed initiative. The author, again speaking as "omniscient narrator," reports that Jesus' washing of his disciples' feet arose from his knowledge that his mission had brought him from God and would carry him to God.

The Evangelist gives Jesus' act of humble service a setting of authority. Jesus knows that his mission had been given him by the Father: *the Father had given all things into his hands.* The phrase *all things* does not refer to a

4. C. K. Barrett, *The Gospel According to St. John* (2nd ed., Philadelphia: Westminster, 1978), 436.

cosmic lordship — an idea that belongs to other varieties of New Testament christology, but not to the Fourth Gospel. Rather, the expression speaks of Jesus having been given plenary authority to be the bringer of eternal life. The redemptive purpose he serves is ultimately the Father's purpose; the Father gives it into Jesus' hands, and Jesus discharges it faithfully.

The theme of Jesus as the Father's agent enters here; it is an organizing motif in johannine christology; and it will figure several more times in the Farewell chapters. It was a principle of Halakhic Jewish thought that one might act through an agent. In an important review of the subject, Peder Borgen reports that "an agent is like the one who sent him." One who is appointed agent *(shaliach)* of another carries the rights and property of the other. The sender and the one sent are so identified that "dealing with the agent is the same as dealing with the sender himself." The principle applied in legal affairs where the agent represented the sender. Some rabbis, however, developed also a more personal "judicial mysticism," in which the sender imparted his own character and qualities to the agent. "The agent ranks as the master's own person."[5] With respect to the work undertaken by the agent, the sender is the superior of the one sent. At the conclusion of his appointed work, the agent reports to his sender.

Johannine christology depicts Jesus as commissioned and sent by the Father (e.g., 8:42; 10:36-38), who has placed all things in his hands (3:35). Jesus is wholly intent on representing him (6:38; 8:29). He has been given full powers (13:3; 17:2). As agent, he is subordinate to the Father (13:16a; 14:28). Yet the agent is so identified with the sender that the way in which the emissary is treated is the way in which the one who sent him is received (12:45; 15:23-24).

It was a part of the principle of agency that an agent could appoint an agent. Thus Jesus, who is himself sent, sends others, who are as himself (13:20; 17:18; 20:21). To receive them cordially or to reject them is to receive or reject their sender (13:20).

Jesus knows *that he had come from God and was going to God.* His act of washing his disciples' feet (like his saving mission of which the act is a paradigm) grows from his relation with the Father who was his origin and his destination.

5. Peder Borgen, "God's Agent in the Fourth Gospel," in J. Neusner, ed., *Religions in Antiquity: Essays in Memory of Erwin Ramsdell Goodenough* (Leiden: Brill, 1968), 138-39. This summary of the theme of agency was reprinted in John Ashton, ed., *The Interpretation of John* (London/Philadelphia: SPCK/Fortress, 1986), 67-78. Although some of the Jewish sources that Borgen cites are later than the New Testament, they are considered reliable sources for Jewish thought in the first century.

On previous occasions Jesus' origin and purpose have puzzled his critics. They asked where he was from (9:29); they wondered where he was going (8:21-24); and they failed to understand his explanations. But Jesus knows that his life and mission have their source and end in the Father. His work has been carried out in oneness with God — a purpose which will lead him to the cross, and the cross is his return to the Father. The johannine christological myth, which is expressed here in compressed form, provides the interpretive setting for Jesus' modest act of service: *Jesus, knowing that the Father had given all things into his hands, and that he had come from God and was going to God, got up from the table, took off his outer robe, and tied a towel around himself* (13:3-4). His servant-act was carried out in awareness of the central and unique place he knew himself to occupy in the purpose of God.

The narrator draws on a common gesture of courtesy for guests whose feet would have gotten dusty from walking on unpaved streets, protected only by sandals. In carrying out this act of a servant, Jesus, in full awareness of his divine origin and destiny, adopts menial garb and takes up the implements of his task:

He prepared himself:

> got up from the table,
> took off his outer robe,
> and tied a towel around himself.

And he performed the work of a servant:

> Then he poured water into a basin
> and began to wash the disciples' feet
> and to wipe them
> with the towel that was tied around him. 13:4-5

Six clauses, six actions by Jesus. Four nouns designating four common things: his robe, a towel, water, and a basin. Walter Brueggemann comments on the act and the appropriate tools:

> The tools define the trade. We can do only what our tools permit us to do. And if we have the tools of a slave, we can do only that kind of work. The towel and the basin are slavely tools. They do the work no "master" would do, i.e., they make contact with the repulsive, abhor-

> rent dimensions of our humanity. The towel and the basin are servant tools. They do the work no reputable, competent manager would do — that is, they make contact with dimensions of our humanity that need personal caring attention.[6]

Peter Objects (13:6-10a)

As Jesus washes and dries the feet of his disciples, they may be startled or puzzled, but they accept his act. Peter, however, openly objects. His objections and Jesus' replies are told in the form of three exchanges.

> He came to Simon Peter, who said to him,
> "Lord, are you going to wash my feet?"
> Jesus answered,
> "You do not know now what I am doing,
> but later you will understand."
> Peter said to him,
> "You will never wash my feet."
> Jesus answered,
> "Unless I wash you, you have no share with me."
> Simon Peter said to him,
> "Lord, not my feet only
> but also my hands and my head!"
> Jesus said to him,
> "One who has bathed does not need to wash,
> except for the feet,
> but is entirely clean.
> And you are clean. . . . 13:6-10a

Peter is shocked at this reversal of roles, and he remonstrates, *Lord, are you going to wash my feet?* Jesus answers Peter by saying that what he is doing cannot be understood now, but its meaning will be grasped *later.*[7] Peter does not ask what Jesus may have meant, but intensifies his objection, saying *You*

6. Walter Brueggemann, *Living toward a Vision: Biblical Reflections on Shalom* (New York: United Church Press, 1982), 134-35.

7. This promise that what Peter cannot grasp now will become clear to him "later" is part of a johannine theme examined in the essay "Not Now, But Afterward," pp. 304-6 below.

will never wash my feet (v. 8a). (The word order in Greek emphasizes *you* and *me: Lord, are you going to wash my feet? You will never wash my feet.*) Jesus replies, saying that an essential bond is established by letting oneself be washed by him: *Unless I wash you, you have no share with me.* Hearing this, Peter overreacts and wants Jesus to wash more than his feet, *Lord, not my feet only but also my hands and my head!* Peter has not been important in the earlier chapters of the Fourth Gospel as he is in the Synoptic Gospels and as he will be in the Passion and resurrection narratives, but when he enters the account here, he is in character as the Peter who runs to extremes.

The words in verse 10 by which Jesus tempers Peter's overreaction hold several puzzles of text and interpretation.

The words *except for the feet* are not in some early manuscripts, and most text critics today think they do not belong in the text. The fact that there is a question about them may suggest that at a very early time this passage was not fully clear. An early copyist may have inserted the words to express his idea of the meaning and to aid his readers.

The sentence at its most literal seems to say: "One who has taken a bath *(louesthai)* is clean *(katharos)* and does not need to bathe again when arriving at dinner. However, walking does make one's feet dusty, and they need washing *(niptein).*" Peter's reaction (in v. 9) was excessive. He does not need to have his head and hands washed. But for one who has walked on unpaved streets, wearing only sandals, washing the feet would be a desirable supplement to a complete bath.

However, foot-washing is a part which can stand for a complete cleansing. Jesus' concluding clause, *You are clean, though not all of you,* lifts the terms out of the literal. He has more in mind than feet. Allowing Jesus to wash one's feet is a sign of union with him. Jesus seems to say that all of the disciples (all but one) are cleansed with a definitive bath; cleanness is the condition to which their association with him has brought them.

Seeking to relate Jesus' words to the community for which the late-first-century Evangelist wrote, some exegetes have taken Jesus' remark about a definitive cleansing to refer to baptism, its completeness and its unrepeatability. Yet the baptized sin. When they do, there is no need of a second baptism. These interpreters, thinking of the penitential practice that grew up in the early church, have seen in the contrast between a complete bath and washing one's feet an allusion to baptism, a definitive cleansing which is not repeated, and penance, which restores baptismal status when it has been forfeited by egregious sin and may be repeated. However, such interpretations read later disciplinary/sacramental developments into this passage.

Yet this verse may refer indirectly to the community's experience of continued sin among the faithful — the experience which in time gave rise to regulations concerning second repentance, restoration of the lapsed, and individual (usually public) penance. It seems significant that no other New Testament writing gives as much attention to the sins of Christians and what can be done about them as does 1 John. Such texts as 1 John 1:5–2:2 and 3:4-10, 19-22 which deal with sin in the church may provide a setting from the johannine community itself in which to place this verse. The author of 1 John seeks to hold the wonder, completeness, and finality of divine forgiveness alongside realism about Christian failure. Perhaps the first-century johannine community for which the Fourth Gospel was written was struggling with the issue. In a sermon, D. M. Baillie caught the idea: "Simon Peter is already a true disciple, he doesn't need to begin all over again, he is one of the clean ones; but he needs time and again, as a pilgrim, to have his feet washed."[8]

Very likely readers are to understand that Peter consented and that Jesus washed his feet.

About Judas (13:10b-11)

though not all of you."
For he knew who was to betray him;
for this reason he said, "Not all of you are clean." 13:10b-11

When Jesus comments that the disciples are "clean," the great exception at once comes to his mind. Although Jesus' followers are a "cleansed" group, one of them would not or could not be made clean, even by Jesus — *you . . . , though not all of you.* Jesus, who in this Gospel always knows, knew that one stood outside the general purity and unity of his followers. Judas was a defiling presence, known to be such by Jesus.

Jesus Explains (13:12-20)

Jesus resumes his street clothing and his place at the table and asks whether or not his followers have understood his act: *Do you know what I have done to you?* What he has done no doubt requires an explanation, and only he can give it.

8. D. M. Baillie, *To Whom Shall We Go?* (Edinburgh: Saint Andrew, 1955), 198.

Verses 13-20 are all in the voice of Jesus and might be thought to be a brief discourse associated with the foot-washing. This explanatory passage holds together around the theme of master and disciples but is composed of brief, somewhat discrete elements, each of which is of interest but which do not flow smoothly from one to the next.

In verses 12-15 the Evangelist reports the end of Jesus' action as circumstantially as he had the beginning (vv. 4-5).

After he had washed their feet,
had put on his robe,
and had returned to the table,
he said to them,
"Do you know what I have done to you?"

Then he explains that his act is an example:

You call me Teacher and Lord —
and you are right, for that is what I am.
So if I, your Lord and Teacher,
have washed your feet,
you also ought to wash one another's feet.
For I have set you an example,
that you should do
as I have done to you. 13:12-15

Jesus, although he is Teacher *(didaskalos)* and Lord *(kyrios)* of his disciples, has washed their feet. They should, on his model, wash one another's feet, *For I have set you an example, that you also should do as I have done to you* (v. 15). Barrett notes: "1 Tim. 5:10 shows that, at the time when John wrote, 'washing the feet of the saints' had become an accepted metaphor for Christian service. The Johannine incident may have grown out of the metaphor, but the metaphor itself must have had some origin, and this may have been the tradition of John."[9]

Jesus cites his act as an "example" *(hypodeigma)*. One returns the humble act of Jesus by serving others as Christ. In the time of the church, response to Jesus is enacted in the corporate, interrelational life.

9. Barrett, *Gospel According to St. John*, 436.

The example of Jesus is also cited in 1 Pet. 2:21, where it is a model of non-retaliation, and is used in Phil. 2:5-11, which commends humility and mutual deference among Christians. The example of Jesus is less prominent in the New Testament writings than it came to be in later Christian devotion and ethics. Romano Guardini remarks that casting Jesus in the role of example should never suggest any posturing on his part. "Christ," he says, "never acts 'moralistically.' The idea that Jesus was constantly setting an example has done much to spoil his sacred picture. Of course he was exemplary, *the* model simply; but the figure of the Lord loses all spontaneity when it is constantly portrayed in pedagogic pose."[10]

Jesus commends his example to his followers in an epigrammatic saying, which is in the form of paired lines:

> Very truly, I tell you,
> servants are not greater than their master,
> nor are messengers greater than the one who sent them. 13:16

Jesus has cast himself as *teacher* and *lord* (v. 14). Here he is *master (kyrios,* which was translated "lord" in v. 13) and *sender (pempsantos),* while the disciples are to understand themselves as *servants (douloi),* and *messengers* or *sent ones (apostoloi).* Nothing is said here about how they serve or what message they carry, only that they are subordinate to their *master* and their *sender.* In both lines, the relation is expressed negatively — what the servants and messengers are not and should not presume to be. Servants and messengers cannot expect better treatment than was given to their master and sender — who is, of course, in the present context the Master who serves.

In v. 17 Jesus speaks of knowing and doing in a beatitude-like comment:

> If you know these things,
> you are blessed if you do them. 13:17

The counsel can seem moralistic, as though Jesus were saying, "Act as you know. Do good, serve modestly, and happiness follows" — which seems unrealistic at any time, but especially on the eve of the crucifixion.

10. Romano Guardini, *The Lord* (Chicago: Regnery, 1954), 362.

Elsewhere Jesus has given another sense of the relation between knowing and doing. He has said *If you will to do God's will, you will know* (7:17), and *If you continue in my word, . . . you will know* (8:31-32). Obeying leads to understanding; knowledge is acquired in commitment or action. The present text, 13:17, gives the more commonplace idea that when something that is important to human well-being is known, if informed actions follow, the result is blessedness. Right understanding informs right conduct.

The Evangelist probably does not regard the two propositions as in conflict. Either way of seeing the relation presents knowing and doing as intimately connected, and the writer may think that either can lead to the other. One can say that truth is known in doing, that obedience leads to discovery; or one can say that one knows in order to do, that truth is validated as it is put into action. In either sequence, truth is not a matter for the disengaged, onlooking mind. Truth is something done; it exists for the sake of action (3:21). If one comes to know through doing, it is also the case that one must do what one knows.

The passive *you are blessed* is a periphrastic way of saying "God will bless you." Blessedness is a divine gift.

A preacher alert to words might think of inverting Jesus' remark to make it say: "If you know what is required of you, miserable are you if you fail to do it." In one of his sermons, the seventeenth-century Cambridge Platonist Benjamin Whichcote did just that. He said:

> As it is the most unsafe, so it is the most uneasy condition for any person to know, and not to do; to know and not to be; to have judgment of right, and conscience of iniquity. I fear no worse hell in the world to come.[11]

After Jesus has explained that his followers form a community of persons who are to serve one another, he turns abruptly (as the narrator also has in vv. 2 and 10-11) to the great exception among the disciples, saying:

11. Almost nothing by Whichcote (1609-83) was published during his lifetime. A volume of *Aphorisms*, gathered from his sermons and other writings, was published in 1703 (with an enlarged second edition in 1753, and a modern edition in 1930 with an introduction by W. R. Inge). The passage quoted here is from a small pamphlet of "Fresh Aphorisms" collected from Whichcote's sermons by T. W. Crafter and published in London, without date (but by appearance late nineteenth century). The editor indicates that this passage is from the third volume of the sermons, p. 216.

I am not speaking of all of you;
I know whom I have chosen.
But it is to fulfill the scripture,
'The one who ate my bread has lifted up his heel against me.'
I tell you this now, before it occurs,
so that when it does occur, you may believe that I am he. 13:18-19

One of those whom Jesus had chosen stood outside the community of mutual service, and could not be reached by Jesus' words about unity with him and with others. Citing Ps. 41:9, Jesus explains that this exclusion of one from his circle is a fulfillment of Scripture. The quoted words, *The one who ate my bread has lifted up his heel against me,* fall in a Psalm that describes conflict with enemies who hate, scheme, and betray. Yet at the end of Psalm 41, the speaker is vindicated by God, upheld, raised, and set in the divine presence.

At the heart of this psalm of conflict are these vivid lines:

Even my bosom friend
in whom I trusted,
who ate of my bread,
has lifted the heel against me. (Ps. 41:9)

Friendship, trust, and hospitality are betrayed. "Lifting the heel" is a somewhat obscure expression, but it may refer to "the action of one who 'shakes off the dust of his feet against' another" in a gesture of insult or contempt.[12]

Jesus' reference to Ps. 41:9 is one of the infrequent Scripture citations in the Farewell chapters. The gospel narrative, as events move toward Jesus' death, raises a question. If Jesus chose his followers (13:18; 15:16), and yet one of them was a traitor (6:70), and if Jesus (who is always informed and in command in the Fourth Gospel) knew who the traitor was, why did the course of events move as it did? Did all the initiatives lie with Jesus' enemies, with Judas and Satan (13:2, 27)?

The Scripture citations in the later part of the Fourth Gospel tend to show that a plan or a determining order is at work in the events of Jesus' life (12:13-15, 38-40; 15:25; 17:12; 19:24, 28, 36, 37). The source of this intentionality which pervades the gospel narrative is the redemptive purpose of God, being carried forward by the Father's will and Jesus' obedi-

12. Barrett, *Gospel According to St. John,* 445.

ence — but also by the slowness of Jesus' disciples, by the plots of his enemies, by the weakness of Pilate, by Peter's denial, and by Judas' betrayal. Here Jesus' citation from the Jewish Scriptures seems to imply that events as they play out are within a divine intention that has been foreshadowed in a Hebrew Psalm. Jesus was the "I" of the ancient Psalm; he was the actualization of God's long-laid purpose to save. The conflict was real, but the opposition could only further the accomplishment of God's intentions. Even the defection of one of the Messiah's close friends has been foretold in the Scriptures, and it could be utilized by God's purpose.

In the midst of the conflicts and stress of the moment, Jesus tells the disciples that in a future time events would confirm his word and thus reveal him: *I tell you now, before it occurs, that when it does occur, you may believe that I am he.* Jesus says that when "it" has occurred — that is to say, after the climactic events of his mission — the disciples would then believe that *I am.* (On "I am" as part of the self-identification of the johannine Jesus see pp. 138-40, and on his assurance that the disciples will later understand, see "Not Now, But Afterward," pp. 304-7.)

Does the Evangelist mean here that Jesus foresees that one of those present at the supper would be disloyal and that when events have proved Jesus right his prediction will demonstrate his identity? He means at least this much. But Jesus' prediction of Judas' disloyalty could in itself indicate no more than that Jesus saw into the character and motives of Judas, and such insight would not be a sufficient basis for the deep recognition of Jesus that is expressed in his *I am.*

A larger meaning is suggested by the Scripture citation. Jesus says that the disciples will later remember not only this event and that he had predicted it but also the Psalm passage to which he calls attention now. It was the coming together of the incident and the interpreting Scriptures that would reveal the rootage of Jesus and his mission in the deep purposes of God.

The aphoristic comment that follows (v. 20) resembles verse 16. Both are preceded by *Very truly.* Both are in paired clauses. Verse 16 speaks in terms of master and servants, verse 20 of being sent and being received. Verse 16 is expressed negatively, *Servants are not greater than their masters.*" Verse 20 is positive:

> Very truly, I tell you,
> whoever receives one I send receives me; and
> whoever receives me receives him who sent me." 13:20

In this couplet, Jesus is both the sender and the one who is sent. The sending of both Jesus' followers and of Jesus himself requires a response. The verb *receive (lambanō)* is repeated four times in the two lines; it is the point of the saying. The sender and the one sent are so united that to receive an emissary of Jesus is to receive him, and in receiving him, one receives the Father who sent him.

Jesus depicts a powerful sequence of being sent and being received. His words here closely resemble a Synoptic saying which forms part of his instruction when he sent out the Twelve (in Luke also the Seventy): *Whoever welcomes you welcomes me, and whoever welcomes me welcomes the one who sent me* (Matt. 10:40; cf. Luke 10:16 and Mark 9:37; Luke 9:48). This epigrammatic saying (or a version of it) may have been embedded in the oral tradition of the communities that shaped the Synoptic Gospels as well as the Community of the Beloved Disciple, and the written texts that came from these independent strains of the early Christian community contained these almost identical expressions.

In the Fourth Gospel, Jesus only sends his followers in the Book of Glory: he twice speaks of his followers as sent as he explains the foot-washing (13:16, 20); in the Second Discourse he says, *I appointed you to go* (15:16); and in the prayer he speaks of his people as being sent as he is sent, *As you have sent me, so I have sent them* (17:18). The theme is repeated, finally, with something like a "commissioning" when, after the resurrection, Jesus says to his disciples, *As the Father has sent me, even so I send you* (20:21). The sentness of the church derives from the sentness of Jesus.

As the Fourth Gospel sees it, the sentness of Jesus' followers is not principally based on his call to them to follow him, nor on his making them associates in his healing and teaching mission (as in Mark 6:6-13); rather it arises as the post-resurrection community of faith, carrying the name of the living Jesus, encounters the world. To that church-in-mission Jesus says that he, the sent one, is also the sending one, and that those he sends are so identified with him that to *receive* them is to *receive* him. Dealings with the sent and obedient church are dealings with Jesus himself and through him with the Father. In its sentness the apostolic community is participating in Jesus' own sentness and ultimately in the *missio dei.*

Essay: Meanings of the Foot-Washing

This incident of Jesus washing his disciples' feet seems to be a simple action, done at a significant occasion, told in a straightforward way, leading to the clear ethical point which Jesus develops in the paragraph that immediately follows. His act of serving is a model for his followers, who should serve one another as he has served them. However, there are suggestions in the text that the act carries meanings beyond this obvious meaning:

> The impressive "preamble" to the incident (v. 3) states a mythic christology beyond anything that would be needed to support a human master-servant relation or a moral example: the Father has given all things into Jesus' hands; Jesus comes from God and goes to God.
>
> The imagery of water and cleansing and Jesus' remark that he must wash those who are to *have a share with* himself (v. 8) suggests that he is speaking of a deep relation with himself, not just of getting dust from the feet of dinner guests.
>
> Jesus says (v. 19) that his action meant more than could be grasped at the time, but that subsequent events would make its significance clear: *later you will understand* (v. 7). A simple moral lesson about serving others could have been grasped readily by a devout Jew.

Significance beyond the apparent is indicated. The Evangelist's attraction to multiple meanings is at work. As subtler meanings interpenetrate the obvious meaning, lines of association mingle. The story suggests four strands of significance.

An Exemplary Meaning

On the model of his washing his disciples' feet, Jesus indicates that his followers should serve one another. Readers might gather this point from the story itself, and it is the central thrust of Jesus' initial explanation in verses 12-17. Jesus, in full awareness of his relation to God and of his mission from the Father, takes a servant role. Knowing himself to be Master, Teacher, and Lord, he voluntarily became servant. Those who are his disciples are to serve each other. Jesus is the exemplar.[13]

While Jesus demonstrates servanthood, he acts out of strong self-assertion: *Jesus, knowing that the Father had given all things into his hands, and that he had come from God and was going to God, took a towel . . .* (13:3-

13. The example of Jesus' conduct is expressly cited in 1 Cor. 11:1; 2 Cor. 8:9; and 1 Pet. 2:18-25. His redemptive mission is cited as a model for Christian conduct in Phil. 2:3-11; see also Eph. 5:22-23. Specific New Testament references to Jesus as example are relatively few.

4). *You call me Teacher and Lord — and you are right, for that is what I am. If I then, your Lord and Teacher . . .* (13:13-14). Jesus did not have to act as he did. No one had been designated to wash the feet of the guests, so the act of courtesy was supplied, not by one who thought himself of no account, nor by one who had been socialized to accept a serving role as all that was open to him, but by one who knew himself to be *didaskalos* and *kyrios.*

Jesus did not serve others out of a conviction that in himself he was nothing — that others had a claim on him while he had no claim on anyone else. He acted, not out of self-negation, but out of self-affirmation. His self-humbling arose from inner authority. It is not that he did not know who he was and therefore had to put himself at the disposal of everyone else; rather, he acted out of self-knowledge and self-possession. As Walter Brueggemann put it:

> He had identity questions, destiny issues, settled in his life. He knew that he was totally empowered by God; all things were given into his hand. And because that issue was settled, he was able to remove the garments, the outward signs of respect and control that the world acknowledges. He was able to take all of that off precisely because the real issues were elsewhere and were settled. . . . He knelt, not in humility or in fear but in strength and confidence.[14]

This feature of Jesus' action suggests that, in the economy of service, one who would give oneself truly and wholeheartedly to others must first possess oneself. Or if that way of putting the point sounds too sequential, it might be better to say that insofar as one's self is securely held, it can be freely shared, and in the sharing of it one comes into the fuller possession of it. The Jesus of this johannine text is model of self-giving service, but at the same time he models inner poise and self-affirmation.

Jesus' followers are called to be a fellowship of mutually serving persons, devoted to one another's well-being and willing to accept menial roles. They are to be a community of persons seeking to serve, rather than of persons who expect service from others; and this interior revolution is rooted in the model of Jesus himself. Such counsel, coming on the best authority, seems to present a simple moral imperative: It ought to be done. It can be done. Do it.

But there are complexities. The common life can be subverted by an egoism that turns everything and everyone toward getting one's own way.

14. Brueggemann, *Living toward a Vision,* 135.

But it can also be subverted by the egoism that expresses itself through consciously casting oneself as servant. Tyrannies are imposed and moral confusion is stirred in the name of "serving others." In such apparent passivity, self-deceptions abound.

Peter's objection suggests a further complexity: *Lord, do you wash my feet?* If some people find it difficult to serve freely and genuinely, other people find it difficult to accept service gracefully. In Jewish society in Jesus' day it was permissible for pupils to wash the feet of their teachers, but when Peter's rabbi approaches him to wash his feet, Peter's very world seems threatened. He clutches his familiar role: *You shall never wash my feet* — not you, not me, not my feet, never! He will remain self-dependent.

One wants a clear order: some people are to be served, while others serve. Roles define one, not least to oneself. One's status, even if it is a subordinate status, can provide one with a measure of security. The revolutionary impact of Jesus can seem threatening to anyone, whatever one's social status. If the mighty are undone by being brought low, the lowly can be made uncomfortable when they are raised up. Jesus cannot reach those who suppose that they are self-sufficient; neither can he reach those who plead that they are not worth his trouble. The precondition of receiving Jesus' help is to acknowledge one's need, realistically and maturely. The English scholar Mark Santer wrote of "being humble enough to accept the divine humility. . . . All Christian service is of a Master who first serves me. Indeed as St. Peter discovered on the eve of his Master's passion, I may not, I cannot be his servant unless I let him first serve me."[15]

This ethical message, with its complexities, is clearly intended; but it is set alongside other meanings. Indeed, if the ethical meaning stood alone it might well assign to Jesus' followers a burdensome demand. He counsels his disciples to do something difficult, and his example shows that it can be done. The other meanings may bring the ethical meaning out of the moralistic "ought" towards which it might otherwise drift.

A Christological Meaning

The foot-washing is sometimes spoken of as an "acted parable," like the actions by which some of the Hebrew prophets dramatized their message. What is it a parable of?

15. Mark Santer, "Diaconate and Discipleship," *Theology,* May 1978, p. 181.

Several verbal clues — the author's preamble to the story (v. 3) as well as his prologue to the Book of Glory (v. 1) — have set the pedelavium within the johannine redemptive myth. Jesus' "acted parable" at the supper does more than demonstrate serving others; it is a subtle proclamation concerning himself as the one who comes from God and returns to God.

The early mention of Judas as already in the devil's control (v. 2) has the effect of placing the foot-washing in the context not only of Jesus' death, but also of the cosmic conflict which is drawing to its climactic moment. Jesus is among his friends, but he and his friends are among enemies, inside as well as outside the room where they are met. A. Jaubert says, referring to 13:1, that "The scene of the washing of the feet is placed under the sign of the Hour."[16]

The Evangelist speaks (v. 3) of what Jesus knows about himself. His self-knowledge is first of all a knowledge of his relation with the Father by whom he had been commissioned and to whom he returns. He acts out of this awareness. Jesus knows *that the Father had given all things into his hands* — again drawing on the idea of "agency." In commissioning an agent, "the sender transferred his own rights and the property concerned to the agent."[17] The Father has conferred on Jesus full powers for his appointed task of bringing eternal life. In the johannine portrait, this hidden giving by the Father is known to Jesus, and Jesus acts in awareness of it.

The Evangelist says that Jesus knows *that he had come from God and was going to God.* This is a concise statement of the descent-ascent formula of johannine christology (which will be considered in the next chapter of this study). The Evangelist sets Jesus' act of washing the feet of his disciples against the contour of the redemptive saga.

As the Evangelist describes Jesus' action, he says that Jesus voluntarily laid aside his outer robe, *himatia* (v. 4), just as his clothes (including his *himatia*) will be taken from him at the crucifixion (19:23). In a brief narrative, told with economy of detail, this author makes a point of saying that Jesus took off *(tithēmi)* his outer robe to become a servant (v. 4) and then put it on again *(lambanō)* when he returned to the table (v. 12). These verbs of divesting and re-vesting are the same as those that are used in 10:17-18 where Jesus says *I lay down (tithēmi) my life that I may take it*

16. A. Jaubert, "Qumran Calendar and Passion in John," in J. H. Charlesworth, ed., *John and the Dead Sea Scrolls* (New York: Crossroad, 1990), 69.

17. Borgen, "God's Agent," 141.

(lambanō) again. The Evangelist narrates Jesus' actions at the table using language that Jesus had earlier used to describe his vocation as redeemer.

"Laying down" is a small, but signficant bit of johannine vocabulary. The verb *tithēmi,* which is used in 13:4 for Jesus putting aside his garments, will appear, with ironic overtones, later in this chapter (13:37-38). Then in the Second Discourse (15:13) Jesus says, with obvious reference to himself, that the supreme love is to *lay down* one's life for another (and see 10:17). This expression is also used in 1 John 3:16 of Jesus laying down his life: *By this we know love, that he laid down his life for us; and we ought to lay down our lives for one another.* It seems that in the late-first-century johannine community *tithēmi* was becoming a common term for Jesus' self-sacrifice. His "laying down" his life was a self-giving to be replicated as his followers gave themselves, as they could, for one another.

In the later developed theological discourse of the church, accounts of the atonement have been developed heavily in Pauline terms (or in terms that have been taken to have been derived from Paul). It is of interest that the Fourth Gospel's presentation of the saving work makes no use of such ideas as sin-bearing, penalty, reconciliation, substitution, justification, or propitiation. When the Fourth Gospel speaks of Jesus' atoning act, it simply says that Jesus "laid down his life for others."

Although the term remains undeveloped in the johannine literature, it is inevitably associated with one piece of theological reflection. For an act of one to be effective for many, there must be a connection between the one and the many. (The connection is suggested by the preposition "for," *hyper,* which is often associated with *tithēmi.*) Jesus speaks of himself as the shepherd who lays down his life for the sheep to which he is bound (10:15); he is the grain that falls into the ground and "dies" for the sake of a harvest (12:24); he lays down his life for his friends (15:13); he is the Vine which contains the branches (15:1-3). Jesus acts for those with whose life he is bound up. The One carries in himself the many.

The entire Fourth Gospel is about salvation, but the simple proposition that Jesus lays down his life for those he loves is its characteristic statement of the work of Christ. There are atonement questions that such a statement does not answer or even entertain, but the johannine proposition is significant for the affirmation it makes so simply.

There is a real "descending" action in the Evangelist's incarnational christology, and the foot-washing speaks of it. Jesus' act of humility is to be seen as "a *katabasis.*"[18] His self-abandonment for others, which shocks Peter's

18. C. H. Dodd, *The Interpretation of the Fourth Gospel* (Cambridge: Cambridge University Press, 1953), 401.

sensibilities, points to "that potent nothingness which overtakes and stops the abysmal plunge away from God."[19] But there is a corresponding "ascending" movement. Jesus is "going to God" (v. 1). Yet he goes by way of the cross. The humiliation of the foot-washing, followed by his resumption of his place at the table, prefigures the glory-in-humiliation of the johannine Passion. The basis for mutual, diaconal love among Christians is not the ethical example of Jesus only, but more deeply, it lies in his entire self-giving, redemptive work. Ethic is bonded to kerygma. The johannine story of Jesus washing the disciples' feet is an indirect but unmistakable telling, through action, of the gospel of the Word made flesh.

A Sacramental Meaning

Sacramental references in the Fourth Gospel are always problematic at best, and any sacramental meaning that may be proposed in the foot-washing act is necessarily somewhat conjectural. Nevertheless, there are hints, and they may be pursued.

Water and imagery of washing and birth are important in this Gospel, as is imagery of bread and wine and of eating and drinking. Yet there is no actual baptism of Jesus (1:29-34) and no act in which Jesus bids his followers to perpetuate the Lord's Supper. Baptismal allusions are largely located in the birth-from-above discourse of chapter 3, while eucharistic meanings are expressed principally in the Bread of Life discourse which follows the feeding sign in chapter 6.

This foot-washing incident of John 13 stands in the place that the account of the Last Supper fills in the Synoptic Gospels. Why this incident appears in this location and why Jesus' words and actions with the bread and wine do not appear has long been discussed, but without a satisfactory conclusion. The johannine story of Jesus washing his disciples' feet has what might be thought of as its own dominical command to "do this" (13:14) as clearly as the Last Supper accounts do. One drastic possibility might be entertained: Did the Community of the Beloved Disciple (a group about whose life almost nothing is known) practice some ritual of foot-washing alongside of, or even instead of, the communal Supper? And did this community root its practice in what it took to be an instituting act in Jesus' ministry?

19. Guardini, *The Lord,* 365.

But the Supper may be in mind. Taking account of the Evangelist's subtleties, a Christian prophet, speaking in the context of the cultic meal, may refer to the Supper indirectly here by referring to what the Supper refers to.

Paul is a witness to some of the understandings of the church's Thanksgiving Meal that had at least some currency in the first-century church. The Lord's Supper, as Paul saw it, was an effective sign of *participation in Christ.* Paul's fundamental religion of *not I, but Christ in me* (Gal. 2:20) was actualized in the Supper (1 Cor. 10:17; 12:13). Similarly, the johannine Bread of Life discourse (ch. 6), with its unmistakable sacramental allusions, underlines the theme of mutual abiding, *Those who eat my flesh and drink my blood abide in me and I in them* (6:56). The realistic language of John 6 virtually says that in the Eucharist the believer ingests Christ. The emphasis on mutual indwelling in the Farewell chapters, *I am in my Father, and you in me, and I in you* (14:20, also v. 23; 15:5, 7; 17:20-23, 26), would have been appropriately understood as a meaning of the Lord's Supper. Jesus' words to Peter *Unless I wash you, you have no share in me* indicate that the foot-washing stands for a profound union with Jesus. The language of washing sounds more like baptismal imagery than like eucharistic imagery, but both the water/birth cluster and the food/sustenance cluster of johannine images speak of an essential participation in Jesus.

The first-century Christian Eucharist also spoke of *unity.* Paul describes the Supper of the Lord as a sign of the oneness of the people of Christ: *Because there is one loaf, we who are many are one body, for we all partake of the same loaf* (1 Cor. 10:17; see also 11:18-19). The *Didache* emphasizes in its prayer over the bread (6:4; 10:5) the gathering of many into one church. The theme of oneness seems to arise naturally from the sharing of food. The reiteration of the petition *that they may be one* in Jesus' prayer (John 17:22-23) may suggest that this Farewell material, with its passionate concern for unity, was shaped, at least in part, in a sacramental setting.

Paul is offended to hear that at the Lord's Supper at Corinth there were selfishness and disregard for those who had little and were hungry; he commends concern for the needy (1 Cor. 11:18-22, 33-34). Perhaps the story of Jesus' act of serving, set in this location, is meant to show the mutual caring among Jesus' followers towards which the Supper must lead.

Such themes and bits of vocabulary can suggest that the meaning of the early Christian Lord's Supper, at least as it is known from Paul, had ties with church themes that are developed in the Farewell Discourses and are enacted in Jesus' washing of the disciples' feet.

An Eschatological Meaning

In this story, the Teacher and Lord takes the place of a slave and washes the feet of the disciples. Does this role-reversal point towards the final great inversion of things, described in apocalyptic literature, when the mighty are brought low and the humble are raised up?

Many interpreters connect Jesus' demonstration of humility in John 13 with Luke 22:27, which mentions a dispute among the disciples at the Supper as to who should be greatest. Jesus rebukes the dispute by contrasting the competitive, status-conscious order of "gentile" society (the *goyim*) with the way it should be among his followers, where the greatest must be as the least and the leader as one who serves. *For which is greater, one who sits at table, or one who serves? But I am among you as one who serves.* Both this Lukan passage and John 13:1-17 are set in Jesus' final meal with his disciples, and both contain the motif of the servant-master.

In Luke's account of the Lord's Supper, Jesus relates his final meal with his disciples to an eschatological banquet. Those who sit with him in the Upper Room in Jerusalem anticipate another meal: *I confer on you, just as my Father has conferred on me a kingdom* (Luke 22:29-30). A reader of Luke will have encountered related imagery in 12:37, where, in a parable of the coming of the Son of man, the eschatological meal mingles with the role-reversal motif: *Blessed are those slaves whom the master finds alert when he comes; truly I tell you, he will fasten his belt and have them sit down to eat, and he will come and serve them.*

Can the eschatological factor in the heavenly meal of Luke 12:37 carry suggestion over into the johannine incident? The later johannine First Discourse will say that the final things are now. Jesus' "coming" to his followers is in the church and the Paraclete. Does this incident in which Jesus washes the disciples' feet carry hints of the "nowness" of things to come? Thinking of Luke 12:37, Jesus' act of washing the disciples' feet can be seen as a prefigurement of the heavenly meal. Jesus' role-reversal suggests that the new order of things does not belong to a far-off time. The master has already begun to serve his servants — in this symbolic act and in the redemptive death to which it points. Where Jesus' followers serve one another, the power of the age to come is actualized. As F. W. Dillistone remarked: "To be united with Jesus in the process of self-emptying and humble service, even to the limit of suffering and death, is to share His glory already and to be assured of entering at length into the glory which Jesus Himself shared with the Father from the foundation of the world."[20]

The Meanings Together

Four strands of meaning — ethical, christological, sacramental, and eschatological — seem to be suggested in this brief account. However, to analyze the text along such lines separates things which are compacted in the text itself. The author tells his story with such density of meaning that readers must cautiously distinguish his overlays of meaning. These strands comprise one textured narrative. A reader should only analyze in order to synthesize.

Ethical obligation is a sharing in Christ, dying and rising; it is a seizing of the new order in which those who reign serve; and it is an enactment of that which is ritualized in the sacraments. *Christology,* Jesus' taking the form of a servant, is the basis for serving others; it is the reality in which the church participates through sacramental life; it is an inauguration of the final things. *Sacraments* are rooted in the reality of Jesus, dead and living; they are validated in mutual service; they are signs of the new age. *The eschatological order* is brought in by a crucified Messiah, apprehended in sacramental life, and demonstrated as Jesus' followers serve one another.

Several of these strands of meaning were in the mind of the great Roman Catholic lay theologian Friedrich von Hügel when he wrote to his niece in 1918, remarking that a fastidious, elitist faith is rebuked by the homely heroism of "a deeply *costingly* realized Christianity," illustrated in Jesus' washing the feet of his disciples:

> I told you of my choking emotion in reading, in St. John's Gospel, that scene of Jesus, the Light of the World (that He is this, is an historic fact), as the menial servant at the feet of those foolish little fishermen and tax-gatherers, what do you think moves me but just that huge life-and-love-bringing paradox, here in its fullest activity?[21]

20. F. W. Dillistone, *The Christian Understanding of Atonement* (Philadelphia: Westminster, 1968), 318-19.

21. F. Von Hügel, letter of Dec. 11, 1918, *Letters From Baron Friedrich Von Hügel to a Niece* (London and New York: Dent and Dutton, 1928), 10.

In the lectionary. The *Revised Common Lectionary* appoints the story of Jesus washing the disciples' feet for Maundy Thursday in all three years. Along with the foot-washing passage from John, the lectionary appoints a Passover lesson from the Jewish Scriptures, as well as the narrative of the Last Supper from 1 Corinthians.

With such a wealth of biblical material, a preacher must decide where the homiletic emphasis will fall. The Passover readings fit the Synoptic accounts in which the Last Supper is a Passover Seder, but not the Fourth Gospel in which the Supper is not the Paschal meal. Paschal significance attaches in John to Jesus' crucifixion, and the foot-washing takes the place of the institution of the Supper. Vivid incidents, which only appear separately in the biblical literature, thus stand side-by-side in the readings that the lectionary appoints for Holy Thursday.

A preacher need not try to reconcile the New Testament chronologies or decide that one of them is right, while being uncomfortable when referring to the sources that give the other. Each of them coheres on its own terms, and "both seem to be operating symbolically, and if historically, only incidentally so."[22] A preacher should not pass between the Synoptic narrative and the johannine narrative as though they told the same story, as they do not. Rather, one should choose one's text or emphasis and develop it on its own terms.

Along with this johannine scripture passage, new service books are commending some act of foot-washing in the Maundy Thursday liturgy. This practice is finding a place within the liturgical life of many congregations in the Christian West, Catholic and Protestant. It has a deep history. The *pedelavium* can be traced to the seventh century. In the Eastern churches, it is carried out dramatically, with persons taking the parts of Jesus, Peter, and Judas. The splendid Latin hymn, the *Ubi Caritas,* was written for the ritual, probably about 800 CE in the Benedictine monastery at Reichenau. The hymn begins:

> Where charity and love are found, there is God.
> The love of Christ has gathered us together into one.
> Let us rejoice and be glad in him.
> Let us fear and love the living God,
> and love each other from the depth of our heart.
> Where charity and love are found, there is God.

Very widely in the West on Holy Thursday the bishop would wash the feet of several poor men. Ritual foot-washing has been widely practiced in monastic communities, with the abbot or abbess taking the lead. In such close-knit groups, along with remarkable unity, there can be contention. The washing of feet can be an expression of the oneness and mutual deference that exist in the community and at the same time it can be a call to bring about a oneness that does not yet exist.

22. G. Sloyan, *John* (Interpretation; Atlanta: John Knox, 1988), 167.

The regular washing of feet has also been a distinctive ritual practice in a few small Protestant groups.

Many of the revised liturgical texts of the later twentieth century have commended this ritual act to congregations at the Holy Thursday liturgy. Following the Gospel and homily, the celebrant begins by washing the feet of some members of the congregation. Sometimes a few persons volunteer to have their feet washed. However, the liturgical directions of most service books are deliberately non-prescriptive, and in some places all members of the congregation take part in washing the feet of others and having their own feet washed. Despite (or perhaps because of) some inevitable clumsiness and even messiness in carrying out the act, it can be deeply moving.

To be sure, the social meaning of having the feet of one's guests washed as they arrive for dinner has disappeared, reducing the connection of the ritual act to ordinary life. Nevertheless, in twenty-first-century society, for one person to wash the feet of another (even where it is done for a few token persons) is a strong, elemental gesture. Feet, hands, water, a pitcher and basin, a towel, and kneeling before someone else are acts that retain their significance through all cultural changes. Twenty-first-century Christians are made present in that first-century room on that momentous night. Jesus' injunction that his followers wash one another's feet is being literally obeyed. This johannine passage about the servant life of the church is a challenge to ceremonial as well as to preaching and ethics.

---

2. Into the Night (13:21-30)

A second incident follows: Judas is dismissed. Jesus permitting him, he leaves the group of disciples and goes to Jesus' enemies, setting in motion the overt steps that will lead to Jesus' crucifixion. The disciples have been treated thus far as a united group. Jesus loved *his own* without exception. He washed the feet of each. But Judas has been an alien presence. He was noted as such in the Book of Signs (see 6:64, 70-71; 12:4-8) and is noted again, as we have seen, three times in the story of the foot-washing (13:2, 10b-11, 18). Now he briefly comes into the center of the story.

A reader passes between these two incidents with a startling sense of their contrast.

- The foot-washing presents a community whose members are bonded in mutual serving on the model of Jesus' humble service.

  The dismissal of the traitor sees one person separated from the group and exposes his disloyalty to Jesus.

- The foot-washing begins with Jesus' confidence in his relation to God: *Jesus, knowing that the Father had given all things into his hands, and that he had come from God and was going to God, got up from the table. . . .*

  The dismissal of Judas begins with Jesus as a troubled leader, making his terrible announcement in human pain: *After saying this Jesus was troubled in spirit, and declared* (emartyrēse, *testified*), *Very truly, I say to you, one of you will betray me.*

After washing the disciples' feet and before he begins his extended discourses, Jesus (who, in the Fourth Gospel, is always in command of events) separates Judas from the other disciples and allows him to go to his enemies. This straightforward yet complex account begins with Jesus, inwardly troubled, announcing that a member of the group will betray him (v. 21). The disciples wonder who it might be, and a request that Jesus identify the traitor is passed from Peter by way of an unnamed person who enters the story at this point and who is referred to as *the Disciple whom Jesus loved* (vv. 22-25). Jesus replies and acts so as to indicate Judas (v. 26). Then he dismisses Judas (v. 27), while the remaining disciples mistake the reason for his departure (vv. 28-29). With no interference Judas leaves (v. 30).

> After saying this
>   Jesus was troubled in spirit, and declared,
>   "Very truly, I tell you,
>   one of you will betray me."
> The disciples looked at one another,
>   uncertain of whom he was speaking. 13:21-22

Jesus makes his startling announcement that one of his followers will betray him (punctuating it with *Very truly*). He knows that he will be betrayed and by whom. In this knowledge, he acts. Although he is troubled, he remains in command of events; he will, in effect, release the traitor (v. 27). When Judas subsequently reappears, leading the arresting party to the place where Jesus can be found, Jesus again takes the initiative, identifying himself to his captors, and placing himself in their custody (18:2-11).

Jesus' announcement is made in emotional distress: *He was troubled in spirit.* The Greek verb *(tarassō)* was used earlier of Jesus' state of mind at the grave of Lazarus, *he was deeply moved* (11:33), and also in 12:27 (a moment of interior stress which is often taken to be the johannine equivalent of the Gethsemane experience reported in the Synoptics: *Now my soul is troubled*). In Ezek. 32:2 (LXX) and elsewhere *tarassō* is used of stormy, agitated water. The next verb, *and declared,* is *martyrein* (the word from which "martyr" would come), a strong word for giving witness or for uttering an avowal drawn by deep conviction. The Evangelist portrays Jesus' loss of Judas as an event that moved him deeply.

There seems a special poignancy in the words *one of you will betray me*. Earlier, the traitor had been spoken of as one of the inner group of Jesus' followers: *Judas . . . though one of the twelve, was going to betray him* (6:71). The betrayal and the fact that it came from one whom Jesus had chosen and taken into his most intimate circle was remembered by those who told the story.

A startling announcement has been made in the room — particularly shocking coming as it does immediately after Jesus had commended and demonstrated self-giving service. The stunned disciples *looked at one another, uncertain of whom he was speaking.*

In the Synoptic accounts, Jesus also announces that he will be betrayed by one of the disciples. But Judas is not pointed out as the traitor (Matt. 26:21; Mark 14:18; Luke 22:21). When, in Matthew and Mark, the disciples hear that there is a betrayer in their midst, they exclaim *Surely, not I?* (Matt. 26:22; Mark 14:19). The Evangelist's statement, *The disciples looked at one another, uncertain of whom he was speaking* (v. 22), may be the johannine equivalent of that question. It suggests, as does the question in Mark and Matthew, that the disciples thought it could be any of them. However, the self-accusing question is not repeated in the Fourth Gospel. The Evangelist (assuming that he knew the Synoptic Passion accounts) may not want readers to suppose that the Beloved Disciple, who is present and is about to enter the story, could have entertained the question *Surely, not I?*

One of his disciples
— the one whom Jesus loved —
was reclining next to him;
Simon Peter therefore motioned to him
to ask Jesus of whom he was speaking.
So while reclining next to Jesus, he asked him,
"Lord, who is it?"

13:23-25

Peter seeks to learn the identity of the betrayer. (Perhaps a reader is to understand that he asks on behalf of the group.) But he asks by motioning to one who is closer to Jesus than he is — a disciple who is described as specially loved and reclining next to Jesus. (The Greek text says that he was *lying close to Jesus' breast,* vv. 23 and 25.) This unnamed person is "the Beloved Disciple," who will figure in the Passion and resurrection accounts and who here enters the johannine story for the first time.

The identity of "the Beloved Disciple" is one of the most persistently discussed topics in johannine studies. He (generally the follower of Jesus is taken to be male) is always close to Jesus — present at the crucifixion (19:26-27) and the first to grasp that Jesus has risen (20:8). Although he is always mentioned favorably, he is never named — neither in 13:23-25 nor in either of his later appearances.

His anonymity has suggested to interpreters that in addition to the places in which he is spoken of as "the disciple whom Jesus loved," he may be the unnamed follower of Jesus in some other places, such as 1:35-37 (uncertain); 18:15-16 (very likely so intended); and 21:2, 24 (again likely).

In all but one (19:26-27) of the places in which he is expressly identified, "the Beloved Disciple" appears along with Peter, but always in such a way as to show Peter at some disadvantage. It is often proposed that this feature of the narrative reflects a time of tension in the first-century faith community between johannine and petrine factions.

There is no counterpart in the Synoptic Gospels for this person or his role. He appears unmistakably only in the late chapters of the Fourth Gospel.

Tradition has been restless with anonymous persons, and many attempts have been made to link "the disciple whom Jesus loved" with known figures. The oldest guess (as early as the second century) is that the Beloved Disciple is John, the brother of James and son of Zebedee. Although in the Synoptic Gospels this John belongs to an inner group of Jesus' disciples, he is not mentioned in the Fourth Gospel, nor is his brother (although "the sons of Zebedee" are spoken of in the appendix, 21:2), and the omission is unexplained. Perhaps John bar Zebedee is the Beloved Disciple. However, objections can be raised to this identification: The Fourth Gospel does not mention a number of events with which, according to the Synoptic record, John was specifically associated. Moreover, the Beloved Disciple is depicted in the account of Jesus' trial as familiar with Jerusalem, and he seems to have had friends among officials there (18:15-16). Would John, or any Galilean disciple, be well acquainted with Jerusalem authorities? To turn the observation around, would an Evangelist with access to sources that are traced to John, Jesus' early disciple, have as little to say about Jesus' ministry in Galilee as the Fourth Gospel does?

In searching for other candidates, Lazarus has been proposed. But while he is spoken of as loved by Jesus (11:5, 36), he is never identified as a disciple. (His sisters, Mary and Martha, are also spoken of as loved by Jesus.) It is, moreover, difficult to see why, having been named freely in the events of which he is part (11:1-44; 12:1-2, 9-10), Lazarus would drop into namelessness in the Book of Glory.

Observing that nothing in the text requires that the Beloved Disciple be thought of as male, the possibility has been raised that Mary Magdalene may be the Beloved Disciple. Mary of Magdala is one of several important women in the johannine narrative — including the mother of Jesus, the Samaritan woman, and Mary and Martha. She is present at Jesus' crucifixion (19:25), and the resurrection accounts record an important exchange between Mary and Jesus at the empty tomb (20:1-2, 11-18, especially v. 17). She is entrusted to tell the disciples that Jesus has risen. These incidents indicate her closeness to Jesus, her dedication to him, and her importance among Jesus' followers. In the Synoptic Gospels she is listed first in a group of women who followed Jesus' ministry in Galilee and supported him with their means (Matt. 27:55-56, 61; Mark 15:40-41, 47; Luke 8:1-3; 24:10). To be sure, she is not designated as one of Jesus' disciples, but the Fourth Gospel makes no point of anyone's membership in an inner group around Jesus. She was a persuasive witness, one who would have been in a position to lend her experience and authority to the composition of a Gospel which might well have differed from the others in substance, point of view, and style. As Sandra Schneiders says, "If there is an eyewitness source behind the Fourth Gospel, the most clearly designated embodiment of that role in the text itself is Mary Magdalene."[23] There is at least as much to be said in behalf of Mary Magdalene as the Beloved Disciple as there is to be said for some other persons who have been proposed over the years by reputable scholars.

It has also been suggested that the writer of the Fourth Gospel is himself the Beloved Disciple. Might the anonymous author have cast himself in the role of this unnamed disciple who was especially close to Jesus? The credibility of this guess depends on whether or not it seems likely that the Fourth Gospel narrative reflects the experience of someone who has seen and heard Jesus. If the Beloved Disciple is the Evangelist, why does he place himself in the story only in its closing events, and why does he speak of himself so indirectly?

Lacking definite figures, it has been suggested that no identifiable person is intended here, but rather that the author introduces in the final incidents of his story an ideal follower of Jesus. However, even though the Beloved Disciple is always presented favorably (at some cost to the reputation of Peter), she/he is thoroughly human; the appendix speaks of her/his death (21:23). There is little to suggest that the Beloved Disciple is a more "made up" or cardboard figure than are other persons the author has placed around Jesus.

It seems likely that the Beloved Disciple is meant to be a definite person —

23. Sandra Schneiders, *Written That You May Believe: Encountering Jesus in the Fourth Gospel* (New York: Crossroad, 1999), 221.

someone who came to be the principal source of the Jesus traditions that were held in the johannine church and who gave to the johannine literature the authority claimed for it in 19:35 and 21:24 (and in 1 John 1:1). As someone who had been important in the founding of the community for which the Fourth Gospel was written and who provided its claim to authority, when the story of Jesus came to be written, it was told in such a way as to place her/him close to the climactic events of Jesus' mission and to suggest the reverence in which she/he was held by the later community.

Surmises about this enigmatic figure are bound up with the understanding one has of the character and historical origin of the Fourth Gospel and the community of faith from which it emerged. In the Farewell chapters the Beloved Disciple makes only this one appearance. The question of this follower's identity and role is less important in a study of the Farewell Discourses than it would be in an examination of the Passion and resurrection accounts, where the Beloved Disciple figures more conspicuously.

It seems significant that this specially loved disciple is brought into the story in the same incident in which Judas leaves.

> So while reclining next to Jesus, he [the Beloved Disciple] asked him,
> "Lord, who is it?"
> Jesus answered,
> "It is the one to whom I give this piece of bread
> when I have dipped it in the dish."
> So when he had dipped the piece of bread,
> he gave it to Judas, son of Simon Iscariot. 13:25-26

When Peter's inquiry is passed to him, Jesus replies that he will give a sign by passing a *piece of bread* (*psōmion,* "morsel" in RSV) to the one of whom he speaks. The term *psōmion* may mean simply a small piece of bread, but it can also refer specifically to bread that wraps the herbs at the Passover. Since in the johannine story this meal is not the Passover, that meaning would not seem to be intended. Jesus dips the bread in wine and gives it to Judas. Thus the identity of the betrayer is made known to the Beloved Disciple (and through the narrator to the reader), but evidently not to the others at the table.

> After he received the piece of bread,
> Satan entered into him. 13:27a

The character of Judas has been a challenge to biblical interpreters, novelists, dramatists, psychologists, theologians, and preachers. In the Fourth Gospel, however, he is simply shown as unaccountable, radical evil — a manifestation of the cosmic opposition, one inhabited by Satan. What he represents is terribly real, but not fully knowable.

The Fourth Gospel explains Judas, insofar as it does, not by exploring his motives, but by setting him in the context of the central johannine myth of conflict and redemption. Judas takes all of his meaning from his relation to Jesus — from his place in the accomplishment of the divine purpose through Jesus and from the cosmic opposition which that divine purpose encountered in its historical outworking and which Judas exemplifies: *Satan entered him* (v. 27). At his trial, Jesus says to Pilate, *The one who handed me over to you is guilty of a greater sin* (19:11).

Judas's commitment to his treachery follows this act of eating and sharing with Jesus. Intimacy and betrayal lie side by side. This Gospel tells of no persons possessed by demons who are cured by Jesus, but both here and in 13:2 Judas is described as in the control of Satan. (The name Satan is used only here; elsewhere the author speaks of the prince/ruler of this world or the devil; see 6:70; 7:20; 8:49-56; 10:20-21.) The abrupt terms seem to say that Satan took control of Judas at the moment he took the bread; as the TEV puts it, *As soon as Judas took the bread, Satan entered into him.* To some interpreters the words carry ironic sacramental overtones — suggesting a johannine equivalent of the Pauline warning against eating and drinking unworthily (1 Cor. 11:27-30). Perhaps sacramental meanings should not be introduced where none are clearly called for by the text, yet it is striking that this stark note of Judas passing into Satan's control occurs at the moment at which he received bread dipped in wine from the hand of Jesus.

A sacramental suggestion may also lie in the application of Ps. 41:9 to Judas in 13:18, *Even my bosom friend in whom I trusted, who ate of my bread, has lifted the heel against me.* In quoting this text, the Evangelist alters the LXX verb from the customary word for eating *(esthein)* to the unusual, graphic, physical term for eating *(trōgein),* which means something like "to crunch." This is the verb which Jesus used in the unambiguously eucharistic paragraph of the Bread of Life discourse of eating his flesh: *Those who eat (trōgein) my flesh and drink my blood have eternal life* (6:54-58). By repeating the verb from chapter 6 (and by using the verb only in these two places in the Gospel) the author may have planted a sacramental allusion in his account of the dismissal of Judas. If one cannot read a sacramental reference in this passage with full confidence, at least one should not fail to take into account its possibility.

This Evangelist, indeed the New Testament generally, shows an obvious difficulty in accounting for Judas. (In the Gospels, Judas says nothing.) For an act so treacherous, so evil, no motivation seems adequate, and this writer supplies none. Paul Duke remarks, "No silver pieces tinge the betrayal in John's Gospel."[24] When the Evangelist says that Satan entered Judas, he is saying that the forces acting in this event lay beyond Judas and what he might have supposed himself to be accomplishing; he was, in effect, being used by brute, inexplicable evil.

> Jesus said to him,
> "Do quickly what you are going to do." 13:27b

Jesus' words read as though he was releasing Judas to get on with his deed, suggesting that neither Judas nor Satan can act except as they are permitted by Jesus.

> Now no one at the table knew why he said this to him.
> Some thought that because Judas had the common purse,
> Jesus was telling him,
> "Buy what we need for the festival";
> or that he should give something to the poor. 13:28-29

The writer's plot has a difficulty. If Jesus says that he will be betrayed (as he does also in the Synoptic Gospels), and if the identity of the betrayer is made clear, even if only to a few disciples near to Jesus (it is not in the Synoptics), why did no one sense what was taking place and act so as to stop Judas? Why did no one grasp what Jesus had made clear enough?

The Evangelist seeks to deal with this narrative problem. Not every reader will think that he has done so with complete success. The loyal disciples, unaware of what is taking place, put an innocent construction on Judas' departure, supposing him sent out on an errand of necessity or of mercy. Their misconstruction depends on Judas's role as "bursar" of the group, which the author introduced earlier (12:6).

24. Paul Duke, *Irony in the Fourth Gospel* (Atlanta: John Knox, 1985), 99.

So, after receiving the piece of bread,
he immediately went out.
And it was night. 13:30

Judas *immediately went out.* The term *went out (exerchomai)* has the ordinary meaning of "he left the room," but it hints at further significance. 1 John is a letter (or homily) from the same Christian community from which the Fourth Gospel came, but written later. At a time probably not long before the writing of 1 John, the johannine community had evidently suffered a grievous loss of members. The writer says of persons who had lapsed or had broken with the community of Jesus: *They went out from us, but they did not belong to us; for if they had belonged to us, they would have remained with us. But by going out, they made it plain that none of them belongs to us* (1 John 2:19). This wounded community seems to have made the ordinary verb "go out" *(exerchomai)* into a quasi-technical term for persons who had been within the believing group — to all appearances, solidly within it — for a time, but had "gone out" from it and toward "antichrist." The same defection which Jesus found among "his own" was experienced in the early church and was spoken of using the same terms that the Evangelist used to describe Jesus' loss to Satan of his "familiar friend."

And it was night: The words seem more than a reference to the fact that the meal was in the evening. This author has a sense for symbols, and "darkness" is a powerful image (see 1:5; 3:19; 12:35; 1 John 1:5; 2:8-11), standing for the negation, for all that is apart from God or against God. There are works that are appropriate to darkness and not to light, because they are evil (3:19-20). Judas leaves the intimate group of Jesus and his followers reclining around a table of sharing, and he passes out into the night, there to find Jesus' mortal enemies. If one may draw a comment from an unusual source, Whittaker Chambers, the enigmatic figure of the Hiss/Nixon era, remarked out of his tormented experience, "On the road of the informer it is always night."[25]

In the lectionary. The Revised Common Lectionary appoints the dismissal of Judas as the Gospel for Wednesday of Holy Week, the day before Maundy Thursday. (Holy Week is a week of incidents. The subsequent *discourses,* which describe

25. Whittaker Chambers, *Witness* (New York: Random, 1952), 456, a sentence that came to my notice through being quoted in Fawn M. Brodie, *Richard Nixon: The Shaping of His Character* (Cambridge: Harvard University Press, 1983).

the community of the new aeon, are not read in Holy Week but are appointed for the weeks of the Easter season.) The presence of Judas at the Supper is noted in all the Gospels, and his dismissal is described rather circumstantially in Matthew, Mark, and John and more summarily in Luke. The events of Jesus' Passion could not be adequately told with Judas's role left out.

This story, coming as it does during Holy Week, provides the preacher and the congregation with a sense of conflict and historical actuality. While Judas opposes Jesus, his motives must forever remain a mystery. Did Judas intend evil, or did he do evil while intending good? He must have been a complex person, but the Gospels do not psychologize. The Fourth Gospel goes to ultimacies and presents Judas as a tool of the cosmic adversary. He collaborated not so much with Jesus' Jerusalem opponents as with Satan.

The johannine story is thrust forward, not by what Judas may have intended, but by what Jesus intended, what God intended.

---

3. About the Discourses

The Farewell chapters of the Fourth Gospel are greatly loved, often read, frequently referred to and preached. What Jesus said to his followers on his last night with them seems to leap over the centuries and to speak of and to the perennial "Christian condition."

Jesus expresses his Farewell approachably, using everyday language. However, as one reads, one becomes aware that some terms are being used in unusual senses. Interior references reach towards one another, producing dense, complex passages in which connections that link one idea to the next are often left unexpressed. Throughout the Fourth Gospel, but concentrating in the Farewell chapters, the author has created a distinctive vocabulary, often adapting words of ordinary speech so that they carry a more than ordinary burden of meaning. These chapters do not hold their themes before a reader in discursive explanations or linear argument, but rather in Jesus' running speech, often using multivalent terms and paradoxical juxtapositions. Simplicity and complexity, accessibility and opacity stand side by side. When in speaking with his followers Jesus is asked for clarification and gives it, his words provide answers and at the same time they often lead to further levels of mystery.

The Fourth Gospel usually means what it seems on the surface to mean, but it also means more than that. It asks and it rewards careful reading.

Character and Origin

From the departure of Judas (13:30) to Jesus' movement with his friends to the garden where he will be betrayed, arrested and taken to trial (18:1), there are no incidents, but rather a sustained body of speech by Jesus to his anxious followers (13:31–16:33), leading to a prayer of summing-up and intercession (ch. 17). This flow of speech is started when Jesus announces that he will soon leave his disciples: *I am with you only a little longer* (13:33). His *hour* is approaching. Jesus knows its meaning as the others in the room cannot guess. He is confident, while they are troubled (14:1, 27; 16:33); he seeks to inform and support them, but he often seems to speak beyond his disciples' ability to understand him.

Lengthy thematic self-presentations by Jesus (usually referred to as "discourses") are familiar from the earlier chapters of the Fourth Gospel. In the Book of Signs, Jesus had presented himself as Light and Life to a world held in darkness and death. He asked for belief in himself. For the most part, his appeals were disregarded. In the Farewell Discourses, however, he does not speak to a public audience, but to followers who do, at least in a basic way, trust him, telling them of his future and theirs.

Thus these Discourses take their place among other occasions, classical and biblical, in which important figures, at the point of death or departure, gather followers and offer parting counsel.[1] The most memorable biblical farewells are Jacob's blessing his sons (Genesis 49) and Moses' blessing the children of Israel (Deuteronomy 33).[2] Such Pentateuchal models were developed in late Hebrew literature in books of "Testaments." Still later, in the Christian Scriptures, the Book of Acts reports Paul's parting words to the Ephesian elders (Acts 20:17-35).

The best-known example in classical literature is Socrates' leave-taking. The original, provocative Greek thinker had been condemned and sentenced to death by the Athenian council (c. 399 BCE). As he faced the end, with his followers around him, he spoke of what might lie ahead for

1. There are discussions of the literature of farewell in Raymond Brown, *The Gospel according to John* (2 vols., Anchor Bible; Garden City: Doubleday, 1966-70), 597-601, and Fernando Segovia, *The Farewell of the Word* (Minneapolis: Fortress, 1991), 5-20. See also the first chapter of William S. Kurz, *Farewell Addresses in the New Testament* (Collegeville: Liturgical, 1990).

2. See Aelred Lacomara, "Deuteronomy and the Farewell Discourse (Jn. 13:31–16:33)," *CBQ* 36 (1974), 65-84. See also Paul Minear, "The Beloved Disciple in the Gospel of John," *NovT* 19 (1977), 108-9. E. Stauffer, *New Testament Theology* (London: SCM, 1965), 344-47, contains an appendix listing a number of characteristics of farewell speeches. However, only a few of the features of the genre identified by Stauffer are found in John 13–17, the most extended instance of farewell in the New Testament.

him. A disciple who was not present asked that the scene and the talk be re-created for him:

> *Echecrates:* I see; but when it came to his actual death, Phaedo — what was said, what was done, which of his close friends were present? Or did the authorities forbid that anyone should be with him, so that he died with no one at his side?
>
> *Phaedo:* No, no: some friends were there, quite a number indeed.
>
> *Ech.:* Well, please do your best to give us a reliable report, unless you chance to be busy.
>
> *Ph.:* No, I am not busy, so I will try to tell you the whole story.
>
> (*Phaedo,* 58D, R. Hackforth trans.)

Such literary farewells often seem somewhat staged. A departing leader assembles persons who represent the community in which he hopes to see his work perpetuated. Jacob called his sons to him, *Gather around, that I may tell you what will happen to you in days to come* (Gen. 49:1). Paul drew around him the elders of the Ephesian church (Acts 20:17). In the johannine Farewell only a few of Jesus' followers who were present are named. Yet the narrative clearly indicates that Jesus is with an inner group to which he imparts the meaning of his leaving.

The Evangelist does not try to establish that a reliable record of Jesus' words was preserved. Since the voice throughout is that of the johannine Jesus, which cannot be distinguished from the voice of the Evangelist, the discourses would seem to be largely the work of the writer. They are an instance of a rhetorical convention widely used in antiquity called *prosopopoeia* — a dramatic re-creation of what a speaker might have said in a certain situation. The Greek historians placed orations in the mouths of political and military leaders; and the speeches of the book of Acts, which read like set pieces, seem to fall within this convention.

To say that these discourses (whatever recollections of Jesus and his words may have found a place within them) are the work of the Evangelist is not to diminish their seriousness. While they may not be literal reportage, they may yet be true in the sense that matters most. As one scholar has put it:

> We can imagine the evangelist seeking to reconstruct the scene and the discourse, not only from whatever oral tradition he had, but through prayerful meditation in search of inspiration. The reality and validity

> of inspiration were widely credited in the classical world, and inspiration was assumed to be a regular feature of poetic and sometime of philosophic composition.[3]

While these speeches by Jesus at the Supper are in style and vocabulary unmistakably johannine, the Synoptic Gospels all set a substantial block of teaching just prior to the passion account:

In Matthew, five chapters of teaching (chs. 21–25) fall after Jesus' entry into Jerusalem and his anointing at Bethany. In the corresponding location, Mark gives two and a half chapters of teaching (11:20–13:37). In Luke, after Jesus enters Jerusalem and cleanses the Temple, a section of teaching runs from 19:47 through 21:38, none of which is given privately. Luke, however, places some private sayings of Jesus at the Supper.

In the Synoptic Gospels, Jesus' Holy Week teaching includes: (1) his public responses to challenging questions, (2) teaching on prayer, which in Matthew and Mark is given to the disciples, and (3) teaching about final events, which is private in Matthew and Mark, but not in Luke.

The johannine Farewell Discourses and Prayer contain non-Synoptic material throughout. Thus the unusual thing about the johannine Book of Glory is not that a unit of teaching comes before the arrest of Jesus, nor that it is long, nor that it is spoken to the disciples. The unusual features are that it is all at the Supper and that it is entirely private (and being private, it is not argumentative). It is principally concerned with his followers and their relation to him, and through him, to the Father. Although the style of thought in the Farewell material is unmistakably johannine, it speaks of prayer, as does the Passion Week teaching in the Synoptic Gospels; and in its emphasis on what is to come, it speaks of the future, as does the very differently expressed apocalyptic teaching of the late chapters of Matthew, Mark and Luke.[4]

Although the Farewell Discourses were probably written for this place in this Gospel, they may have drawn on pre-existing material. Early Christian sources mention prophets who occupied an honored place in the Lord's Day assembly. It seems probable that the johannine believers formulated

3. George A. Kennedy, *New Testament Interpretation through Rhetorical Criticism* (Chapel Hill: University of North Carolina Press, 1984), 78.

4. C. H. Dodd, *The Interpretation of the Fourth Gospel* (Cambridge: Cambridge University Press, 1953), 390-96, discusses the relation between the Farewell section of the Fourth Gospel and the teaching material of the Synoptics, giving special attention to the "reinterpretation, or transmutation, of popular eschatology" in the johannine discourses.

the innovative features of their developing christology at least in part through gifted persons who spoke (perhaps sometimes in ecstasy) in the gathered church. These discourses may have been first articulated in that setting. David Aune writes: "The discourses of the Johannine Jesus bear unmistakable marks of having been formulated by prophetic or charismatic individuals within the context of the pneumatic worship of the johannine community."[5] Themes that were probably first explored in Spirit-given oral form were found to give sharable words to the community's faith, and the writer of the Fourth Gospel shaped them into written discourses.

Structure and Organization

The Farewell material that runs from 13:31 through chapter 16 has no clear linear organization. No argument or sequence of thought unifies Jesus' discourses; in a few places the thought seems to come to an ending or to take on a fresh beginning, but units of content are not clearly marked off. A few passages stand out because of their imaginative vigor. For example: Jesus' departure to his Father's house and his return for his friends (14:1-12), the image of the vine and its branches (15:1-7), or of the woman in childbirth (16:20-22). But no image is sustained for long. Short units of thought pass rapidly from one to the next, the connections between them often being left implicit.

In attempting to analyze these Farewell Discourses, several difficulties are encountered:

Duplications. A reader cannot help but observe that certain themes, after being mentioned once, circle back into attention.

Some of the repeated themes of chapters 13–16 are:

- Jesus' impending *departure*, which provides the "farewell" occasion, is spoken of in 13:33 then in 14:1-6, 25-27 and again in 16:5-7. (It occurs in Jesus' prayer, see esp. 17:11 and 13.) The idea that Jesus will be accessible to his followers in the old way for only "a little while" ap-

5. David E. Aune, *The Cultic Setting of Realized Eschatology in Early Christianity* (Leiden: Brill, 1971), 101. On the role of prophecy in the first-century church (but without much discussion of the Fourth Gospel) see M. Eugene Boring, *The Continuing Voice of Jesus* (Louisville: Westminster/John Knox, 1991).

pears briefly in 13:33 and 14:19 and then insistently in 16:16-22. It is not surprising that such a situational factor should be repeated; thus it is unexpected that the "I am about to leave you" theme is absent between 15:1 and 16:5, about one third of the discourse material.

- Jesus' *new commandment* that his followers love one another is introduced in connection with the foot washing in 13:12-16, and then it reappears in the discourses in 13:34-35 and again in 15:12-15, 17.
- The promise of *answered prayer* and the invitation to use *Jesus' name* in prayer appears in 14:12-14, returning in 15:7, 16 and again in 16:23-24 and 26-28.
- The theme of mutual divine-human *indwelling* is found in 14:20-23, in 15:1-11, 12-17 (and in 17:21 and 26). The Father is in Jesus; Jesus is in the Father; believers are in Jesus; and both Jesus and the Father are in believers.
- The *Spirit-Paraclete* is spoken of first in 14:15-17 and in 25-26, then again a chapter later in 15:26-27, and the theme is extensively developed in 16:7-15.
- *Joy* is promised in 14:28, in 15:11, and later in 16:22-24. And *peace* is mentioned in both 14:27 and 16:31-33.
- The sense that Jesus' followers live in *conflict with the world* is expressed in 15:18–16:4 and later in 16:33. The opposition is led by the "Prince of the World," 14:27-31 and 16:11; and "the evil one" is spoken of in 17:15.

The duplications in chapters 14 and 16 are most frequent.[6]

Earlier chapters of the Fourth Gospel have shown the author to be a craftsman. But this self-critical writer seems in these Farewell chapters to have said things well, and then within a few paragraphs to have said some of them again.[7] This repetition of themes has led some commentators to look for an organization of the discourses on a "circular" or "spiral" pattern, but the repetitions do not seem to follow any consistent scheme.

Non-Consecutive Passages. In addition to these duplications, a reader could hardly fail to observe several unexpected breaks in the text. At the end of chapter 14, after some verses which have the sound of a summing up,

6. Brown, *John,* 588-94, has a discussion and chart of these duplications.

7. The comment suggests one writer whose style of thought was to say a thing once and soon say it over again, the author of that rambling, associational, almost garrulous work, 1 John.

there is an unmistakable ending: *"Rise, let us be on our way"* (14:31). Yet three more chapters of speech by Jesus follow before the narrative moves ahead at 18:1, *After Jesus had spoken these words, he went out with his disciples across the Kidron valley.* Later, one notes that chapter 16 shows a similarly convincing finality in verses 31-32. Yet this verbal cadence is followed, not by advancing incident, but by a lengthy prayer in chapter 17. Why are there in this Farewell material two conclusions, neither of which concludes?

Another indication that an author or an editor nodded (at least by the standards of a modern copyreader) is that in 16:5 Jesus says, . . . *but none of you asks me 'Where are you going?'* Yet that question had, in fact, been expressly asked by Peter in 13:36, and Thomas had asked a similar question in 14:5.

Such puzzles in the text suggested to some early-twentieth-century commentators that chapters 14–16 come from an original unity whose parts had somehow gotten separated and out of sequence. Yet the manuscript tradition gives no evidence that blocks of text have become disordered, and the corrective rearrangements that critics proposed seem to raise as many questions as they answer.[8] It seems more likely that, rather than our present text containing dislocated parts of an original unity, several passages that originally existed independently have been brought together. Raymond Brown says, "There can be no doubt that the chapters that form the Last Discourse were not always united."[9]

Three Discourses and How They Came to Be

Although the text keeps its secrets, it does offer itself for analysis. The understanding of the origin and structure of the farewell material that is used in this study goes along these lines:[10]

8. The detection of disarranged sections of text was common in the early years of the twentieth century. One might cite the Moffatt translation of the New Testament, the commentary based on it (G. H. C. Macgregor, *The Gospel of John* [Garden City: Doubleday, Doran, 1929]), and the commentary by J. H. Bernard, *The Gospel according to St. John* (2 vols., International Critical Commentary; Edinburgh: Clark, 1928).

9. Brown, *Gospel according to John,* 582.

10. Careful readers of this Farewell material must try to account for its structure and purpose. Some scholars have thought that chapter 14 is one unit, while chapters 15–16 form another. There are differing ideas as to how 13:31-38 relates to what follows. In this study, the discussion of the origin and character of the Farewell Discourses is heavily indebted to John

The Evangelist drafted three texts of a Farewell Discourse, each one expressing somewhat different Jesus-and-his-people emphases and exhibiting different aspects of the Spirit-Paraclete. They appear to emerge from successive situations in the life of the johannine community:[11]

The *First Discourse* begins at 13:31, after Judas is sent out; and it continues to the obvious closure at 14:31: *Rise, let us be on our way.* This first version of a farewell speech would have been followed appropriately by 18:1, *When Jesus had spoken these words, he went forth with his disciples across the Kidron valley, where there was a garden.*

This first draft of Jesus' Farewell follows from Jesus' announcement that he is leaving. He seeks to support his followers in their sense of abandonment, telling them of his Father's house to which he is going and to which he will in time bring them. He develops the undiminished ties that will hold between himself and the disciples following his departure, albeit under changed circumstances. Jesus describes the divine Advocate who will be sent to them and who will keep him in their memory (14:25-26). The Discourse is concerned with continuity and with the relation of the absent/present Jesus to the company of those who had come to believe in him.

The Evangelist, however, has a second matter in mind. The johannine community of believers in Jesus had evidently been begun by apostolic witnesses who traced to the figure who is known in the Fourth Gospel as the Beloved Disciple (21:20-25, in this study, see pp. 53-55). Spiritual authority in the community and its contact with the story of Jesus had come through those original evangelists. As the community of the Beloved Disciple continued and grew, it could always refer its life to the trusted persons under whom it had been founded. But now this young church was losing its first generation of witnesses, and their passing raised questions of continuity and spiritual guidance. The Evangelist writes at two levels. When he tells what the departing Jesus said to his disciples, he refers at the

---

Painter, "The Farewell Discourses and the History of Johannine Christianity," *NTS* 27 (1981), 525-43. Painter's analysis gives an economical and satisfactory account of a text that contains many puzzles.

11. With the rough outline of stages in the history of the johannine church that is suggested here, one should compare the more developed (and perhaps necessarily exploratory and conjectural) work of Raymond Brown in *The Community of the Beloved Disciple* (New York: Paulist, 1979), which detects four phases in the development of the community and its theology. In an appendix (pp. 171-82) Brown explains the conclusions of other scholars who have also been at work reconstructing this history.

same time to his first-century readers who are losing their original witnesses and who fear lest the immediacy of their contact with the roots of their faith would be weakened.

Some authors revise a great deal; others do not. Yet anyone who has done much writing, especially on a project that takes a long time, is likely to have on hand several drafts of important passages. An initial effort gets down the heart of the matter, but if the work does not leave the author's custody, after a time, one has second thoughts. One's own mind has moved on, and new circumstances suggest a different angle of vision. In rereading, the author becomes convinced that the original work needs revision, but a little altering and adding will not do. One must start freshly. Yet the old text was good; one keeps it on hand. So an author has two, or in time more than two, drafts of material.

To speak of written texts and drafts is not an injection of modernity into this account. These Discourses, while they may have had an origin in oral address, by the time they entered the Fourth Gospel, were obviously written. The principal author of this Gospel concludes his work saying, *these [signs and words of Jesus] are written* (20:31), and the epilogue says that there is no limit to the *books* that would be needed to record all that Jesus did (21:24-25). Readers have here the work of an author who writes with care for people he knows.

Before the Evangelist's Gospel was ready for circulation, the believers in Jesus (who were at the same time practicing Jews) were shocked by the acute tensions that developed between themselves and the synagogue. This situation required the voice of Jesus.

The author did not discard the Farewell speech which he had already written. But he prepared a Second Discourse which addressed the new situation.

The conflict with the synagogue that occasioned the Second Discourse is spoken of in its second half — the passage that runs from 15:18 to 16:4a. Verse 16:2 refers clearly to the expulsion of the believers in Jesus from their local Jewish synagogue. When those who believed in Jesus as the Christ were read out of the Jewish community, they were exposed to peril. But in addition, when they were cast on their own, they had to sort out their independent identity. They drew their sense of themselves from their conviction that they were deeply united with the living Jesus. The writer explores this union between Jesus and his people in the first half of the discourse (15:1-17) — in the vine and branches image of 15:1-6 and in the themes that follow from it. Few persons could have felt confident in this time of challenge. Some Christians defected, while others remained (15:4-5, 7), but under conditions of stress. The Paraclete strengthens the church for courageous witness (15:26-27). The closing part of the Second Discourse (15:18–16:4a) develops more circumstantially the theme of the people of Jesus living with opposition and threat.

The end of the Second Discourse falls at a "literary seam" which comes in the middle of 16:4. The *this* of *I have said all this* in 16:1 and the *these things* of 16:4a both refer to what Jesus had been saying in the foregoing paragraphs. However, the *these things* of 16:4b seems to have forward reference to what he is about to say. Thus 16:4a is a conclusion, while 4b opens a new unit of thought; Jesus' Second Discourse begins at 15:1 and ends with 16:4a.

That a break was made between chapters 15 and 16 is understandable. When in the twelfth century, chapter units were entered in the Bible, an editor evidently noticed that at what we now call 16:1 Jesus begins to speak of his own speaking: *I have said all this to you to keep you from falling away.* He continues his self-reference in verse 4a with *But I have said these things to you,* and in 4b *I did not say these things to you from the beginning,* and in verse 6 *But because I have said these things to you.* So the start of this series of references by the speaker to his own speech (at 16:1) was made the beginning of a new chapter.

At some later time, after the composition of the Second Discourse, the crisis of the separation of the Jesus-people from the synagogue had largely passed. The believers in Jesus were living on their own, face-to-face with an unfriendly world. A Third Discourse was prepared. In this new composition (which begins at 16:4b and ends at 16:32-33) the Evangelist helps the young church, living now apart from the synagogue, to face its uncertain future in a hostile society. He tells the believers in Jesus that they can count on the Paraclete, who engages the world and contends with it in behalf of God (16:7-11). The Spirit is also a living voice, leading the disciples into truth which is both new and is at the same time the truth of Jesus (16:12-15). Some Christian believers seek to withdraw from an uncomprehending and threatening world. The Third Discourse urges the church to hold fast, for the anxiety and bewilderment of the present will not have the final word.

Before Jesus re-engages in public events, he offers a lengthy prayer (ch. 17). The prayer has its own somewhat abrupt opening and conclusion (17:1, 18:1); it looks both backward and forward. It may have been composed for its present location, quite possibly emerging from the same conditions that gave rise to the Third Discourse. In it, Jesus summarizes his completed work, and he prays for his people. The world can be seductive, and "the evil one" threatens. Christians under testing risk falling into disunity. But the Great Intercessor prays for them.

This rapid analysis of the structure of Jesus' Farewell will be filled out in closer detail in the following sections of this study.

Chapter 21, which contains post-resurrection incidents, seems to be by a second writer; it constitutes something like an "Appendix" to the Gospel. A reader may conjecture that the principal author of the Fourth Gospel died before his work had left his hands. A literary executor (a disciple who had absorbed the Evangelist's mind and style and who cherished every word he had left) found among his parchments three versions of Jesus' farewell speeches as well as a substantial prayer. There was also a scrap of writing material containing an incident of a woman taken in adultery, whose accusers brought her to Jesus; it might fit in somewhere. (It has for many centuries usually been set at 8:1-11.) The Farewell addresses were all of approximately the same length. Each seemed to have been written at a different time and to carry marks of the situation for which it was composed. Each was of great value — a veritable gift of the Spirit. Such duplications as they contained were not serious. Nothing this author had left should be set aside.

It seemed to this cautious editor that the three drafts could all be retained for the text of the Gospel and that they could be placed in the order in which they appeared to have been composed. The first version ended with an emphasis on the union of believers with Jesus and the Father (14:18-31), while the second version began with Jesus describing himself and his people as a vine and its branches (15:1-7). Similarly, the second version ended with Jesus speaking about his own words, *I have said all this to you . . .* and *But I have said these things to you . . .* (16:1, 4a), and the third version began in much the same way, *I did not say these things to you . . .* (16:4b). They too could go together. The prayer, a self-contained unit with much retrospective material, suited a location before the account of the passion events resumed.

Of course, before the composition would leave the hands of this conscientious editor there would be time to deal with such problems as the *Arise, let us go hence* at the end of the first version and the troublesome *None of you asks me . . .* in the third version. But his Gospel was in demand, and there was not time for such final editing. There never is.

Special Features of Situation, Themes, and Vocabulary

Some features of situation, emphasis and terminology set the Farewell material apart from the twelve chapters that precede it and give it its distinctive character and its place in the design of the Fourth Gospel:

From and to a Community of Faith

The Book of Signs tells that while there was a general public rejection of Jesus, there was some positive response as well. Repeatedly the Evangelist says: *There was a division; some believed, but some refused* (6:66; 7:43; 9:16; 10:19-20; 11:45-53). At no point, however, has attention come to focus on those who were receptive. Although Jesus specifically calls a few followers (1:37-51), there is no list of his disciples' names; the term "the twelve" is used twice and only in passing; and Jesus at no point gives a commission to his disciples to share in his work. The disciples are expressly mentioned at several incidents: They are present at the wedding at Cana (2:2); they baptize, although Jesus himself does not (4:1-2, a somewhat puzzling reference); they go into a Samaritan village to buy provisions (4:8); at the feeding of the multitude they distribute the loaves and fish and gather the fragments after the meal (6:3, 12-13); they are in the boat during the storm when Jesus comes to them (6:16-21); they go with him to Bethany and are on hand when Lazarus is raised (11:1-44); they are present at the anointing at Bethany (12:1-8) and at Jesus' entry into Jerusalem (12:12-22). These are hardly prominent roles. This Gospel conveys no sense that Jesus' followers were associated in his mission or were a special object of his care or that he said things to them that he did not say in public.

Yet a leader's thought can be most fully expressed to a sympathetic community. A reader of the Fourth Gospel realizes that even the story of Jesus' rejection is told by those who had "received" him (1:12). The account of the general blindness is given by the sighted. In the Prologue, the author says *we have seen his glory* (1:14), indicating that he writes from and for a community of believers. If, however, the author's presentation of Jesus is to be complete and convincing, he must give attention to the sighted and to what they saw.

It is the special function of chapters 13–17 (as of chapters 20 and 21) to focus on the disciples and their relation with Jesus. The "you" that Jesus addresses in these chapters is obviously, in the first instance, his disciples who had associated with him for many months, but who were now about to lose him. These men, several of whom are named, had been close to Jesus *from the beginning* (15:27), and now he is leaving. However, as he speaks to them, Jesus' references occasionally become more general; he refers to the wider community of those *who have my commandments and keep them* (14:21a). Even as Jesus speaks to his disciples, he speaks beyond them. While the "you" of these discourses is Jesus' immediate followers, it is also a larger community of consent. In the mind of the Evangelist, the disciples are the church, and the church is present in the disciples. If Jesus' disciples are themselves, they are also representative. Except in a few matters that bear on the primary, unrepeatable witness-bearing role of Jesus' immediate associates, his companions are (or they can represent) the community of believers which grew from their foundational witness.

Although Jesus speaks specifically to his disciples, their understanding of him is inadequate. When certain of them speak (in ch. 13, early in ch. 14, and again towards the end of ch. 16), they do not grasp what Jesus is saying. Like Nicodemus or the Samaritan woman or Mary of Bethany, their literalness misses Jesus' subtleties. Consistently they understand neither him nor themselves:

> You will never wash my feet. . . . Lord, not my feet only, but also my hands and my head! (13:8-9).
>
> Some thought that, because Judas had the common purse, Jesus was telling him, "Buy what we need for the festival" (13:29).
>
> Lord, why can I not follow you now? I will lay down my life for you, (13:37).
>
> Lord, we do not know where you are going. How can we know the way? (14:5).
>
> Lord, show us the Father, and we will be satisfied (14:8).

> What does he mean by saying to us, "A little while, and you will no longer see me, and again a little while, and you will see me," and "Because I am going to the Father?" They said, "What does he mean by this 'a little while'? We do not know what he is talking about" (16:17-18).

Then at the end of the Third Discourse, the disciples say *Yes, now you are speaking plainly, not in any figure of speech! Now we know . . . ; we believe . . .* (16:29-30). But Jesus' response is equivocal: *Do you now believe?* (16:31). A reader is quite sure that even then the disciples do not grasp much of what Jesus has been telling them. The disciples are not men of ill-will nor duller than others, but their incomprehension makes it clear that what the johannine Jesus knows about himself and his destiny no one else in the Fourth Gospel narrative knows.

Of course, the fact that these things are said about Jesus' knowledge and about the disciples' impercipience at the time of the story means that, by the time this Gospel was written, Jesus' community had come to know, and it could only have come to know through the testimony of the disciples themselves. These Farewell chapters, in effect, imply that what the disciples did not know then, they later came to know; and through them the readers of this Gospel now can know as well. The Evangelist, writing *now* as he does about the disciples *then,* gives evidence of a revolution in the consciousness of the followers of Jesus. The Paraclete's work — informing, reminding, clarifying, correcting, vitalizing — is implied. The Jesus who speaks to the disciples at the Supper is at the same time the first-century johannine church articulating what it has learned. Moreover, the circle of witness that grew from Jesus to the disciples, and from them to the first-century johannine community, continues to grow. Through the written Gospel, readers too are brought within this circle of privileged understanding (20:31).

Vocabulary Shift

In passing from chapters 1–12 to the Farewell chapters, a reader of the Fourth Gospel encounters several changes in vocabulary. Some words that had previously been important are reduced, while other terms move to the fore — indicating a shift in the writer's emphasis and purpose.

Several words that are of diminished importance in the Book of Glory may be identified:

"Believe." The term *believe* has been one of the organizing words of the Book of Signs. The verb *to believe* (it is never the noun "faith") is used more than 90 times in the Fourth Gospel, approximately 70 of its occurrences coming in the first twelve chapters. In the first large division of this Gospel the importance of believing is apparent not only in the frequency with which the word is used, but also in the urgency it conveys. Jesus' signs and his words are intended to elicit belief (2:11, 23; 4:42, 50, 53; 11:45); to believe in him is to have eternal life (1:12; 3:15-16, 36; 5:24; 6:40, 47; 11:25-27); unless one believes, one perishes (3:16, 18, 36; 8:24); through believing in Jesus one is delivered from the profoundest hunger and thirst (4:10-15; 6:35; 7:37-38); to believe in Jesus is to believe also in the one who sent him (10:37; 11:42). Jesus urges his hearers to believe in himself as the one from God. His mission has set before humanity life or death, and in the spirit of Israel's prophets, he, in effect, asks "Why will you die?" Yet the Book of Signs concludes saying, *Yet they did not believe in him* (12:37).

This word "believe" which has punctuated the first twelve chapters is used much less frequently and less urgently in chapters 13–17. (It is used in 13:19; 14:1 twice, 10, 12, 29; 16:9, 27, 30, 31; 17:8, 20, 21. It is missing altogether in the Second Discourse.) The basic importance of believing is not forgotten when Jesus converses with his followers; the relation to God is always secured and sustained by faith. However, in the Farewell Discourses Jesus is talking to persons who at least in a basic way have consented to him. Although their believing may need to develop, they have responded to him with trust, *They have believed that you sent me* (17:8). He does not urge upon them the life-or-death issue of believing so much as he describes for them the life that is opened to them because they have believed.

"Hear." The Fourth Gospel is a notably aural book; *hearing* appears more than thirty times in the Gospel as a whole. A relational fabric of speaking and hearing is described: Jesus hears the Father (8:26), and what he hears, he makes known (8:26; 15:15). Jesus' followers hear him (10:3, 16). The Father always hears Jesus (11:41-42); those who hear Jesus hear the Father (14:24); those who hear the Father come to Jesus (6:45); the dead will hear the voice of the Son of God (5:25, 28). Of course, there are those who do not hear (8:43, 47; 10:8). This urgent johannine emphasis on *hearing* to a great extent drops away in the Book of Glory. Twenty-seven of the appearances of *hear* fall in the first twelve chapters. The appeal to believe is an appeal to hear, and believing and hearing are emphases of the Book of Signs.

"Voice." Related to hearing is the noun *voice.* Chapters 1–12 mention the *voice (phōnē)* of John the Baptist (1:23), of the bridegroom (3:29), of the

Son of God (5:25, 28), of the (unheard) Father (5:37), of the Shepherd (10:3, 4, 16, 27), Jesus' voice at the grave of Lazarus (11:43), and a voice from heaven (12:28, 30). The Evangelist has in mind a living voice, a call. The voice is not merely the conveyor of a message; it is itself a part of the message. It is a vital reach of one person towards another. Thus it seems significant that *voice,* after having appeared more than a dozen times, often with marked theological significance, in chapters 1–12, disappears in the farewell chapters and returns only in 18:37. Although Jesus' words and his commandment(s) are emphasized in chapters 13–17, an urgent voice seeking response is not a theme of the Book of Glory, but of the Book of Signs.

"Life." Associated with the reduction in the terms "believe" and "hear" and "voice" is a reduction in the use of the term "life." In the early chapters of the Fourth Gospel, persons are urged to believe and live. The coming of Jesus was to make life available to those who receive him (1:4; 3:15-16, 36; 4:10-14; 5:21, 24, 40; 6:33-40, 51, 52-59, 63, 68; 8:12, 51-52; 10:10, 28; 11:25-26; 12:50). When at chapter 13 the story is no longer of Jesus' appeal to his hearers and his conflict with his enemies, but of his sharing with his followers, the term "life" all but vanishes. Of the 56 instances of "life," "live," or "living" in this gospel, only five occur in chapters 13–17: in 14:6, 19 (twice) and in 17:2, 3. At the conclusion of the book, the term returns, stating that the purpose of the Gospel as a whole is to impart belief and life (20:31). "Life," however, is principally a word of the Book of Signs.

"Light." The term *light* is used more than twenty-five times in the Fourth Gospel, in at least nineteen instances as an image referring to Jesus. The Prologue connects the light with the creative Word (1:4, 9). Jesus is the light of the world (8:12; 9:5), a light whose coming creates a crisis (3:19) in which some, having the light of life (8:12), can walk in the light (12:35-36), while others are exposed as deeply committed to darkness (3:19-21). But the light which came would withdraw. Before the darkness again closed in, persons were called to believe in the light and become its children (9:5; 12:35-36). The image of light and its corollary, darkness, is crucial in the thought of the first half of the Fourth Gospel. However, in chapters 13–17 the term simply disappears. *Light* is entirely a term of the Book of Signs.

"Witness." "Witness" (as verb, *martyrein,* or as noun, *martyria*) is an important term in johannine thought. Jesus himself is witness (5:36; 8:18; 18:37); others witness to him (1:15; 4:39; 5:32). Yet of the more than forty-five instances of this term in the Fourth Gospel, twenty-six appear in chapters 1–12, while only three occur in chapters 13–17, where in 15:26-27 they speak of the Paraclete and the church as witnesses. Similarly, while the

terms "to judge," *krinō*, or "judgment," *krisis*, are found twenty-six times in chapters 1–12, in the Farewell chapters they appear only in the passage in which legal terminology is used to describe the work of the Paraclete (16:8-11, three times). The dropping away in these chapters of "witness" and of "judge" suggests that in the second part of the Fourth Gospel the juridical imagery that has described the public ministry of Jesus has finished its part.

Two christological terms that speak of Jesus' revelational functions and that have been conspicuous in the Book of Signs are significantly reduced in the Book of Glory:

"Christ." The term "Christ" — the Messiah, the divinely anointed One — is used eighteen times in the Fourth Gospel, more often than in any of the Synoptics. Six of these occurrences fall in the bitter polemics of chapter 7 where the argument circles around whether or not Jesus is the Messiah. This title is often used in connection with confessing, believing, knowing or bearing witness (1:20; 3:28; 4:42; 6:69; 7:26; 9:22; 11:27). Even though the extensive use of the term by Paul indicates that in the early Christian decades, "Christ" had become a characteristic word of the church's vocabulary, it does not appear at all in the Farewell chapters of the Fourth Gospel. It does return in 20:31, where the Evangelist tells that his purpose in writing was to draw readers to believe that Jesus is the Christ, the Son of God. Yet in the Fourth Gospel, the title "Christ" belongs distinctively to the public self-presentation of Jesus in chapters 1–11.

"The Son." The term "the Son," used of Jesus as the Son of God, appears in the Fourth Gospel in the Prologue (1:14, 18) and thereafter 23 times in chapters 1–12. By contrast, it occurs only three times in the Farewell chapters (in 14:13 and twice in 17:1). (Later it can be found in 19:7 and 20:31.) The term "the Son" is characteristically used by the johannine Jesus in speaking of himself, affirming that he is uniquely rooted in the Father; he is one with the Father and acts by the Father's direction; in his acts, the Father acts. The Evangelist introduces the term in the Prologue, saying: *No one has ever seen God. It is God the only Son, who is close to the Father's heart, who has made him known* (1:18). Carrying such meaning, "the Son" is distinctively a term of the Book of Signs. (However, the term quickly came to be characteristic of the post-resurrection johannine community, as is indicated by the fact that Christ is designated *his Son* or *the Son*, or *the Son of God* 22 times in 1 John.)

If some terms are reduced in importance in the Farewell chapters, other terms come to the fore.

"Love." Perhaps the most conspicuous of the words that come into prominence in the Book of Glory is "love." Of the 36 times this word occurs in the Fourth Gospel, 33 are in chapters 13–17. It appears in the first verse and in the last verse of the Farewell chapters: *Having loved his own who were in the world, he loved them to the end* (13:1); . . . *so that the love with which you have loved me may be in them, and I in them* (17:26).

Instead of the urgent appeals to believe that mark the Book of Signs, there is a development in the Book of Glory of the theme of love. Standing among those who do believe, Jesus sets forth the relation with the Father and himself in terms of love: the Father's love for the Son (15:9-10; 17:23-26) and for those who believe in him (14:21-23; 16:27; 17:23); Jesus' love for the Father (14:31) and for his people (13:1; 15:9-10, 12); believers' love for Jesus (14:15, 21, 28; 16:27) and his command that they love one another (13:34-35; 15:12-13, 17).

"In" Phrases. The Fourth Gospel as a whole contains at least fifty-three theologically significant "in"-phrases: Jesus' people are "in" him, as he is "in" the Father. (This trait of johannine thought and style becomes even more characteristic of the First Epistle, where persons are described as "in" one another almost fifty times in five chapters.) The "in"-phrases of the Fourth Gospel speak of the union of the Son with the Father and of the Father and the Son with Jesus' people. (These more than fifty instances appear in only thirty-two verses, for eleven of them are double, expressing the mutual indwelling of two or more parties, *you in me, and I in you,* while four [13:31-32; 14:10, 20; 15:4; 17:21] speak of three parties.)

Similar "in"-phrases had appeared in the Book of Signs, notably in the unmistakably sacramental passage in the Bread of Life discourse where Jesus had said, *Those who eat my flesh and drink my blood abide in me, and I in them,* 6:56, but also in 10:38, where he had said *The Father is in me and I am in the Father.* However, such expressions become much more frequent in Jesus' Farewell — 42 of the 53 instances falling in chapters 13–17. Fourteen of them occur in the First Discourse, especially in 14:10-21. Fourteen fall in the Second Discourse (ten of them concentrated in 15:2-7, where the idea of persons being "in" one another is often expressed using the verb *remain* or *dwell,* as *remain in me*). Only one such phrase (16:33) occurs in the Third Discourse, while twelve appear in the Prayer of ch. 17. In addition to the phrases which speak of persons dwelling in one another, there are others which say that Jesus' word (15:7), his love (15:9-10; 17:26) and his joy (15:11) are "in" his followers. These things that are interior to Jesus' people are tokens of their participation in Jesus himself. In the Fourth

Gospel these "in"-phrases identify a divine-human coinherence that is constitutive of the church's very life.

"Know." Know is one of the deep words of johannine vocabulary. There are two principal Greek verbs for knowing in the Fourth Gospel, which are together used more than 110 times in the book as a whole. (The two Greek words were once thought to refer to different kinds of knowing, but they are now considered virtually interchangeable.) The noun, *knowledge,* does not occur.

There is a slight increase in the frequency of the word *know* as a reader passes to the Book of Glory. It is used 38 times in chapters 13–17. (One third of the occasions of the word occur in one fourth of the book.) But as the term appears in the Farewell, the greatest change is in the richness or significance it carries. The Discourses and Prayer emphasize what Jesus knows (13:1, 3, 11, 18; 16:19, 30; 17:25). They speak frequently of what the disciples know, or of what they ought to know, but do not, or of what Jesus has made known to them (13:7, 12, 17; 14:4, 9; 15:15, 18; 16:18, 30; 17:7, 8, 25, 26). They speak also of what the world does not know (14:17; 15:21; 16:3; 17:25).

Clearly the most important kind of knowing is interpersonal knowing — not a knowing about, but a subject-to-subject knowing of another person. The Farewell Discourses speak of knowing Jesus (14:7, 9), of knowing the Father (14:7; 17:3), of knowing (of being brought within) the relationship that persists between Jesus and the Father (14:20, 31; 17:7, 8, 23, 25-26), of knowing the Paraclete (14:17), of knowing Jesus' mind (15:15). The theme comes to its climax in the conclusion of Jesus' prayer, *Righteous Father, the world does not know you, but I know you; and these know that you have sent me. I made your name known to them, and I will make it known, so that the love with which you have loved me may be in them, and I in them* (17:25-26).

This profoundest knowing — a knowing which is a mode of indwelling — is not the result of inquiry nor the conclusion of a line of reasoning; it is revelational. Jesus is known because he has made himself (and the Father) known. In johannine terms, to be a believer is to be a knower (cf. 1 John 2:20). (See the essay, "Believing Is Knowing Is Hearing Is Seeing Is Believing . . . ," pp. 142-49.)

Some other terms come into prominence in the second half of this Gospel:

All six instances of the word *peace* (14:27 twice; 16:33; 20:19, 21, 26) fall in the Gospel's concluding chapters.

While in the Synoptic Gospels Jesus speaks often about prayer, all of the johannine references to *asking* things of God (14:13; 15:7, 16; 16:23-26) appear in the Farewell chapters. (See the essay "Prayer in the Farewell Discourses," pp. 217-21.)

In the narrative of the first twelve chapters some persons are spoken of as rejoicing over something, however, all of the references to *joy* as a quality of life appear in the Book of Glory (14:28; 15:11; 16:20, 22, 24; 17:13; 20:20).

Reduction in Rhetorical Vividness

In addition to words or expressions which decrease or increase in prominence, one may remark the changed rhetorical character of the second part of the Fourth Gospel. George MacRae observed, "The language of sign and symbol so familiar in the first [half of this gospel] is virtually abandoned in the second." The fairly well-developed image of the vine and branches begins the Second Discourse; and the brief illustration of a woman in childbirth comes in the Third Discourse (16:21). But aside from these, vivid images are absent in the Book of Glory. "There is no more appeal to the imagination in talk of bread, wine, water, life, light, shepherd, and the like."[12] Sharpness and concreteness are replaced by a characteristic johannine plainness. The author's fondness for words that can have more than one meaning continues; there are juxtapositions of paradoxical elements (*I go away . . . I will come,* 14:2ff, 12, 18, and *you will not see me . . . you will see me,* 16:16-19); the practice of advancing Jesus' thought by means of his hearers' misunderstandings is continued. These, however, are relatively low-key rhetorical devices. It is almost as though, in considerable measure, the author, now that Jesus is speaking to *his own,* has him explain, as directly as language concerning the divine/human relation permits, the character of the life that has been presented in arresting images in chapters 1–12.

A reader may note also the absence in the Book of Glory of the strong, and at times bitter polemic that had given intensity to the speech of the later parts of the Book of Signs, notably in the argument with the synagogue in chapters 8–10. Jesus is not now accusing or arguing with anyone. The intent of the departing Jesus is to support or to encourage listeners who are united with him, as he is with them. Jesus continues to elude and

12. George W. MacRae, *Faith in the Word* (Chicago: Franciscan Herald, 1973), 52.

mystify, but in his Farewell, he and the persons with whom he speaks stand, so to speak, on the same side.

Reduced References to the Scriptures of Israel

Several explicit quotations from the Jewish Scriptures appeared in the Book of Signs:

- in 1:23 (citing Isa. 40:3);
- in 2:17 (citing Psa. 69:9);
- in 6:31 (citing Psa. 78:24, with other echoes);
- in 6:45 (citing Isa. 54:13);
- in 7:38 (citing Isa. 44:3; 55:1; 58:11, uncertain)
- in 10:34 (citing Psa. 82:6);
- in 12:13 (citing Psa. 118:25-26);
- in 12:15 (citing Zech. 9:9);
- in 12:38 (citing Isa. 53:1);
- in 12:40 (citing Isa. 6:10).

In the first twelve chapters of John, there are nine unmistakable quotations (and one questionable quotation). Four of these occur in chapter 12. Five (including 7:38) cite Isaiah; four cite the Psalms; and one cites Zechariah. (In the Passion account there will be four more: 19:24, 28-29, 36, 37.) In addition to the clear quotations, in these opening chapters Jesus argues from the Scriptures, using them to vindicate his claims (10:31-39, et. al.). The figure of Moses is brought in repeatedly (1:17; 3:14; 5:45; 6:32; 7:19-24; 9:28-29); Abraham (8:39-40, 52-59) and Jacob (1:51; 4:5-6, 12) and David (7:42) appear, but less often. There are several Temple and tabernacle references. The exodus and the bread in the wilderness motif are important in the Bread of Life discourse (esp. 6:25-55). The serpent in the wilderness image in 3:14-15 refers to Moses and the exodus; and very likely the promise of water for the thirsty in 7:37-38 alludes to Moses and the water from the rock. Events and themes of the Fourth Gospel are organized around Jewish feasts and observances. The Shepherd image of chapter 10 suggests a background in Israel's divine Shepherd (Psa. 23; Ezek. 37). The Book of Signs opens with a Prologue (1:1-18) which echoes the creation story of Genesis 1, and it closes with a long composite quotation from Isaiah (12:38-41).

By contrast, in chapters 13–17 there is only minimal explicit use of the

Scriptures of Israel. We have noted that in 13:18 Jesus cites Psalm 41:9 as his comment on Judas. In 15:25b, Psalm 69:4 (or 35:19) is cited as *a word written in their law* — an ancient Jewish Psalm anticipates the hatred for Jesus. But these are the only places in the Farewell chapters in which the Jewish Scriptures are quoted expressly. (One may remark that there are no clear citations of the Jewish Scriptures in the johannine epistles.)

Even though the Book of Glory opens with a reference to the Feast of the Passover, thereafter, the Farewell Discourses make no significant use of Exodus-Passover motifs; none of the references to Moses are developed; there are no cultic or sacrificial references (unless there is a suggestion in Jesus' prayer, 17:19), and there is no drawing on the Jewish theme of presence. These things are known to and used by this author in the first half of his work. Yet in these later chapters where a reader might expect such material to be drawn together and developed further as a factor in the self-understanding of the community of believers in Jesus, none of it reappears.

To be sure, the thought and vocabulary of the Farewell chapters owe much to Jewish terminology and modes of thinking. The Vine image derives some of its pertinence from the use of the vine as a symbol for Israel in the Psalms and the prophets, but no attention is directed to such associations by the author. Jesus' new commandment suggests former commandments, but again the connection must be supplied by the reader. The woman in travail, 16:21, echoes a prophetic image, but it does not do so expressly. Wisdom allusions are present, but they are indirect. The author writes as he does because his mind is full of the Jewish Scriptures. Yet he does not in these Farewell Discourses make clear quotations or validate his presentation of Jesus and his people by citing Yahweh and Israel.

Shift in Christological Emphasis

In moving from chapters 1–12 to chapters 13–17 one observes a change of emphasis in the Gospel's christology. An aspect of the presentation of Jesus which has been entered previously but has not been developed comes to the fore, while the emphasis that dominated the Book of Signs recedes. Since christology is central in the Fourth Gospel, this shift is an important indicator of a change in the author's purpose.

It oversimplifies johannine christology to look at it through any single scheme. However, one can observe that the Evangelist sets the historic mission of Jesus — his calling of his followers, his signs, his offer of life, his stirring of opposition, his trial, crucifixion, and resurrection — within a redemptive myth-scheme which frames and pervades the events of his life. The scheme, which is often expressed in spatial terms, is presented as a twofold movement:

— a *descent:*
Jesus is the one who *comes from* God,
and who *comes to* the world.

answered by:

— an *ascent:*
Jesus is the one who *leaves* the world,
and *goes to* God.

Throughout the Fourth Gospel there are about fifty places in which either Jesus' descent or his ascent is mentioned — instances such as:

- . . . judgment that the light has *come into the world,* 3:19;
- The bread of God is that which *comes down from heaven* and gives life to the world, 6:33;
- I am *going to the Father,* 14:28;
- It is to your advantage that *I go away,* 16:7;
- I came *from God,* 16:27.

Sometimes the descent and the ascent are set side by side in capsule summaries, as: *I am going* [ascent] *to him who sent me* [prior descent], 7:33; or *I know where I have come from and where I am going, but you do not,* 8:14. Indeed, the Farewell Discourses are bracketed by such concise summaries, one at the opening: *Jesus, knowing . . . that he had come from God and was going to God* (13:3), and one toward the close, *I came from the Father and have come into the world; again I am leaving the world and am going to the Father* (16:28).

Both Jesus' origin and his destiny are a mystery (8:14). His opponents think that they know where he is from (7:27) and hence they can explain him. But their grasp of Jesus' "whence" is inadequate (8:26-28; 9:16, 29-30; 19:9). Similarly, when Jesus speaks to his disciples of his departure, his meaning is missed (14:5; 16:16-18). The Evangelist seeks to help his first-century readers to understand what no one understands in the story he tells.

The two christological movements — to humanity from God and from humanity to God — are interdependent. The one who ascends is the one who has descended. The one who comes from God and whose mission is given him by God at the end returns to God. A reader often feels that when either movement is mentioned the other is at least suggested.

This motif of descent and ascent interpenetrates the narrative of the Gospel, creating terms that can be read in more than one way. One might cite the "thickness" of the meaning of the johannine language about Jesus' *lifting up,* his *glorification,* or his *coming into the world,* or the questions about where Jesus is "from" and where he is "going," and Jesus' repeated emphasis on himself as sent from the Father, on his role as witness of what he has seen with the Father.[13]

The Fourth Gospel contains approximately as many passages which speak of Jesus as having *come from* God as it does passages which speak of him as *going to* God, but the two emphases are differently sited in this Gospel. Of the passages which speak distinctively of Jesus as *from God,* more than two thirds fall in chapters 1–12, while well over two thirds of the passages which speak of Jesus as going *to* God fall in chapters 13–17, one fourth of the book.

The One Who Comes from God. In chapters 1–12, Jesus refers approximately 30 times to himself as sent by the Father, or he refers to the Father as the one who has sent him. To identify a few such references: In the Bread of Life discourse, Jesus describes himself as the bread which *came down from heaven* (6:33, 41, 42, 50, 51, 58). He says, *I have come down from heaven . . . to do the will of him who sent me* (6:38). *Not that anyone has seen the Father except the one who is from God; he has seen the Father* (6:46). In chapter 8 Jesus says that he knows whence he has come (8:14, 38) and that he declares what he has seen in the Father's presence. Summarily, he says, *I came from God and now I am here* (8:42). Elsewhere the Gospel affirms that because Jesus' origin is from beyond the world he holds universal authority to save and judge; his voice will be heard by those in the tombs (5:22, 26, 28).

13. Two writers who particularly develop this organizing from-God and to-God movement in johannine christology are Eduard Schillebeeckx, *Christ, the Experience of Jesus as Lord* (New York: Seabury, 1980), chapter 5 (pp. 305-432), and Godfrey Nicholson, *Death as Departure: The Johannine Descent-Ascent Schema* (Chico: Scholars, 1983). There is a summary of sources for this pattern in the appendix "Descending-Ascending Redeemer Figures in Mediterranean Antiquity," in Charles Talbert, *Reading John* (New York: Crossroad, 1993), 265-84.

The dominating christological emphasis in the Book of Signs is that Jesus is sent by God. He is *from the Father,* representing the divine initiative, challenging darkness, offering life, and seeking a human response. Significantly, chapters 13–16 contain only three references to Jesus having come from God. (However, there are six such references in the prayer of chapter 17.)

The One Who Is Going to God. By contrast, in the Book of Glory — or more specifically in the Farewell chapters — Jesus says repeatedly that he is *going to God.* The motif of Jesus' *ascent* is the principal christological emphasis of his Farewell. Speaking in private he tells his followers of a destiny that is first his, and then is theirs in him.

Jesus' departure to the Father is the fundamental way in which the johannine Jesus speaks of the climax and completion of his work. The crucifixion and the resurrection events (chs. 18–21) fill their place in the story, to be sure. However, Jesus' death and resurrection are subsumed in his movement to the Father; his crucifixion is the return. As Godfrey Nicholson put it, "The crucifixion receives its 'meaning' by being understood as a part of a larger schema: the crucifixion was the beginning of the ascent to the Father, the means by which the Son of Man left the world *kato* (below) to return to the world *ano* (above)."[14]

The theme of Jesus' departure was entered, in the author's voice, in the Prologue to the Book of Glory: *His hour had come to depart from the world to the Father* (13:1) and *knowing that he has come from God and was going to God* (13:3). Thereafter, Jesus himself speaks of his *going,* saying *I:*

I am going . . . , 13:33.

Where I am going you cannot follow me now, 13:36.

I go and prepare a place for you, 14:2, 3-4.

I go away, 14:28.

I am going to the Father, 14:28.

(The departure motif does not appear in Jesus' Second Discourse.)

I am going to him who sent me, 16:5.

14. Nicholson, *Death as Departure,* 143.

I go away . . . , 16:7, twice.

I am going to the Father, 16:10, 17.

I am leaving the world and am going to the Father, 16:28.

I am coming to you [to the Father], 17:11, 13.

The language that describes Jesus' *going* is not visual; it is only minimally spatial; and it might be thought somewhat undramatic. Two verbs are used most:

hypagō, to go one's way or depart. This verb is used often in the New Testament to speak of Jesus' ascension to God or to a heavenly throne. It is the commonest verb in the departure sayings, being used ten times in the Farewell chapters; see 13:3, 33, 36; 14:4, 5, 28; 16:5 twice, 10, 17. But it does not use dimensional language of going up.

The verb *poreuomai,* to proceed or journey, is used six times to speak of Jesus' departure, all of them in chs. 14 and 16 (see 14:2, 3, 12, 28; 16:7, 28).

Five other verbs are used less often:

anabainō, ascend or go up (the term which the New Testament writings commonly use for Jesus' ascension, see e.g. Acts 2:34; Rom. 10:6; Eph. 4:8-10), is used in this Gospel only four times for Jesus' "ascending," none of them in chs. 13–17. The related word *metabainō,* leave or depart, is used only in 13:1: *His hour had come to depart from this world and go to the Father.*

erchomai, come, is used in 7:34-36 and in 13:33 to say *you cannot come,* and twice in the prayer in ch. 17, *I come to you,* where *coming* to the Father means "going" from the world. *aperchomai,* go away, is used twice in 16:7: *It is to your advantage that I go away. . . . If I do not go away.*

aphiēmi, leave, occurs in 16:28: *I am leaving the world.*

Several of these verbs (particularly *anabainō* and *poreuomai*), in addition to their christological use, are used in the narrative to speak of a person simply leaving one place and going to another.[15] Jesus' departure to the Father is described in what must be considered rather ordinary terms.

The johannine vocabulary of Jesus' departure also includes "lifting up" *(hypagō)* — the play on words which speaks of Jesus' crucifixion as being at the same time as his going to the Father. This paradoxical and characteristic expression does not occur in the Farewell chapters.

---

15. Dodd, *Interpretation,* 385, asks whether the Evangelist uses even the common verb for "going up to Jerusalem" (2:13; 5:1; 7:10, 14) casually. The term *anabainō* may have overtones of the *anabasis* of the Son of Man.

In describing Jesus' departure, the Fourth Gospel uses familial and relational rather than political, spatial or cosmic terms. While Jesus is spoken of as leaving the world and going to the Father, he is not spoken of as going to a heavenly throne or temple or as taking an exalted place in the cosmos. (The term "lord," *kyrios,* is used of Jesus in the Fourth Gospel narrative, but always with the social sense of an honored, but clearly a human person. Unlike the vocabulary of Acts and Paul, the image of triumphant Lordship is nowhere brought into connection with the departed, living Christ.) Jesus' association with the Father is not spoken of in terms of victory or splendor.

Readers of the New Testament and singers of Christian hymns are familiar with texts that picture the living Christ in terms of royalty, enthronement, power, victory, acclaim, and glory.

Some of these terms trace to a very early christological reading of Psalm 110:1. The Psalmist depicts a victor, virtually an associate ruler, seated at God's right hand. It is noteworthy that when the Fourth Gospel refers to the living Christ, it makes no use of terms of monarchy, empire, conquest, honor, a throne, or splendor, and it does not allude to Psalm 110.

The only places in the Fourth Gospel in which terms of kingship are associated with Jesus are (1) when Nathanael meets Jesus and exclaims, *You are the King of Israel!* (1:49), and (2) when after the Sign of the Bread the people want to seize Jesus and make him king, but he eludes them (6:15). And, most notably, (3) in the narrative of his trial when Pilate asks *Are you the King of the Jews?* 18:33; *So you are a king?,* 18:37. (Is Pilate curious? Is he sarcastic?) He asked the crowd, *Do you want me to release for you the King of the Jews?* 18:39. The Roman soldiers mocked Jesus, saying *Hail, King of the Jews!* 19:3. When Pilate comes out before the people, he says, *Here is your King!* 19:15; and he places on Jesus' cross the inscription *The King of the Jews,* 19:19-22.

Language of kingship that the Fourth Gospel excludes from its depiction of the post-resurrection Jesus it concentrates ironically in the heart of the passion narrative. This location of christological language of royalty seems to be a part of the Evangelist's ironic presentation of Jesus' crucifixion as glory in the abandonment of glory. In his mind, it is as a tortured prisoner and an executed criminal that Jesus is most regal.

The Fourth Gospel does virtually nothing to portray the risen living Jesus, the place he now occupies, or the prerogatives he now exercises. It says only that Jesus is living, that he is with the Father, and that he and the Father live in the church. Jesus is not so much going to someplace as to someone. As his coming was a sending from the Father, and as his mission was carried out in union with the Father, so his departure is a going to the Father (in the Book of Glory, seven times), to God (twice), to the one who sent him (twice), and to the Father's house (once). He says, *I am coming to you [to the Father]* (twice), and he goes to a glory he had left (three times, all in ch. 17). The dominant idiom is that of relationships — Jesus lives with the Father, and Jesus and the Father live with Jesus' people.

In certain respects the descending and the ascending movements of the johannine christological myth seem symmetric. Jesus returns *where he was before* (6:62, and compare 17:5). Yet in one important respect they are asymmetric. Jesus' sending was solitary; his work, his signs, his teaching, his challenge to darkness, his death, were his alone. He took initiative; others responded to him. He did not speak for a movement or seek the authorization or consent of others. He and his work were attested by the Scriptures, by John the Baptist, and by a voice from heaven (12:28). They were finally legitimated by the one who sent him (8:18). He said at the end in utter isolation, *It is finished.* His initial passage to the Father, by way of death, is alone: *Where I am going you cannot come* (13:33).

However, as the Son's work culminates in his return to the Father, it associates others with it. A people is the beneficiary of his solitary work; *you will follow* (13:36). The single grain, by yielding life, brings forth much fruit (12:24). Others are united with the Son in the movement "to God" as they were not in the movement "from God." As Jesus will be with the Father, his followers will ultimately be with him (14:3; 17:24). The people who are associated with the living Jesus do not share his destiny because they also shared his heavenly origin; rather, in the midst of a world in the grip of death, they have been met by Life itself. They have trusted the Way and have passed from death to life. They are *born of God* (1:13, cf. 1 John 3:9; 4:7; 5:1, 4, 18). They live in relation to Jesus and through him in relation to God.

As the Fourth Gospel has it, the dealings of God with humanity are always through the Eternal Word who having united with humanity, remains in union with humanity. In the Christ-myth of the Fourth Gospel, Jesus' departure to the Father is for him a return to a former glory, but as his "descent" was his en-fleshment (1:14), and his dying was for others, so his "ascent" retains his bonds with humanity. The ways in which the bonds between the risen Jesus and his people are lived are the subject of the Evangelist's necessarily suggestive and somewhat indirect exposition in chapters 13–17. The discourses which begin with words of parting, *I am with you a little longer* (13:33), end with Jesus and the Father united in love with Jesus' people, *So that the love with which you have loved me may be in them, and I in them* (17:26). The dramatistic christology of the Fourth Gospel depicts a union of the divine with the human which makes possible a union of the human with the divine.

The Farewell chapters depict this sharing of others with the departed Jesus in two ways:

Future and Transcendent. Jesus is the way to the Father (or to the Father's household). His going opens a route which others will follow (14:3-6), so that they will finally be with him in the place to which he goes (14:3; 17:24). He came where others were, so that ultimately they might be with him where he is.

Present and Immanent. But in a second idiom, the departed Jesus is with his followers now (14:18). He and the Father come and make their home in the community of disciples (14:23). Jesus' followers do greater works because he has gone to the Father (14:12). Their prayer is effective because they have the use of his name (14:13-14; 16:23-24). They are united with him now like parts of a biological organism (15:1-11). They have his peace (14:27). Their suffering is his (15:18-21). His victory is theirs (16:33).

These two idioms mingle. In depicting the ultimate destiny of Jesus and his people, the language of the Fourth Gospel is reticent — it could seem to lack visual imagination. If the purpose of the writer had been to depict a cosmic victory of the Redeemer or to project a golden vision of the destiny of the redeemed, a Dante or a Milton could have done it better. The Evangelist's flatness, however, may be deliberate. If he is a mythologizer, he is at the same time a demythologizer. If in speaking of Jesus and his work he must use terms that suggest departure to a distant place, he will hold such terms in check, setting them alongside non-spatial terms, so that a reader will look for meanings rather than be dazzled (and perhaps misled) by visions. Yet one is struck with what a weight of significance these elemental, spatial/relational terms carry for johannine thought. Since the human mind must use the language of space, time, and social order, this author will use it, but he will use it in his own way. To be where another is is to be in union with that other. *Where I am, there will my servant be also* (12:26). For this writer, when one has said that Jesus is with the Father, one does not go on to say more. Rather, one stops because no more can be said.

In setting forth who Jesus is and what his being with the Father means, the church and its experience form a part of the Evangelist's material. The mission of Jesus created a community of persons who shared a transforming experience. The Farewell chapters suggest a process of christological/ecclesiological discovery. In chapters 1–12 Jesus had said: "This is the way that I am to the Father, and the Father is to me." Then in chapters 13–17 he enlarges the relation to include the disciples, who in this matter represent all believers. In effect, Jesus says, "As the Father and I are towards one another, so we are towards you. As we are in one another, so you are in us, and we are in you." Through Jesus, the receiver and the giver, the relationship that persists between the Son and the Father becomes a divine-human relation, open to anyone who believes and loves. For the community of faith, the relation between Jesus and the Father is not known from the outside, as though the knower were an observer who had been given privileged information. Rather, the relation between Jesus and the Father and between Jesus and the Father and the church is known and confessed from the inside; the knower has been made a participant in the thing known.

Thus johannine christology is bound up with ecclesiology. In the Book of Glory, the living Jesus is depicted in terms of his continuing relation with the church in the world. Jesus who is with the Father is the correlative of the church firmly set on earth. He is known as he makes a difference to the faith, prayer, witness, unity, self-understanding, courage, and destiny of the church living in history. He is grasped as the church claims his adequacy for itself. Knowledge of him and relation to him are accessible through the life he shares with his people.

The life of believers witnesses to Jesus' life, as his life is demonstrated in theirs. Jesus lives in, for and through the church, as it exists in, by and for him. With respect to these two, reciprocally existing realities, to know either is to know the other. To enter deeply into the life of the church is to enter deeply into the life of the Christ who is departed to the Father, but who at the same time indwells the church.

What developed presentation the Fourth Gospel gives of the living Jesus is given in terms of Jesus' continuing relation to the believing community. His life after he has "gone away" is a life that continues to be bonded with his people. What he is doing now he is doing in, for and through them. When one seeks, in johannine idiom, to imagine the living Jesus, one does not search for symbolic material — royal or priestly, or cosmic — whereby to picture an essentially unimaginable world beyond this world. One looks to the rich interior of the church — the community whose ultimate life cannot be described except as life in relation to the living Christ: he in it and it in him.

4. The First Discourse: Absence and Presence (13:31–14:31)

Jesus has only begun to speak when he makes the brief announcement from which his First Discourse takes its rise: *My children, I shall not be with you very much longer* (13:33 TEV).

Jesus' notice that he is leaving is unanticipated. As the disciples realize what Jesus is saying, they are dismayed. They are losing the person who has given meaning and purpose to their lives. He does not say where he is going — only that they cannot go with him. Why not? Will they see him again? Without him present, can his followers keep their unity and focus? Indeed, will the company of Jesus' disciples survive his departure? His work with them was surely not finished! Jesus speaks a lengthy Farewell to support his followers in their apprehension and loss. *Do not let your hearts be troubled* (14:1).

Jesus' First Discourse (13:31–14:31) is one of the most complex and closely written portions of this complex and closely written Gospel. The composition is unified; some themes that are introduced early return later, often somewhat expanded. The text does not explain; it presents, it affirms, in the voice of the departing Jesus, often moving rapidly from one image or idea to the next, leaving implicit the connections between them. Complex realities are expressed in an everyday vocabulary, often, however, introducing words that carry more than one level of meaning. This Discourse keeps a reader's interest in part through the suggestion and indirection of its manner.

Looking at the sweep and character of the First Discourse, three general observations can be made:

a. One notes the christocentric character of the thought. Jesus sets himself in the center of the continuing relation of his followers with God. What the disciples will be depends on their attachment to him. But the

Evangelist sees the disciples as representative. He often looks beyond them to a larger community comprising *those who have my commandments and keep them.* Broad human hungers and quests are met in Jesus. A true presence of or vision of God is accessible, not to an elite who arrive at it by speculative thought or spiritual disciplines or who experience ecstatic states of consciousness. Rather, all is accessible to every believer. To know Jesus or to be in relation to him is to participate in the divine life.

The centrality of Jesus in this First Discourse is remarked by Bruce Woll, who observes that in this passage of 39 verses, Jesus appears as the subject of a clause forty-six times. He uses the emphatic "I" ten times. He is the object of verbs more than twenty-five times. "Jesus refers to 'my Father' 4 times; 'my name' 3 times; 'my commandments' 2 times; 'my words' 3 times; 'my peace' once; 'my disciples' once."[1] All centers on Jesus; all other authority, all other relation and guidance derives from or is given through him.

A corollary of the christocentrism of the Discourse is that in the relation into which one is brought by Jesus, God is characteristically spoken of as *the Father* (or more frequently as *my Father*). In the Farewell material up to this point, God has been spoken of as the Father only in the author's prologue to the Book of Glory (13:1-13). The brief introduction to the discourses (13:31-35) speaks only of "God." However, references to the Father become very frequent in chapter 14; there are twenty-three in thirty-one verses — more than in chapters 15 and 16 combined. Jesus reveals the Father (14:8-10). The Father dwells in Jesus and acts through him (14:10-11, 20). Jesus for his part lives in the Father and obeys the Father (14:31). He goes to the Father (14:2, 12, 28), and through him others are brought to the Father (14:2-3). They come to know (14:7), to see (14:9), and to be loved and indwelt by the Father (14:21, 23). This Discourse is full of Jesus as the one who makes God known and of God as made known through Jesus.

b. This Discourse describes a profound, intimate, mutual sharing between persons. The preposition "in" takes on theological significance. Persons are spoken of as being "in" one another: *I am in my Father, and you in me, and I in you* (v. 20). The "in"-phrases sound as though two persons occupied the same space or as though they enclosed one another — an impossibility in bodily life that the text uses to suggest a union of persons.

1. Bruce Woll, "The Departure of 'The Way': The First Farewell Discourse in the Gospel of John," *JBL* 99 (1980), 234, n. 40.

(Such expressions put one in mind of the term "intersubjectivity," which figured in the thought of the French philosopher Gabriel Marcel.)

The fabric of relationships that Jesus describes is complex. It is rooted in the primal relation which persists between Jesus and the one he refers to as his Father — Jesus is *in* the Father and the Father is *in* him (v. 11). This relation is then opened to include Jesus and his people; believers are *in* Jesus, and he is *in* them (v. 20). Jesus tells his disciples that the Spirit of truth *will be in you* (v. 17). Jesus and the Father together will *in*dwell believers (v. 23). In this Discourse, persons (human and divine) are not conceived as bounded, or separate from, or armored against one another. Persons can share themselves and be shared. Jesus' followers are fulfilled as they live in him and he lives in them.

The relation of persons, as it is developed, is not set forth in a new, quasi-technical vocabulary. Rather, in addition to the "in-phrases," the author describes the relation between Jesus and believers using a few common verbs:

> *knowing* and *being known* (ten uses, seven of them in vv. 4-9),
> *believing* (seven times, four of them in vv. 10-12),
> *seeing* (seven times, four of them in vv. 17-19),
> *revealing oneself to another* (twice, both in vv. 21-22),
> *loving* and *being loved* (nine times, seven of them in vv. 21-24).

These terms, appearing in advancing, overlapping clusters, describe ways in which one internalizes the world and the persons around oneself and permits oneself to be shared with others. The words of this small, accessible vocabulary pass into one another, enlarging and modifying one another. The author never steps outside his terms and explains them through another terminology. Probably for him no other terms could be more clear, ultimate, or authoritative than these which have grown up with and carry the elemental insights of the community's faith (see pp. 142-49 below for further discussion of this johannine vocabulary of relations).

c. This Discourse is full of movement. The God it describes is not the summit of the order of reality, discoverable by persistent human search. The relation with God, as the Evangelist presents it, does not come about because the long religious quest has made a forward leap. It is revelational, occasioned by a stir from the other side, and all of it in Jesus. C. H. Dodd notes that the passage "is dominated by the ideas of going and coming. Verbs expressing these ideas . . . occur at least fourteen times, with Christ as subject; and the longest passage without direct reference to going and coming is not more than five verses."[2]

This Discourse places no emphasis on Jesus being "sent" or his being "from the Father." Indeed, none of the Farewell Discourses says much about Jesus as the Father's "sent one." The point may have been taken for granted since it was the principal christological emphasis of the Book of Signs. The Prayer of chapter 17 will reintroduce the theme.

In our psychologically minded age we might take this language of "coming" and "going" to refer to religious experience of the kind familiar to devout persons in many times and traditions. On occasions of distress or spiritual dryness or personal uncertainty, God can seem distant, while at other times God can seem near. A Psalmist pleads, *O Lord, do not be far away!* (Ps. 22:19). However, such perceived closeness or remoteness is not what this author has in mind.

When the Evangelist speaks of movement he refers to the God who acts in human affairs, faithfully, but under divine freedom. As heirs of modernity, today's readers can find such ideas of the stir of God within human life to be clumsy or naïve. Yet at the heart of the biblical story is the intellectual scandal of this visiting, speaking, acting God, who stands in personal relation with the creation, who loves with a holy love and judges with a righteous judgment, who seeks the trust and the prayer of any, and who moves in the time-and-place specificities of human affairs. But this God works through the ordinary processes of nature and history, with no compelling insignia of divine agency. The Roman Catholic theologian Romano Guardini wrote of the God who is given to us by the revelation in Christ:

> Certainly, God is omnipresent, exalted over time and space; yet he also can come when it pleases him; can live among us, and when the hour has struck, can depart and return — with a new countenance. . . . Certainly God bears all things, speaks through all things; yet at a certain period in history he also proclaimed an explicit message which demands differentiation and decision, and which separates mankind into the obedient and disobedient, believing and unbelieving. . . . Certainly, everything that occurs is activated by his eternal power beyond the reaches of time; yet there are specific acts of God in time; the acts

2. C. H. Dodd, *The Interpretation of the Fourth Gospel* (Cambridge: Cambridge University Press, 1953), 403.

founded in sacred history, which every human is invited to enter but is also free to reject.[3]

The First Farewell Discourse will be discussed in three sections of this long chapter:

1. In a compressed introductory prologue (13:31-35), Jesus speaks of the glory he shares with the Father and of his solitary departure; and he commands mutual love among his followers. Then Peter says that he will follow Jesus, even to death; but Jesus predicts that before the night is over, Peter will deny him three times (13:36-38).

2. In the first part of the Discourse (14:1-17) Jesus assures his followers of continuity and explains that his departure will not be a loss for them. Although he is leaving, the bonds with himself and with the Father will hold. He goes alone to his Father's house, where he will prepare a place for them, and later he will return for them. Thomas asks about the destination and the way (vv. 5-6). Jesus says that his disciples have known and seen the Father. But Philip is doubtful and asks to be shown the Father. Jesus responds, saying that in knowing him they have known the Father (vv. 7-11). These exchanges advance Jesus' thought through the questions or misunderstandings of his followers. The personalities of the questioners are not developed. The dialogic form suits the thought of the Evangelist, and he seems to have liked a variety of names. In vv. 11-17 Jesus goes on to speak of works — his own and those of his followers — and of prayer in his name, and he introduces the Spirit-Paraclete.

3. In the second part of the Discourse (14:18-31) Jesus passes to the startling disclosure that in a sense he will not really be absent from his disciples at all. He will "come" to them. He must explain this seeming contradiction. A question from Judas (not the betrayer) leads Jesus to say that he will be manifest to his followers, but not to the world (vv. 22-23). In vv. 18-24, Jesus says that, rather than being distanced from his followers, he and the Father will "come" to indwell the community of obedience and love. The Paraclete is introduced a second time, and the Discourse ends with benediction and encouragement.

3. Romano Guardini, *The Lord* (Chicago: Regnery, 1954), 423-24.

1. Glory and Denial (13:31-38)

Jesus' Prologue: Glory, Departure, and Love (13:31-35)

When he had gone out,
Jesus said, 13:31a

The narrator begins with a note of circumstance: *When he* [Judas] *had gone out.* There will not be another such notice until Jesus and his disciples go to the garden at the beginning of chapter 18.

There are things that Jesus can say now that Judas's troubling presence has been removed. Jesus' opening words give a rapid series of ideas — ideas not prepared for in the foregoing material and not developed here, but introduced in compressed statements. Three themes relate to one another and to Jesus' coming passion and departure:

1. The Son is *glorified* now, and in him God is *glorified* (vv. 31-32).
2. Jesus is departing alone (v. 33).
3. Jesus gives his followers a *new commandment* (vv. 34-35).

"Now the Son of Man has been glorified,
  and God has been glorified in him.
  If God has been glorified in him,
God will also glorify him in himself,
and will glorify him at once. 13:31b-32

Jesus begins with five tightly worded clauses which have "almost poetic value."[4] This brief passage may be thought of as a "prologue" to Jesus' Farewell. The change of tone is abrupt: the betrayer goes out into the night, and then Jesus speaks of an exchange of glory between himself and God. He sets forth here the relation that persists between God and himself — the relation in which his life is rooted and out of which his mission has come, the relation which will be demonstrated in the coming events, and a relation constituted in a shared glory. The verb "glorify" (not the noun "glory")

4. Rudolf Schnackenburg, *The Gospel According to St. John* (3 vols., New York: Crossroad, 1968, 1980, 1982), 3.49. Mark L. Appold describes the passage as "hymn-like" (*The Oneness Motif in the Fourth Gospel: Motif Analysis and Exegetical Probe into the Theology of John* [Tübingen: Mohr, 1976]). Bruce Woll, *Johannine Christianity in Conflict* (Chico: Scholars, 1981), 38, speaks of a "hymn of triumph," drawing on Heitmueller's term *Triumphlied.*

appears in all five lines. The first two gather up the past into the present, saying "now." The verbs are passive; the Child of Humanity and God have been glorified, each by the other. The last two lines look forward, and the future verbs are active: God will glorify (see further "Glory and Glorifying," pp. 369-75 below).

Jesus speaks of himself in this passage as *ho huios tou anthrōpou.* The NRSV (the text that is generally followed in this study) translates the expression by the well-established Tyndale/KJV wording, *the Son of Man.* This translation — although it is deeply lodged in the tradition of the English-speaking world — carries inevitably the problem of generic "man." The biblical expression, *the Son of Man, ho huios tou anthrōpou* — which is important in the christology of the Gospels — speaks of Jesus' humanity, not of his maleness. Regrettably, the two ideas are merged in the English term "man." Searching for a translation that might convey the thought of the expression while avoiding these misleading suggestions, interpreters have proposed such wordings as "the Truly Human One," or "the Child of Humanity," or, in the address to Ezekiel, "O mortal." In this commentary either the Greek phrase or one of these translations will be used.

Several ties link this prologue to the First Discourse with the final section of chapter 12, the end of the Book of Signs. Themes that belonged to the conclusion of Jesus' apparently failed public ministry are reintroduced as he begins to explain to his disciples that his work is a victory, but not a victory such as the world can grasp.

- the emphatic *now* (31a): compare 12:27, *Now my soul is troubled,* and 12:31, *Now is the judgment of this world.*
- the glorification of the Child of Humanity (31a): compare 12:23, *The hour has come for ho huios tou anthrōpou to be glorified . . .*
- the Father is glorified in the Son (32a): compare 12:28a, *Father, glorify your name.*
- Jesus is with his followers only a little longer (33a): compare 12:8, *You do not always have me with you,* and 12:35, *The light is with you for a little longer.*

Now the Child of Humanity is glorified. The Evangelist's emphatic *now* indicates that time is gathering to a moment of intensity. Earlier the narrator said that Jesus was *not yet glorified* (7:39), but here *not yet* is overtaken by *now* (cf. 12:31).

The *"now"* means that the dismissal of Judas has set in motion actions toward Jesus' arrest, trial, and death. The final events of Jesus' life are a unity which has begun to unfold. At one level the *"now"* speaks of Jesus'

Farewell, his crucifixion, and his return to the Father. However, at another level, this *"now"* is an eschatological *"now." Glory* speaks of final things, things that are to be unveiled. It suggests that which is true of God, but hidden — hidden, and yet apprehensible and declarable in anticipation of that which will be revealed in the end. Ultimate glory is manifest in Jesus and paradoxically in the events of his passion which begin to develop *now.*

These opening words of glorification now, spoken on the eve of the crucifixion, are an indication that the whole Discourse, which is begun here, is spoken from the standpoint of the accomplished work of Jesus and from within the new condition that it opens for Jesus' followers. As C. H. Dodd put it, "In all that follows it is Christ crucified who speaks, the living Christ who has already passed through death, although dramatically he speaks on the eve of his death."[5]

The Child of Humanity is glorified. Jesus speaks of himself as the Child of Humanity *(ho huios tou anthrōpou)* who is *glorified.* The words contrast sharply with the Synoptic Gospels in which Jesus, speaking of his future and referring to himself as "the Child of Humanity," anticipates his death, saying *"The Child of Humanity must undergo great suffering . . . be killed . . . rise again"* (Mark 8:31-32; 9:12; 10:33-34, and parallels). Here in the Fourth Gospel, as he moves towards the climactic event of his work, he calls it the *hour* for his *glorification* (7:39b; 12:16, 23; 17:1). Earlier (in 12:23-24) he spoke of his *hour,* saying, *The hour has come for the Child of Humanity to be glorified.* Then, anticipating his death, he at once said, *Very truly, I tell you, unless a grain of wheat falls into the earth and dies, it remains just a single grain.* Unlike the Synoptists, the writer of the Fourth Gospel never speaks directly of Jesus' crucifixion except in the passion story itself. Although 1 Peter indicates that already in the first century Jesus' "sufferings" had become a summary description among Christians for the climax of his career (1 Peter 1:11; 2:21, 23; 4:1, 13; 5:1), neither the Fourth Gospel nor the johannine epistles speak of Jesus' suffering. The johannine Jesus speaks only of his *"glorification."* The use of the expression *is glorified* in 13:31 and 12:23 may be taken as a "divine passive," indicating that in the events that are beginning to unfold, God is the glorifier of "the Child of Humanity."

This perception of crucifixion as glorification belongs to the special vision of the Fourth Gospel. Some early strata of the New Testament speak of Jesus' redemptive actions as humiliation, which is followed by exaltation: suffering passes over into glory. *Was it not necessary that the Messiah*

5. Dodd, *Interpretation,* 403.

should [first] suffer these things and [then] enter into his glory? (Luke 24:26, and see Phil. 2:8-9). In a divine reversal, the human verdict of Jesus' condemnation and death was overturned by God's verdict of resurrection and vindication — as when Peter proclaims in Jerusalem:

> This Jesus . . . you crucified and killed by the hands of those outside the law.
> But God raised him up . . .
> God has made him both Lord and Messiah,
> This Jesus whom you crucified (Acts 2:22-24; see also 2:36; 10:38-41).

In the mind of the Fourth Evangelist, however, things go together differently. Glory does not follow the crucifixion and, in effect, overturn it. Rather, glory is exhibited in the crucifixion itself. (The TEV translates v. 31, *Now the Son of Man's glory is revealed.*) The coming trial and crucifixion show forth Jesus' glory. However, the glory in Jesus' death does not stand apart from the life that preceded it. His life continuously displayed the glory of the enfleshed Word; he lived *among us* and *we have seen his glory* (1:14). Even though as he is presented in the Fourth Gospel Jesus carried no unambiguous evidence of his divine origin and mission, and while he could be seen and rejected, his glory was recognized by a community of belief (the *we* of 1:14). Although Jesus' glory was especially apparent in his "signs," as they were apprehended by the eyes of faith (2:11; 11:4, 40), his entire life was, to believers, a demonstration of the radiant presence of the divine. For a time, the sun blazed in the darkness and made it as the day (8:12; 9:5). The divine *shekinah* had made its tabernacle in the flesh of Jesus; it *tented among us* (*skēnoō,* 1:14, a reference to the exodus tabernacle). The bringing of Jesus' life — a life devoted single-mindedly to the will of the Father and the redemption of the race — to its climax in his departure to the Father by way of the cross was, in the vision of the Fourth Evangelist, an intense focusing of the glory that pervaded it all.

There is no Transfiguration story in the Fourth Gospel and no account of Jesus' birth. These incidents — both in the Lukan nativity story and in the Synoptic narratives of the Transfiguration — are suffused with outward radiance. In the Fourth Evangelist's mind, the glory, which was present in the whole life of the Word made flesh (1:14), but which was closely veiled, was shown forth supremely, if only to the eyes of faith, in Jesus' crucifixion.

When the Evangelist speaks of Jesus' crucifixion as his "glorification," he shows the way in which things interpenetrate in his mind. He sees and holds before his readers paradoxical unities between seemingly discrepant things — sighted persons who are blind, living persons who must be born, discrete persons who are "in" one another, absent persons who are present, a cruel trial and death that are a showing forth of splendor. This trait of language and thought is more than a Chestertonian love of paradox. It was shaped by encounter with something deeply transforming. When Jesus died on the cross, an instrument of human cruelty and injustice became a sign of divine tenderness and victory. A "conversion of the imagination" is at the heart of the New Testament message. Paul in his idiom says that the wisdom and power of God are demonstrated in Christ crucified (1 Cor. 1:21-25). Similarly the Fourth Evangelist's perception of glory in the abandonment of glory has transformed systemically the way in which he understands and retells his gospel story. The revelation of glory transforms the meaning of Jesus' life. His unsuccessful mission, his rejection, torment, and death were a demonstration of divine splendor. Beneath the horror, the glory.

The Child of Humanity is glorified. In the Synoptic Gospels Jesus often refers to himself as *the Child of Humanity (ho huios tou anthrōpou)* — which is characteristically spoken in the third person. (For Jesus' use of the expression to refer to himself, see 9:35-37.) The title is used as often in the Fourth Gospel as it is in any of the Synoptics; 13:31 is the last instance of the term in the Fourth Gospel and is its only occurrence in the Farewell chapters. A reader of 13:31 may be expected to gather its meaning from previous occurrences in this Gospel.

The specifically johannine understanding of *ho huios tou anthrōpou* can be identified by setting two groups of instances of the term as it is used in the Fourth Gospel alongside similar groups of uses in the Synoptic Gospels. Some interpreters continue to trace the title *ho huios tou anthrōpou* to Jesus himself; most exegetes, however, think that it represents a very early Christian interpretation of him. It would be important for other purposes to pursue this historical issue, but here it is enough if we sketch some of the ways in which the term the Child of Humanity is used in the Synoptic Gospels and in the Fourth Gospels as finished literary texts.

We identify here two groups of Child of Humanity sayings, gathering from the Synoptics and from John: (1) sayings in which *ho huios tou anthrōpou* links earth and heaven, and (2) sayings which connect the Child of Humanity with Jesus' passion.

Eschatological sayings: One group of occurrences in the Synoptic Gospels presents the Child of Humanity as an epochal figure who "comes" dramatically to bring one age to an end and to inaugurate another, as: *Then they will see ho huios tou anthrōpou coming in clouds, with great power and glory* (Mark 13:26; 14:62 and parallels). This strange intrusive figure seems to trace to the apocalyptic image of Dan. 7:13-14. (The quotation marks in the NRSV of Mark 13:26 indicate that the translators thought that the passage from Daniel was in the writer's mind.) In Daniel's vision, the great pagan empires that controlled the ancient world are represented by grotesque animal-like figures. They are subdued by a human figure *(one like a child of humanity)* whose coming brings in an everlasting kingdom. This vision, coming from late exilic Israel, linked the fortunes of the nation with a coming divine self-vindication in history; they provided hope for a proud, but exiled, scattered, and oppressed people. This suggestive but undeveloped figure of Jewish apocalyptic was taken up in the Synoptic Gospels (whether by Jesus himself or by his earliest followers) and was filled with the content of Jesus' unique mission. In the Child of Humanity the new age had broken in.

In the Fourth Gospel a group of instances speak in non-apocalyptic terms of a commerce between earth and heaven centering on the Child of Humanity. The Fourth Evangelist entertains no apocalyptic vision of the coming of *ho huios tou anthrōpou* from heaven; but, citing Jacob's dream in Genesis 28, Jesus says that heaven and earth are joined in *ho huios tou anthrōpou. You will see heaven opened and the angels of God ascending and descending upon the Child of Humanity* (1:51). *Ho huios tou anthrōpou* is the one who has descended (3:13) and who ascends to where he was before (6:62). He is the bread from heaven which gives life to the world (6:27-34, 53). *Ho huios tou anthrōpou* executes judgment with plenary authority (5:27, cf. 9:35-37). In summary, in the non-apocalyptic idiom of the Fourth Gospel, in the Child of Humanity, the heavens are opened, and a descent and an ascent, a heavenly banquet, and a final judgment are all accessible in Jesus, the Truly Human One, and in him now.

Passion sayings. The Synoptic Gospels bring *ho huios tou anthrōpou* into Jesus' sayings about his own death. He is reported to have predicted, *Ho huios tou anthrōpou is to be betrayed into human hands, and they will kill him, and three days after being killed he will rise again* (Mark 9:31, cf. 8:31; 10:33 and parallels). This image of a rejected, suffering, but ultimately vindicated and redemptive Child of Humanity had roots in the "Servant Songs" of Second Isaiah. In Isa. 42:1-9 "The Servant of God" is specially called and gifted to summon Israel to its vocation. His obedience to his appointed task leads to conflict in which the Servant is cruelly treated (Isa. 52:13–53:12). Yet he and his mission are bound up with a community, and out of his suffering, healing benefit comes to many. Inevitably this prophetic text was interpreted by early Christian Bible readers to refer to Christ.

The Fourth Gospel refers several times to the redemptive death of *ho huios tou anthrōpou,* but again in its own way. The Child of Humanity will be *lifted up* to give life to whoever believes (3:14). His *lifting up* will make clear his identity (8:28). The Fourth Gospel associates *ho huios tou anthrōpou* with several images from the Jewish Scriptures. The Child of Humanity is lifted up, just as the bronze serpent was lifted up in the wilderness (Num. 21:4-9). Alluding to the bread in the wilderness, the life-giving food from heaven is the flesh of the Child of Humanity (6:53, cf. v. 27). These uses center around the paradox of a redemptive death. The Child of Humanity is "glorified," but he is "glorified" paradoxically like a grain of wheat that falls into the ground and dies in order to yield a harvest (12:23-24).

The term "lifted up" (the Greek verb is *hypsoō*) which figures in some of these johannine *ho huios tou anthrōpou* sayings (but not in the Farewell chapters) carries multiple associations. At its most literal, crucifixion lifts its victim from the earth. But "lifting up" can also mean to set one in a place of honor, to raise one to recognition or power. The same Greek verb (or a cognate) is used in Phil. 2:9 and Acts 2:33, among other places, to speak of the risen Jesus' exaltation. The johannine "lifted up" (a play on words by the Evangelist) probably traces to Isa. 52:13, *My servant shall prosper, he shall be exalted and lifted up, and shall be very high.* In the christology of the Fourth Gospel, Jesus' crucifixion is the triumphant "lifting up" of the Child of Humanity whereby, his work "finished," he resumes his glory.

The glory of *ho huios tou anthrōpou* has been apparent to the eyes of faith throughout Jesus' ministry and is about to be decisively shown in his passion. In the johannine presentation of him, the Child of Humanity is the one who brings heaven to earth and who by his death (his "lifting up") opens salvation; he is the heavenly nourishment of all who believe. When Jesus' Farewell monologue opens affirming the glorifying now of the Child of Humanity, this characteristic self-designation of Jesus carries a weight of johannine christology.

In the glorification of the Child of Humanity, another is involved: *and God has been glorified in him.* The verb in the first clause, *ho huios tou anthrōpou is glorified,* may (as in 12:23) be understood as a "divine passive," meaning "God glorifies the Child of Humanity" (cf. 12:28). God is the implied actor there and expressly the actor in the last two clauses *(God will glorify him . . .).* God is the glorifier of the Child of Humanity, but in the glorifying of the Child of Humanity, God is glorified. That is the thrust of the second and third clauses *(God has been glorified . . .).* Anything that deeply affects the Son and his purpose involves the Father as well. The glory of either is the glory of both. God is party to Jesus' *hour.* God is the glorifier and the glorified (see "Glory and Glorifying," pp. 369-75 below).

The two glories or gloryings are not rival, as though the glory of one party diminished the glory of the other. (The complementariness of the two glories was expressed in 11:4, *This illness . . . is for God's glory, so that the Son of God may be glorified through it.*) The Father and the Son live in one another, toward one another, for one another. Between them there is a deep unity — loving and being loved, speaking and hearing, giving glory and receiving glory. The Father and the Son, though they are distinct, are one. Based in their coinherence, Jesus' glorification is God's glorification; as God is glorified, the Child of Humanity is glorified. The two share one life and one glory (see 17:1). This crucial event in the life of the Word made flesh is, so to speak, an event interior to God.

Some manuscripts omit the clause *If God has been glorified in him,* which repeats as an "if" condition the thought of the previous main clause. Most text critics think that it is a genuine reading, arguing that it is easier to imagine that a copyist would inadvertently drop a repeated expression from the author's text than to guess why a copyist would insert it.[6] Even if the clause is genuine, it adds only emphasis to the thought.

Jesus glorifies God in carrying out the work of human redemption, a work given to him by God. And God glorifies the faithful Redeemer. God will glorify him *in himself,* that is "in his own being, in a new act of mutual indwelling."[7]

The linked set of five clauses about glorifying which began with *now* ends with *at once.* An emphatic present brackets Jesus' hymn-like prologue. The mutual glorifying of Jesus and the Father is taking place in the events that are unfolding in the Gospel's passion sequence, which has begun.

After this affirmative, visionary opening, which speaks of an exchange of glory between the Father and the Son, Jesus turns to the here-and-now situation, telling his followers that he is leaving them.

> Little children,
> I am with you only a little longer.
> You will look for me;
> and as I said to the Jews

6. Commentators disagree. Barrett omits the words; Brown and Lindars accept them; Metzger argues for them; Schnackenburg thinks the line serves the structure of the thought.

7. G. B. Caird, "The Glory of God in the Fourth Gospel: An Exercise in Biblical Semantics," *NTS* 15 (1968-69), 271.

so now I say to you,
'Where I am going, you cannot come.' 13:33

Jesus' address, *little children,* expresses endearment and reassurance appropriate to his leave-taking. He does not speak to his disciples as "little children" anywhere else in this Gospel, and the expression does not appear in Jesus' speech in the Synoptics. (In the Synoptic Gospels, he speaks of people as God's children, Matt. 5:45, and often, but not as his own children, and he calls his followers a "little flock" in Luke 12:32, but not "little children.") This address appears, however, seven times in 1 John. The use of "little children" there and here is one of the verbal links between this Gospel and the Epistle. Jesus does not develop the familial image as though he were to his disciples as a parent (unless there is a hint of such imagery in the term "orphan" in 14:18).

Jesus announces that he will soon leave his followers, *I am with you only a little longer.* With these words Jesus begins to prepare his disciples for his impending departure — which will be the central christological emphasis in the First and Third Discourses and the Prayer. The word "with" figures importantly in johannine speech. Jesus is "with" others, as others are "with" him (see 1:1-2; 17:24, etc.). The phrase *a little while (mikron)* will return in 14:19 and then insistently in 16:16-19. Jesus has in mind its background in the prophetic writings where it indicates the imminence of divine acts (see Isa. 10:25 and Jer. 51:33).

Jesus adds that when he is gone his dismayed followers will seek to perpetuate the known, old relation: *you will look for me.* This brief expression seems to record the immediate pain of separation that the disciples experienced at Jesus' leaving. The meaning of his "going" and of the different, but not reduced condition of the disciple is not explained here but is a major theme of the ensuing discourses.

As Jesus tells his disciples that they cannot accompany him, he refers to two earlier statements he made to hostile groups: "Where I am going you cannot come" (7:33-34; 8:21-22). (Jesus speaks now of "the Jews" as though he were not himself a Jew speaking to Jews. The Evangelist here represents Jesus as speaking in the vocabulary of the first-century Christian community.) On the first of these two occasions Jesus' opponents understood him to mean that he was leaving the country *(go . . . and teach the Greeks)* to avoid arrest (7:35-36). On the second occasion (8:21-22) his hearers again misunderstand, thinking he may mean that he is about to vanish, perhaps even to take his own life.

Jesus' opponents were *from below* (8:23) and they could grasp neither where he was "from" nor where he was "going." This failure meant that their condition was irremediable: *You will die in your sin* (8:21, 24). Yet this misunderstanding of Jesus by his enemies carries the irony of this Gospel. Limited and mistaken as these reactions were, the enemies of Jesus (like Caiaphas the high priest in 11:49-52) spoke more than they knew. Jesus would indeed, through the church, go to the Greeks and teach them. He would in fact lay down his life.

Now at the opening of his Farewell, Jesus, speaking with his loyal followers, uses almost the same words — *as I said* to others who could not understand, *so now I say to you.* Even though he speaks now to his friends, his words will again not be fully understood (13:36-37; 14:5). In this setting, however, he can go on to explain. The cryptic comments which were unproductive among hostile listeners are turned here into significant disclosures. Jesus says nothing at first about where he is going — only that his disciples cannot accompany him. Even though his departure eventually will involve others, no one shares his initial going. The principal christological theme of the Book of Glory — Jesus' going to the Father — has now been introduced, but only introduced.

Jesus gives his disciples a rule to guide them when he is gone:

I give you a new commandment,
that you love one another.
Just as I have loved you,
you also should love one another.
By this everyone will know that you are my disciples,
if you have love for one another." 13:34-35

Jesus' followers will no longer have him to unite them. Whether they hold together will depend on them. Jesus gives them a single parting command: *love one another,* a command that constitutes virtually the entire johannine ethic. (It does not stand alone. It has been concretized in the foot-washing — "wash one another's feet" — and it will receive its fullest demonstration in the cross, in which Jesus gives his life for others.) The commandment is highly specific; it is given among the followers of Jesus and expresses no general concern for the neighbor, the poor, or the many. Although the focus of the commandment might be thought narrow, no one could argue that it is vague or easy. The first-century readers of the Fourth Gospel may have thought Jesus' parting commandment spoke pertinently to them inasmuch as they were losing their earliest and most authoritative leaders. The voice of Jesus urges them to remain bonded to one another.

Jesus' directive that his disciples love one another is not arbitrarily imposed; but it arises from and is patterned on his prior love for them: *as I . . . you also.* Jesus points to his own love to the uttermost and says, in effect, "Love as you know yourselves to have been loved." Jesus will be gone, but the community formed by his call, his love, his care, and ultimately by his final self-giving remains. He remains in it because he and it are bound up in a single life. Jesus' followers, as they love one another, constitute a continued mode of his presence. As his own love is in them, he is in them.

Although the commandment to love is called "new," the counsel is old. General parallels can be found in Jewish Scriptures, in rabbinic tradition, and indeed in classical moralists. But the command is spoken here for a new era. It is obeyed out of a new motivation and in a new relation to the commandment-giver.

Love among Jesus' followers is a sign to the world: *by this everyone will know.* The public presentation of Jesus, whose coming was for the world's sake, ended in a rejection which will be carried to its conclusion in the terrible events of the crucifixion. However, the living Jesus (the post-resurrection Jesus of chs. 13–17 and of the johannine church) continues to have dealings with the world, but now through the divine Advocate and the church. Hence, the convincing sign of love is crucial. Love among believers constitutes Jesus' credentials before the world. Although Jesus will not be directly apprehensible by the world (14:20-23), where his community demonstrates love among its members, reproducing the love that he shows for them, it will gain the world's attention. Something profound and universal in humanity is awakened: *All will know.*

In the lectionary. The Revised Common Lectionary appoints 13:31-35 as the Gospel reading for the Fifth Sunday of Easter in Year C. Thus these verses, which come in the johannine text in a pre–Good Friday setting and carry an unmistakable "departure" sound, are encountered in the liturgy during the season after Easter. When it is read during Easter, the "now" of Jesus' "glorification" (13:31) can be heard as the "now" of the church, of the Spirit, and of present-day faith and witness. This is the age in which, although Jesus is departed, Christians are bound to one another, and their love is a sign to the world.

The lectionary also appoints this passage for Wednesday of Holy Week and for Holy Thursday, where it stands in close association with the foot-washing incident of 13:1-17, making its "new commandment" pertinent.

A preacher would probably find that the non-narrative character of the Evangelist's prologue, its involuted construction, and the quasi-technical terms such as "glorify" and *ho huios tou anthrōpou* make these verses difficult to read aloud and rather full and knotty as a source for preaching. Yet in lectionary-based preaching one should seek (especially in Holy Week) to remain in some measure engaged with the ideas and vocabulary that figure in the Evangelist's presentation of Jesus.

Hardly any other text in the New Testament states so directly the rootage of Jesus in the Father and the generous mutuality of the glory-filled relationship between him and the one he refers to in this place as *"God."* The johannine term "glorify," in all its paradoxicality, is a proclamation of the gospel. It speaks of a glory shared between Jesus and the Father and demonstrated in Jesus' cross and resurrection, and through the cross and resurrection it catches up humanity into itself.

On Easter V a preacher might want to explain why Jesus' telling his disciples that he would soon depart (13:33) occurs in a reading appointed during Easter. But (disregarding the scrambled chronology) it is just this *I am going* — Jesus' universalization — which is the precondition of the present situation of the community of faith. The Fourth Gospel would have its readers understand that the church is what it is and Christians are what they are because the risen Jesus has gone to the Father.

The love command (13:34-35) is an accessible and always pertinent theme for preaching. On Holy Thursday this command would stand in close relation with the foot-washing and with Jesus' word, *If I your Lord and Teacher have washed your feet, you also ought to wash one another's feet.* The loving community is the earthly correlative of the living, glorified Jesus and is his evidence before the world.

Jesus and Peter (13:36-38)

Jesus has spoken of the mutual glorifying of the Father and the Son and of the love that is expected among his followers. He now must attend to human weakness and failure. The opening affirmations and counsel of vv. 31-33 are preceded by Jesus' awareness of the treachery of Judas (vv. 21-30) and followed by his prediction of Peter's denial (vv. 36-38).

The dialogue between Peter and Jesus is the first of several exchanges at the start of the Farewell chapters: Jesus and Peter (13:36-38), Jesus and Thomas (14:5-7), Jesus and Philip (14:8-11), then later, Jesus and the other Judas (14:22-23). Of these exchanges, the one with Peter is the longest and the most interactive. None of the later exchanges includes a "follow-up" question, so none can develop the character of the questioner. The dialogical character of the Discourse is soon dropped, to be partially resumed in the Third Discourse.

Simon Peter said to him, "Lord, where are you going?"
Jesus answered, "Where I am going, you cannot follow me now;
  but you will follow afterward."
Peter said to him, "Lord, why can I not follow you now?
  I will lay down my life for you."
Jesus answered, "Will you lay down your life for me?
  Very truly, I tell you,
    before the cock crows,
    you will have denied me three times.   13:36-38

This tightly knit passage consists of three compound units, each containing a question and a statement.[8]

1. a Peter asks: *Where are you going?*
   b Jesus replies: *You cannot follow now; you will follow later.*
2. a Peter asks: *Why cannot I follow you now?*
   b Peter pledges: *I will lay down my life for you.*
3. a Jesus questions: *Will you lay down your life for me?*
   b Jesus predicts: *Before the cock crows, you will deny me three times.*

The statements in 1.b and 2.b introduce words that become important in the questions that immediately follow in 2.a and 3.a.

Jesus has said, not very informatively, that he is "going." Peter asks the natural question, *Lord, where are you going?* Jesus does not answer directly, only saying that the others cannot go with him. He speaks here of his going to the Father by way of the cross. His departure completes the course of his appointed work. Peter (and no doubt not Peter alone) does not understand and asks, literal-mindedly, in effect: "We have gone everywhere with you all these months. Where could you be going now that we cannot go also?"

Again, Jesus does not answer Peter's question directly, but says that while Peter cannot follow him now, Peter will truly follow *afterward* (1.b). Je-

8. The pattern of this exchange will be repeated in 16:29-32a, where, at the end of the Third Discourse, (1) the disciples collectively make a confident overstatement (v. 29), (2) Jesus questions, repeating their statement (v. 31); and (3) he predicts that his followers will desert him (v. 32a).

sus is not referring to continued companionship with himself, but to his own passage to the Father, in which he is the lone redemptive figure — though others will ultimately be associated with him (14:1-13; also 17:24). But the author is fond of multiple meanings, and Jesus' words may refer also to a coming time when, the failures of the passion events behind them, others, including a fully restored Peter (21:18-19), will in fact go courageously where Jesus has led the way. Peter cannot follow now but will follow afterward.

This exchange opens a leading theme of the First Discourse: Jesus' initial departure is alone, *You cannot follow now* (1.b); but his solitary going will in time involve others, *You will follow afterward* (1.b). The idea that others will "follow" was not expressed in Peter's question (1.a); Jesus introduces it in his reply (1.b).

This passage seems to couple Jesus' prediction of Peter's imminent failure (v. 38) with a prediction of his eventual faithfulness (vv. 36-37). It is clear that the author knows of a time when Peter has occupied a fully vindicated place in the leadership of the Christian community. (In the Synoptic Gospels, Jesus gives no indication that he knows of Peter's ultimate loyalty.)

The second exchange (2.a and b) is built around another expression with complex reference: Peter says, *I will lay down my life for you.* Jesus questions, *Will you lay down your life for me?* Peter says that he will "follow" to the point of sacrificing his own life for Jesus. He is not boasting recklessly; his brave but futile gesture when Jesus is arrested (18:10) indicates that he is willing to act against great odds in support of Jesus. He has begun to grasp that Jesus is not going away in any casual sense. Jesus is threatened, and Peter will stand with him, wherever that might put him.

Peter's pledge to Jesus, *I will lay down my life for you,* is an instance of johannine irony. It is Jesus, not Peter, who lays down his life for others. He has spoken of himself so earlier (10:11-15), and he will again (see 15:13). 1 John 3:16 suggests that Jesus' *laying down his life (tithēmi)* had become in the first century a term by which the johannine community spoke of Jesus' self-sacrifice (see the note on p. 44). The author, who has put a remark of unconscious tribute to Jesus in the mouth of an enemy (11:49-52), now puts a remark of great incomprehension in the mouth of a disciple. Peter fails to grasp the unique role and competence of Jesus. He can do nothing to put Jesus in his debt. Yet may there be a double irony here? In the "after-time" would Peter lay down his life for Jesus? Did the Evangelist know that in fact he had done so? (The Appendix in 21:18-19 indicates that Peter's martyrdom preceded the final editing of the Fourth Gospel.)

In 3.a-b Jesus repeats Peter's words as a question: *Will you lay down your life for me?* Then he says what he knows will happen. Before dawn, Peter will deny Jesus three times. He will have evidenced a weakness of which he himself is unaware, but which Jesus knows and Peter will soon know. All the New Testament Gospels tell that on the night of Jesus' arrest, Peter denied Jesus, and they all say that Jesus predicted this (Matt. 26:33-35; Mark 14:29-31; Luke 22:33-34; John 18:15-18, 25-27), but only John tells of Peter's reinstatement (21:15-19). This failure of the most prominent of Jesus' followers (who had by the time of writing become one of the early church's leaders) must have burned itself so deeply into the memory of the early Christians that no one could tell the passion story in any detail and omit this incident. The realism of Jesus' prediction is matched by the realism of the Evangelists in including the story in their narratives. Some years ago the English theologian L. W. Grensted remarked, "The Christian Church, as it seems, was founded by a group of men who had loved, misunderstood, and denied their master. And not only they, but their followers, continued to lay an inconvenient and injudicious stress upon the fact."[9]

Essay: The Love Commandment

The Synoptic Gospels portray Jesus as an itinerant rabbi who gives wide-ranging ethical teaching, directed to everyone who is willing to hear him. In the spirit of the prophets, he speaks in behalf of the poor, and he inveighs against empty religious practice. The Jesus of the Synoptics speaks of inner truthfulness, of prayer and fasting, of charity and impartiality in performing it, of duty to God and to Caesar, of non-retaliation, of forgiveness. The greatest commandment, he says, is that one love God supremely, and the second is that one love one's neighbor as oneself. Those who belong to the reign of God should extend their love even to their enemies. What the in-breaking reign of God requires, Jesus says, is radical change — new persons who belong to a new age. The Jesus of the Synoptic Gospels urges repentance, a new mind.

In the Book of Signs, Jesus gives no comparable ethical counsel. He contrasts people who walk in darkness and do evil with others who walk in the light and do the works of light, and he engages in some discussion of keeping the law (5:9-18; 7:19-24). But he gives no directions for the conduct of those who believe. The johannine Jesus urges people to inward change

9. L. W. Grensted, *The Person of Christ* (London: Nisbet, 1933), 37.

brought about by their recognition of the divine light, which he himself is. He does not urge repentance, but he says that persons as they are are living a life that is not life. They must be born from above.

This absence of ethical teaching in the opening portion of the Fourth Gospel makes it notable when, in the Book of Glory, speaking to the disciples in private, Jesus repeats several times his single commandment: *Love one another.*

This commandment is first spoken in association with the foot-washing (13:14-15). The meaning of the commandment is demonstrated in Jesus' act; the act is informed by his commandment. The commandment is repeated in the "prologue" to the First Farewell Discourse (13:34-35). It returns twice in the Second Discourse (15:12, 17). Additionally, when Jesus speaks of his "commandment" (15:12) or his "word" or "commandments," as he does in 14:15, 21-24; 15:10, a reader may assume that although Jesus may refer broadly to the revelation he has brought, this specific counsel is in mind, for it is the only element of his teaching that he refers to as a commandment.

This commandment seems to have held continued authority in the johannine community, for it is cited in 1 John 3:23 and 2 John 5, and the discussions of love in 1 John 2:10; 3:10-18; 4:7-12, 16-21; 5:1-3 seem, in great measure, to derive from it.

The Departure Setting

Jesus' command that his followers love one another enters the Fourth Gospel at his leave-taking. During his ministry he has himself been the focus of the unity of his followers; their loyalty to him has united them with one another. When he is no longer with them, will they hold together?

A departing leader's plea for those who remain behind to continue in love is among the conventions of farewell speeches. In the *Jubilees,* Isaac says to Esau and Jacob, "And this I command you, . . . love one another, my sons, . . . as a man loves his own life." In the *Testament of Gad* the patriarch says, "Now, my children, each of you love his brother. Drive hatred out of your hearts. Love one another in deed and word and inward thoughts."[10] Jesus, in much the same way, leaves as his final testament his requirement that his disciples love one another.

10. See Raymond Brown, *The Gospel according to John* (2 vols., Anchor Bible; Garden City: Doubleday, 1966-70), 613 for some of these parallels.

The community of Jesus' followers is the sign in history of what he has been and done and intended. When he has gone, it remains a people of witness. Moreover, as the writer and as the first readers of the Fourth Gospel knew, the community would grow and spread and come to encompass greater human variety. As it did, the problems of cohesion would become more difficult. Jesus' followers — the immediate disciples and those who would believe through them — needed to know that continued unity in love was the will of Jesus, who was still present in the community. What each member did to each was, in effect, done to Jesus.

The Paradox of Freedom and Command

A question comes to mind: Can love be commanded? Can mutual service be made a matter of requirement? It might be thought that the idea of "commandment" subverts the spontaneity and freedom that love and humility presuppose. Is not love that is given in obedience to an "ought" inevitably qualified as love?

To reply briefly: Jesus stands in the tradition of the Bible when he commands his followers to love. The Creator, who knows the constitution of humanity and what is in the interest of the creature, says, *Hear, O Israel, you shall love* (Deut. 6:4-5; Lev. 19:18). It is true that love arises from the deepest levels of humanity; it is an affirmation of freedom and cannot be itself if it is compelled. But it can be drawn forth; it has a "because of" element. Paradoxically, at the same time that love is spontaneous, it belongs to the very structure of humanity; it is part of the life of justice and obligation. One can know one ought to love, and one can learn to love and to love more wisely and devotedly. As an expression of one's character, love is very powerful, yet it is subject to control; it can be brought under discipline. Love is a matter of behavior, of life in community, of social expectation, and it is a subject for critical thought. When we love, we are most free and at the same time most compelled. T. F. Torrance, speaking of life in the church, put the point: "The great characteristic of all Christian service or *diakonia* is that while it is certainly fulfilled under the constraint of the love of Christ it is a service *commanded* by Him and laid by Him as a task upon every baptized member of His Body."[11]

11. T. F. Torrance, "Service in Jesus Christ," in *Service in Christ: Essays Presented to Karl Barth on His 80th Birthday,* ed. James I. McCord and T. H. L. Parker (Grand Rapids: Eerdmans, 1966), 1.

A New Commandment

Jesus' term "new" suggests former commandments. The ancient and fundamental "ten words" were marks of Israel's covenant with God — a covenant whose ethical implications were developed in the prophets, especially their passion for justice. The basic mandate was given in Lev. 19:18, *You shall love your neighbor as yourself. I am the Lord.* The rabbis had long counseled love.

Jesus' commandment is "new" because it belongs to the people of the new age, because it is from a new commandment-giver, because it is set on a new theological basis, and because it asks a new kind of love. Augustine once said, "This love renews us, so that we are a new people, inheritors of the new covenant and singers of the new song."[12]

Writing later in the first century, the author of 1 John plays with this "oldness" and "newness" (see 1 John 2:7-8). By the time of the Epistle, the commandment which in the Gospel is called "new" has become "old," in the sense that it has been with the Christian community from its beginning and is familiar through oral tradition as well as through the written Gospel that was held in the johannine community. Yet the "old" commandment is "new" (1 John 2:8) because it belongs to the age that is dawning. Although it may have been heard often among the johannine Christians, it remains a commandment of life for the new people. Whereas in the Fourth Gospel those who *believe* have passed from death to life (5:24), in 1 John it is those who *love: We know that we have passed from death to life because we love one another* (1 John 3:14). In 1 John love is a sign of new and transformed life: *Whoever says "I am in the light," while hating a brother or sister, is still in the darkness. Whoever loves a brother or sister lives in the light* (1 John 2:9-10a). *Everyone who loves is born of God and knows God* (1 John 4:7b). In the johannine church, as evidenced by both the Gospel and the Epistles, love within the family of faith is the actualization of the new age.

Responsive Love

The love which Jesus asks among his followers is their response to a love which has come to them. He says that his followers should love one an-

12. Augustine, *Tractates on John*, LXV.1.

other *just as I have loved you* (13:34b). In the Second Discourse, Jesus' love command (15:12, 17) occurs in a context of his demonstrated love in laying down his life (15:13; cf. 1 John 3:16; 4:9-11), of his calling his disciples his friends (15:14-15), and of his choosing them (15:16). His sovereign requirement is set in the midst of his sovereign giving. Love arises from prior love. When Jesus says that his disciples are to love with a love which was demonstrated when he laid down his life for them (15:13), he means that their love for one another, like his love for them, "is to be limitless in its self-giving."[13] In 1 John too Jesus' sacrificial love is the model for love among Christians: *He laid down his life for us — and we ought to lay down our lives for one another* (1 John 3:16).

The johannine writings describe love among Christians as their participation in a love which originates in the Father and is demonstrated finally in Jesus' cross. 1 John says that Christ's love exhibited the loving initiative of God. *In this is love, not that we loved God, but that he loved us and sent his Son to be the atoning sacrifice for our sins. Beloved, since God loved us so much, we also ought to love one another* (1 John 4:10-11). Johannine thought unites kerygma and ethics. J. L. Houlden remarks that the love command is spoken "in the setting of a profound and highly integrated theological perspective."[14]

Particular Love

The johannine Jesus asks his followers to love one another. Although the Evangelist in 3:16 roots his Gospel in God's love for the world, Jesus in the Fourth Gospel says nothing about his people showing a broad, undiscriminating love for the neighbor, such as is commended in the Synoptics (Matt. 5:43; 22:34-40; Mark 12:28-34; Luke 10:25-27), nor is anything said of love for one's enemies (cf. Matt. 5:43-45; Luke 6:27, 32-36; cf. Rom. 12:20). Other passages in the New Testament also commend love among believers (Rom. 13:8-9; Gal. 5:14; 1 Thess. 3:12; Heb. 10:24; 13:1; Jas. 2:15-16; 1 Pet. 2:17). The johannine ethic is unusual, not because it urges believers to care for one another, but because the love it commends is so exclusive. Neither the Fourth Gospel nor the johannine Epistles speak of the poor, of hospitality,

13. D. Moody Smith, *Johannine Christianity* (Columbia: University of South Carolina Press, 1984), 178.

14. J. L. Houlden, *Ethics in the New Testament* (Harmondsworth: Penguin, 1973), 72.

of family relations, of the community of justice, of masters and slaves, or of doing good to all. The focus is entirely on mutual, self-giving love toward one's fellow believers.

In 1 John the object of benevolence is always a "brother or sister" in need (3:17). The term *adelphos* (translated inclusively as *brother or sister* in the NRSV) refers to one's fellow Christians, with whom — with all of whom — one is united as children in a family are united.

If a reader judges that this johannine ethic of love is narrow, one could reply that Jesus' terms do not forbid or discourage wider sympathy and charity. Clearly they do not require one to hate or regard ungenerously those outside one's group. Perhaps the first lessons about loving are only learned in a fairly close-knit community. Indeed, unless the love commandment is seen to be operative in the close-at-hand community, nothing that Christians do or say to their pagan neighbors will carry any credibility. However, if community is to be developed intensively as a preparation for demonstrating love in more extensive relations, Jesus' farewell words do not say so.

A sociological factor undoubtedly influenced this johannine particularity. The first-century church was marginalized by Hellenistic society, had been expelled from at least some Jewish synagogues, and was thus relegated to an "outsider" status. It was regarded with hostility and stood open to persecution. Such an excluded community inevitably develops a strong internal loyalty. Standing at odds with the supporting, meaning-imparting structures of the general society, it had to create and hold to an alternative order of interpersonal bonding and articulated meaning.

Identification with the Christian faith and community would, for many converts, of both of Jewish and Gentile background, break former solidarities of family, occupation, civil identity, and shared values. New and fulfilling ties had to compensate for such disruptions, and positive new loyalties had to unite new converts in mutual support. As Houlden put it, "In the tightly-knit Christian body, with its strong dependence on and loyalty to Christ, the duty of fostering the cohesion of the community is intensified: it becomes, in its new form, a major strand in the meaning of love."[15] This johannine emphasis could seem narrow; yet it deals with love in the specific, near-at-hand level where it must be lived and where it is often most difficult.

15. Houlden, *Ethics,* 18.

Witness to the World

Love among Jesus' followers is to be a demonstration to the world: *By this everyone will know that you are my disciples, if you have love for one another* (13:35). Although the command to love may focus on the close-at-hand group of one's fellow believers, it looks beyond to "everyone." Jesus' words assume that something in the world is capable of recognizing the love which vitalizes the community of disciples. It will recognize too that this love points beyond itself to the community's rootage in Jesus.

In the early centuries, the love that was demonstrated among Christians was, in fact, observed and admired. Minucius Felix, in his *Octavius* dialogue, section 9, says that "Christians love one another before they know one another." Tertullian, in a well-known passage from *Apology* 39, says sarcastically that the Christians' reputation for love is held against them: "It is the exercise of this sort of love which, among some people, chiefly brands us with a mark of evil. 'See,' they say, 'how they love each other.'"

Love as an Adequate Ethic

A modern reader may grant that this highly particular ethical injunction may have been suitable for the first-century johannine church and yet question its adequacy for a community of faith situated in society as it has developed in later generations. Aside from the repeated love commandment, virtually nothing is said in the Fourth Gospel about interpersonal relations. The foot-washing implies humility and mutual deference, but nothing is said about patience, kindness, sharing, weeping with those who weep, rejoicing with those who rejoice, speaking the truth, or forgiving. Yet the faith of the Fourth Gospel is obviously a community-making faith. It is spoken by and for a collective life. The response to the rather individualizing "whoever" of the Book of Signs unites believers not only with God, but with others who are also united with God through Jesus. *That you may have fellowship with us; and truly our fellowship is with the Father and with his Son Jesus Christ* (1 John 1:3) — a "you" and an "us" and an "our." The bonding established on this basis goes to the roots of existence. Common tokens of recognition unite persons within a new *koinonia.* When one speaks the deepest secrets of his or her inward life, others respond, for faith brings one into a life that is deeply shared.

Moreover, based as it is in a great act of divine self-giving, the community of faith has resources for meeting and overcoming divisive forces, which are rooted in egoism. The restraints on egoism, at this early stage of the church's development, were not institutional, but worked, rather, through the overwhelming recognition: Remember that we are loved, and how and by whom we are loved. The simple command to love one another is a rule from Jesus that arises from the very existence of the redeemed community — a rule of love, evoked by love, and expressive of life and freedom.

Jesus' command falls not on some of his followers, but on all. It is not qualified, so that love is appropriate in some situations, but not in others. Obviously, circumstances will affect the way in which love comes to expression, but no circumstances make some other law supersede the law of love. The church lives always under the constitution of love. Its law is mutual, reciprocal love, alert to the strengths and the frailties of others. It requires each to love and each to receive love. It is a severe and deeply testing command.

Almost at once, forms for ethical catechesis developed in the church — such as the New Testament "house tables" or "the two ways." In a fairly short time the church would begin to think and act in larger-scale terms. Within the structures of common life, such regulative factors would develop as episcopal counsel, common deliberation seeking direction for the church, and decretals or canons that provided discipline, fairness, or means of reconciliation. However, the first-century johannine community shows no signs of such regulative pastoral developments. It begins where it must begin — in concrete, face-to-face, long-term relations of persons with one another in local, space-time-specific communities of faith. Christians had the demanding task of learning and demonstrating love in the close-at-hand context in which it is always hardest. As Hugh Montefiore remarked, "You cannot learn love in large groups."[16]

Jesus' rule for his people was not detailed, yet what it said was so central that it said all. Jesus' requirements are implicitly contained in the obligation to love, and all violations of the common life are at root abridgements of love. Apparently in its first years, the johannine church was adequately guided and informed in its internal life by this single commandment. The intensity, joy, and vitality of its shared life made further explicit regulation unnecessary. The rule of mutual, serving love was sufficient to guide Christians' life together. It was the johannine church's entire *Corpus Juris Canonici.*

16. H. W. Montefiore, *Awkward Questions on Christian Love* (Philadelphia: Westminster, 1964), 118.

2. Because Jesus Goes to the Father (14:1-17)

Jesus' Departure and Return (14:1-3)

Do not let your hearts be troubled.
  Believe in God,
  believe also in me. 14:1

Jesus' announcement that he is leaving has set the disciples' minds racing. "Where is Jesus going? Will he come back to us? Will we go to him? Is this the end of our relationship with him?" Sensing his followers' dismay, Jesus turns from Peter to the disciples as a group, speaking words of emotional support, *Do not let your hearts be troubled.* His word *be troubled* is the graphic term *tarassō,* which is used in the Greek text of Ezek. 32:2 of a stormy sea. The disciples' hearts are in tumult.

Reassurance and the calming of distress have a natural place in farewell speeches, for example, in *The Testaments of the Twelve Patriarchs,* which contains a series of final leave-takings: "My children, grieve not that I am dying . . . for I shall rise again in the midst of you . . . and I shall rejoice" (*Testament of Zebulon* 10). The immediate setting in the Gospel has shown much that might trouble the disciples: The plans of Jesus' enemies give a foreboding tone to the occasion (11:57); Jesus has said that he is leaving, and leaving alone (13:33); there is a traitor in the group (13:21); and that very night there will be a testing in which Peter will fail (13:36-38). Jesus, who is himself calm and self-possessed, assures his followers that a firm belief in God and in himself should quiet their hearts; his going from them is not the end of their relationship with him.

When Jesus says *Believe in God, believe also in me,* his verbs may be read in Greek as either indicative, "you do believe," or as imperative, "believe." Most commentators think that the imperative is intended. The Jewish trust in God was (and is) exclusive, unshareable. Yet Jesus bids his followers to have an undivided trust in God and in himself: *believe in God, believe also in me.* Jürgen Moltmann reproduced the thought when he said, "Christians believe in Jesus for God's sake, and in God for Jesus' sake."[17]

Jesus speaks of where he is going:

17. Jürgen Moltmann, *Jesus Christ for Today's World* (Minneapolis: Fortress, 1994), 71.

> In my Father's house are many dwelling places.
> If it were not so, would I have told you
> that I go to prepare a place for you?
> And if I go and prepare a place for you,
> I will come again and will take you to myself,
> so that where I am, there you may be also. 14:2-3

These words project a powerful image, weakened for many Christian readers by its familiarity: Jesus is going to his Father's house, a place for which others too are destined, although he first goes alone. There he will act as something like a guest-master, preparing a place for others. He will come back for them and take them to be with himself.

No other New Testament passage casts its view of the future in such essentially domestic imagery. These words deal, however, with aspects of the Christ-myth that appear elsewhere in the New Testament, but expressed in other idioms. The two movements of this johannine imagery ("I will go from you/I will come again for you") can be compared with christological affirmations which are made in the New Testament, but in terms that differ markedly from these in the johannine Farewell.

Jesus speaks of his going to the Father, but he does not go in a moment of "ascension." Jesus here identifies his destination in familial terms as *my Father's house.*

In speaking of the Christ beyond the cross, the faith community must use metaphor. No literal, univocal terms can describe the living Jesus or his relation to God or to his people. The church's discourse must use language of time, place, social roles, and human relations (since that is the most significant language at hand) to speak of that which is not part of time, space, or human society. The metaphors that speak of Christ beyond time and space always express something about him and about his people living in relation to him. They also draw their image-material from the lived world of the image-making and image-using community. The church's metaphoric speech is born out of the depth of existence in faith, and it bears the weight of Christian living and believing. All systematically expressed accounts of Christ derive from primary, elemental images. Nothing is true in discursive theology that is not first true in imaginative vision.

Most of the early Christian descriptions of the living Jesus (descriptions made familiar by Acts, Paul, the deutero-Pauline epistles, Hebrews, and the Apocalypse, and perpetuated by creed and doxology) used spatial imagery — Christ is "ascended," he is "above," at the supreme place in the cosmos (see, for example Acts 1; Eph. 1:20-23; Phil. 2:9-11; 1 Pet. 3:22; Revelation 1). In these early images, the living Christ occupies a place of supreme authority, power, and splendor emblematic of his victory. This picture derived in some measure from a christological reading of Ps. 110:1, which depicts a priestly, royal figure at the right hand of God. *The Lord said to my lord, "Sit at my right hand until I make your enemies your footstool."* The earliest Christians read this opening of Psalm 110 as a God-given description of the absent-present Lord with whom they were linked (see Acts 2:34-35; Rom. 8:34; 1 Cor. 15:25; Eph. 1:20; Col. 3:1; Heb. 1:3, 13; 8:1; 10:12, 13; 12:2). He is associated with God in a place of honor and power. Christians have immediate access to him, and through him to God. The triumph through death that set Jesus in this place of glory will in the end be shared by believers and by a renewed cosmos.

This imagery of Jesus as the one at the right hand of a heavenly throne — which is common in the New Testament, in the creeds, in biblically derived hymns and preaching — has no place in the depictions of the living Christ in the Fourth Gospel. Johannine symbolism owes nothing to Psalm 110 or its priestly-kingly images, and it contains no post-Easter event of "ascension."

The johannine presentation of the living Christ draws on the scale and idiom of the household. Jesus is going to his "Father's house," which is, however, a place of abundant room for which others too are destined, albeit dependent entirely on him. He has gone ahead to the place where others will join him. He is getting it ready; he will return for them and take them there.

The Father's house, with its many rooms, is a somewhat problematic image. At first reading, it can suggest the Temple, which Jesus earlier described in this phrase (see 2:16-17). Perhaps in 14:2 he has in mind a heavenly Temple to which he goes. But Jesus' description of his destination has no overtones of grandeur, and nothing suggests a place of sacrifice. It seems unlikely that Jesus speaks of going to a heavenly Temple.

Jesus' reference in 14:2 to *dwelling places* in his Father's house uses the Greek noun *monai* ("rooms" in RSV and TEV). The term is related to the verb *menō*, meaning to remain, stay, or continue (rather like the old English noun "abode" and verb "abide"). Jesus pictures his destination as a large, hospitable household. When he refers to his departure, he usually speaks of going *to the one who sent me* (as in 7:33; 16:5) or *to the Father* (as in 16:10, 17; 14:12, 28; 16:28; in the prayer of ch. 17: *I come to you*). Emphasis falls on Jesus' relation with the Father rather than on his going to a place. The Father to whom he goes is a generous householder, who has room in his home for his Son and for others who are associated with him. Jesus is going, he says, to where a son, unlike a slave, remains forever (8:35) and where there is room for others.

As to the "many rooms," there are instances in late Judaism of heaven pictured as a many-chambered residence.[18] The source of this johannine language may, however, lie closer at hand. The term "dwelling places," *monai,* and the verb "dwell," *meno,* bring 14:2 within a rich circle of ideas around remaining, continuing, "abiding," "abiding in," and "abiding places." The terms speak of places where persons permanently reside. (See 15:5-10 and in 1 John *menō* appears 24 times in the first four chapters.) With *monai,* Jesus is saying that where he is going there are abiding places for many. As G. C. Caird remarked, "John is not here dealing in pictures, but in an association of sound."[19]

The translation of *monai pollai* in 14:2 as "many mansions" was long familiar in English speech through the KJV and goes back to the pioneering translation of William Tyndale, who had in his ear the Latin *mansiones multae.* The Latin noun *mansiones* was related to the verb *manere,* to dwell, and it simply meant a place of residence. It had no connotation of an especially palatial home, and in the sixteenth century the English word "mansions" — "places to stay" — would have been a defensible translation of *monai.* But later changes in the language made the word suggest an especially lavish home, which was a misleading image for 14:2.

The comfort of Jesus' words is that, in ways that he only suggests, although he will be gone, his care and love will continue. In time, he will bring his followers to be with him in the place to which he goes.

Jesus follows his *I go* by saying at once *I will come again.* His words in 14:2-3 restate in an original form an eschatological pattern that appears also in 1 Thess. 4:14-18 — Paul's earliest statement about the return of Christ. There are similarities in profile between the two scenarios: Jesus, who is departed, is yet risen and living. He will come for his people

18. See Brown, *Gospel,* 625.

19. G. B. Caird, *The Language and Imagery of the Bible* (London: Duckworth, 1981), 47.

(1 Thess. 4:16a; John 14:3b, the only express New Testament reference to Jesus' "coming again"). His return will unite believers with him (1 Thess. 4:17a; John 14:3b), to be with him (1 Thess. 4:17b; John 14:3c). This confidence is a comfort to his followers (1 Thess. 4:18; John 14:1a).

While this essential contour of events is similar, the two visions of Jesus "coming again" differ significantly in standpoint and idiom. In 1 Thessalonians the voice is that of an apostle who speaks to believers, saying "we," while in the johannine text it is Jesus himself (the johannine Jesus) who speaks, saying "I" and "you." Furthermore, the action in 1 Thessalonians is laid out against a two-level cosmos. Paul, speaking from the vantage of earth, describes Jesus' "descent" from heaven with its dramatic visual and auditory accompaniments: a cloud, a cry, a call, an archangel's trumpet. The dead in Christ will rise first and meet Jesus in the air. They will be joined by living believers. In the Fourth Gospel, by contrast, the setting is domestic. Jesus is simply "going" to his Father's house, where he prepares a place for others. When in v. 3b he speaks of his "coming" for others, there is no cosmic, apocalyptic drama — no sounds, no clouds. The Fourth Gospel depicts eschatology without trumpets.

Was the author of the Fourth Gospel familiar with Christian apocalyptic writing and preaching like that of Paul's early years, and did he for some reason develop an alternative to it? Or did the tradition from which the Fourth Gospel arose simply grow along independent, non-apocalyptic lines? Is it possible that the sort of statement expressed in the Farewell Discourse, rather than being a modification of earlier apocalyptic, represents the earliest idiom for describing Christ's "coming again"?[20] One can only surmise this writer's relation to other strands of first-century Christian thought and remark that he wrote as he did.

The focus in this passage is on Jesus. The initiative is with the *one* who acts in behalf of the *many.* His distinctive work is unshared: *I go, I prepare, I will come, I will take.* Yet his actions are for others: *I go . . . for you. . . . I will come and take you. . . . Where I am there you may be also.* In depicting the destiny of believers, there is nothing of natural immortality nor of metaphysics. All is Jesus, all is grace.

Jesus says that his parting from his followers in "a little while" is not

20. In an early work, *Jesus and His Coming* (2nd ed., Philadelphia: Westminster, 1979), J. A. T. Robinson advanced the thesis that the unified johannine eschatology was early and traced to Jesus, while the apocalyptic idiom represented a somewhat questionable development in the early church. Robinson restated this position, with varying degrees of insistence, throughout his scholarly work, culminating in *The Priority of John* (London: SCM, 1985).

the end of his relation with them. These johannine valedictory speeches contain penultimate words about Jesus' departure, leaving his disciples in the world, where they bear witness, encounter opposition, and experience pain and joy. Yet the ultimate emphasis is on reunion. The parting is endurable because beyond it Jesus' people will be with him where he has gone.

A pledge that believers will finally be "with Jesus" is expressed in several strands of New Testament thought.

In two passages, Paul (in both places writing about himself and writing under internal pressure) describes in a few words what he thinks of as the ultimate destiny of believers. In 2 Cor. 5:6-9, he speaks of this life as being *at home in the body, but away from the Lord.* He says that he would prefer to be *away from the body* and *at home with the Lord.* In Phil. 1:23, he weighs the alternatives of life and death that are before him. Taking account only of himself, his *desire is to depart and be with Christ, for that is far better.* (For related expressions, see Jesus' pledge to the penitent thief, *Today you will be with me in Paradise,* Luke 23:43; and compare Jesus' prayer that his followers *may be with me where I am,* John 17:24.)

To be sure, popular piety (picking up imagery from the Book of Revelation) has associated much scenery and even music with the confidence of heaven. All such scene-setting is relative to culture and tastes. One person's vision of blessedness, circumstantially described, may sound to another person like sustained discomfort or utter boredom. Yet for the New Testament the heart of the matter seems to be that heaven is less a place than it is the open, enduring, fulfilling relation with Christ in an order of things of which he is vital center.

These deceptively simple opening verses of chapter 14 show a powerful creative mind dramatically refashioning the Christian account of the ultimate future of Christ and his people. (And the Evangelist has not yet given his readers the end of it. Before this First Discourse ends the images of these opening verses will have been further reworked.) Jesus is going — not to a heavenly throne, nor to the innermost sanctuary of a heavenly temple, nor to the supreme place of the cosmos, but simply to the Father's house. He will come again — not with an archangel's call, nor in the clouds, but as one who has gone ahead might return for friends he has left behind but not forgotten.

The Way, the Truth, and the Life (14:4-7)

And you know the way to the place where I am going."
Thomas said to him,
"Lord, we do not know where you are going.
How can we know the way?"
Jesus said to him,
"I am the way, and the truth, and the life.
No one comes to the Father, except through me.
From now on you do know him and have seen him. 14:4-6

As Jesus speaks of his going and of its importance for others, he introduces a new term: *the way.* Assuming that he will be understood, he says, *You know the way.* Thomas interjects, pleading that the disciples ("*we*": he speaks for the group) *do not know.* They do not know Jesus' destination — as Jesus himself has suggested in 13:33, 36. How can they know how to get there?[21] Goal and route are interdependent. It is a fair question.

Jesus' term *the way* is not understood. Some exegetes refer to these sayings of Jesus that the disciples find difficult as "riddles" — sometimes as "departure riddles," implying that his words really were obscure, perhaps intentionally so. The disciples' need for explanation holds back the pace of Jesus' speech for a moment, requiring him to restate what he has just said. His restatements lead to three of the strongest christological affirmations in the Discourse, in vv. 6, 9, and 23. Literarily, these affirmations seem to be the purpose of the delaying exchanges which prepare for them.

Thomas, with no introduction, enters the dialogue, asking to be shown the way. Jesus replies, strongly injecting himself: *I am the way, and the truth, and the life.* He is *the way* to the Father — a route, an access for others. He is *the truth,* for he is the faithful revealer of God. He is *the life,* for he brings to a world in the grip of death the eternal life that comes from God. Jesus' simple, provocative words are ten monosyllables in English.[22]

21. William Temple comments: "We do not go to a railway station and ask the officials to recommend a direction and a train; it is only because we know where we mean to go that we can reasonably even ask for advice how to start." *Readings in St. John's Gospel* (London: Macmillan, 1939), 229.

22. The Latin is also terse, and it alliterates: *Ego sum Via et Veritas et Vita.*

How are Jesus' words related? Do they form a series of three equal terms: way, truth, and life? Or is the series cumulative, with emphasis falling on the last: life? It could seem so, for in the Book of Signs, "life" is virtually the supreme good. Perhaps the first two lead up to and modify the last: "the true way to life."

However, the series has been introduced in v. 4 by *the way* — the term that baffled Thomas. The clause that follows the triad (v. 6b) concerns others coming to the Father through Jesus. The emphasis of the series, as indicated by what leads to it and by what follows from it, is on *the way.* The theme is movement — movement toward. James Moffatt made "the way" a noun and reduced the other terms to modifiers when he translated, "I am the real and living way." Jesus is the true way, as he is the true vine (15:1) and the true light (1:9; 1 John 2:8). He is the living way, as he is the living water (4:10) and the living bread (6:48). The emphasis belongs on the start of the series — on Jesus as a way, a reliable and vital way.

This is one of several *"I am"* sayings in the Fourth Gospel, three of which fall in the Farewell chapters. *"I am,"* which Jesus uses in speaking of himself, is often used in elemental metaphors that catch up meaning-bearing things into the presentation of Christ: *I am the bread of life, the good shepherd, the door of the sheep, the light of the world, the resurrection and the life, the real and living way, the true vine.* Sometimes, however, Jesus uses the expression alone, saying simply *I am* (as seen in 13:19).

Jesus' "I am" sayings invite inquiry. Similar expressions can be found in nonbiblical religious texts.[23] Evidently this turn of speech or something close to it was so diffused in ancient religions that first-century readers of this Gospel coming from different traditions could find the language evocative.

However, the first background for this usage in the Fourth Gospel is no doubt the Jewish Scriptures, in whose rhetoric "I am" appears not frequently, but importantly, as a divine self-characterization. God says "I am," and thus the mystery of divine hiddenness and revealedness is presented. A central text is the vividly narrated theophany in Exodus 3. Moses, who is reluctant to accept the divine call to lead the Israelites, asks on what authority he might put himself forward: *"When the people ask me 'What is God's name?' what shall I say to them?" Then God said to Moses, "I AM WHO I AM." He said further, "Thus you shall say to the Israelites, 'I AM has sent me to you'"* (Exod. 3:13-14). These words must be understood in Hebrew idiom — not as metaphysical terms speaking of Being or Is-ness, but as terms of divine self-assertion and promise. The divine "I" — while shrouded in

23. See Brown, *Gospel,* 255.

mystery — is self-disclosed. God is met on God's own terms. "I am" speaks of the self-existent one, the singular one, the one whose purposes come from within and will be carried out in faithfulness. "I will prove myself to be what I will be." (See also Deut. 32:9; Isa. 41:4; 43:10; 46:4; 49:12.)

Expressions with "I am" occur in the Jewish Scriptures as an idiom of divine self-affirmation. In Isa. 43:25, the voice of God says, *"I, I am he who blots out transgression."* (The Septuagint translated this using *egō eimi* twice: *"I am, I AM, who blots out. . . ."*) This turn of speech shows the God of the biblical faith to be an "I" — one who acts and speaks from within. God initiates encounter with human selves, making liberating demands and opening severe possibilities. Divine ways are mysterious and surprising. The first person "I" of divine self-expression is not defined, captured, or categorized by any third-person pronoun (not "he," nor "she," "she/he," nor "it"). The divine "I" can only be suggested by metaphor; indirect speech is inevitable. The divine reality can be met primarily by listening as one is addressed by the divine "I" and then replying with an awed personal "you." The God who says "I" is self-disclosed, self-defined, even while remaining self-concealed. God, and no other, is God. God pledges to be to the creation now as in the past, and to be the promise of future faithfulness.

A related way of speaking is attributed in later parts of the Jewish sacred writings to Wisdom. This personified, quasi-divine power (which becomes important in post-exilic Judaism and is a formative factor in New Testament christology) speaks in strong self-affirmation. Wisdom's "I" idiom (which is not exactly "I am") is expressed (among other places) in Proverbs (as in *I, wisdom, live with prudence, and I attain knowledge and discretion,* Prov. 8:12) and Sirach (as in *I will make instruction shine forth like the dawn,* Sir. 24:32a).

This characteristic of what might be called the Hebrew rhetoric of divine address is used in the johannine presentation of Jesus. (That is, it is used in Jesus' self-presentation. Only Jesus says *"I am."*) The expression belongs, of course, to the christological reflection of the johannine community rather than to an actual pattern of the speech of Jesus the rabbi of Nazareth, though the johannine line of reflection could have developed out of hints in Jesus' words, some of which were retained in the Synoptic tradition. In Mark 14:61b-62 the high priest asks *Are you the Messiah?* and Jesus replies, *I am* (see also Mark 6:50; Matt. 14:27). The johannine Jesus speaks of himself in some of the same ways in which (according to the rhetoric of the Jewish Scriptures) the living self-revealing God speaks. The expression *I am* depicts Jesus as so rooted in God and so attuned to the speech of God that he can take to himself without presumption this distinctive, authoritative divine self-designation.

Jesus assures Thomas that he does know the way, saying, in effect, "You really do know, for you know me, and I am the way. You know more than you know you know." Thomas has protested that one has to know the destination in order to know the way. Jesus answers that the certain way includes the goal. While Thomas wants a map showing the destination and the way to get to it, Jesus says it is enough if one can know and trust a reliable way.

The crucial term "way" in this place is to be understood not as a manner of life but as revelation, as offer, as gospel. The Jewish Scriptures sometimes spoke of the "way" of God as commandments that lead to life: *You must follow exactly the path that the Lord your God has commanded you, so that you may live* (Deut. 5:33; cf. 8:6; 10:12; 11:22; 19:9; 26:17; 28:9). The "way" as Jesus speaks of it, like the Jewish Torah, is gift or invitation. Isaiah spoke of a God-given, accessible way: *A highway shall be there, and it shall be called the Holy Way. . . . It shall be for God's people; no traveler, not even fools, shall go astray* (Isa. 35:8). The desert barrier would be subdued and a new exodus would pass along a safe and unmistakable route. The God-given "way" was redemption, a "way" opened in the wilderness for the restoration of Israel (Isa. 40:3, quoted in John 1:23). God will lead the blind by a way they do not know (Isa. 42:16). (The divine electing purpose acts among the nations: it also makes a "way" for the Persian emperor Cyrus, Isa. 45:13.) The way was followed inwardly; God gives his people *one heart and one way* that they may fear him (Jer. 32:39). In a much later tradition, the members of the Qumran community described themselves as "those who have chosen the Way" (1QS 9); their regulated life in the desert was understood as the way in the wilderness spoken of in Isa. 40:3 (1QS 8).

Jesus, drawing on this biblical term, and uniting it with his unique mission, presents himself as the way to the Father. The way is in him and through him; indeed, he *is* that way. He himself is from the Father (so 7:29; 8:42, etc.) and is one with the Father (10:30). At the same time, he is one of and one with the human race (1:14; 6:42; 1 John 1:1). He is going to the Father (7:33; 13:1, 3; 14:12, 28), and as he does his going opens access for others (12:24). His unique, solitary work creates a people.

Jesus is not saying that he knows and points others to the way; he *is* the way. To speak of a person as a way corrects any naïve spatial understandings of Jesus' "going" or of its consequences for others. The movement-talk of "from" and "toward" is useful; perhaps it is indispensable for creatures of space and time; but in johannine idiom, space-talk speaks of relationships of persons, of union between persons, brought about through a person.

Turning to the second term of Jesus' triad, What of *and the truth* —

or, if "truth" is understood as modifying "way," what of "and the true (or real) way"? "Truth" holds different meanings in different cultures and contexts. In the johannine writings it does not mean accuracy of observation, fact, or reportage. It is not meant in the more intellectualized sense of correct representation — of having pictures or concepts in the mind that correspond with things as they are. It does not mean (as it did among some Greek thinkers) "real, not illusory." Rather, the johannine sense of "truth" derives from the Hebraic sense of truth as characteristic of persons and of relationships among persons. The root term carries the meaning of firmness or durability, suggesting personal characteristics of faithfulness, trustworthiness, sureness, constancy, or reliability.

This johannine sense of "the truth" informs the christological affirmation of 14:6:

Truth is in God, of God (3:33; 7:28; 8:26; 17:3). God is always true — true in the divine character and reliable in divine self-disclosure.

Jesus, the Incarnate Word, is the true manifestation of God (1:14; 7:18; 8:26, 40, 45-46; 18:37). He truly represents the character and bears the very reality of the divine (1 John 5:20; see Heb. 1:1-3).

Truth is not static, waiting to be discovered. It is active, self-imparting. It challenges illusion and asks for discrimination (3:21; 1 John 4:6). It is saving and judging. Truth is grasped in venture, in moral commitment. It is something to be done. It is known in the doing (3:21; 8:31-32; 1 John 1:6; 3:18).

The whole movement of revelation and redemption is in truth. God is self-disclosed in Christ, the eternal Logos (1:14, 17), who is God's reliable self-representation in terms of humanity, but is also humanity's true way to the Father (14:6). To believe, as the Fourth Gospel has it, is to become a participant in the truth. Truth, accessible through believing, requires interior revolution. But for those who commit themselves to it, the truth is salvation (8:32; 1 John 3:19; 2 John 1-4).

Fr. Congar summarizes this "inspired johannine synthesis":

> The truth goes from God to God, passing through the incarnate Word and the people of God. God the Father is true, authentic, stable, in his very being. His eternal Word is true because it is his Word. It became flesh in Jesus Christ and was communicated to me through him and his Spirit. By receiving and keeping the Word and the Spirit, we can walk (2 John 4; 3 John 3-4), have grace and truth (2 John 1-3), love (1 John 3:18), be consecrated (John 17:17, 19), worship (4:23) and be free (8:32) in truth or in the truth. We can, in a word, live truly.[24]

---

24. Yves Congar, *The Word and the Spirit* (San Francisco: Harper and Row, 1986), 46.

In the claim *I am the truth* Jesus sets himself in the center. The one in whom God's truth is declared and in whom the true human response is made says *"I am."* He claims, in effect, to be the trustworthy way — a way that does not mislead or stop short of the destination.

Jesus completes the triad with *and the Life* (or "the living Way"). "Life" too is a foundational johannine term — particularly an emphasis of the Book of Signs. Jesus has frequently spoken of life, and now he identifies it with himself. Rather than being the one who tells how life can be found, he *is* the life.

The ultimacy of the category "life" in the thought of the Fourth Gospel may derive from theological reflection (perhaps largely intuitional in character) on the basic, irreducible place of life in nature and human existence. Life (which is shared with all biological species) is the precondition from which human beings experience or attend to anything at all. Where life is, much is possible — meaning, relation, art, play. Without it, nothing. Life is self-propagating; life begets life. Yet it is elusive. We cannot isolate life or quantify it. Life never occurs abstractly; it inheres in things that live. Moreover, we cannot make it. We can only receive it, value it, and seek to transmit, enhance, and preserve it. And, of course, we can diminish it, and ultimately we can destroy it. It is a precious, vulnerable thing, given into the custody of the creation.

In the Fourth Gospel, life is in God. In the johannine view, humanity is made for God, and it only truly lives in relation to God. Apart from a conscious, trusting relation with God, life is a life without living, a pseudo-life. It is life so defective that it requires, not encouragement for one to go on as one is or counsel to modify one's conduct. Rather, more drastically, it requires that in the midst of life one be born again (3:1-14). To persons in the midst of such death-in-life, true life has come: *In him was life* (1:4).

Life is a reality that belongs to the deep structure of the Evangelist's thought:

God, the ever-*living*, self-existent one,
  brings the divine *life* itself,
    by the *living* Word,
      to those in *death*.
      Those who are in *death*
    are awakened to *life*
  by the *life*-giving Word,
who is the very *life* of God.

At least part of the configuration of John 14:6a can be found in a saying, not by Jesus, but by his critics, reported in all three Synoptic Gospels. In Mark 12:14 it comes in a section of questions set by Jesus' enemies to entrap him. Flatteringly, they preface their question about tribute to Caesar, saying, *Teacher, we know that you . . . teach the way of God in accordance with truth* (see parallels in Matt. 22:16 and Luke 20:21). J. D. G. Dunn gives his opinion: "It is quite likely that those who shaped the Johannine tradition knew this Synoptic exchange and transformed the words of flattery into a truth claim of Jesus himself."[25]

This Evangelist sometimes says a thing positively and then restates his point in the form of a denial of its contrary. (This stylistic trait is encountered as early as the Prologue in 1:3.) Usually the not-construction introduces no new ideas; it only adds emphasis. In 14:6b, however, Jesus' words seem to bring a sense of particularity and even of exclusiveness to his claim. In addition to putting himself forward as the way, Jesus denies that there is any other way: *No one comes to the Father except through me.*

Jesus' unique place as revealer is not stated here for the first time; it has been claimed earlier (e.g., 1:18; 3:5; 6:44, 46, 53; 10:1, 9). It would be quite possible for a twenty-first-century reader to affirm the positive statement of 14:6a (that Jesus is the Way) while at the same time being uncomfortable with the apparent implication of the negation in v. 6b (that there is no other way). Yet the Evangelist probably thought that the negation flowed from and was implied in the affirmation. Its apparently exclusivist claim might be offensive in our religiously plural world. The text seems to say that the concentration of the divine redemptive purpose in one person — Jesus Christ, first-century Jewish rabbi, enfleshment of the eternal Word, and subject of the Christian message — means that salvation or access to God is simply not available apart from Jesus and his story. He is not one way among many; he and only he, is the Way.

Such a reading universalizes the text, taking *No one come to the Father except through me* as speaking of Christianity (a cultural construction unknown in the first century) vis-à-vis non-Christian religions and post-Christian unbelief. But is 14:6b responsibly interpreted by such universalizing and modernizing?

Christians articulate their conviction that Christ is the only way most urgently when his lordship is challenged — as by a Caesar, a Hitler, or

25. J. D. G. Dunn and James P. Mackey, *New Testament Theology in Dialogue: Christology and Ministry* (Philadelphia: Westminster, 1987), 73.

present-day relativism or syncretism. When the Fourth Gospel was written, the negation of 14:6b probably referred to a specific challenge that the original readers did not need to hear mentioned but that is not now recoverable with any certainty. The context for which the negation was written is unknown. A concise comment by New Testament scholar Fred Craddock speaks to the present-day applicability of the text:

> What is not clear is whether the expression "no one comes to the Father, but by me" is a polemic, and if so against whom. One can rather safely assume the writer's awareness of both the synagogue and the Baptist sect in such a statement, but in view of the statement about the Holy Spirit (14:15–16:15), the remark about Jesus as the only way to God could be addressed to pneumatics or charismatics who discounted the historical Jesus in favor of new revelations in the Spirit. If an interpreter extends the meaning of "no one comes to the Father, but by me" as a polemic against other religions (Moslem, Hindu, etc.), then responsibility must be taken for the application rather than giving the impression that this was what the Evangelist had in mind.[26]

The apparent particularism of 14:6b, moreover, must be held alongside the universalism characteristic of the johannine message itself. In fact, the tension between particularity and universality in the thought of the Fourth Gospel provides some of the vitality of the book. The same tension runs through biblical literature. The earliest of the writing prophets said that God, who made an exodus for Israel, also led the movements of the other nations of the ancient Near East (Amos 9:7). God is the one God of all, having a purpose that gathers up the human race. The very singularity of God which Paul derived from his Jewish inheritance opened him to the unity of all under God: *Is God the God of the Jews only? Is he not the God of the Gentiles also? Yes, of the Gentiles also, since God is one* (Rom. 3:29-30). The johannine Prologue connects Jesus of Galilee with the eternal creative Word, who gives light to every person who comes into the world (1:3-4). The particular life-story that the Fourth Gospel tells is the decisive manifestation within history of the one who is the source and goal of all history. The God who acted toward the world in Jesus, the Incarnate Word, not to condemn, but to save, is the God who has created and who loves all and who meets the human depths of each person — albeit in modes of encounter at which biblical language and biblically informed speculation can barely hint.

26. Fred B. Craddock, *John* (Knox Preaching Guides; Atlanta: John Knox, 1982), 103-9.

In 14:7, which brings this unit of thought to its end, Jesus' idiom passes from talk of himself as *the way* to the Father to talk of *knowing* the Father through knowing himself. Images of space, movement, and destination give way to relational terms of knowing and seeing.

> If you know me,
>   you will know my Father also.
> From now on you do know him and have seen him." 14:7

Jesus again says that he and the Father are so united (cf. vv. 10-11) that to know him is to know the Father. But such knowing is participatory. To know Jesus and the Father is to be in union with Jesus and the Father.

Some Greek manuscripts give v. 7a as *If you had known me, you would have known . . . ,* making it a reproach, saying, in effect, "You might have known me, but you did not." This wording, which is chosen by the RSV, echoes 8:19, in which Jesus, speaking to a hostile audience says, *If you had known me, you would have known my Father also.*

Other manuscripts, however, make it not a reproach but a promise: *If you know me, you will know my Father also. . . .* This construction says, in effect, "Since you know me, you will know my Father as well." This is the choice of NSRV and TEV, and it leads convincingly into the second half of the verse.

Jesus seems to be doing again what he did at the beginning of his Farewell, where he took words that he had spoken in a negative sense to his opponents in the Book of Signs and repeated them in a positive sense to his disciples. *As I said to the Jews* [in rebuke, 13:33], *so now I say to you* [in explanation and support]. In effect, he says: "Since you know me, you know the Father also."

Jesus says that to know and to trust him as the way to the Father is to "know" and "see" God: *From now on you do know him and have seen him.* The deep interior knowledge of Jesus is the equivalent of the authoritative theophanies of the Jewish Scriptures or the vision of God pursued by the mystics. *No one has ever seen God. It is the only Son . . . who has made him known* (1:18). (For further discussion see pp. 142-49 below.)

The words *from now on (ap' arti)* refer to a time beyond the passion and the resurrection. The post-resurrection church sees and knows, as Jesus' disciples did not during his lifetime. The knowledge of the Father that had not been brought about by long association with Jesus will be brought about by his departure.

Jesus and the Father (14:8-12)

Philip said to him,
"Lord, show us the Father,
and we will be satisfied."
Jesus said to him,
"Have I been with you all this time, Philip,
and still you do not know me?
Whoever has seen me has seen the Father.
How can you say, 'Show us the Father'? 14:8-9

Thomas (responding to Jesus' introduction of the term "the way") asked about a journey and a destination (v. 5). Jesus, in reply, turned away from spatial metaphors and spoke of seeing and knowing the Father (v. 7). These terms puzzle Philip, who interjects, *Lord, show us the Father, and we shall be satisfied.* (While Philip's request seems to begin a new unit of thought, it obviously is continuous with what has gone before; Philip's question in v. 8 is enclosed by vv. 7 and 9, in both of which Jesus says that to know and see him is to know and see the Father.) The character of Philip is not developed; his request simply leads Jesus to restate and enlarge the claim that Philip found unsatisfying. Jesus (speaking at his own level — the level of reality, the truth of things) has said *you know the Father and have seen him* (v. 7). Philip, lagging (and speaking no doubt for others), says *show us.* If the disciples have been shown so that they know and have seen, they do not know that they have been shown.

Philip's request for a demonstration beyond anything that the disciples have so far had seems to represent a kind of longing that is restless with the sorts of evidence for the reality of the divine life that are available under the terms of the human condition. The desire of the disciples, voiced by Philip, to see the Father indicates that although they *have been with Jesus all this time,* insofar as they have not recognized the Father in him, they still *have not known* him. Long association has not brought the sort of perception that Jesus says it might have brought.

From Philip's inquiry, Jesus develops a lengthy statement about himself, the Father and believers. (The Father is mentioned nine times in five verses.) Jesus' advancing themes are showing, seeing, speaking, believing and doing. The exchange with Philip suggests the complexity of seeing. Earlier, Jesus spoke of a seeing in which nothing is seen — a seeing which evidences blindness (9:35-41). There is, however, a seeing which gives access to the truth of things. When Jesus says *Whoever has seen me has seen the Father. How can you say, "Show us the Father"?* he says that a true seeing of him is the *visio dei.* The words put forward a central johannine claim: with respect to God made known and accessible in human terms, Jesus is all that humanity has and as much as humanity can expect to have. Less is inadequate. More is impossible. No one will see more of the Father than is seen in Jesus. Yet at the same time, in our unperceiving world, there is a "knowing" and a "seeing" him which do not yield true knowledge of either Jesus or the Father.

> Do you not believe that I am in the Father
>   and the Father in me?
> The words that I say to you
>   I do not speak on my own;
> but the Father who dwells in me
>   does his works.
> Believe me that I am in the Father
>   and the Father in me;
> but if you do not,
>   then believe me because of the works themselves. 14:10-11

In this tightly worded passage, Jesus, who has said (v. 9) that in knowing and seeing him one knows and sees the Father, explains (vv. 10-11) that he can say this because of the deep mutual indwelling that persists between himself and the Father, *I am in the Father and the Father in me* (v. 10a; he repeats the words in v. 11a, and compare 10:38).

The Father's indwelling comes to expression in Jesus' words, which are given to him by the Father: *The words that I say to you I do not speak on my own* (v. 10b). Words shape thought and feeling into intelligible units which reach from one person toward another, imparting the self and creating a world of discourse that is shared between the speaker and the hearer. One discovers what lies within another person by attending to that person's speech. (Indeed, to a great extent, one discovers oneself through one's own speaking.) Jesus' words are his own; they arise from within himself *(ap' emautou, from myself).* They are *the words that I say to you;* they seek to create a bond of understanding with others. Jesus' words, however, are not only from himself; they originate from his oneness with the Father (cf. 3:34; 8:47; 12:47-49). Unlike the utterances of Israel's prophets, which came from the intermittent prompting of "the word of the Lord," Jesus' words arise from his persisting oneness with *the Father who dwells* (*menō*, "abides") in him.

Having spoken in terms of seeing (v. 9b) and in terms of speaking (v. 10b), Jesus changes his idiom in vv. 10c-12 to speak of his *works (erga)*, which, like his words, arise from the indwelling Father (cf. 4:34; 5:19-20, 36; 9:4; 10:25, 32, 37). Jesus virtually equates his words and his works. His words are actions; and his works — his signs, his self-revelation, his claim — are in part carried out by words. Jesus' performative words and his articulate works are effective on the world, and together they attest the rootage of his life in the Father (vv. 10b-11).

In the Book of Signs, Jesus spoke of his unity with the Father and claimed a divine origin for his words and works. He repeatedly urged his hearers to believe (see especially the close parallel between 14:10-11 and 10:37-38). However, the high claims he made during his public presentation of himself were largely rejected. They are restated in 14:10-11 for the disciples, again with a call to believe; and (as Jesus will soon explain) his followers, as they respond to his appeal, are themselves brought into the unity that persists between the Father and himself (14:20-23).

The johannine writings (as we have observed) use the idiom of mutual indwelling — describing persons as "in" one another. The words *I am in the Father, and the Father in me* are repeated twice (vv. 10a and 11a; and compare 10:38 and especially 17:21). The "in" formula speaks of two personal centers that are distinct and nameable. But the two intend and act as one; they are bound in mutual loving, listening, understanding, willing, and giving. The Son is utterly, transparently grounded in — is one with — the Father (10:30), and at the same time, the Father is uniquely, fully present and manifest in Jesus (14:8). The Father speaks and acts in the words and actions of Jesus. In Jesus' words and deeds, the unheard, unseen God is made audible and visible (1:18). These two, although they are distinct, are so *for* one another that neither can be known or dealt with apart from the relation. The Father and the Son interpenetrate; to know or "see" Jesus truly is to see him in his mutuality with the Father. It is to be brought through him to "see" the Father. Contrarily, if one looks at Jesus and sees no more than Jesus, one has not truly seen Jesus.

When Jesus says *Believe me that I am in the Father and the Father in me,* both the verb "believe" and the note of reciprocal indwelling of the Father and the Son are repeated from 14:10a (and the call to believe echoes the more remote 14:1). The first evidence for Jesus is Jesus himself: *believe me. But,* Jesus says, *if you do not, then believe me because of my works.* His "works" — particularly his signs — are grounds for belief. His "signs" *(sēmeia),* are revelatory acts that so demonstrate his oneness with the Father as to give rise to faith. They are written in this Gospel so that its witness too will occasion faith on the part of the reader (20:30-31). Jesus' works attest him and his oneness with the Father. Yet, even with his signs to attest him, he has been rejected.

The continuity within this closely written section, 14:10-17, follows along these lines: Jesus asks for belief in the mutual indwelling that persists between himself and the Father (v. 10a). That indwelling comes to expression in his words and works (v. 10b). If the indwelling seems difficult to grasp, one can credit it as it is demonstrated in Jesus' words and works (v. 11).

The theme of Jesus' works introduced in vv. 10-12 then unites the following sequence of thought. Those who believe on account of Jesus' works (as the two previous verses have described) will themselves do the works that Jesus has done and even greater works because he is with the Father (v. 12). The works of Jesus' followers will, like his, be a demonstration of the divine indwelling (see vv. 20-23). Jesus' followers pray, assured of answer (v. 13). Their works are accomplished through prayer in Jesus' name, which makes those works the works of Jesus himself (vv. 13-14). Love and obedience shape a disciplined life of asking (v. 15). The indwelling, the works, the prayer, and the obedience are all by the Spirit (vv. 16-17). While they are responsible human actions, they are at the same time divinely given.

Very truly, I tell you,
the one who believes in me
will also do the works that I do,
and, in fact, will do greater works than these,
because I am going to the Father. 14:12

Jesus turns from himself and the Father to his followers and their relation to him. He explains that his departure is not the loss they fear it to be, but a gain. Those who believe in him (vv. 10-12) will, he says, replicate and even exceed his own works — but all because he goes to the Father. His departure is the ground and cause of the new possibility in the lives of his followers, and they enter the new possibility as they believe in him.

Jesus has just said that his own works are done in the Father and now says that his followers will do the works that he does. He is model or prototype of his people; their works are of the same kind as his, and their works, like his, will be the works of God. Louis Martyn has noted characteristics of Jesus that are also characteristics of the church — both are divinely sent, both are hated by the world, both bear witness. Martyn refers to the church as Jesus' "double."[27] The early church proclaimed, challenged, healed, and forgave sin, as Jesus had. It saw itself as, in some sense, the continuator of Jesus' mission and heir of his prerogatives.

When Jesus says that his followers will do *greater works* than he has done, his words give a reader pause. Jesus is Redeemer; the church is entirely dependent on him. Can its works in any sense surpass his? A present-day interpreter can bring to this issue from an ancient text some observations informed by modern observation of human groups.

Any stirring of new collective life — religious, political, social, artistic — begins locally and particularly. It originates either in the mind of one creative person or else in a small, closely knit group, usually of young adults. Ideas and visions are lived intensively before they become expansive. The germinal words and ideas of the time of beginnings are often so visionary and forceful that they will be appealed to for many generations. If a new movement deals with basic human issues, it carries an implicit claim to an extended hearing. Perhaps it dreams of universality. The founding figure may not in her or his own inaugural career (or the founding figures may not in their initial effort) have been able to move much beyond the culture-boundedness of the time and place in which the ideas germinated. The original impulse is inevitably expressed in the idiom of the thought world in which it came to birth, and that idiom may be somewhat provincial. But, if there is genius in the new idea, something in the inaugurator's vision leaps beyond its early cultural confinement and gives promise of what later generations will see and do. If the new impulse persists, it will move into new cultural settings, and it will incorporate new human variety and create innovative forms of expression and action. *Greater works* will develop — indeed, if the movement is to last, they must develop.

27. J. Louis Martyn, *History and Theology in the Fourth Gospel* (New York: Harper and Row, 1968), 140-41. Martyn also make the point in other places.

Such observations may illuminate the text, but the Evangelist no doubt sees Jesus' promise not in terms of social processes (which, as described here in somewhat sociological terms, would have been strange to his way of thinking) but in the context of the basic christological message that informs his Gospel. The "greater works" are done by the church living in the world, but they are done because Jesus has passed beyond the world. Yet he remains united with the church, and its works are his works in it.

The church's "greater works" — probably implying in the Evangelist's mind its numerical growth and geographical spread, the barriers it had overcome, the signs and wonders it had witnessed — were Christ's works, done because his followers asked in his name (vv. 13-14). And the glory of such works was the Father's in the Son. Seen from a modern and detached point of view, many of the actions of the church, ancient as well as modern, carry sobering ambiguities both of motive and of achievement. Yet one can point, in every community of faith in every age, to miracles of quiet courage and compassion and to acts which attest the hand of the departed, glorified yet always present Jesus.

In the lectionary. The Revised Common Lectionary appoints the book of Acts as one of the liturgical readings during the weeks of Easter in which the Farewell portion of John provides the Gospel readings. In this record, the Holy Spirit leads the young church in unexpected directions. *Awe came upon everyone, because many wonders and signs were being done by the apostles* (Act 2:43). Despite obstacles, the gospel prevails. One can read this New Testament account of the advance of the earliest church as the story of the unfolding of the greater works.

Asking in the Name (14:13-14)

I will do whatever you ask in my name,
  so that the Father may be glorified in the Son.
If in my name you ask me for anything,
  I will do it. 14:13-14

Jesus has said that his works were performed by the indwelling Father (14:10). On this model of the Father working in the Son, Jesus says that his followers do not accomplish their "greater works" as self-reliant actors, but as persons who, out of their dependence, ask in prayer: *whatever you ask*

. . . *if you ask.* The same works which were spoken of in v. 12 as done by those who believe are spoken of in vv. 13-14 as Christ's works which he will do in response to his disciples' asking. It is the disciples, yet not the disciples, but Christ in them. This brief passage on prayer opens and closes with Jesus saying *I will do it.*

One aspect of the new era, the church era, is the use of Jesus' name. The departing Jesus leaves to his followers the custody of his name: *I will do whatever you ask in my name . . .* and *if in my name you ask me for anything.* The use of this name in faithful "asking" brings into effective action the one whose name it is; he will do it. The universalized Christ, who is with the Father, can act through those who have been given his name — a name which is as himself, a name that holds authority in heaven and earth.

When the disciples' prayer is answered, *the Father [is] glorified in the Son.* Prayer exhibits a deep mutuality of interest: believers ask in Jesus' name. When they do, the one whose name is used will himself respond and act: *I will do it.* The acts that Jesus performs in response to prayer are for the glory of the Father in the Son. Prayer is described as a joint action of believers, the Son, and the Father. When the community asks in the name, human interests and the interests of the Son and the Father unite.

If it stood in isolation, this passage, with its unqualified terms "anything" and "whatever," might seem to assign almost talismanic power to Jesus' name and to invite indulgent prayer. But the Discourse will soon turn to the love and obedience that bind believers to Jesus and will speak of observing his "commandments" (14:15, 21). Clearly Jesus' name is a caution, a discipline, or a judgment as much as it is an enabling or an empowerment. Hoskyns says: "The prayers of the disciples will be heard because the faithful petitioners belong to Christ, and, being united with him, offer only such prayers as are agreeable to him, the formal mention of his name proceeding from a real correspondence with him."[28]

Introduction of the Paraclete (14:15-17)

If you love me,
you will keep my commandments.
And I will ask the Father,

28. Edwyn Clement Hoskyns, *The Fourth Gospel,* ed. F. N. Davey (London: Faber and Faber, 1947), 458.

and he will give you another Advocate,
to be with you forever.
This is the Spirit of truth,
whom the world cannot receive,
because it neither sees him nor knows him;
you know him,
because he abides with you,
and he will be in you. 14:15-17

Jesus continues to describe life in the new age, saying that even though he himself departs to be with the Father, he still acts through the legacy of his name (v. 14) and through the abiding gift of the Advocate (vv. 15-17). It is by the request of Jesus, his work complete, that the Father will send the Advocate to those who love and obey: *I will ask the Father, and he will give you another Advocate.* (A reader may observe the "triadic" language: the Son will ask the Father, who will give Jesus' people another Advocate, the Spirit of truth.)

When Jesus speaks of *the Advocate* (Gr. *paraklētos*), a new word enters his speech unprepared and largely unexplained. The theme of the Advocate will return in each of the other Discourses of the Farewell (chapter 7 below will be devoted to "The Paraclete"). But a few words here may introduce this new johannine term.

The Evangelist's word makes difficulties for translators. *"Paraclete"* was a term of law and the courts; and some equivalents have been derived from this legal background. The promised divine presence is to be "counselor" (RSV) or "advocate" (NEB, NRSV). But the word *paraclete* was not confined to the courtroom, and some translators and interpreters have drawn from the language of personal relationships more than from law and have used terms such as helper, strengthener, inspiriter, one who stands alongside, one who takes another's part, or one who speaks in another's behalf. The one who will be sent from the Father is *another paraclete,* implying that Jesus has himself been a *paraclete,* and the one who comes to the disciples will be to them as Jesus has been. The term "the Spirit of truth" (which was in currency among the covenanters of Qumran, who distinguished "the Spirit of truth" from "the Spirit of error") is also used in explanation in v. 17.[29] This is the Spirit who does not deceive, who

29. The Scrolls describe a conflict between the Spirit of Light and Truth and the Spirit of Darkness and Falsehood. See 1QS 3.17–4.6. The Fourth Gospel uses the expression "the

conveys the reality of things, who is truth for the disciples, as Jesus has been the truth.

The Paraclete is particularly given to the community where Jesus is loved and obeyed. The Evangelist speaks of *the Spirit of truth, whom the world cannot receive, because it neither sees him nor knows him.* The world — the alienated socio-cultural order that is set in contradiction to God — cannot accept or engage with (it cannot *receive* or *see* or *know*) the divine power that demonstrates things as they truly are. However, the community of Jesus has enduringly lodged within it (it *knows*) the *Spirit of truth.* Although Jesus' ministry belongs to its own moment of history, the coming Paraclete will remain with his people, a resident teacher and counselor. (John the Baptist earlier witnessed, at Jesus' baptism, that the Spirit *remained* on Jesus, 1:32-33.)

Jesus says in this place only that the Paraclete will *be with you forever* — a presence which will remain with his followers when he is gone. While Jesus says that the community will be indwelt by the Spirit of truth, he does not say that the community cannot go grievously wrong or err. The text does not say as much here, but the indwelling Spirit of truth, in addition to inspiring the people of Jesus, may have to correct them.

In the situation of the first-century church, which the Evangelist always has in mind, the words pledge also that the divine presence will remain with the johannine community after the loss of its original witnesses has deprived it of the authoritative guidance on which it had depended since its beginning. The Spirit is pledged to the church, but especially to the church when human authorities are swept aside and confidence is shaken.

The sayings concerning the Paraclete which are written here as Jesus' farewell promise originated in the post-resurrection church and express its discoveries. Jesus' community had moved into new situations and had experienced inevitable hesitations, false starts, and uncertainties. Yet the withdrawal of Jesus' presence had been followed by a new, divinely given power, leading the community, giving it confidence, and uniting it with the very life of God.

---

spirit of Truth," but not "the spirit of Error." 1 John, however, approaches such dualism with "the children of God and the children of the devil" (3:10), "the spirit of God and the spirit that is not from God" (4:2-3), and "the spirit of truth and the spirit of error" (4:6).

In the lectionary. The Revised Common Lectionary brings this Farewell material before the church in the Easter-to-Pentecost season.

The opening of chapter 14 is thrice-familiar. The preacher's task will be to see it freshly. The image of Jesus going to his Father's house and returning for others is commonly used to interpret the deaths of Christians. The lectionary offers it as post-Easter interpretation of life in Christ. Can it be presented as Easter-season proclamation?

What depths of the divine-human mystery are opened when Jesus is understood as the way, the truth, and the life? What do the ordinary verbs, believe and know and see, tell about a believer's relation with Christ? Is Jesus' promise that his disciples will do greater works than his an invitation to presumptuous triumphalism, or is it gospel? The preacher will find profound themes and substantial difficulties lodged in words that are closely packed and deceptively simple. A sermon that will stick in the mind must grow from a single idea or image from this Discourse. One does not want to overload the sermon or the hearers' minds.

The lectionary's choice of 14:8-17 as the Gospel reading for Pentecost clearly intends an emphasis on the Paraclete theme of vv. 15-17. A preacher who uses this passage may have to clarify. The Feast of Pentecost falls in the Church Year fifty days after Easter because liturgical time follows Luke-Acts, which gives a staged-out account of the post-Easter events. A timeline separates the cross, the resurrection, Jesus' ascension, and the coming of the Spirit. Churchgoers who encounter the events in liturgical time have come to think of them as sequential. Yet in their lives of devotion and service many thoughtful Christians, with unconscious sophistication, know that the realities signified by these liturgical occasions form a unity. Believers live in the light of the whole story, which is opened progressively in the Church Year. They realize that the story is one, for they know it from the vantage of its climactic events.

The Fourth Gospel — unlike both the Synoptic Gospels and the liturgical year — unites the redemptive events and the redemptive divine action: the cross is Jesus' return to the Father. The Spirit is promised at the Supper and then is given on the Sunday after Easter (20:22-23). Good Friday, Easter, Ascension, and the giving of the Spirit form a complex but unitary event.

A preacher using 14:8-17 at Pentecost will find that the liturgy has set a johannine passage in a non-johannine time-scheme. The two should not be casually conflated. The Fourth Gospel knows nothing of tongues of fire, the sound of a mighty wind, and the apostles speaking in other languages. If these two New Testament narrative sequences lie side by side in the minds of listeners, there is probably no need for a preacher to distinguish them. However, if the johannine material appointed for Pentecost is to be used with integrity, it should be used in its Gospel context and not be transferred to a setting in Jerusalem fifty days after the resurrection. Much can be said on Whitsunday about the Holy Spirit from John 14:15-17 without going to Pauline or Lukan sources, which on other occasions may be heard on their own.

In this liturgical Gospel for Pentecost, Jesus pledges the Paraclete, who will be to the church as he has been. These words of Jesus, when they are read today, fall in a time in history when serious people search, often in remote, recondite, and even bizarre ways, for divine immediacy. Jesus describes the Paraclete as the Spirit of truth, who must work in a world in which truth (trustworthiness) is scarce. This Paraclete, given from the Father on the request of the Son (the triune God's self-investment in humanity) will be with and in the church — especially at those times in which the church undergoes a shaking of the foundations on which it has depended. The church, eager for a touch of authenticity and power, may be reminded by this passage that the Spirit of truth is given not on human demand, nor can she be induced by disciplines or programs. But she belongs to the community that loves Jesus and obeys him.

A preacher who concentrates on the johannine text will not lack for suggestion.

Essay: Believing Is Knowing Is Hearing Is Seeing Is Believing . . .

Believing, knowing, hearing, and *seeing* are among the deep words of the Fourth Gospel. The Evangelist often uses these words as though, in the crucial matter of establishing a relation between Jesus and the Father and Jesus' people, they come to much the same thing. In 12:44-45 Jesus equates believing and seeing: *Whoever believes in me believes not in me but in him who sent me. And whoever sees me sees him who sent me.* In 14:7 he similarly joins knowing and seeing the Father: *If you know me, you will know my Father also,* then he adds *from now on, you do know him and have seen him.* A little later, Jesus repeats his shift from knowing to seeing, *Have I been with you all this time, Philip, and still you do not know me? Whoever has seen me has seen the Father.* Then he adds a reference to believing: *Do you not believe that I am in the Father and the Father in me?* (14:9-10). Not-seeing and not-knowing are similarly equivalent, as when Jesus says that the world neither sees nor knows the Spirit of truth (14:17). In Jesus' prayer following the discourses he will describe his disciples, beginning his thought with the metaphor of receiving his words, that is, of hearing: *They have received [my words].* Then he will pass to the metaphor of knowing: *and [they] know in truth that I came from you.* Finally, he will enter the language of believing: *and they have believed that you sent me* (17:8). The Evangelist is able to say many of the same things using *believe* or *know* or *hear* or *see* or by passing from one of these terms to another. (Attention here is on the Farewell chapters, but there are instances of this interchangeable "epistemological" vocabulary earlier in the Fourth Gospel. Knowing and believing are taken to be equivalent in 6:69: *We have come to know and believe that you are the Holy One of God.* See also 6:40; 10:38.)

The general equivalency of these verbs tells something of what the Fourth Gospel means by each and clarifies some central themes of johannine thought. All four speak of ways in which we apprehend all that is not ourselves, the world of physical things, other persons, events, language, imagination, and ideas — the multiform world we encounter from birth onward. Trusting, knowing, listening, and seeing are basic ways in which we "take in" the reality that is outside our heads. The Fourth Gospel sometimes speaks of believing as "receiving," and at least once "seeing" is an equivalent of "tasting" — virtually ingesting (8:52). And the Bread of Life Discourse speaks vigorously of eating and drinking — the mysterious process by which we take into ourselves non-living things that are not ourselves so that they become part of us and give us life.

We may internalize and engage with this world outside ourselves by knowing, seeing, hearing, and believing; or we may fail to know, see, hear, or believe. In our commonsense way of understanding things, one does not bring the world into existence by one's knowing, seeing, hearing, or believing. But until one apprehends it, that great vivid world of persons, happenings, words, things, ideas, and pictures in the mind might as well not be. A usable, inhabitable, sharable reality is given to us as we come to know, see, hear, and trust.

But, passing beyond the level of common sense, it has become a philosophical commonplace that the world is not an objective reality which is what it is and which we appropriate inwardly and more or less accurately as we encounter it. The world we live in is not the world as it is but the world as we shape it in the rough processes of our experience. Knowing is not passive but active and interpretive — even creative. We bring to all our knowing, seeing, hearing, and believing a socially formed reality-sense and a personal history of perception. The self discovers itself through its engagement with that which is not itself. Our knowing, seeing, hearing, and believing are, to some extent, a process of self-making and world-making. We live at the vital point at which our inner self is breaking into the world of not-self and at which the outer world is becoming internalized — the disappearing point of subjective and objective.

The nexus of our engagement with the world is elusive. Our encounter with the world of not-I can be deeply informing. But at the same time, our believing, knowing, hearing, and seeing can be mistaken or even delusional. One can be persuaded of what is not true and see what is not there. We can be victims of the corporate "blind spots" that belong to the collective constructions of reality in which we perforce live and which shape us. We bring a history of past misperceptions, some of them deeply embedded. But we also have a real but limited ability to recognize and correct our faulty perceiving.

All these terms — know, see, hear, and believe — which might be thought to constitute the "epistemology" of the Fourth Gospel, can be used for a range of human experience. Some knowing, seeing, hearing, and believing can be quite casual, while other knowing, seeing, hearing, or believing can revolutionize the self and the world it inhabits. One must examine the human context of any act of perception. What meaning is yielded when one believes, knows, hears, or sees? What does the act do to the believer, the knower, the hearer, the seer?

To explore this vocabulary as an aspect of Jesus' Farewell, one should examine not only these terms as they are used in the Fourth Gospel, but also, at least at an ordinary-speech level, the human experience to which they point.

Believing

"Believe" is one of the characteristic organizing words of the Fourth Gospel. *Believe, pisteuō,* occurs more than ninety times in the Fourth Gospel, approximately seventy of them in the first twelve chapters. (The noun "belief" or "faith," *pistis,* is never used in the Gospel.) The verb is used more often in John than in all of the Synoptic Gospels combined. In the New Testament, only Acts and Romans begin to use the word as frequently as does John. Jesus seeks belief in himself (John 3:14-16, 36; 5:24; 6:34-40; 7:37-39; 9:35-38), and the author indicates that the entire Gospel was written to bring its readers to believe (20:31).

Believing is not a response that is in itself given by the senses, yet it draws on and interprets the world that is known to us through sense experience. One sometimes believes because one has seen. In the Fourth Gospel, some persons believe in Jesus because they have witnessed his signs (2:23; 6:2). Thomas, after the resurrection, sees and believes — although others will believe without having seen as he has (20:29). It is part of the sacramentality of the Fourth Gospel that when one has an opportunity to see, one should see. Sight is not opposed to faith; one is not called on to believe against appearances. But believing, in the johannine sense, involves a "seeing" or a "knowing" beyond anything derivable from sensory experience alone. Believing is like insight, imaginative grasp, or recognition. "Believing in" another person (as Jesus asks people to "believe in" him) means gathering the resources of the self and coming to an unreserved commitment to the other. Such "believing in" is always a venture. In 6:35, *believe in me* is equated with *come to me;* it can be described in spatial terms as a decisive movement of the self. In establishing a trusting relationship with another person, one cannot withhold one's commitment until proof is in hand that the relationship will be found lasting and rewarding — that is, until one "knows." Under such conditions, wholehearted commitments would never be made, for prior evidence is always incomplete. Validation develops, if it does, on the basis of commitment. One does not seek to know first and then to extend one's trust. As the Fourth Gospel sees it, believing is prior to and provides an access to knowing.

Knowing

To *know,* in the Fourth Gospel, is represented by two Greek words, *ginōskō* and *oida,* each of which is used about sixty times. Again the author's mind runs to verb forms; the noun "knowledge," *gnōsis,* simply does not appear. Modern scholarship judges that the two Greek verbs have a wide area of meaning in common. There are, of course, many kinds of knowing, but in construing the johannine text the significance of knowing in any instance depends on the human situation in which one comes to know rather than on which of these verbs is employed.

The rough equivalence of trusting and knowing is clearest in the way in which one comes to know another person — one's friend or one's spouse. No amount of information about that other person will bring one to know her or him. Two subjects must stand in mutual address. A word spoken from one person to another creates a situation of crisis. Response must be made. From a cordial response, a relationship of deeper trusting and knowing may grow. And, of course, the relationship may be brought to an end by an unfriendly response. One comes to know another person as that other person makes herself or himself known. In coming to know another person, one comes to know oneself. Thus, in interpersonal knowing, one always knows "from the inside" or not at all. One is formed by the relationship. One can never come to know another person if one holds oneself outside a measure of commitment.

While the interdependence of trusting and knowing is most apparent in interpersonal relationships, in his great study *Personal Knowledge,* the scientist/philosopher Michael Polanyi speaks of what he calls the "fiduciary element" in all knowing. "Human knowledge," he says, "rests on a belief element." All things we know beyond simple undigested information "we know by dwelling in them. All understanding is based on our dwelling in the particulars of that which we comprehend. Such indwelling is a participation of ours in the existence of that which we comprehend."[30]

Such an understanding lies close to the ancient Hebrew sense of what it means to know. In the thought of the Bible, knowing does not arise from a subject making a detached examination of an object and drawing careful, tentative conclusions. The knowing that matters to us is less a cognitive perception than it is our passionate, involved relation with a thing or a person we seek to come to know. It is a knowing in which we venture ourselves and in which we become known to ourselves. Such knowing has an indefinite capacity to grow.

The Fourth Gospel describes the relation between Jesus and his people as a mutual and profound knowing: *I know my own, and my own know me, just as the Father knows me and I know the Father* (10:14-15); *on that day you will know that I am in my Father, and you in me, and I in you* (14:20). Jesus is saying that to know him is to be united with him. One knows that Jesus' life is shared with the Father as one is brought into that life oneself. In the terms of the Fourth Gospel, one does not begin to believe where knowledge reaches its limit, but believing is a mode of knowing.

Hearing

The Fourth Gospel speaks of revelation and response in the metaphor of *speaking and hearing. To hear, akouō,* can be a virtual equivalent of believing. *If I tell you the truth, why do you not believe me? Whoever is from God hears the words of God* (8:46-47). Hearing is a primal human act. In infancy, the voices of others may be our first and most basic contact with the

30. Michael Polanyi, *Personal Knowledge* (New York: Harper and Row, 1964), "Preface to the Torchbook Edition," ix-xi.

world of persons and relationships outside ourselves. Others speak to us out of their interiority. From such speech we gradually discover those strange others outside ourselves and at the same time we discover our own interiority. The spoken voice establishes a presence; someone else has drawn close — even if it is the remote "drawing close" that modern electronics makes possible. The words and tone of voice disclose the speaker — the voice within the voice. Our awareness of what matters to anyone else is obtained almost entirely aurally. We can hear, as we can see, at a great range of receptivity. Sensitive listening is a learned skill — and not always easily learned.

Hearing — especially the human hearing of divine speaking — is one of the great metaphors of biblical religion: *Hear, O Israel* (Deut. 6:4). Or *the Word of the Lord came to me* (Jer. 1:4). In the Fourth Gospel, hearing is virtually an equivalent of believing; the appeal to hear is an appeal to believe. The hearing that is believing is not a superficial taking in of words but a deeply formative response. Speech arising from deep in the speaker's self can communicate to another person at an equivalent level. To "hear," as Jesus presents it in the Fourth Gospel, is to give consent to another who addresses one. The Fourth Gospel puts forward a relational fabric that is constituted in speaking and hearing: Jesus hears the Father; others hear Jesus; the Father hears Jesus; those who hear Jesus hear the Father; those who hear the Father come to Jesus; the Spirit hears and speaks; the Father hears the asking believer. Yet, as we know from common human experience, speaking and hearing are fragile, and there may be a failure to hear.

The term "hear" is used thirty-one times in the Fourth Gospel, often with theological significance. It is, however, almost entirely a word of the Book of Signs. *Akouō* is used only four times in Jesus' Farewell (14:24, 28; 15:15; 16:13).

Seeing

As to "seeing," the Fourth Gospel uses forms of three principal Greek words for see: *blepō, theaomai,* and *horaō. Blepō* is common in the Synoptic Gospels as "watch" or "take care." Although the word is used in the Fourth Gospel nineteen times, it is never used in this sense. "See," as *theaomai,* appears twenty-nine times, and as *horaō* (in its various forms) more than sixty-five times. In the past, linguists sought to distinguish these Greek terms as referring to different levels or kinds of seeing. Modern scholarship, however, finds no consistent and important differences of meaning among them. Of course, the experience of seeing is exceedingly varied — from a casual glance to vision that is life-changing. But it seems that all of these Greek words can be used for a range of seeing.

"Seeing" might be thought of as a passive act; one simply opens one's eyes and "takes in" what is there. However, much modern philosophy and psychology have made us aware that seeing is active, interpretive, and participatory. In much of human experience, seeing is a presiding sense, providing a deep, varied, immediate engagement with the world outside ourselves. Everyday experience shows that what we see depends heavily on what we expect to see. Every act of seeing carries with it a cultural point of view, preexisting categories of the mind, and an observer's past personal history. Even to see what is before one's eyes is, to a great extent, a learned skill. It is not only necessary to understand what one sees; one must see what one sees.

Even scientific inquiry advances not because new data come to notice so much as because shifts in interpretive categories or "paradigms" give an observer new ways of looking at data — often data that have been accessible for some time but not "seen."[31] Because we always bring to it different selves, living in different worlds, asking different questions, seeing is a task that is always unfinished.

Yet seeing is more than a demand. Vision often seems to come as an unexpected gift. After a frustrating struggle, there can be a moment when, with a sense of wonder, a patient observer says "I see." Perhaps one could have seen earlier, but did not. However, once one has seen, nothing is as it was.

The Fourth Gospel is a very visual book. Jacques Ellul remarked, "John's Gospel is the biblical book which most continually deals with the matter of sight and vision."[32] It speaks positively of seeing, even though it recognizes that some seeing can be inadequate. In the metaphoric world of the Fourth Gospel, seeing is not contrasted with some other and better mode of apprehension. Blurred and faulty seeing needs to grow and develop, not into something else, but into better seeing.

Sometimes the Fourth Gospel speaks of the new life as beginning with seeing. There is something that must be seen, and there must be those

31. See the argument of Kuhn, *The Structure of Scientific Revolutions* (Chicago: University of Chicago Press, 1970).

32. Jacques Ellul, *The Humiliation of the Word* (Grand Rapids: Eerdmans, 1965), 242.

who (like John the Baptist, 1:34) see and bear witness. The early chapters of the Fourth Gospel carry the repeated invitation *"come and see"* (1:39, 46, 47; 4:29). Jesus' signs and works are a starting place. As the theologically informed sociologist David Martin has said, the signs "direct attention to the person who performs them; they can arouse a first interest in the person of Jesus himself and bring men to a 'crisis': to decide for or against Jesus who claims that he is doing all this by virtue of his unity with the Father."[33] While seeing can give rise to believing, it does not do so inevitably. Jesus speaks to those who think they see, but are self-deceived (9:40-41). He describes a seeing that does not lead on to belief: *But I said to you that you have seen me and yet do not believe* (6:36). *Now they have seen and hated both me and my Father* (15:24).

Sometimes, however, in the Fourth Gospel, seeing is not presented as a prelude to belief. Rather, it signifies the profoundest engagement with the most significant and most elusive realities. Those who see the Son and believe have life (6:40). At times, seeing is described not so much as the starting place from which believing arises as the culminating point to which the dialectic of disclosure and response leads. One sometimes sees for the sake of believing, but at other times (in the metaphoric scheme of the Fourth Gospel) all is for the sake of seeing. It is manifestly possible to see and not to see. But it is also possible to look where one has looked before and see what one has never seen. David Martin says, "Redemption is recognition: Seeing again, noticing that which was always there for the first time."[34]

Through this powerful metaphor of seeing, the author speaks confidently of the mystery of seeing that which cannot be seen: "seeing" life (3:36), "seeing" the Spirit (14:17), or "seeing" the kingdom of God (3:3, a "seeing" which is also an entering, 3:5). *If you believed, you would see the glory of God* (11:40). All culminates in the seeing of the Father (14:7, 9) — the Father, whom, in another sense of seeing, no one has ever seen at any time (1:18; 5:37; 6:46). Jesus' final prayer for his people is that they may behold his glory (17:24). Productive seeing passes at length, not beyond seeing, but to the ultimate seeing of the kingdom which is the true seeing of Jesus. To see in this final sense is to be united with what one sees.

33. David Martin, *The Breaking of the Image* (New York: St. Martin's, 1979), 76.
34. Martin, *Breaking*, 76.

3. On Interrelations (14:18-31)

This First Discourse takes its rise largely from Jesus' opening saying that he is leaving his disciples: *I am with you only a little longer* (13:33). Having made this announcement, Jesus begins to explain to his disciples the new situation that follows for them from his departure.

But mid-way through his explanation, Jesus' thought takes a new direction. He makes an unexpected and seemingly contradictory statement: *I will not leave you. . . . I am coming to you* (14:18). Jesus reverses his metaphor of movement. He will not "go," he will "come." Further ideas grow from this freshly introduced theme. The new ideas as they develop do not expressly set aside the earlier "I am going" motif; they seem more like an overlay of new thought. It is as though the earlier proposition "I am departing" should not stand alone. This second half of the Discourse withdraws nothing, but what it adds transforms what had gone before.

Although the emphasis shifts markedly at 14:18, the First Discourse comprises a unit. The end gathers up the beginning, and the beginning foresees the end. As Jesus concludes (14:28), he draws together the principal christological affirmations of the Discourse, reminding his hearers of what he had said earlier about himself: *You heard me say to you, "I am going away, and I am coming to you."*

As earlier themes are restated, they are enlarged and reconfigured. For instance: In 14:10, Jesus spoke of his own oneness with the Father, saying *I am in the Father and the Father in me.* In 14:20 he brings the subject back but now includes the disciples: *I am in my Father, and you in me, and I in you.* And in 14:2 Jesus described "rooms" in the Father's house to which he would take others so that they would be with him. The image returns in 14:23, but it is reversed; Jesus speaks now of believers themselves as "rooms" in which both he and the Father will come to dwell.

Jesus' theme, especially in this second part of the Discourse, is the complex interior bonding between himself and his followers and between the Father and his followers, through him. He describes human life remade in a new body of relationships.

The theme calls forth a varied, but simple vocabulary. To identify some of the terms in which Jesus describes the relation between himself and his people:

- In vv. 18 and 23, Jesus says that he will *come to* his own. The Fourth Gospel often speaks of interpersonal relationships using the language of movement and place — where one is from, where one is going, where one dwells, being where someone else is. In this idiom, to be where another is means to be united with that other.

- In v. 19a, Jesus' followers will *see* him. Jesus adds that he cannot be seen by the world, but only by the community of preparedness and recognition. Clearly he refers to an interior, sympathetic seeing.
- In v. 20a, the disciples will *know;* they will know because they are themselves part of the thing known. *You will know that I am in the Father and you in me and I in you.* Jesus has in mind a participatory knowing.
- V. 20 speaks of persons who *indwell* one another. In vv. 10-11, two parties, Jesus and the Father, were "in" one another, but now, in v. 20, three parties, Jesus, the Father, and Jesus' people, are "in" one another. V. 23 puts the relation graphically, saying that Jesus and the Father will *make their home* in believers.
- The relation of *loving and being loved* spoken of in v. 15 returns in v. 21. In the community of mutual love, Jesus will *manifest himself* to his own.
- It was said in v. 15 that the relation between Jesus and his people is mediated and regulated by his "word" or "commandments." The relation with Jesus is a disciplined, faithful, covenanted relation. When Jesus reintroduces the theme in v. 23, he adds that the relation is with the Father as well as with himself.

The Discourse is introducing a new life, which is described as a complex of new relationships. But the Evangelist does not devise a new quasi-technical vocabulary; rather he uses words from common speech. The terms that he employs — *coming to, seeing, knowing, indwelling, loving, being loved, disclosing oneself,* and *keeping the word of another* — flow from one into the next, touching and enriching one another.

As the unity that persists between Jesus and the Father (vv. 10-12) is widened to include Jesus' people (vv. 20-22), a distinction is introduced between the community of consent and the world which rejects. The world was first mentioned in v. 17, where it was said only that the world could not respond to the Paraclete. But Jesus now adds that the world stands outside the circle of revelation and response which he is describing. He does not refer to the world as antagonist (as he will in the Second Discourse, 15:18–16:4a). He says only that the world is unable to see or receive the witness of God. His showing is a self-communication that depends on receptivity. In this First Discourse the world is not described as hostile, but simply as impercipient.

In the Book of Signs, while Jesus was making a public presentation of himself, he claimed that his words and works were rooted in his unique relation with the Father. Such claims gave offense and stirred division. Now, speaking to the disciples, who have begun to consent to his claims, he again sets forth his oneness with the Father. His words will now have a hearing because the hearers themselves are brought within that oneness.

Taking this new direction, Jesus continues:

> I will not leave you orphaned;
> I am coming to you. 14:18

In the opening words of this First Discourse Jesus told his disciples that he was leaving them but that they should not be troubled because he would return for them (vv. 2-3). Now he says unexpectedly that he will not leave his followers, but will "come" to them. A negation, *I will not leave you orphaned,* is followed by an affirmation, *I am coming to you.* (The NRSV wording "orphaned" renders the Greek word *orphanos.* Some English translations do not try to reproduce the image of the text but use less graphic terms such as "abandoned," "friendless," or "forlorn.") The "orphan" image casts Jesus as a parent or teacher and the disciples as children or pupils who, with his departure, may feel themselves forsaken and left without guidance. In cultures in which instruction was personalized, teachers were revered, and pupils were deeply loyal, such an image would come to mind ("the disciples of the rabbis were said to be orphaned at their death"[35]). In *Testament of Isaac* 13:5, a book in the Jewish valedictory literature, a pupil asks a dying rabbi, "Will you then leave me an orphan, Father?" From a different tradition, shortly before Socrates is to take the hemlock his grieving disciples speak "of the great sorrow that had come upon us; for truly we felt like children who had lost a father, condemned to live henceforth as orphans" (Plato, *Phaedo* 116a). The loss of a parental figure suggests frustration of hopes, the loss of a guiding relationship and a dependable order, inward emptiness and pain, anxiety concerning the future, and perhaps in some cases a feeling of having been deserted.

This image of being orphaned seems to say that after Jesus' departure his disciples at least briefly went through a painful period of bereavement. Does this brief image in John record an otherwise lost touch of history? In time, as this Discourse will show, the disciples' sense of loss was compen-

35. Brown, *Gospel,* 640.

sated by the realization that in a deep sense Jesus was present, although not in the old way. But for a time, the disciples experienced painful separation.

In addition to preserving a memory of a desolate period in the experience of Jesus' disciples, the Evangelist is speaking in v. 18 to a first-century community of believers that was losing its first witnesses. The "orphaning" of Jesus' disciples to which the writer refers no doubt has in mind at a second level the sense of abandonment which the first-century johannine Christians were feeling with the loss of those who had begotten them in the faith. The writer seeks, through Jesus' words, which he sets a generation earlier, to deal with his community's traumatic experience of aloneness.

When Jesus says *I will not leave you orphans,* he adds *I am coming to you.* It is a surprising pledge on this night of parting. The Discourse which has spoken of going and absence turns to speak of coming and presence.

One meaning of these enigmatic words *I am coming to you,* spoken on this occasion of farewell, would seem to be that Jesus' coming is the Paraclete's coming, which has been promised in the immediately foregoing verses (14:16-17) and will be spoken of again in vv. 25-26. Jesus who pledged *another Paraclete* here says *I am coming to you.* The Paraclete will be his alter ego. In the Paraclete's coming, Jesus comes. The Advocate was introduced in 14:15-17; then that subject is set aside while Jesus says in 14:18-24 that he will *come to* his disciples and that he and the Father will dwell in believers. Then in vv. 25-26 Jesus returns to the Paraclete theme. Thus two Paraclete passages are separated by Jesus' radical reinterpretation of his going and his coming. Clearly they should be read together. Jesus' going to the Father, the coming of Jesus and the Father to believers, and the sending of the Paraclete are ways of speaking of a single event in which the divine work is brought to its completion and in which the life of the believing community is constituted — indwelt by the Father and by Jesus, with the Spirit present in and to it.

Additionally, Jesus' "coming" may involve time and events that will take place in sequence; he will leave and will later return (NEB: "I am coming back to you"). We may read here a short-term reference to Jesus' "coming" to his disciples in the resurrection appearances (chs. 20–21). He leaves the disciples in his death and burial, but after a short time he returns. However, keeping in mind Jesus' use of *I will come again* in 14:3, a reader may find in v. 18 a long-term future reference to the final "coming" of Jesus to take his followers to be with him. C. K. Barrett remarks, "It is by no means impossible that John consciously and deliberately used language applicable to both resurrection and the *parousia,* thereby emphasizing the eschatological character of the resurrection."[36]

But in v. 18 Jesus simply says *I am coming to you,* making no reference to time. Perhaps rather than setting the two movements — the going and the coming — in sequence, Jesus is holding them up against one another, suggesting that his departure is at the same time his coming. The same movement of Jesus in relation to his disciples which takes him from them brings him to them. Jesus "coming" does not here refer to a "coming" at the resurrection, nor to a future "coming" which, in effect, closes the era of the church, but to a present "coming" which pervades and indeed defines the era of the church. As the Discourse develops, Jesus' "coming" will be accomplished in the "seeing" that will be possible for his followers but not for the world (v. 19a), in the *knowing* that will occur *in that day* (v. 20), in Jesus' *self-manifestation* to those who love him (v. 21), and in the *coming* and *dwelling* of Jesus and the Father with believers (v. 23).

The Evangelist lets his terms of "going" and "coming" — a "going which is at the same time a "coming" — stand alongside one another. His images of movement contain tension, vitality and interest. He says enough so that a reader knows that he is not speaking in literal place terms. He will not, however, tell all, but leaves his readers with a paradox — a stretching of the law of non-contradiction — which is full of suggestion. The absent one will not be absent.

In the first part of the Discourse, as we have seen, the Evangelist refashioned the apocalyptic imagery of movement in space, of angels, clouds, and trumpets, and of catching up believers into the air; and he rewrote it as a domestic parable of Jesus' journey to his Father's house where he will prepare a place to which in time he will bring his friends (14:1-3). But when he carried out that revision, the Evangelist's reworking of early Christian apocalyptic was not finished. In this later part of his First Discourse he recasts eschatology even more radically. The "coming" of Jesus may be future. (The Evangelist nowhere openly sets aside the future-orientation of the Christ-myth as he received it.) But Jesus' "coming" is also *present* as he comes now in and to the church.

In the opening part of this First Discourse, Jesus, using spatial terms, spoke of the Father as though he were remote; Jesus leaves his disciples and goes to the Father's house, from which he will return (14:2-3). But now Je-

36. C. K. Barrett, *The Gospel According to St. John* (2nd ed., Philadelphia: Westminster, 1978), 464.

sus speaks of his own "coming," with the Father (v. 23), to dwell in his people. The words by their very paradoxicality make it clear, as John Fenton says, that the Evangelist's "language of movement was metaphorical."[37]

> In a little while the world will no longer see me,
> but you will see me;
> because I live,
> you also will live. 14:19

Jesus' phrase *in a little while (epi mikron),* is more than a time notice. It is "a prophetic expression, indicating that Divine action is imminent, in judgment or in deliverance."[38] It is used by Isaiah (Isa. 10:25) and Jeremiah (Jer. 51:52), and it is echoed in Hebrews 10:37 (citing Isa. 26:20). The term *mikron* will return insistently in the Third Discourse (at 16:16-19).

Jesus says that *the world* (which he has said does not know the Paraclete, v. 17) *will no longer see* him, but the disciples *will see* what the world cannot. When Jesus "comes" to his followers (v. 18), it will not be a public event, accessible to general observation. Knowledge of the risen and coming Jesus is a knowledge held within the community of his followers — a knowing that is a believing. The Jesus of the community's faith has no compelling evidence that can persuade those who stand outside the *koinonia* of consent. When one comes to "see" the living Jesus, one does so by identifying in the same act with the constitutive confession of the people of faith. One sees in a community of shared seeing.

Although Jesus speaks of departing in a little while, he does not speak of dying. He departs, not to die, but to live — breaking his association with the disciples in order to be with the Father. However, in being with the Father, he is also with the disciples, and with them in such a way that his life secures theirs. *Because I live, you also will live.*

Similar language about living because Jesus lives appeared in the unmistakably sacramental portion of the Bread of Life discourse: *Those who eat my flesh and drink my blood abide in me, and I in them. Just as the living Father sent me, and I live because of the Father, whoever eats me will live because of me* (6:56-57). In the

37. J. C. Fenton, *The Gospel According to John* (Oxford: Oxford University Press, 1970), 155.

38. R. H. Strachan, *The Fourth Gospel: Its Significance and Environment* (London: SCM, 1941), 286.

mind of the author (or in John 6 it may well have been in the mind of a redactor) the Christian Eucharist (which is clearly referred to in 6:56-57, but not in 14:19) was a locus of the mutual indwelling that persisted between the living Jesus and his people.

The believing community which will "see" and "live" will also "know."

> On that day you will know that
> I am in my Father,
> and you in me,
> and I in you. 14:20

Jesus' expression *on that day* refers to the new situation for believers that follows his going to the Father — his going which is also his coming. His going/coming will bring to his followers an access of new understanding, *you will know.* The phrase "that day," which customarily speaks of final events (see Mark 13:32; Matt. 7:22; Luke 17:31), here refers to life in the post-resurrection community of faith (cg. 16:23, 26). The knowledge that is pledged for the end is accessible now in the life of the sign community of the new age.

The fuller knowledge that becomes available to believers by the Spirit is knowledge of life in a fabric of new relationships — knowledge of Jesus' relation to the Father and to his people, and knowledge of themselves in relation to him, and through him with the Father. Earlier in this discourse (using his characteristic "in-phrases") Jesus said that he is in the Father and the Father is in him (14:10). The idea is repeated in v. 20, but now it catches up the disciples in the mutual indwelling: *I am in my Father, and you in me, and I in you* — Jesus in his Father, believers in Jesus, and Jesus in believers. The theologian Robert Jenson remarked: "The Christian God, the triune God, has room in himself for us, in our full communal and individual personhood as the spouse of the Son the respondents of the Logos."[39] The knowledge which is pledged for "that day" is a sharing in life; the relationship will be understood and its divine character will be authenticated because Jesus' followers will themselves be participants in it. Jesus' relation with the Father becomes known as it reaches to include his people.

39. Robert Jenson, "The Christian Doctrine of God," in G. Wainwright, ed., *Keeping the Faith* (Philadelphia: Fortress, 1988), 41.

In the setting of the Gospel narrative, Jesus speaks of the future, saying *you will know.* The Evangelist, however, is writing from that post-resurrection time; he says, in effect: "We now do know. We know the relation of Jesus to the Father because we have been brought within it, and through our relation to Jesus — we in him and he in us — we have come to recognize the prior relation that persists between him and the Father."

Jesus has been saying "you." But with v. 21, the terms of his speech reach beyond the close-at-hand situation of himself and his disciples and address Everybeliever. As W. H. Cadman put it, "Jesus gives the assurance that he will love and manifest himself not only to those whose feet he has washed, but to all lovers of himself who should become so by their response to the preaching of the johannine 'word.'"[40]

> They who have my commandments and keep them
> are those who love me;
> and those who love me
> will be loved by my Father,
> and I will love them
> and reveal myself to them." 14:21

The unifying reality in this compact statement is love, which appears in all three clauses. Obedience, Jesus says, is an expression of love — of loving him and being loved by the Father (first two clauses), and love leads to self-disclosure (the last clause).

Vv. 20 and 21 describe an interpersonal and reciprocal bonding that involves Jesus, the Father, and Jesus' people. The "in" terms of v. 20 use quasi-spatial expression, speaking as though two parties enclosed one another — virtually interpenetrated one another. But, as v. 21 clarifies, the relations that are spoken of are freely created and sustained in love and obedience. Personal centers are united without being lost, qualified or diminished. Persons who love can live "in" one another; the needs and concerns of another become interiorized; one takes strength from the strengths of another. What we love never stands altogether outside us.

Some themes in this idea-filled passage may be identified:

- Jesus holds love and obedience together. Commandment-keeping is not a matter of demand. It arises from love for the commandment-

40. W. H. Cadman, *The Open Heaven* (Oxford: Blackwell, 1967), 169.

giver. Ceslaus Spicq has commented, "The only love for him which Jesus can recognize as valid is the *agape* which accepts his spirit and conforms itself to his will."[41] Love, while it is an expression of freedom, at the same time always contains an element of covenant. Those who keep Jesus' commandments out of love are delivered from the futility of love in a moral vacuum.

- Jesus says that *those who love me will be loved by my Father, and I will love them.* He describes an exchange of love between himself and his people in which the Father too is involved. In this three-part relationship, God extends love and receives love. The God of the Bible is characteristically depicted as the initiator of relationship with humanity — God is maker, lover, speaker, guide, provider, judge, savior. But God is also portrayed as a listener, a responder, or a rewarder. The Fourth Gospel has often said that the Father loves Jesus (3:35; 5:20; 10:17; 15:9-10; 17:23); it now says that the Father's love for Jesus extends to those who are bound to Jesus in love. The disciples have been brought within the exchange of love which prevails between Jesus and the Father. Since Jesus and the Father are one, to love Jesus is to love the Father also. Since Jesus and his people are one, the Father, in loving Jesus, loves Jesus' people as he loves Jesus himself.
- When Jesus says *I will reveal myself to them,* he indicates that he is known as he is self-disclosed. He will make himself known, not to any and all alike, but to those who love and obey him. Such self-disclosure is the way of personal relationships. One only comes to know another person as that other persons makes herself or himself known. When self-disclosure is cautious and measured, the other will be known only partially and selectively; but in a context of love and trust, self-disclosure can be free, unreserved and expansive. Jesus speaks here of a free, glad self-disclosure that opens within love and trust. Believers form the community which has received Jesus' self-imparting in which nothing is held back.

This passage speaks of a "showing" (Gr. *emphanizō*) of Christ to "his own" — an insider's knowledge of Jesus, opened by trust, and based on self-disclosure. This manifestation no doubt refers at short range to the resurrection, where Jesus *shows himself* (21:1) to those who are bound to him in faith. However, the language refers also to a continuing, intimate self-

41. C. Spicq, *Agape in the New Testament* (St. Louis: Herder, 1966), 3.63.

manifestation in the later believing community, which is a people of the resurrection. Spicq describes this elusive but self-authenticating manifestation:

> Charity makes the Christian know and feel the presence of Christ. Each loving believer experiences Christ's love for him. In the active communion which mutual love creates, the invisible itself is grasped and made near; there is contact. The illumination is of a spiritual order . . . neither physical sight nor speculative knowledge, but knowledge of the heart.[42]

The johannine Christians may well have thought that their developing christological understanding (of which the Fourth Gospel is witness) was not so much their own daring theological construction as it was the living Christ showing himself to them.

Jesus' term *reveal* in v. 21, *I will reveal myself to those who love me,* puzzles one of the disciples and elicits a question.

A second Judas, called "the son of James," is named among the disciples in Luke 6:16 and Acts 1:13, but not in the lists in Mark and Matthew. He enters here, designated only as *not Iscariot.* Lindars remarks, "It is difficult to see any reason why John should mention this name, except for a liking for variation, as Peter, Thomas and Philip have all played their parts."[43]

> Judas (not Iscariot) said to him,
> "Lord, how is it that you will reveal yourself to us
> and not to the world?" 14:22

Judas seeks clarification, asking how important things can be known to some persons and not belong to the pool of information that is accessible to everyone.

In fact, Jesus has said only that he would disclose himself to those who love him. Yet he accepts the distinction in Judas's question. The world as it is can neither know the Spirit (v. 17) nor accept Jesus' manifestation of himself (v. 22).

Perhaps Judas's words express a question that was in the minds of

42. Spicq, *Agape,* 3.66.

43. Barnabas Lindars, *The Gospel of John* (New Century Bible Commentary; Grand Rapids: Eerdmans, 1972), 482.

some of the Evangelist's first-century readers: "Why is Jesus' Messiahship — something that is so clear to us — evidently hidden from others? Could not Jesus, who has shown himself savingly (albeit often paradoxically and puzzlingly) to a few, show himself convincingly to all? Why is he rejected by many and accepted by few?"

Jesus replies to Judas that receptivity depends on loving him and keeping his words, which are the Father's words. While Jesus' manifestation necessarily originates in himself (*reveal myself*, v. 21), nothing is effectively revealed until the initiating party's disclosure meets with recognition.

The dynamics of Judas's question in 14:22 resemble those of Peter's statement in Acts 10:40-41 about the resurrection. It occurs in the narrative part of Peter's sermon in the House of Cornelius: *But God raised him [Jesus] on the third day and allowed him to appear, not to all the people but to us who were chosen by God as witnesses, who ate and drank with him after he rose from the dead.* Christ is revealed (the verb is *emphanizō* in both John and Acts), not generally to "all the people," but to his followers. The mystery of the risen Jesus is held within and is shown forth through the mystery of the church.

If a tradition of the resurrection is being drawn on here, it is enlarged and carried forward. The receptive, perceiving community in which Jesus is recognized continues beyond the immediate disciples and the Easter experience into the extended people of faith, of which the original readers of the Fourth Gospel were part. Jesus is known to and among believers, but by a hidden, interior knowing. As the Evangelist would have seen it, the only way in which the world can come to know the living Jesus is by believing, and thus ceasing to be world.

> Jesus answered him,
> "Those who love me
> will keep my word,
> and my Father will love them,
> and we will come to them
> and make our home with them. 14:23

Continuing to speak of receptivity, Jesus answers Judas with a positive statement emphasizing love and union (v. 23), which he follows with some clarifying negations (v. 24).

Jesus' reply does not expressly use or explain the term *"reveal"* which was in both Judas's question (v. 22) and in Jesus' statement that had occasioned it (v. 21). Nonetheless it is a reply. The private manifestation about which Judas asks consists, Jesus says, in himself and the Father jointly *coming to* and *making their home with* persons who *love him* and *keep his word.*

Jesus implies that holding to his word is not an imposed burden, but is conduct freely impelled by love. Love evokes love. The loving self-disclosure that takes place between Jesus and his people involves the Father as well (compare v. 21). The Father loves those whose love has made them one with Jesus.

In an affirmation that lies near the heart of this First Discourse, Jesus says that he and the Father will come and dwell where he is loved and his word is kept: *We will come to them and make our home with them.* Love for Jesus and obedience to him open the way for divine indwelling. At the beginning of this Discourse, when Jesus was speaking of his departure, he described the Father's house as a destination to which first he, then others through him would move (*I go for you. . . . I will take you,* 14:2-3). In 14:18, Jesus reverses his spatial terms and says that he will not leave, but will *come* to his people. In vv. 19-21 he set aside the idiom of going and coming and had spoken in relational terms of seeing, loving, obeying, and self-disclosure. With v. 23, the idiom of location and movement returns. Now, however, Jesus extends the earlier image, saying that he and the Father will *come* to make believers their *dwelling places.* When he speaks of "dwelling places," he uses the very word, *monai* — "rooms," or "abiding places" — which he used in 14:2 for the places in his Father's house that he would prepare for his followers.

Now in a radical inversion of the image of 14:2, Jesus speaks of believers as the *monai, residences,* in which he and the Father will dwell. At the beginning of this First Discourse, 14:1-6, Jesus presented himself as the believer's way to the Father; in this second part of the Discourse, love for Jesus opens the way for Jesus and the Father to come to reside in the human heart.

The opening verses of this Discourse had reinterpreted apocalyptic eschatology, turning dramatic, cosmic images of clouds, archangels and trumpets into a familial, domestic picture of the Father's house to which Jesus is going and to which he will bring his followers. Now Jesus further interprets his own interpretation. From the evidence of the Farewell, one cannot gather what the Evangelist's attitude was to the apocalypticism of Judaism, of the early Paul, and the earliest church. Assuming that the apocalyptic idiom preceded the johannine idiom, is the Evangelist repudiating it? Supplementing it? Embarrassed by it? Reacting against it? Going beyond it? Offering an alternative to it? Whatever may have been his motive and intention, the Evangelist in this First Discourse presents a highly original reworking of eschatology. A union with God described as distant and future in 14:2-3 is now depicted as a relationship brought about in the present. Jesus does not here describe his "coming" as an event to which the disciples look forward. Rather, his "coming" is a present, intimate relation in which the faith community and the individual believer are constituted. It is not a public manifestation accompanied by disruptions in nature and high visibility (*Every eye shall see him,* Rev. 1:7) — but, as C. F. D. Moule put it, it is "a secret, private coming to each individual as he [or she] realizes the fact of the resurrection, loves God in Christ, and accepts him."[44] Jesus' "coming" is actualized where he is loved and obeyed. A powerful experience of life in the new community has led to this original reconceiving of eschatology.

The terms of this passage imply that humanity can sustain the divine presence. The thought is not expressed in technical theological language; it says simply that the Father and the Son make their home in humanity. The words are relevant, nonetheless, to the later scholastic and post-Reformation debates about the human capacity or incapacity for the divine. They side with Richard Hooker's great affirmation of Christian humanism: "Capable we are of God."[45] The capacity for God is not alien, but is the deepest characteristic of humanness. While the indwelling described in 14:23 is gift or grace, it is rooted in the *imago dei* and in the divine intention for humanity. There is room in the divine life for humanity and room in the human self for God. Romano Guardini put it:

> Christian existence contains a mystery which can be grasped only by faith. Here is a human being, a creature, a piece of the world. But in that one arises the living God. . . . God is God and lives in his own interiority. But God grants to human beings the privilege of participating in it. Not of themselves or as their own, but by grace and as grace. When persons step into this relationship, believing, loving, hoping, then there awakens within them a life that does not come from themselves. But it is realized in them and so they become the persons their Creator intended them to be.[46]

---

44. C. F. D. Moule, "The Individualism of the Fourth Gospel," *NovT* 5 (1968), 173.
45. Richard Hooker, *Of the Laws of Ecclesiastical Polity,* I.xi.3.
46. Romano Guardini, *The World and the Person* (Chicago: Regnery, 1965), 46-47.

This affirmation that Jesus and the Father dwell in humanity carries forward a persistent theme of the Jewish scriptures. The fullness of divine presence in the people was part of Israel's hope. Zechariah foresees a day when, beyond the failures and lapses of the nation, God will come and dwell in the midst (2:10). Through Ezekiel, God says, *I will set my sanctuary among them forevermore. My dwelling place shall be with them* (37:26-27). Indeed, Ezekiel's prophecy ends with the glory returning to the Holy City, which will be called *God is there* (48:35).

The johannine affirmation that God makes a home in the people of faith continues and interiorizes this Jewish heritage. As the tabernacle in the wilderness was a sign of God's presence, leading and moving — a "tent of meeting" between God and Israel, the place of the *shekinah* — so in Jesus Christ, the eternal Word was made flesh and "tented" or "tabernacled" *(eskēnōsen)* among us (1:14). The johannine prologue adds *and we beheld his glory;* the incarnate Word was for a time the dwelling place of the divine glory. Jesus was the true Temple, *He was speaking of the temple of his body* (2:21). Then the world's light withdrew (12:23-36), and the people that he has summoned to himself thenceforward form the dwelling-place of God. The Evangelist sees the hope of God present in humanity fulfilled as Jesus and the Father make their home in the believing community. As E. K. Lee put it, "In the Christian community, as in the heavenly Jerusalem, there is no temple needed, 'for God Himself and the Lamb are the temple thereof.'"[47]

The Evangelist closes his great affirmation of v. 23 by negating its contrary (a rhetorical trait of his, previously encountered in 1:3 and 14:6).

> Whoever does not love me does not keep my words;
> and the word that you hear is not mine,
> but is from the Father who sent me. 14:24

Having spoken of the community of acceptance, Jesus notes again the reality of rejection. As obedience arises from love (vv. 21, 23), failure to obey Jesus' words derives from failure to love. But why do some persons love and some do not? The Evangelist does not say. It is part of the mystery of the relation of humanity to God; human beings can say "no" to the invitation to life. God cannot enter where God is not welcomed. With the affirmation of v. 23 and the negation of v. 24a, the Evangelist leaves his readers

47. E. K. Lee, *The Religious Thought of St. John* (London: SPCK, 1962), 196.

with the mystery of the relation of heeding-and-unheeding humanity to the out-reaching, self-imparting God.

Schnackenburg remarks that these words provide "a resounding conclusion" to the principal portion of this Discourse.[48]

Gift and obligation stand in complementary relation in the structure of thought of this second half of the First Discourse. What God/Jesus gives and pledges interplay with what God/Jesus requires.

Jesus points up human responsibility when he speaks of those who "keep" or who "have" and "keep" his commandments (15, 21a). His word asks for decision; some persons keep it (23a), as some do not (24a). Obedience follows from love: *If you love me* (15, 23), *those who love me* (21). And the text takes account of those *who do not love me* (24). Jesus' words do not illuminate the mystery of why some persons love and others do not.

Yet at the same time, Jesus emphasizes the initiative that he and the Father take in establishing bonds with persons of faith: *I will pray* and *the Father will send* (16, 26). *He [the Paraclete] will dwell with you . . . be in you* (17). *I will come to you* (18). You will *be loved by my Father* (21, 23). *I will love . . . and will manifest myself* (21). *We will come to them and make our home with them* (23).

In the paragraph vv. 15-24, Jesus, emphasizing divine initiative, says, "*I will*" (in vv. 16, 18 twice, and two times in v. 21); and he says *my Father will* (16, 21, 23 three times); and *we will* (23) and *he [the Paraclete] will* (17). But speaking to human responsibility, he says, "You will" articulating it as requirement (15, 23) and as promise (19 twice, 20, 21).

14:25-31 is made up of brief, somewhat discrete thoughts in anticipation of Jesus' departure: Jesus again promises the Paraclete (vv. 25-26); he reassures the disciples by his own peace (v. 27); he repeats things he has said previously about himself — his going and his coming — bringing back the "I am about to depart" theme (v. 28); he foretells a time when, beyond the missed communication of the present, his words will be understood (v. 29); he speaks of the conflict with *the ruler of this world* (v. 30) and of his own final loyalty to the Father (v. 31). Jesus passes rapidly from one thought to the next; nothing is developed. When he urges his followers not to let their hearts be troubled (v. 27), he returns to the opening words of chapter 14; and v. 28 is a christological summing up. Jesus is gathering his

48. Schnackenburg, *Gospel*, 3.82.

thoughts to a conclusion. The sense of an ending is confirmed by the dismissal *Rise, let us be on our way* (v. 31b).

> I have said these things to you
>   while I am still with you.
> But the Advocate, the Holy Spirit,
>   whom the Father will send in my name,
>   will teach you everything,
> and will remind you of all that I have said to you. 14:25-26

The Advocate was introduced in vv. 16-17, but only to say that while Jesus is departing, the Spirit of Truth will abide with believers forever. Here the Advocate is reintroduced, described now as the Holy Spirit, a teacher who continues Jesus' prophetic, disclosing, instructing ministry. Jesus has necessarily spoken incompletely; the Advocate will teach more fully.

Jesus contrasts the particular, limited (albeit basic and crucial) character of what he could impart during his lifetime with the fuller sustained teaching that will be given by the Paraclete who will be sent in his name and who will teach *everything.*

There are deep continuities: The Paraclete will be to Jesus' people as he has been. She will teach the disciples as Jesus has taught them. The Paraclete will be sent from the Father as Jesus has been sent, and she will be sent in Jesus' name. The Paraclete's teaching will be derivative, not novel: she will *remind* Jesus' followers of what he has taught. The Spirit (like the Son, v. 24) is the Father's gift — sent in Jesus' name to be in and to the community of faith as he has been. Yet the Spirit will not be Jesus, but Another who will represent him.

The New Testament provides wordings (wordings which name basic experience of divine action) out of which the church of the first four centuries formulated the classic doctrines of trinity and incarnation. The christological controversies and developments drew heavily on the vocabulary of the Fourth Gospel — especially chapters 14–17. The johannine language is undefined, uncriticized, and unsystematic. It belongs to a level of discourse that some theologians used to refer to as "immediate utterances of faith."

In the debates of the early centuries, spokespersons for different sides had to appeal to the same biblical texts. The johannine vocabulary is less a solution to the later dogmatic controversies than it is evidence that a fundamental reworking of the understanding of God arose in the community that came into being as a result of the mission of Christ. The later theologians did not find in the johannine terminology a body of answers to their questions so much as they found encounter with radiant mystery and a challenge to thought.

The Paraclete is identified as *the Holy Spirit* — the only instance of this term in the Fourth Gospel. When this Discourse was written, *the Holy Spirit* may have been becoming a common Christian designation of the new divine reality — the breath of God. The Evangelist may have brought in the more familiar name to explain to his readers his own more vivid but less familiar term.

The Spirit, Jesus says, *will remind you of all that I have said to you.* The new era is a time of new understanding, and the understanding is at the same time a remembering. The words and work of Jesus require constant interpretation in new situations. The interpreting Spirit does not strike out independently, but brings the work and words of Jesus into a critical present. Bruce Woll expressed the tension, "The continuity of the Son who transcends time is given a specific shape and structure, an 'anchor' in the past, a past which receives a protological character, mysterious and hence in need of subsequent illumination and interpretation, but seed and source nevertheless."[49]

The time of the disciples' association with Jesus was a time of momentous events, but it was also a time of incomprehension. As the Fourth Gospel has indicated, even Jesus' closest followers grasped little. However, the Spirit will bring about a recognition of his life-and-light-giving work. The later time — the time of the Paraclete — is a time of insight, of recalling and repossessing. Through the interpreting Spirit, fresh understanding breaks forth. Such Spirit-given interpretation should not, however, be thought of as inquiry into inert material, held in the past. As Barrett remarks, the Paraclete, in recalling all that Jesus has said to his followers, "recreates and perpetuates the situation of judgment and decision that marked the ministry of Jesus."[50]

The Evangelist again has his first-century community in mind. The believers in Jesus are losing their authoritative teachers. The writer, at the second level at which his mind is working, assures them that the Holy Spirit, sent from the Father, who compensated the original disciples for

49. Woll, "The Departure of 'The Way,'" 239.
50. Barrett, *Gospel,* 467.

their loss of Jesus, compensates similarly for the loss of the living links the johannine church has had with the Beloved Disciple, and through him with the historical reality of Jesus.

Without transition, Jesus passes on to say,

> Peace I leave with you;
> my peace I give to you.
> I do not give to you as the world gives. 14:27a

The departing Jesus leaves his followers his gift of peace — *shalom,* the just order of God, inner well-being, divine favor. The word which is used here at the end of the First Discourse will be the first thing that the risen Jesus says when he sees his disciples (20:19, 21, 26). *Shalom* is both greeting and farewell.

Jesus gives his own peace, *My peace I give to you.* J. A. T. Robinson remarks, "What seems to have impressed his contemporaries was precisely his self-possession, his poise, his authority, his 'peace' — what he made *out* of the inner tensions and the outward conflicts that marked and scarred his entire public life."[51]

The peace which Jesus has he gives. The peace he offers is not a state of contentment which his followers are to achieve. Peace, as it is understood in the Bible, is not so much absence of conflict as it is righteousness, justice and wholeness; it has its basis in the knitting up of the broken divine-human relation (Psa. 85:8; Rom. 5:1; Eph. 2:14). It is God's peace, the *shalom elohim,* which flows into the broken human community. In johannine terms, Jesus' peace is the peace of union with himself, and to be in union with him is to share his union with the Father.

Jesus' promise of peace follows immediately after his promise of the Spirit (v. 26), suggesting that the two are linked. The next sentence will speak of joy (v. 28), and the immediately preceding context (vv. 21, 23) has spoken of love. Paul, in his different theological idiom, links these things when in Galatians 5:22 he identifies love, joy and peace as fruit of the Spirit; and in Romans 14:17 he says that the reign of God is *righteousness and peace and joy in the Holy Spirit.* These characteristics — love, joy, peace and righteousness — always in short supply, were no doubt united with one another and associated with the Spirit in the mind of the earliest Christians because they belong to the ultimate accomplishment of God's promises,

51. J. A. T. Robinson, *The Human Face of God* (Philadelphia: Westminster, 1973), 88.

and in the thought of the first Christians the Holy Spirit is the actualization now of the age to come (Rom. 8:23; 2 Cor. 1:22, 5:2-5; Gal. 5:5; Col. 1:20). Peace, *shalom,* is among the final things, belonging to the time of accomplishment or fulfillment. (See Ezek. 37:26, *I will make a covenant of peace with them; it shall be an everlasting covenant.* See too Isaiah 57:19, *Peace, peace, to the far and the near, says the Lord; and I will heal them.* And see the prophetic vision of the right ordering of things according to the purpose of the creator in Isaiah 11:6-8, echoed in Revelation 7:15; 21:1-14.) When Jesus bestows his peace, he implies that the final reconciliation of all things does not lie in a distant future, but is accessible now, in himself.

Jesus says *I do not give to you as the world gives.* (It is unclear in the Greek wording whether it is Jesus' *giving* that is different from the world's giving or Jesus' *peace* that is different from the world's peace. Some English translations decide the point, but some reproduce the indefiniteness of the original. Perhaps the grammar contains "a purposeful ambiguity which will allow for both alternatives.")[52] The world, organized apart from God, and therefore apart from its own good, has no final peace, and it can give none. The peace it offers is illusory. Walter Brueggemann comments, "The world wants *shalom;* but . . . the world cannot have *shalom,* cannot possibly have it, on the present terms."[53]

> Do not let your hearts be troubled,
> and do not let them be afraid. 14:27b

Jesus turns again to the troubled hearts of his followers. He offers his gift of peace to quiet their inner turmoil and fear. He speaks to the disciples on an occasion when deep disturbance *(tarassō)* and opportunity to play the fearful coward *(deiliaō)* were close, as events would show. Jesus' words have behind them the disclosures of the Discourse as a whole. His hearers (and the Evangelist's readers) are to know a union with him and with the Father that is greater than the troubling things that are in and around them. Perfect peace casts out fear.

Jesus, suggesting that his disciples' peace grows from his redemptive work, reminds the disciples of what he said earlier:

52. Richard Jeske, "John 14:27 and 16:33," *Interpretation* 38 (1984), 405.

53. Walter Brueggemann, *Living toward a Vision: Biblical Reflections on Shalom* (New York: United Church Press, 1982), 119.

You heard me say to you,
'I am going away, and I am coming to you.' 14:28a

He sets side by side the two metaphors of movement that he had introduced earlier in the Discourse — *I am going away* (13:33; 14:2), and *I am coming to you* (14:3, 18) — as though they gathered up what he has sought to say about himself. We have suggested earlier that these two metaphors of movement, although they seem formally contradictory, refer to the same event — the death/glorification of Jesus. His leaving his followers is at the same time his coming to them.

Jesus does not in this place describe his movement in "descent/ascent" terms. His spatial metaphors do not speak of passage from the Father to the world and back to the Father. (He is not using the organizing redemptive myth that was described in chapter 3 of this study. See pp. 81-89.) Rather, here at the end of Jesus' mission (as also in 13:1), the Evangelist sums up the contour of the christological movement in "up-down" and "ascent-descent" terms. Jesus leaves his disciples, and he returns to them. The viewpoint is earth and history. The disciples pass from desolating loss to re-encounter with Jesus. (One may observe, by contrast, the shape of the christological summary at the end of the Third Discourse, 16:28.)

Jesus has been consoling his disciples, who have been made anxious and fearful by his talk of departure. Now, as he ends, he says that *if they loved him* they would *rejoice* that he is going to the Father. Jesus seems to say that the disciples are distressed because they are thinking of their own loss; if, however, they were, in love, able to consider what his departure meant for him *(if you loved me),* they would rejoice.

If you loved me,
you would rejoice that I am going to the Father,
because the Father is greater than I. 14:28b

Jesus seems to be asking his disciples to think of the conclusion of his mission as he sees it — not an easy act of the imagination. From his point of view, his going to the Father is the completion of his commissioned work, but it is at the same time a personal fulfillment. (Compare the account Jesus gives to the Father in the opening of his prayer, 17:1-4.) Jesus' solitary, unshared work has been given him by the Father. It has been carried out faithfully during his single lifespan. Its final movement — his parting from his followers and his going to the Father — as he has sought to explain, will bring about a new and better condition for his people. Here he adds that for himself too this completion brings satisfaction.

This interpretation of Jesus' words suggests what Jesus' departure looked like from the point of view of Jesus, the redemptive figure of the Fourth Gospel. Such a venture inside the awareness of the one who uniquely came from God is clearly a construction in the order of myth. Yet it need not be thought of as speculative — as though the Christian mythmaking imagination had run where it would. How might the Evangelist have come to such an understanding of the inmost mind of the Redeemer? And how might modern-day readers find it convincing?

The functional or economic christology of the apostolic generation may have led the Evangelist's mind along lines like these:

Christians know themselves to be the recipients of a divine work, and they know the difference — the death-to-life difference — that work has made. The redemptive work has made known the character and purpose of God. God acted savingly because God loved (3:16). The Son, the Redeemer, carried out the Father's appointed task to bring eternal life. He is now returning to the Father. Jesus' work (as the johannine church was beginning to understand it) was a divine act — rooted in God's purpose in Israel and in universal history, and finally in the divine intention in creation through the Eternal Word.

The Evangelist and his community may have asked something like, "Could humanity be brought into a new and transformed condition and the divinely sent agent of that redemptive work not himself be fulfilled in accomplishing it?" Perhaps one can, without irreverence, conjecture the johannine Jesus saying, "It is to your advantage (the beneficiaries) that I go away, and it is also to mine (the benefactor)." P. T. Forsyth, using the christological theme of a redemptive divine *kenosis* (self-emptying), developed the answering sense of a divine *plerosis* (self-fulfillment).[54] Something of the sort may be suggested here. If a Hebrew prophet can speak of God as afflicted in the afflictions of the loved people (Isa. 63:9), the same divine empathy and identification may allow one to think of the Redeemer as fulfilled in his people's being brought to wholeness.

When the Evangelist has Jesus explain that *the Father is greater than I*, it seems to have been clear to him that the lesser person is fulfilled in return-

54. Peter Taylor Forsyth, *The Person and Place of Jesus Christ* (London: Hodder and Stoughton, 1910): the phrase is the title and the theme of the final chapter.

ing to the greater. He holds that with respect to the redemptive work, all is from the Father; the Father gives to the Son, sends the Son, instructs the Son, supports the Son, loves the Son. The Son, for his part, receives from the Father, hears, obeys and loves the Father; and then, his work completed, he returns to the Father. The Evangelist's understanding of Jesus is again illuminated by the idea of agency; the agent is subordinate to the sender; he is directed by, and reports to the sender. Now Jesus is returning to the one from whom all has been received and with whom all has been shared.

This language of the lesser Son and the greater Father is a part of the johannine Christ-myth. If this passage speaks of the subordination of the Son to the Father, other passages imply their equality, oneness and mutuality. The Father and the Son live in an exchange of listening, of acting, of loving and of glory.

Formally, if one is thinking in terms of status or ontology, the proposition *the Father and the Son are equal,* and the proposition *the Father is greater than the Son* are contradictory. Yet if one is thinking in the functional, non-metaphysical terms of the New Testament, it could be put forward that only God can discharge the central, restorative work of God. If God delegates this work, it is also to God that the work is delegated and by God that it is carried out. The exegete Robin Scroggs (speaking to another johannine text) proposes that equality and subordination are not discrepant. He argues that, in the elusive, paradoxical johannine idiom, "Jesus is so perfectly a mirror of God that he really has no independent existence. . . . If Jesus is perfectly a mirror of God, if he does only what God is doing, if he wills only what God wills, then he is the very act and will of God himself."[55] Then, summing up the johannine theme in a way that illuminates 14:28b, Scroggs says, *"Complete subordination means complete equality!"* (italics in the original).

Jesus, again commenting on his own speech, continues:

> And now I have told you this before it occurs,
> so that when it does occur, you may believe. 14:29

Although Jesus' followers do believe in him, he seeks from them a fullness of belief that eludes them now. That fullness will come, he says, and when it does, it will build on what he has been telling them. Yet for now, Jesus'

55. Robin Scroggs, *Christology in Paul and John* (Proclamation Commentaries; Philadelphia: Fortress, 1988), 79.

words are not fully effective, and the disciples' believing is incomplete. He tells them, in effect, "I tell you now, but your grasp of what I am saying must wait."

Since v. 29 is part of a summation, it seems likely that the *this (I have told you this)* refers to the entire First Discourse. Jesus has told the disciples the mystery of his departure and of the new situation for them to which it will lead. Their comprehension of what he tells them must remain undeveloped until the events take place: *when it does occur, you may believe.* Events of the spirit are experienced before they are conceptualized.

What will occasion the disciples' understanding? What is the *it* which Jesus says will occur? Doubtless Jesus speaks of the climax of his work — his glorification and the coming of the Paraclete. Insight that is not possible prior to these events will follow from them. The statement implies an "after" condition — the time of the church and the Spirit. By the time this Gospel was written these crucial events have taken place, and Jesus' followers are beginning to understand and believe as they did not when he was with them. When he says that those who now believe will believe, his words suggest that there is an indefinite depth in believing; persons who believe do not, as they grow in their relation with God, pass to something beyond belief, but they grow into more informed believing.

> I will no longer talk much with you,
> for the ruler of this world is coming.
> He has no power over me;
> but I do as the Father has commanded me,
> so that the world may know that I love the Father. 14:30-31a

Beyond Jesus' unfaithful disciple and his enemies in Jerusalem, his opponent is *the ruler (the archōn) of this world.* Jesus is about to pass from intimate conversation with his followers to deep, solitary contest with another. As the Fourth Gospel sees it, the crisis of Jesus' historic mission is at the same time the crisis of an unseen cosmic conflict.

When Jesus speaks of the malign force that moves in the final events of his mission, he says *the ruler of this world is coming.* The expression suggests evil mimicking good. The powers of heaven have their *coming;* John the Baptist *came* (1:6-7); Jesus *comes* (1:9, 11; 6:38; 10:10; 11:27, and often); his "hour" *comes* (2:4; 7:30; 13:1); Jesus and the Father *will come* (14:3, 23); the Paraclete *comes* (16:7, 8, 13). As these powers have their "coming," in the divine-human drama of the Fourth Gospel, Jesus' enemy, *the ruler of this world* also *comes.* Jesus describes an Advent of evil. In the moral history of the race, redemptive and destructive forces which are always present have times of quiet and times of intense conflict. They *come* in moments of crisis.

In the face of this *coming,* Jesus is confident, saying that the world's ruler when he comes, *has no power over me.* The Greek is "has nothing in me," which is a legal expression; the world's ruler has no charge that will hold. As always in the Fourth Gospel, Jesus is in command. Even in his final, terrible conflict, no power takes from the johannine Jesus what he does not himself yield.

Jesus has asked his followers to keep his commandments (vv. 15, 21, 23, 24). He now says that he is himself a commandment-keeper: *I do as the Father has commanded me.* He does not ask of others what he does not do himself. In this coming conflict, Jesus is not driven by the initiative of Satan to which he must respond. Rather, he willingly and steadily obeys the Father.

In the unique terminology of the Fourth Gospel, the "commandments" of the Father are not for Israel, nor for humanity at large. They are for Jesus, and they are obeyed by him. They consist in his commission to bring salvation to the world. The "commandments" that are directed to Jesus' people are those that are given by Jesus himself.

Jesus' obedience gives visible evidence of his love for the Father. He acts *so that the world may know that I love the Father.* As the disciples who love Jesus are to keep his commandments, so Jesus obeys the Father. Jesus' obedience is witness to the world of the Father in whom his own life is transparently grounded. In obeying and loving, Jesus acts *so that the world may know.* In a world taking its own errant way, to have an obedient person in its midst is a fact of universal significance.

At the close of this Discourse, on the night of his arrest, when Jesus speaks of doing as the Father has commanded him, he doubtless refers principally to his going on to his trial and crucifixion. His suffering and death might look as though *the ruler of this world* has, at a moment of crucial importance, prevailed. But it was not so. W. H. Cadman put it,

> Satan's greatest assault upon Him was also His own greatest opportunity to obey the Father's will. . . . In the judgment of the Cross the world and the world's prince were to lose their case. The coming of Sa-

> tan, just because it would give Jesus the opportunity to show the perfection of His love and obedience to the Father's will, would spread throughout Satan's domain, the world, the knowledge that the conqueror had come. Henceforth all who believed in Him would be in union with the Victor in the decisive conflict; and to that union Satan's fatal power could not extend.[56]

Rise, let us be on our way. 14:31b

The words sound as though Jesus is proposing that he and the disciples leave the room where they have eaten and to move on to the next place of appointment. But there is no movement until 18:1; rather, three more chapters of speech by Jesus follow before the group goes on to the garden where the guard will arrest Jesus. In chapter 3 of this study we argued (as most modern commentators argue) that these apparent words of dismissal are an indication that the johannine Farewell is a composite body of text, the first part of which comes to its natural end at 14:31.

However, from the beginning of historical commenting, attempts have been made to give these words of ending an understandable setting in the flow of Jesus' speech and in the events of this night. Some rather "novelistic" exegetes have proposed that Jesus and his followers did, at this point, leave the room in which they had met, and as they walked to the garden, Jesus continued to talk. Other commentators, seeking to connect these words with the immediately foregoing context, suggest that Jesus is calling his followers to rise and advance to engage the *ruler of the world.* (This argument gives the johannine text some connection with a similar wording in Mark 14:41-42.) These proposals seek to provide a context for the words as they stand in the received text, and some of them have been well-argued. But most modern commentators do not find them persuasive.

In the lectionary. The Revised Common Lectionary appoints 14:15-21 for the fifth and 14:23-29 for the sixth Sundays after Easter in Year A.

These passages are dense with thought, and they often carry a reader from one idea to the next quite abruptly. The language is not narrative, concrete, graphic, or pictoral; indeed, especially when they are read aloud, the Farewell speeches can sound repetitive. Yet the thought of these Discourses goes to the ultimacies of the divine redemptive work. They give the richest depiction any-

56. Cadman, *Open Heaven,* 174.

where in the New Testament of life in the post-Easter church in union with the living Jesus. They are relevant to Christians in any age. However, to make that relevance clear, a preacher needs to read and reread the large units of the Discourse, and then focus on one thesis for each sermon.

The first passage, 14:15-21, begins with a Paraclete saying (14:16-17) and proceeds to Jesus' *I will come to you* (14:18). The climax of Jesus' mission is his going *from* his followers and *to* the Father, but (as we have seen) his going *from* them is at the same time his coming *to* them. He comes in the coming of the Spirit. The text passes from the idiom of spatial movement to the idiom of sharing in life — obeying, knowing, self-disclosure, and love. Jesus is not distant, but richly present.

The passage for the sixth Sunday after Easter, 14:23-29, opens with Jesus' pledge that he and the Father will make their dwelling in those who believe and love (14:23-24). The oneness that persists between Jesus and the Father includes Jesus' people also. The lection passes to another Paraclete saying (14:25-26), to Jesus' bestowal of peace (14:27), and to sayings that are associated with his departure (14:28-31). This passage is not long, but its content is rich and diverse.

These passages are all clearly about Christian existence in the living Christ; they suit the Sundays of Easter. However, links between this johannine presentation of the church's relation to the living Jesus and Christian life in tumultuous twenty-first-century society do not lie on the surface of the text. Such links develop in a preacher's mind through prayer and reflection. What does it mean for Christians to live in the world drawing on a life that is beyond the world? Is the church really taught by the Spirit? If it is, how is it taught? What does it mean that the Father and the Son have their home with and in believers? What can Jesus' *shalom* mean in a world of conflict and militarism? What affirmations does this Discourse make concerning the Spirit's work, and what misunderstandings does it seek to head off? What does it mean that Jesus' cross is the climax of his conflict with "the ruler of this world"?

These liturgical readings are so full of ideas and of arresting, if soberly stated, expressions that a single sentence, phrase or image, if it is thought about deeply enough, can start a preacher's mind moving in the direction of a message of good news. A preacher's task is to see this biblical material, much of it very familiar, as though one were seeing it for the first time.

The First Discourse is a literary unit. It has its own beginning; it passes from questioning and dialogue to monologue. It is held together by the unified christological themes of Jesus' *going* (13:33; 14:1-3) and his *coming* (14:18, 23), and by the juxtaposition of the two in the opening at 13:1 and in the summary at 14:28. It develops the new condition — the age of the Spirit — that will compensate the disciples in their seeming abandonment.

Although this First Discourse is full and complex, it seems to hold together around the theme of the legacy of the departing Jesus. He is going. Can anything compensate for the loss of this epochally creative figure, this emissary from heaven? He is leaving, but unmistakably the human situation is different because of him. He has set events in motion. Will they continue without him?

The Discourse may be summarized by pointing to what the departing Jesus leaves:

First of all, Jesus leaves a people — a community of trust, of love and obedience, of asking, and of remembering. This community represents the result of his work, his teaching, and his self-investment. He is present in the community, which will be to the world as he has been.

The community of Jesus is built around a few close associates who have been with him throughout his ministry. His Farewell is spoken particularly to them. Yet the Evangelist knows and speaks indirectly of a wider community of faith. The immediate disciples form the center of an extended people — a people created by witness. Jesus' disciples are essential, but they are called for the sake of those that will follow them. The concrete fact of this vital, multi-generational community is crucial. The record of who Jesus was and what he said and did was carried by the church, and only by it. The faith-community is his evidence, his witness. Without the church, history would be as though Jesus had never lived. His impact on the world will be through a people which bears his name.

To this community (and through it to the world) Jesus leaves:

- his words (the words he has received from the Father) and the words he speaks at his departure (14:10, 23-24, 25).
- His works — his creative, healing and revealing acts — and the pledge that his own works and greater works will be done by his people in his name (14:12).
- His name and the authorization to ask in his name, assured that, as believers do so, they will be heard (14:13-14).
- His commandments (14:15, 21-23), centrally the commandment that his followers love one another (13:34).
- His peace (14:27), the unassailable well-being that is in God and from God.
- The Paraclete, who is to be to the community what Jesus was (14:15-17); she is to teach and to remind (14:26) and to make the Jesus-event contemporaneous with every age.

Finally, through Jesus, the church is left the assurance of the Father's own direct love and presence (14:20-23).

These elements of Jesus' legacy are not separable. Rather, they cohere as aspects of Jesus' leaving to the church himself — not only the promise of eventual reunion with him in the Father's house (14:2-3), but also the powerful conviction that he lives now with his people in a relation of love, self-imparting and indwelling (14:18-21, 23). He is in them, and they are in him.

The Evangelist wrote urgently of this legacy in part because the first-century community for which he wrote was losing the original witnesses who linked it with Jesus. It was anxious over what would happen to its faith and its very identity when this link was broken. The Evangelist tells his readers that as Jesus left his disciples he promised them that their new state would not be impoverished, but enriched. The first-century writer, drawing a parallel between these cases of loss, tells his immediate readers that the features of Jesus' legacy which he has presented do not take the place of Jesus as though he were absent; rather, they are means by which Jesus' continual presence is actualized in the community. The Evangelist pledges the believers of the johannine church that, as Jesus' disciples after he left them were in a richer rather than a poorer condition, so, following the death of the witnesses on whom they have depended, their life in Jesus will not be diminished. Like Jesus' first disciples, the first-century believers will be driven by an experience of absence to discover presence. The Jesus of the First Farewell Discourse speaks not only to his immediate disciples, but beyond them to the first-century community of johannine believers and to the unimagined generations that lay beyond.

Essay: The Father and the Son

The Fourth Gospel, in its distinctive metaphoric idiom, speaks repeatedly of God as Father and of Jesus as God's Son. Although Father and Son terms are also used in the Synoptic Gospels, in the letters of Paul, and widely in the New Testament, they appear with greater frequency in the Fourth Gospel than anywhere else in the Christian Scriptures, and more concentratedly in the Farewell Discourses than anywhere else in the Fourth Gospel. Carrying the authority of the New Testament (and especially of John's Gospel) these Father/Son terms entered the doxological, creedal and theological traditions, providing a primary idiom for classical christology and for the formulation of the divine Father, Son and Holy Spirit — a naming that has, since early centuries, pervaded Christian prayer, doxology and doctrine.

In the Synoptic Gospels Jesus is referred to as Son at significant events, such as his baptism (Mt. 3:13-17; Mark 1:9-11; Luke 3:21-22), his Transfiguration (Mt. 17:1-8; Mark 9:2-8; Luke 9:28-36), Peter's confession (only in the version of Mt. 16:13-20), and the centurion's attestation at the crucifixion (only in Mark 15:39).

Jesus refers to God as Father more than one hundred times in the Fourth Gospel — more than in the Synoptic Gospels combined and far more than the references to the Father in the entire Pauline corpus. The term "the Father" which appears only once in Mark is used by Jesus more than sixty-five times in the Fourth Gospel. "My Father," which appears fifteen times in Matthew, but not at all in Mark, occurs twenty-six times in the Fourth Gospel. Jesus addresses the Father in 11:41; 12:27, 28; 17:1 and see 17:5, 11, 21. God is referred to as Father fifty-two times in the Farewell chapters and twenty-three times in chapter 14 alone, more than in any other chapter in the New Testament.

The correlative image of Jesus as Son runs similarly through the Fourth Gospel. The term "the Son" is rare in the Synoptic Gospels, but common in the Fourth Gospel (where it is usually taken to be a shortened form of "the Son of God"). The stated purpose of the Fourth Gospel is to persuade readers that Jesus is the Son of God (20:30-31), and in the Gospel as a whole Jesus is referred to as the Son (usually by Jesus speaking of himself) more than forty times. However, we may note that in the Farewell chapters, Jesus is only spoken of as "the Son" three times. The Evangelist's broad strategy seems to be to present Jesus' sonship in the Book of Signs, often attested by signs and supported with vigorous argument, while in the Book of Glory he gives greater emphasis to the divine Fatherhood. The Farewell Discourses draw the Father image to the center of speech concerning God as nowhere else in the Scriptures.

The Father-Son terms not only appear frequently in the Fourth Gospel, they appear in distinctive ways.

The Fourth Evangelist establishes his pattern of naming in his first chapter. As he opens his Prologue, he speaks only of *God,* and of the relation of *the Word* to *God* (1:1-3). He says that divine power makes human beings children of *God* (1:12). But in 1:14, as the Evangelist introduces the

Word becoming flesh, he also begins to speak of *God* as a *father* and of God's *only-begotten.* V. 18 says that the Son reveals the unseen Father, *No one has ever seen God. It is the only Son, who is close to the Father's heart, who has made him known.* Thereafter, Father/Son talk pervades the Gospel, but in its own idiom. The Fourth Gospel does not describe a judging, forgiving, caring God who is father to all people, nor even to a select few. The divine fatherhood is presented in John as particular and exclusive. God is Father in relation to one who is to him a Son. As the Fourth Gospel presents the redemptive work, human beings are not, by reason of their humanity, children of the divine father, whose relation to themselves they must learn to recognize and whose character they must emulate. Rather, the Son alone is begotten of God; he is an only Son (*monogenēs,* 1:14, 18; 3:16, 18; cf. 1 John 4:9). The Son and the Father are to one another as neither is to anyone else. Derivatively, God gives life to others who are identified with Jesus (1:12; 20:30-31, and often). In the Fourth Gospel the one who imitates the Father is the Son, who grows up in his father's home, where he learns and does only what his father is doing (5:19, cf. 8:38).

In the Fourth Gospel, the Father and the Son are bound by mutual loving, listening and glorifying. The two persons interpenetrate one another; they are turned towards one another; they are "in" one another. The Father is not the Father nor the Son the Son apart from the relation in which each stands to the other. In johannine terms, human search can run to no depths of the Father where it is not in touch with the Father as known and dealt with in the Son, nor does anyone know the Son truly except as one who is perfectly united with and who demonstrates the Father.

With respect to mission, however, the Father and the Son are not described as equal. The Father sends, and the Son is sent (5:36-38; 6:44; 8:18, and often); the Father commands, and the Son obeys (10:18; 12:49b; 14:31; 15:10); the Father works, and the Son imitates (5:19); the Father speaks, and the Son hears and tells what he has heard (8:26, 38; 14:24); the Father, out of a self-dependent life, has power to judge and to raise the dead, but he has given these powers to the Son (5:22, 26; 6:40).

Yet, after concentrating attention on this relation of the Father and the Son, the Fourth Gospel does speak of divine life imparted to humanity. The Prologue describes persons who are *children . . . born of God* (1:12-13, using the term *children, tekna,* rather than *sons, huioi,* which is the preferred term of Paul and of Hebrews). Jesus does not propose that his followers address God as their *"Father"* until after the resurrection when he speaks of *My Father and your Father; my God and your God* (20:17), opening to others the relation in which he stands. This single reference to a shared fatherhood is a strategically placed indication that when the Fourth Gospel uses the image "Father" as richly and independently as it does and uses it of Jesus' relation with God, it is speaking out of the relation to God which was opened to believers by the risen Christ. (One may observe the frequent references — church references — in 1 John to persons who are begotten by the divine Father.)

The johannine Father/Son terminology has a background in the ancient world where emperors in Egypt and Babylon were spoken of as sons of God, as was the Roman Emperor in Jesus' day. In the Jewish Scriptures the image "son(s) of God" may refer to quasi-divine beings (a sort of heavenly council, e.g., Gen. 6:2; Job 1:6; 38:7). But more often the term Son of God refers to Israel collectively (e.g., Exod. 4:22; Hos. 11:1) or to Israel's king (e.g., Pss. 2:7; 89:26-27). More than one exegete (beginning with the author of Hebrews, see 1:5) has noticed the strikingly "johannine" comments in 2 Sam. 7:14 in which God says of David, *I will be a father to him, and he shall be a son to me.* In Jewish sources, the title "son of God" does not in itself set its bearer on the divine side, but it "characterizes groups or individuals who stand in a peculiar close relationship with God."[57]

God is referred to as father very sparingly in the Jewish Scriptures — no more than a dozen instances and never in direct address. Moreover, in Jewish awareness, divine fatherhood is not domineering. Sandra Schneiders describes the biblical picture of God as father.

> The father metaphor in the Old Testament is nowhere used to present God as a patriarch dominating the people or exercising coercive power over them. On the contrary, the father metaphor is evoked precisely to describe the compassionate love of God who is like a parent spurned by ungrateful children but who is endless in patience and loving-kindness to a rebellious people.[58]

Some conservative interpreters continue to think that this designation of Jesus' relation to God as a Son to a Father traces to Jesus himself. Other exegetes, however, think that the terms arose as a very early Christian interpretation of Jesus. In the Synoptic Gospels, as in John, Jesus is reported to have spoken of God as his "Father" and of himself as in some exclusive sense as God's "son." (The most conspicuous instance, and

57. Vincent Taylor, *The Names of Jesus* (London: Macmillan, 1953), 54.

58. Sandra Schneiders, *Women and the Word* (New York: Paulist, 1986), 29-30.

hence the most subject to question is Jesus' strangely "johannine" comment in Matthew 11:27, *All things have been handed over to me by my Father, and no one knows the Son except the Father, and no one knows the Father except the Son and anyone to whom the Son chooses to reveal him.*) It should be noted that, rather than the formal and somewhat distancing expressions common in Jewish address to God, the Gospels say that Jesus used, at least at times, the intimate, endearing Aramaic term "Abba" (Mark 14:36, and others).

These images of God as a father acting in relation to a son and of Jesus as a son acting in close union with a father confront twenty-first-century readers with an issue that has not previously been felt with the force it now has. The symbol-system of the Fourth Gospel describes the divine action for human redemption in terms of two personal forces, both of which are identified in masculine images: God is a father, a male parent; and Jesus Christ is his son, a male child. Some modern-day readers have difficulty focusing on this divine redemptive action; their attention is drawn by the fact that in the charter Christian literature, male images are predominantly used to portray the acting parties. This use of almost exclusively masculine imagery to speak of divine being, character and agency seems to represent a projection into the working of the divine of the patriarchal social order of the ancient world, and indeed of much social history to the present time.

It might be observed that, alongside this personal and masculine imagery for God and for Christ, no New Testament book uses as much non-personal, nature-derived imagery to describe Christ and the redemptive work as does the Fourth Gospel. The saving figure is portrayed in terms such as: word, light, water, wind, bread, way, vine, door, a bronze serpent, a seed that is placed in the ground. By setting these impersonal images alongside the personal images of "Father" and "Son," the author helps a reader recognize that they all are images.

We approach the ancient biblical literature now in a time of change in social order and in consciousness. In marriage and the family, as well as in society at large, men and women are coming to greater equality. Leading, acting, achieving public roles that once fell, not exclusively, but preponderantly to men may now be filled by women. Moreover, people are less role-defined than they once were, and they live longer than they once did. During one's lifetime, one may function in quite different ways. One who is a teacher may also be a parent, a wife or husband, a civic activist, a neighbor, a care-giver, a hobbyist, and an artist. One who is heavily defined for part of one's life by parental roles may do something else before the children are born, while they are growing, or when they are grown.

Presumably if the Bible were being written now and if the presiding images of the tradition were being coined now, so that today's experience informed the common imagination, things that were said in the past about the initiating, acting God using role-images that were specific to males would be said today by female images or by role-terms that would not be sex-specific. In a symbol-system formed out of today's life, the rich experience of women, which has been muted in the past, would figure strongly in God-talk.

Yet with regard to the precise matter at hand, while many roles in society can be filled by either men or women, the specific role-images that dominate the Fourth Gospel are those of Father and Son; and it is an irreducible human reality that only males can be fathers, and only males can be sons. The relation of a child to her or his father is, moreover, among the most powerful emotional factors in shaping personality. One's relation to one's father carries the ambiguity of all human relationships. It can provide a positive model, and it can leave ineradicable scars. One may note that in the relational but somewhat uncircumstantial way in which the Fourth Gospel presents divine ways, hardly anything is said about God as Father that could not be said as well by imagery of Mother. Yet were substitutions to be made, it would replace one set of hermeneutical problems with another. For motherhood is limited and flawed, as all human roles are limited and flawed, and many persons carry emotional burdens from a relation with an inadequate or an overbearing mother. The situation of the people of the biblical traditions is that God must be pictured, but always pictured out of image-material taken from flawed people who are shaped in defectively ordered societies.

The Christian church is a continuing historical community which took its rise from determinative inaugural events. It still reads, interprets, and proclaims its gospel from an ancient but indispensable witness literature which in characterizing God did not say "mother" and did not say "Jupiter" or "Diana" or "First Cause" or "The One." It said such things as "shepherd," "vinegrower," "judge," "defender," "king," and "father" and "son." It also said, somewhat secondarily, such things as "mother" and "nursemaid." The Bible was written when it was; its writers drew on the cultural resource at hand, using the available vocabulary. Out of their deep experience of the divine, the authors formed language which has leaped beyond the situations of its coinage and has spoken with revelatory power to persons in unimaginably different cultural contexts.

The question arises whether in order to have the realities to which the biblical literature bears witness the community of faith must continue to use the culture-conditioned language-forms of the Bible itself. If the language-forms are questionable, to what extent are the realities they signify questionable as well?

Thoughtful people understand this fundamental question of interpretation differently. Some take offense if any change in basic God-talk is proposed, while others are offended if wholesale change is not introduced at once. All parties may feel strongly about the matter. The Christian community is, with respect to its own charter literature, dealing today with a criticism that is new, fundamental, and many-sided. One should neither charge categorically that the biblical texts are hopelessly "sexist" nor ignore the fact that of course they are. The characteristic terminology of the Farewell chapters of the Fourth Gospel puts the issue before a reader in an almost aggressive manner. (It does so quite unintentionally, of course.) It would be remiss if an expository, largely descriptive treatment of these chapters such as this present study failed to recognize the problem, but unrealistic to expect that it could solve it.

5. The Second Discourse: Jesus and His People (15:1–16:4a)

A first draft of Jesus' Farewell had been prepared for the Gospel text when new events shook the community. The believers in Jesus' messiahship were (as they saw it) being thrust out of the Jewish synagogue. The Evangelist's work had not yet been sent to its intended readers when this shattering event suggested that new Discourse material should be prepared, taking account of these new circumstances. The voice of Jesus was needed in this bewildering situation. A Second Discourse was drafted. It is about the same length as the first and was conceived in two divisions of approximately equal size and of related but contrasting subject matter.

In the first part of the Discourse (15:1-17) Jesus, in an extended image of a vine and its branches, describes the life-imparting unity that persists between himself and his followers. In the situation that is upon them they must remain faithful "branches" in the "vine." Then the vine figure drops away, but themes of "abiding," of love and obedience, and of "friends" flow from it and into one another. Jesus depicts in varied terms a people united with himself.

Then at 15:18 Jesus' topic and tone change markedly. From the interior bonding between believers and himself, the Discourse passes abruptly to speak of the world's animosity. After saying *love one another* (15:17), the text turns at once to say *If the world hates you* (15:18). In the second part of the Discourse (15:18–16:4a) the community of Jesus is confronting hostility. At first the language is general, offering support for Christians in the face of outside "hatred" or "persecution." Jesus says, by way of support, that the world's treatment of his people replicates its treatment of him. Then in 16:1-4a, the terms become more circumstantial and clearly refer to a break with the Jewish synagogue and even suggest that martyrdom is a near threat.

Even though the expulsion from the synagogue of those who confessed Jesus is mentioned specifically only towards the end of the Discourse, the conflict which led to that event (late in the first century CE) doubtless had been building for some time, and it formed the situation for which the entire Discourse was written. The early passages on remaining in union with Jesus and on mutual love among believers were written from and for a community in crisis. In a hostile environment, the believers in Jesus, having lost their Jewish supports, are driven to explore their own interior resources. When the structures on which they had depended were withdrawn, the followers of Jesus had to count on a transcendent resource as well as on one another.

Jesus does not in this Discourse repeat the future-oriented counsel of the First Discourse, but speaks in the present — the community's, the believer's present. He develops the bonds that exist between himself and his followers. This Discourse is given urgency not by Jesus' imminent departure and the changed conditions that will follow, but by events that are taking place as the Evangelist writes — events that he does not refer to, however, until he has gotten well into the Discourse.

1. Branches in a Vine (15:1-6)

Jesus' Second Discourse opens with a vigorous self-assertion in the "I AM" form — *I am the true vine.* (The "I AM" form appeared at 14:6; see the notes at pp. 124-25 above.) The image develops, describing believers who live by their relation to Jesus as "branches" which only live by their attachment to a vine. The vine image does not continue for long, but when it drops away, the following material seems to rise from the imaginative impulse it provided. It leads into the themes of remaining ("abiding") in the fundamental life-giving relation to Jesus (vv. 4-10), of praying with confidence (vv. 7, 16), of the practice of self-giving love among Jesus' followers (vv. 12-13, 17), and of being Jesus' friends (vv. 13-16). These themes which characterize life in the community of Jesus flow from one to the next. (Did the author draw on a previously existing unit of thought and rhetoric — perhaps using material that was first spoken, by divine insight, at the Lord's Day assembly?) Fenton says that this first half of the Discourse (15:1-17) explores "the essence of church membership."[1]

1. J. C. Fenton, *The Gospel According to John* (Oxford: Oxford University Press, 1970), 158.

The Vine figure which dominates the first eight verses is the most vivid and developed image in the Farewell chapters. The image is given explanatory equivalences (rather like those in the Good Shepherd image; see 10:7, 9, 11, 14): *I am the Vine . . . My Father is the vine-dresser . . . You are the branches.* But this metaphor with its assigned meanings does not form an allegory. The image has no story, no beginning and end. Unlike a parable taken from agriculture, in it nothing happens; it is not a story of planting, tending and harvest. Raymond Brown puts this passage in the literary category of the Hebrew *mashal* — meaning loosely, illustration, figure, or image.[2]

The figure of the vine draws on common life in the ancient Near East. Vineyards were everywhere, and practices related to their cultivation would be familiar. A speaker could assume knowledge of planting good, domestic, bearing stock; tending the vines; protecting the vineyard against thieves; harvesting the grapes, pressing them and making them into wine. However, this johannine passage makes almost no use of this readily-accessible lore. The author emphasizes only the connectedness or living structure of the vine — a vine whose many parts comprise a productive, fruit-bearing organism.

The vine, in its complexity and unity, could represent a social unit. The vine had, in fact, become something of a national emblem of Israel. Josephus describes a large, golden vine of splendid workmanship that was set over one of the doors of Herod's temple.[3] The image drew on the Jewish Scriptures which speak of Israel as God's vine.

To cite three instances:

Psalm 80:1-18 tells a story of God bringing a vine out of Egypt. God cleared the ground and planted it. The vine flourished. But its protections broke down, and the vine was ravaged. The Psalm ends with a plea to God to regard the vine and destroy those who have burned it and cut it down.

Isaiah 5:1-7, a passage often called "The Song of the Vineyard," tells of a vine that was planted with care, protected, and watched expectantly. But it yielded wild grapes. The singer accuses the vine. The vinedresser did all he could, yet the results were disappointing. He will reject the vineyard; its protections will be removed; it will receive no more care and watering. Then the prophet tells what the perceptive reader has known all along: The

2. See Raymond Brown, *The Gospel according to John* (2 vols., Anchor Bible; Garden City: Doubleday, 1966-70), 668-69. Other commentators work with such terms as "allegory," "image," and "figure."

3. See Josephus, *Antiquities* 15.11.3; *War* 5.5.4; see also Mishnah *Middoth* 3.8.

story is of God and his people. *For the vineyard of the Lord of Hosts is the house of Israel* (v. 7).

The thought of *Ezekiel 15* also uses the image of Israel as God's vine, but it makes the observation that the wood of a vine is weak and useless. When the vine proves unproductive, its wood is cast into the fire. God will give up Jerusalem as a branch of a vine is given up to the fire. He will be against its inhabitants and make the ground on which it grows to be desolate.

These and other vine passages, through the image of a vineyard in relation to a vinegrower, speak of Israel's tumultuous relation with Yahweh. They express love and care but also accusation and anger. Although Israel is the object of God's special tending, concern, and expectation, its history, as the prophets tell it, is one of collective failure and divine disappointment. These prophetic units often end with the destruction of the vine, actually or by anticipation.[4]

In this Second Discourse the Evangelist was drawing on an evocative image which would, in a general sense, have been familiar to most of his readers. However, no specific passage in the Jewish Scriptures seems to have been the direct source for the johannine vine image. The life-in-Christ reality determines how the picture-language of Israel's tradition is used. The vine image is developed under the control of the writer's christological/ecclesiological purpose. As C. H. Dodd put it, "The symbol is almost absorbed into the thing signified."[5]

The agricultural images of the Bible usually involve time and seasons. A story is implied — a story of planting, watering, tending, waiting; of barren soil, drought, weeds, pests, thieves; all leading to the eventual harvest, abundant or disappointing. But as this agricultural material is caught up in the johannine *mashal,* the vine has no history or destiny.

In the literature of Israel, agricultural images do not characteristically speak of repetitive cycles; rather, the drama, the linear movement and climax of a single growing season are used to interpret history, *The harvest is the end of the world* (Matt. 13:39). Thus it is striking that in the vine image of 15:1-6 *all is now.* There is no development. Even though something may happen to individual branches, nothing happens to the vine. There is

4. An observation made by J. H. Bernard, *The Gospel According to St. John* (2 vols., International Critical Commentary; Edinburgh: Clark, 1928), 2.478.

5. C. H. Dodd, *The Interpretation of the Fourth Gospel* (Cambridge: Cambridge University Press, 1953), 137.

no planting, no maturation to harvest, no destructive enemies, no degeneration or barrenness, and there is no final gathering of grapes for wine-making. It is as though the branches are always in fruit-bearing season. By eliminating time from the image, the writer is suggesting that *the final things* — life, fruit, joy, but also judgment — *are now.*

The Evangelist develops only one feature of the vine — its connectedness or structure, on which the vitality of the individual parts depends. The vine produces through the branches; the branches are dependent on the vine. This organic unity and multiplicity suggests a community of many persons who are sharers in a single life. None of the vine passages from the Jewish Scriptures which might be thought of as sources (or partial sources) for this johannine image contains this one-and-many emphasis.

> I am the true vine,
> and my Father is the vinegrower. 15:1

Jesus expresses the mystery of himself and his people in one of his christologically significant *I am* sayings. (The *I am* idiom has been encountered at 13:19, and see the notes at 14:6, pp. 124-25.) He refers to himself as a collective reality. The vine is a totality of organically united parts, and Jesus puts himself forward as a communal unit, saying that the one holds in himself the many. Behind Jesus' expression is the Hebrew sense of "corporate personality" which thought of a community as so bonded that it could be known and designated as an individual person.[6] The vine image is simultaneously both christological and ecclesial. The Discourse represents Jesus as saying "I," "I am." This passage is not an apostle urging believers to grasp "You are a people in Christ." Rather, it is Christ saying "You are a people in me."

From the vine images that occur in the Jewish scriptures a reader gathers that *I am the true vine* means "I am true Israel." The biblical pictures of the vine are full of divine calling and passion, but also of human failure and unfaithfulness. A good, productive vine of God's own planting is destroyed by enemies, or it becomes wild and degenerate, fit only to be burned. Yet God continues to care. When Jesus says "true" here, he means

6. The point is especially associated with the British biblical scholar H. Wheeler Robinson. Two of his articles on the subject were reprinted in *Corporate Personality in Ancient Israel* (Philadelphia: Fortress, 1964).

that he is faithful or reliable. Jesus is the one in whom the planting and tending intention of the Vinegrower/God is realized. The affirmation *I am the true Vine* puts forward the claim that Jesus, the Messiah, enters and fulfills the intended destiny of Israel. He is true to his calling, obedient, steadfast. He will "bear much fruit."

The corporate image which turns in one direction saying "I am Israel" turns in another to say "I am the church." When Jesus, speaking of himself and to his disciples, says *I am the true Vine,* his words make an ecclesial statement. They depict a sharing of life and the utter dependence of believers on Jesus. As Paul Minear put it, "christological reality is absolutely basic to ecclesiological reality."[7] The two are so united that the church-reality rests in the Christ-reality, and the Christ-reality is found and known in and through the church-reality.

This vine image, which speaks simultaneously of Christ, of Israel, and of the church, no doubt formed a part of the self-understanding made necessary for the johannine community by its break with the synagogue.[8] At first it was clear who the Jesus-people were. They were Jews who confessed Jesus as Messiah (cf. 1:41, *We have found the Messiah*). They told their own story and were no doubt distinguishable in a number of ways. In fact, they may have been from the first an irritating presence; the bitter divisions that are indicated in 16:2 must have come after an extended period of conflict. Many Jews of the synagogue must have become convinced that this new movement in their midst was unassimilable. As long as the believers in Jesus were part of the synagogue, they could understand themselves through Jewish categories. They did not need to inquire urgently of their own sources as to who they might be as a distinct folk. However, when they were set outside the synagogue and put on their own, in addition to the immediate necessity of surviving new risk, there was the theological task of explaining themselves to themselves.

Jesus is not described in the Vine image as a discrete individual — even a basic and organizing individual. Rather, he is universalized; the one holds in himself the many. He is the vine in its totality of parts. The Vine and its branches — Christ with his people — form one connected, interdependent life. Christ, who unites and imparts life to all the parts of the vine,

7. Paul Minear, *Images of the Church in the New Testament* (Philadelphia: Westminster, 1960), 42.

8. The expulsion of the believers in Jesus from the synagogue is not mentioned explicitly until 16:2. This action may have been either local or widespread. It is often thought to have been the occasion for the Second Discourse.

lives through those parts, and they live by their attachment to him. In terms of this image, neither he nor they have a self-dependent identity.

To the mind of the Evangelist, a satisfactory Christian self-definition, independent of the synagogue, must relate life-in-faith to the purpose of God, to Jesus Christ, to Israel, and to the ends of human life. The *mashal* of the True Vine does these things. It presents to the imagination the essential mystery of the living Jesus and of a believer's relation to him in a community to which he imparts his own life.

Jesus next turns to the ultimate reference of the life in the vine: *my Father is the vinegrower.* In the vine pictures in the Scriptures of Israel, God is the owner, the planter, the cultivator; and Israel is God's cherished vine. But it is not an untroubled relationship. God is a passionately engaged vinegrower: selecting good stock, bringing it to a chosen vineyard, clearing the ground for it, defending it from plunderers, disappointed in its barrenness, pruning it, addressing it, appealing to it, and sometimes accusing it, abandoning it, burning it. When Jesus here cites the Father's role as the vine-dresser, he implies that God who chose and cared for Israel is similarly active in the Christ-and-his-people event — its foundational moments and its subsequent development. God superintends the process; the total life of the vine depends ultimately on divine initiative and divine care.

The vinegrower acts on the vine:

He removes
  every branch in me that bears no fruit.
  Every branch that bears fruit
he prunes to make it bear more fruit. 15:2

With the words *every branch,* the image becomes distributive. Only at v. 5 is it clearly said that the branches are persons, but a reader has probably guessed the equivalence at once. Jesus speaks now not of the one but of the many in the one.

The Father/cultivator watches the vine; he knows and judges. He acts on the vine in two ways: (1) He removes *(airei)* the branches that bear no fruit. (2) He prunes (*kathairei,* a play on the Greek verbs) the bearing branches to increase their productivity.

More will be said about both the bearing and the non-bearing branches as the passage develops. But a reader can observe at once:

1. The Father/cultivator exercises sovereign control over the vine. (The agricultural image allows no reciprocity; branches cannot object

when they are pruned.) The trunk and branches of the vine are useless in themselves. No one plants a grapevine for its wood; the insubstantial, but tough stems are for the sake of the fruit. But when some branches bear no fruit, the vine-dresser cuts them out for the good of the total life. The Evangelist speaks (but at this point only by suggestion) of divine judgment active within the community of believers, excising parts that carry no life.

2. The bearing branches are acted upon as well. They are cropped back. Left unattended, the productivity of the vine will decrease. There is a severe realism in this image. The Evangelist is saying that the conditions of believing existence are not easy. Jesus does not describe an automatic unfolding of an intrinsic life — from bud, stem and branch, to leaves and grapes. The branches, for the good of the vine, must be selectively cut back. The Father is a diligent tender of the vine. This pruning by the vinedresser suggests that, in the author's view, limitation, discipline, struggle — possibly even opposition and suffering — are potentially redemptive (the Greek verb says "cathartic") instruments of God. But the idiom of the Vine image is very indirect.

The terms "fruit" and "bearing fruit" are conspicuous in this passage, appearing six times in vv. 1-8 and returning twice, without the rest of the image, in v. 16. Moreover, they are crucial to the substance of the thought:

- The removal or retention of a branch depends on whether or not it yields fruit, vv. 2 and 6.
- Much fruit is the goal, v. 5.
- More fruit is desired by the vine-dresser, v. 8.
- Fruit glorifies God, v. 8.

Yet this term is left unexplained throughout the vine-and-branches passage.

Perhaps "fruit" was a bit of first-century in-talk which would have been understood in the Evangelist's community despite its indefiniteness. It may have meant something like: "Believers in Jesus are expected to do what believers in Jesus are expected to do." Barrett describes fruit along such general lines: "The bearing of fruit is simply living the life of a Christian disciple."[9] In a closely knit community which actively instructed its members and was bound together by a vital tradition to which it held in

9. C. K. Barrett, *The Gospel According to St. John* (2nd ed., Philadelphia: Westminster, 1978), 474.

the face of opposition, such terms could convey significant ethical and spiritual guidance through implicit understandings that "we do/don't do that sort of thing."

Some specificity may be given to the idea of Christian "fruit-bearing" when later in the passage reference is made to such things as: answered prayer (vv. 7 and 16b); keeping Jesus' commandments, specifically the commandment that his followers love one another (vv. 10-13, 17); joy (v. 11); sharing privileged knowledge (v. 15); and converts to the faith (v. 16a). All of these obligations and rewards are results of or evidences of the divine life within — of being "in the vine," united with Jesus. Such terms are suggestive; "fruit" would seem to include all of these, but not to be confined to them.

> You have already been cleansed
> by the word that I have spoken to you. 15:3

Jesus steps outside the indirect medium of the vine figure and speaks *of* himself and *to* his disciples.

The disciples, Jesus says, *have already been cleansed (katharoi)* by the active (the *"cathartic"*) *word* which he has spoken and which they have received. Through their initial calling and response, their months of following him, learning to understand and growing in trust, the disciples had become deeply united to Jesus. The vitalization and fulfillment — as also the discipline and restraint — of this association have been for them the equivalent of the vine-dresser's pruning of the healthy branches of the vine.

Jesus turns to speak directly and imperatively of the need to remain faithful:

> Abide in me
> as I abide in you.
> Just as the branch cannot bear fruit by itself
> unless it abides in the vine,
> neither can you
> unless you abide in me. 15:4

The image of the vine allowed nothing to be said about responsibility. A branch cannot change or determine itself; it cannot either question or consent to its treatment by the vine-dresser. The vine image drops away so that the interpersonal relationships to which it has referred can be spoken of directly, and the speech begins with an imperative, *Abide in me.* Although one cannot tell a branch "Stay attached to the vine," Jesus can urge his followers: "Be faithful in your relation with me."

The Evangelist's "in-phrases" occur throughout the Farewell passages, but they concentrate in this section of the Second Discourse as they do nowhere else in the Fourth Gospel. (Fourteen such expressions occur in vv. 1-10.) Using the language of space to speak of that which is not defined by physical space, the writer speaks of believers who are in Jesus, as he is in them; he is in the Father, as the Father is in him; he and the Father are in believers; his love is in them.

These in-phrases are suggestive.

As embodied beings, we live and move in space; we occupy space. If someone else seeks to intrude on the space we consider ours, we feel crowded or violated and we resist. Our niche in space is our own and no one else's. Of course, we can invite others into our space. To a limited extent, we can make our space, ourselves sharable. But one way of speaking of our individuality is to say that we are, as no one else is, the space we inhabit.

The johannine idiom of persons who are (indeed, who may remain) "in" one another moves along different lines. The mutual "in-ness" of persons is not spoken of as invasive — something to be refused or resented. Rather, it is freeing and fulfilling. The terms of the idiom do not depict persons as discrete beings who must hold off intrusion, as though one's personal space were under siege. One's space is not conceived as bounded, but open. The psychic space which is one's self is given to be shared.

The relation of the believer with the living Jesus is described in the Fourth Gospel as a pooling of selves. A believer's unique, inhabited space has become a shared space. Personal existences can be "in" one another.

The metaphoric language of Jesus' Farewell says nothing about believers being "in" one another. It speaks only about believers being in Jesus and Jesus in them. Jesus' person is inclusive; he can indwell others, as others can indwell him.

The term *"abide"* which enters at 15:4 unifies the passage through v. 10. Jesus urges his followers: "continue, stay, rest in the life that is yours-and-not-yours." The abiding is reciprocal — *I abide in you* and *you abide in me.* The mutual abiding contains a requirement and a promise. The "you must abide in me" rests on Jesus' prior and utterly dependable "I shall abide in you."

Jesus' request may seem unheroic. But the johannine community knew the importance (the life-or-death importance) and at times the difficulty of simply remaining. Describing the urgency of "abiding," Jesus uses a series of negatives: *As the branch cannot bear fruit by itself unless it abides in the vine, neither can you unless you abide in me. . . . Apart from me you can do nothing.* Jesus says that anyone who does not *abide* in him *is thrown away like a branch and withers.* A detached, isolated branch is unproductive and of no use to anyone. It cannot bear fruit *from itself* — as though it were its own source of life. It is cut out and lies on the ground, a cluster of unrealized possibilities. Whatever "fruit" there may be does not come from the branch, but from the branch-in-the-vine — from the total, interconnected, one-and-many unit of life that is Jesus and his people. The vine lives and produces through the branches, and the branches only live and bear fruit in union with the great life in which they are held.

The image continues — changing, however, to positive language and to the mode of explanation. The "I am" expression is reintroduced. When in v. 5 Jesus says expressly *I am the vine, and you are the branches,* the equivalences have probably been apparent to his readers from the start.

> I am the vine,
> you are the branches. 15:5a

Jesus says, in effect, "The vine is myself; the branches are you who share my life." These two affirmations are interdependent. As Paul Minear put it, "The decisive 'you are' can be said to the church only by the decisive 'I am' of Christ."[10] The "you" refers to the disciples *as representative.* The Evangelist is addressing second-generation Christians. To be a member of Christ's people (at whatever remove from first-century Palestine) is to stand in vital relation with Christ. He is known, and bonding with him is accessible, not as an individual union achieved through an inner quest, but in the concrete, societal life of the community of faith. And the community of faith everywhere derives from the small group that was associated with Jesus. The Evangelist's language is apostolic and ecclesial.

The vine image makes a one-sided presentation of the believing people. Although it speaks of a community, the only relationship it keeps in view is the member's relation with Jesus. A "you" must abide in "me." Nothing is said about responsible, supportive relationships between or among Jesus' followers. The point at which

10. Minear, *Images of the Church,* 42.

the branch is joined to the vine is the only relational nexus to which Jesus here gives attention.

In the immediate context, there are some emphases which may compensate for this one-sidedness.

The foot-washing incident gives Jesus' followers a model of serving one another (13:1-20).

The commandment to love one another — which is announced at the opening of the discourses (13:34-35) and is repeated in the development of the vine passage (15:12, 17) — speaks of other believers and only indirectly of Jesus, while the vine image speaks of Jesus and not of other believers.

> Those who abide in me and I in them bear much fruit,
> because apart from me you can do nothing. 15:5b

Speaking first positively, then negatively, Jesus says that believers who remain in the life that they share with him are productive, while those who seek to live on their own become barren. Apart from the word "fruit," he is drawing away from the vine image and speaking directly of his relation with his people. His living in them and they in him is the essential precondition of the "fruitfulness" for which the common life exists.

The word "abide" (the Greek word is *menein,* which simply means to remain, dwell, or live on) is a characteristic term of johannine vocabulary. (It is used ten times in vv. 4-10. It appears in important connections both in this Gospel and in 1 John, but nowhere else is there such a concentration of uses as in this passage.) The word appears first in the Gospel in 1:38 where the first two persons who follow Jesus ask him *Where are you staying?* But this ordinary Greek word passes over to more than ordinary significance. Jesus refers to the enduring relation between himself and the Father, *I am in the Father and the Father is in me* (14:10), and to a sustained, mutual, divine-human indwelling, *you will abide in my love* (15:10). Translations such as "stay" or "remain" seem too characterless to carry this depth of meaning. The NEB uses the somewhat old-fashioned term "dwell." The NRSV retains from the Authorized Version the older, Anglo-Saxon derived, evocative translation "abide" to suggest the uniqueness and depth of the relationship which the Evangelist has in mind.

The abiding things are not spoken of in the Fourth Gospel in terms of a Platonic contrast between an eternal, unchanging realm and a realm of transiency. The johannine reference to lasting things is personal, intentional, relational and responsible. Human life at its truest, as the Bible sees it, is not self-sustaining. It is from God, and is most fully itself when it recognizes its creaturely, dependent relation to God. What enters at v. 4 is not so much the word "abide" as the phrase "abide in" — *abide in me . . . I abide in you . . . my words abide in you . . . abide in my love . . . I abide in my Father's love.*

The divine-human relation described in the phrase "abide in" is complex: Seen as gift *(I abide in you),* the term *menein* expresses deep indicatives and pledges. Jesus' bonds with those who are "in" him are enduring and are sustained in faithfulness. His self-giving is not withdrawn. Jesus is supremely the Abiding One. His words, his love, his very self are life-givingly invested in his people.

But this abiding of Jesus, on which the disciples can depend, rests in turn on the Father's abiding which undergirds Jesus. *I abide in [my Father's] love* (15:10). The lasting quality of the relation of God with believers — a relation which Jesus mediates — is rooted in the lastingness of the unity that persists between Jesus and the Father.

On the human side, to abide requires responsibility and intentionality. Abiding is not passivity. There are imperatives, as when Jesus says, *Abide.* And there are conditional expressions, *If you abide . . . unless you abide.* And there is the possibility of inconstancy, *Anyone who does not abide.* Such alternatives go to the heart of the relation with Jesus. Abiding in him — in his words, his love — is life, productivity, and the open relation to God in love and joy. Failure to abide is barrenness, rejection and death.

Jesus points up the importance of "abiding" by a contrasting "not" statement:

> Whoever does not abide in me
> is thrown away like a branch
> and withers;
> such branches are gathered,
> thrown in the fire and burned. 15:6

The negative *whoever does not abide* brings back the subject mentioned in v. 2, the removal of unproductive branches; but the pruning is now described more vividly. This discriminative cutting out and burning of fruitless branches is an important feature of the johannine image, and it doubtless drew on familiar agricultural practice. Some branches are removed, and some are not. The skilled vinedresser decides which it should be. The vine remains intact, not only surviving the loss of the branches, but becoming more productive because of the pruning.

This feature of cultivation does not figure in any of the passages from the Jewish Scriptures which might have served as source for the Vine image. In Ezekiel 15, Israel has become the useless wood of the vine, which God will give up to the fire, but in the prophet's vision, the whole vine is destroyed. The Evangelist's picture of selective excision and burning does not seem to be a touch suggested by his presumed literary sources; it was original in his Christian development of the image.

What in first-century community life might have led the author to bring to the foreground this previously unused feature of vine-tending?

The image of the vine-grower's "pruning" would seem to be an oblique reference to a problem in the johannine community over spiritual discipline and lapsed members. The author writes very indirectly here, but this passage falls in the first part of a two-part discourse which in its second half will speak of opposition and persecution. The believing community was under stress. Surely the collective trauma that is indicated in 15:18–16:4a is in the author's mind when he alludes in 15:6 to internal losses. He does not analyze the community's external situation nor its response to opposition, nor does he explain, with some compassion, the terrible pressures that many believers were under to turn back from their new-found faith. He does, however, seek to give some meaning to the baffling, dismaying mystery of Christian defections.

In his signs and teaching Jesus has extended an offer of abundant life — of water for the thirsty and light for those in darkness. A new fulfilling condition is accessible to "whoever will" enter it. Those who believe are spoken of as "given" by the Father to the Son. The new life is at the same time a work of God and a human act of believing. It seems enduring. *No one can snatch them out of my Father's hand* (10:28-29).

Yet constancy cannot be taken for granted. When believers are urged to "abide," it implies that in the first-century johannine community simply staying had become problematic. Some believers who seemed to be solidly, organically in the new life (*every branch in me,* v. 2) had left it; or else they had brought scandal on it and had to be excluded. Branches (by their own volition, or by the determination of the community) were separated from the vine (*is cast forth, eblēthē,* was used in 9:34 of expulsion from the synagogue).

Lapsed Christians and the terms on which they might be readmitted to the community of faith and practice became a preoccupying internal problem for the church in the second and third centuries, but Matthew 18:15-18, Hebrews 6:4-8 and 10:26-29, and the present text indicate that the issue needed to be addressed in the first century. In this Gospel the loss of one of Jesus' disciples is spoken of in 6:66 and 13:30. 1 John 2:19 and 4:1 indicate that the johannine community had suffered a substantial loss prior to the writing of the Epistle. The writer of 1 John commented *They went out from us, but they did not belong to us.* (The author's final reflection, *they did not belong to us,* suggests that in his judgment the defectors' attachment to the community and its faith, since it failed under testing, had been more apparent than real.)

The Evangelist, speaking indirectly, seeks to give meaning to Christian defection. The separation of the branch, he says, is the doing of the Vinedresser, who prunes the vine for its own good. The statement that the branches *are thrown in the fire* seems to be a "divine passive," meaning that God acts (see v. 2). However, God's excluding judgment is not arbitrary, but is a consequence of the death that the branch has already imposed on itself when it sought to live in detachment. The divine judgment seems to be a ratification of the death-in-life into which one has been brought by the quest for self-dependence.

The Evangelist is saying that the life of a believer who seeks to live out of contact with Jesus and his people deteriorates. The separation, the "pruning," is a joint action of a fruitless branch and a careful tender of the vine. As it is developed here, the image of cutting out a "branch" provides no roles for the community. The "branches" are not depicted as related to one another. There is no suggestion of communal discipline nor of the weighing of cases by collective authority; there is no institutional mechanism of exclusion; and there is no concern for restoration. (Were cases at this stage of the church's development handled by an un-formalized "sense of the meeting"?) All is between God and the member, and (as the Evangelist tells it in this passage) exclusion seems to be final.

When Jesus says that the one who does not abide in him *is thrown away like a branch and withers,* he expresses his presentism once more. Life and fruit-bearing are now. But so are death, judgment and exclusion.

An ecclesiology of at least a rudimentary sort seems to be implicit in the Vine image. Jesus and his people form a unit of life, a societal whole. The members of this many-in-one unit stand in a life-giving relation to Jesus, and through him they are related to one another. The life of the church is not from itself, but is Christ's life in it. The purpose of this common life is to "bear much fruit."

Within the collective life, the "branches" are all directly and equally attached to the Vine and must remain so. In the Farewell Discourses the only reference Jesus makes to relations of his followers to one another is his repeated command that they love one another (13:34-35, 15:12-13, 17) and his prayer that they be one (17:11, 21). Mutual love might be thought to include such things as kindness, forgiveness, truth, patience, and support. The johannine love command, however, does not draw out such implications.

It seems that any community, no matter how spontaneous its origin may have been, once it has come into being, tends quite quickly to develop internal order and differentiation of functions. The Pauline and deutero-Pauline literature indicates that such developments were taking place in other first-century Christian communities, but if they were under way in the johannine church, the Farewell Discourses give no hint of it. The Fourth Gospel seems to assume an undifferentiated, egalitarian community. In the Vine image, all the branches are equally set in the life of the vine. A later writing from the same community says that all members are taught by the Spirit and all know (1 John 2:27).

In the order of the earliest church, Jesus' immediate disciples, who have been with him from the beginning of his ministry, inevitably occupy a unique place. All subsequent Christian witness will necessarily derive from them. The church is "founded on the apostles and prophets." But the place the disciples occupy arises from their participation in a unique moment of history, and (despite the concern in the First Discourse for succession) nothing in the johannine text indicates that they hold an "office" that could be transmitted to others. There is no hint in the Second Discourse that in the johannine community some persons were recognized as filling, either by charism or by appointment, places of leadership. None of Jesus' disciples speaks to or for the others. Insofar as Jesus' close followers are appointed to be witnesses, the most conspicuous witness is Mary Magdalene, 20:1-2, 18. Peter, on the evidence of the "appendix" of chapter 21, is called to "feed" Jesus' "sheep," 21:15-19. But nothing indicates what his "feeding" role is nor that it could be passed on to anyone else.

The community that is implied in the johannine literature seems to have taken on very little structural definition. (The second and third letters of John speak of a presbyterate, but they tell nothing about the authority or functions of an "elder.") At the time of the writing of the Fourth Gospel, the community of the Vine seems to have been extending itself in space and perpetuating itself in time, while retaining its identity as Jesus' people. It seems to have done so with a minimum of articulated structure, designated authority figures, or an express rule of faith. Was the johannine church an immature community that for its self-preservation and mission would need in time to develop ministry and order? Or was it an intentionally non-hierarchical community that was so carried by the Spirit that it worked, at least for a while?

In the lectionary. The Common Lectionary appoints 15:1-8 as the Gospel reading for the Sixth Sunday of Easter in Year A. Its situation in the Liturgical Year is not that of Jesus reassuring his disciples on the night of his arrest, but that of the living, universalized Jesus, known to be present, giving vitality to a community of faith and love — clearly appropriate scripture for Easter season preaching.

The vine image seems to be a sermon waiting to be preached. The readily grasped picture of a people comprising an organically connected unit of life establishes a communicative bond between the biblical text, the preacher, and the congregation. But there are perils. The image of the vine and its discerning cultivator can seem remote and bucolic. Many persons who encounter this passage today live far from sharp pruning knives and hot brush fires, and they have not seen the almost shocking sight of a severely cropped vineyard in early summer. Without some such realism, thought associations arising from the image can suggest clipping faded blossoms from one's house or garden plants rather than looking closely at the vigor of a vine on whose productivity one's life and livelihood may in considerable measure depend.

Present-day preachers encounter this text as authoritative scripture from which they try to help Christians — often fairly comfortable Christians — to gather a sense of their living relation to Jesus. But the passage was born out of extremity. It does not represent a first-century writer sharing a few thoughts suggested by a roadside vineyard. It represents interior discoveries made in a deeply threatened church. What did the community's faith have that could hold it up in the face of opposition and of loss of roots? How could the defection of apparently once committed members be given some meaning? In the midst of change and loss, what truly "abides"? One does not touch the heart of this passage until one touches the existential forces from which it sprang. It was written for a church experiencing conflict, pain and loss; and it speaks of resource greater than the conflict, the pain, and the loss. It will be heard most profoundly by those who read it in the spirit, if not necessarily the circumstances, in which it was written.

---

2. Sharing in Life (15:7-17)

The *mashal* of the vine and its branches — the figure which has given imaginative impulse to the theme of remaining in Jesus — now falls away. The image, with its indirect speech about vines, branches and vinegrowers, would be limiting if it were continued longer. (An image which is sustained after it has done its disclosing work risks becoming contrived. Only a special sort of mind can write allegory convincingly.) There are limits to what can be said about interpersonal relations as long as one is speaking in terms of plants and their care.

The language also turns away from the "not" constructions of vv. 1-6; it no longer speaks of branches that bear no fruit and are cast aside. Jesus now describes positively the life of those who know him and are bound to him and who live as his people in the world.

Vv. 15:1-17 present a succession of themes that seem to grow from one to the next. Vv. 1-6 have described Jesus and his people as a biological unit, a vine and its branches. Although the vine figure ends at v. 6, the key term "fruit" returns in vv. 8 and 16.

The idea of "abiding" in an organic life, which is introduced in v. 4, continues as the main thread through v. 10, the term "abide" being used five times in vv. 4-6, always in the third person: "those who abide."

In vv. 7-10, however, the language changes to "you who abide," spoken directly to the disciples (and by implication to the readers of the Gospel). V. 11, which reads like a summary, suggests that vv. 7-11 are a unit. The theme of association with Jesus continues in vv. 12-17, but in a rapid succession of ideas: mutual love (vv. 12 and 17), laying down one's life for others (v. 13), being friends of Jesus, not servants (vv. 14-15), and being chosen (v. 16). The section begins and ends with Jesus' command that his disciples love one another (vv. 12, 17).

Formally, vv. 7-17 shape a verbal *inclusio*, the themes of vv. 7-10 reappear in vv. 12-17 in reverse order. The rhetorical device turns at v. 11.

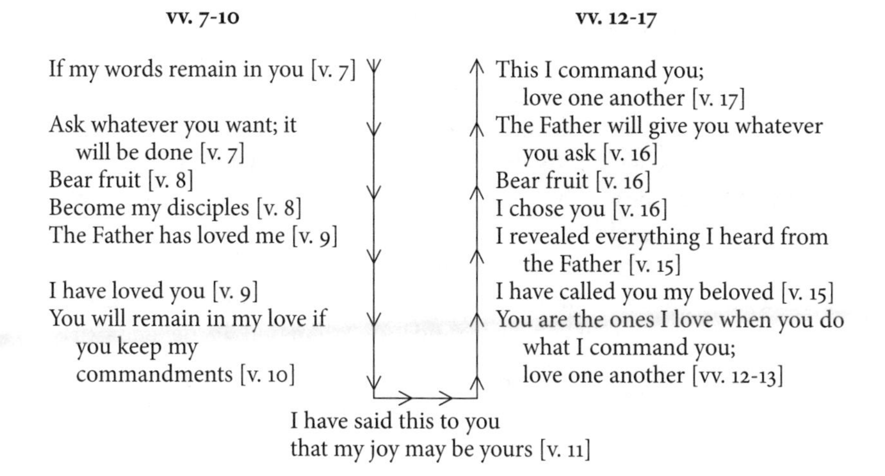

The arc of this inclusio suggests that the elements of experience that are named within it are not separable, but follow from one another. The things that are spoken of at the end are implied also at the beginning.

Although Jesus has established the cruciality of *abiding* (vv. 4-6), he has done little to describe life "in the vine." He now speaks of life in relation to himself, mentioning: prayer, informed by his word and receiving answer (v. 7); glorifying the Father in true discipleship (v. 8); love and obedience (vv. 9-10); and joy, full joy (v. 11). Remaining in Jesus is a demanding and a rewarding existence.

The relation between Jesus and his people is a deep engagement that draws him into them and them into him. Personal interaction is suggested by the language. In five verses, Jesus says "me" or "my" nine times and "you" or "your" eleven times. Moreover, the things which are Jesus' own ("mine") are shared with others; they become "yours": *my words abide in you,* v. 7; *abide in my love,* vv. 9-10; *my joy may be in you,* v. 11. Jesus is deeply invested in his followers through his words, his love, and his joy.

These verses contain six "in" constructions: *abide in me; my words abide in you,* v. 7; *abide in my love . . . you will abide in my love as I abide in the Father's love,* v. 9b-10; *that my joy may be in you,* v. 11. Indeed, between vv. 2 and 11 there are fourteen "in" phrases, four of which are double — two parties, each being "in" the other. Nowhere else in this Gospel are these "in" expressions concentrated as they are in this portion of the Second Discourse.

Ceslaus Spicq describes this New Testament "in" expression as

> . . . a technical locution of the Christian life and divine realities. "To be in Christ" and "to be in the Spirit" (Rom. 8:9) are definitions of Christian being, of the unique way of existing in union and community with Christ. It is a question not only of immanence but also of vital relationship. The believer responds by seizing and making his own the word, the charity, the joy, the life which the Father and the Son communicate to him. Consequently, to say that the Holy Spirit "is in" the disciples suggests a living, interior presence in the most profound communion, like the union by which the Father lives in Christ and Christ in God — by their relations of knowledge and love — and both Father and Christ are united with the Paraclete in his dwelling in souls.[11]

If you abide in me
and my words abide in you,
ask whatever you wish,
and it will be done for you. 15:7

11. C. Spicq, *Agape in the New Testament* (St. Louis: Herder, 1966).

Life in Jesus and his people ("abiding in the vine") is a life of prayer. It finds expression in human words. It is not passive, passionless, indifferent, nor without desire. It wills and seeks and asks, while God listens and responds.

Jesus' expression here, however, carries a qualifying "if." *If you abide in me and my words abide in you, ask. . . .* Christian prayer is disciplined and given its character as the one who asks abides in Jesus and as Jesus' words abide in the one who asks. Prayer that receives response arises from the indwelling words of Jesus.

A reader expects a parallel here, as in v. 4, which said *If you abide in me, and I in you,* but the form is: *If you abide in me, and my words abide in you.* (Compare the accusation in 5:38, *you do not have his [God's] word abiding in you.*) The language suggests that Jesus' remembered words were an informing, regulative presence among Jesus' followers and in their life of asking. (One thinks of the Q material of the Synoptic tradition or of the sayings held in memory, though unwritten, of which Paul's *remember the words of the Lord Jesus,* followed by an otherwise unrecorded saying, Acts 20:35, provides an instance. The johannine community probably held sayings sources of this kind.) The church's memory must have treasured the remembered sayings that were Jesus' legacy to his people. As an enfleshed presence, he was gone; the things he said remained and still carried authority. The grammatical parallel presents Jesus' words as a mode of the indwelling of Jesus himself. Where his words abide, the person whose words they are abides.

Jesus' words were not, however, so much remembered pronouncements of a departed leader as they were words by which he still lived and led and taught and shared himself. Jesus was not merely effective through words he had spoken in past situations. Rather, the one who had spoken still spoke (as the johannine discourses themselves witness). The demands on his followers of unprecedented situations are met as they listen to the living and speaking Christ.

This Discourse presents Jesus' words as a powerful, active force (see 6:63, 68; 14:10), yet they are vulnerable, as spoken words are always vulnerable. Jesus says "if." Whether or not his words find an effective lodging-place in the consciousness of his hearers depends on their response.

When Jesus' words engage persons in a sustained relationship, human asking is effective. Being prompted by the words of Christ within (words which are from the Father), true prayer is, in a sense, given. In the mysterious exchange of life in Christ, the effective prayer which is addressed to God ultimately comes from God.

As to the divine response, the expression *It will be done for you* may be considered a passive construction with God as the unexpressed subject: "God will do it for you."

The sequence of ideas in vv. 6 and 7 is of interest. Even though v. 7 begins the new rhetorical section which continues through v. 17, clearly there is no abrupt break between vv. 6 and 7. The negative warning of v. 6, *If you do not abide . . .* , is answered by a positive pledge in v. 7, *If you do abide. . . .* The idea of judgment and exclusion (the useless branch that is burned, v. 6) is followed by the contrasting idea of remaining in Jesus' words as a condition of answered prayer (v. 7).

In Matthew 18:15-20 — one of the unmistakably "ecclesiastical" passages of Matthew — these two topics follow one another in this same order. Jesus' mention of the exclusion of an offending member (18:15-18) leads him to speak of answered prayer, secured by his presence (18:19-20).

It does not seem likely that the Evangelist knew the matthean passage or its sources. But one may ask, Is there some reason why these two quite disparate subjects were related in the mind and experience of the early church? One passage is as clearly matthean as the other is johannine. Yet the sequence of subjects and their internal dynamics seem similar enough to rouse a reader's curiosity.

My Father is glorified by this,
  that you bear much fruit,
  and become my disciples. 15:8

The "fruitful" church, Jesus says, is the glory of the Father (cf. Matt. 5:16). The church doing its appointed work is a demonstration of the final divine splendor. Yet the church cannot live or be productive except as a people in Jesus. As Barrett puts it: "The Father is glorified in the Son — in his obedience and perfect accomplishment of his work. It is therefore but a short step to see the glorification of the Father in the obedience and fruitfulness of those who are united to the Son."[12]

When Jesus tells persons who are his disciples that they can become his disciples, his words suggest the depth and complexity of discipleship. As the open johannine "whoever" (common in the Book of Signs) indicates, there is no one who is not a follower of Jesus who cannot become one. And the present text suggests that no one who is a follower cannot be-

12. Barrett, *Gospel,* 475.

come a more faithful one. The God-glorifying, fruit-bearing church is a community of disciples who are growing into discipleship.

> As the Father has loved me,
> so I have loved you;
> abide in my love.
> If you keep my commandments,
> you will abide in my love,
> just as I have kept my Father's commandments
> and abide in his love. 15:9-10

Abiding is now clarified as a relation sustained in love and obedience — a point that could not be made until the useful but limiting analogy of vine and branches was dropped. (The term "love" which is introduced in v. 9, becomes the governing theme of the next five verses.) The love of which v. 9 speaks passes in v. 10 to commandment-keeping: Love yields obedience, and obedience issues from love. The themes are interwoven in language, suggesting their closeness in experience. The love-in-obedience to which Jesus summons his followers is their participation in the relation in which he stands to the Father. As the Father has loved the Son, so the Son has loved his own. As Jesus obeys the Father and abides in his love, so the disciples are to obey Jesus and abide in his love. However, the mutual love of Father and Son is more than model. As David Stanley has said: "It is the creative cause from which all Christian love necessarily springs. . . . Divine love is redemptive, indeed a creative, transforming act, when directed towards creatures."[13] Jesus' followers are caught up into the vital exchange of loving and obeying which persists between himself and the Father.

Vv. 9-10 are closely woven. It was said earlier that the Father loves the Son (e.g, 3:35; 5:20; 10:17), and the emphasis will return later in the final prayer (17:23, 26). A central christological affirmation of the Fourth Gospel is that Jesus is uniquely the Beloved One. It has also been said that Jesus loves his followers (13:1). In these verses, the two relations and the three parties and the one love are expressed together. *As the Father has loved me, so have I loved you.* Jesus' love to his disciples is as the Father's love to himself. He is the loved one and the loving one. As he loves, he mediates a love which comes to him.

The constant, self-imparting love of the Father for the Son and of Je-

13. David Stanley, "I Am the Genuine Vine," *The Bible Today* 8 (1963), 489.

sus for his disciples is to be answered by his followers remaining in Jesus' love. But their response to him is free, and hence fragile. So he urges: *abide in my love.* The response of Jesus' followers to him is continued and renewed in love and obedience. *If you keep my commandments, you will abide in my love, just as I have kept my Father's commandments and abide in his love* (15:10). Jesus has urged his followers to "abide." Now he says that he too "abides." The relation between himself and the Father is sustained intentionally and in obedience.

The terms "command" and "commandments" which enter in v. 10 begin a theme that runs through v. 17: *If you keep my commandments, as I have kept my Father's commandments* (v. 10); *This is my commandment* (v. 12); *If you do what I command you* (v. 14); *This I command you* (v. 17).

The idea that God is self-imparted in commandments and that persons are held in relation to God through keeping them lies deep in the Jewish sense of covenant and Torah. If divine commandments are demands *(You shall . . .),* they are also revelation, bonding and love *(I am . . .).* Jesus who has spoken of himself as a commandment-keeper, now shows himself as a commandment-giver.

In the thought of the Fourth Gospel, Jesus and his disciples have an important commonality in that both are obedient — their obedience rooted in love and abiding. It is clear that the intimate relation between Jesus and believers and between them and God through Jesus "is a preeminently moral union."[14]

Jesus' "commandments," which were introduced earlier (13:34-35), return at the beginning and at the end of the second part of the inclusio passage of this Second Discourse (vv. 12 and 17). In the Jewish mind, the divine Torah meant more than a code of moral or cultic duties. It meant teaching or counsel. It was a sharing of the life of God with the life of Israel. The dignity of being a Jew was rooted in consent to a divine self-imparting in the Torah. W. H. Cadman suggested that there is a link between this emphasis on commandments and the "friends" passage which follows:

> In vv. 14-15 we are told that the disciples are friends of Jesus because he has made known to them everything he has heard from the Father, and that they are his friends if they do what he commands them. There is surely an indication here that what he commands them to do is what

14. Barnabas Lindars, *The Gospel of John* (New Century Bible Commentary; Grand Rapids: Eerdmans, 1972), 490.

he has made known to them, namely, the whole revelation he has accomplished, his word comprehensively understood. By his obedient response to all that he had heard from the Father, that is, to the Father's purpose for salvation, Jesus has remained in the Father's love; and he is now calling for a similar response from his disciples.[15]

Jesus says that the relation with the Father derives from shared love (v. 9); and it passes over into shared joy (v. 11). The obedience, no less than the love and the joy, is a human participation in the life exchanged between Jesus and the Father.

Johannine christology represents Jesus' oneness with the Father as a union, carried out in the initiative of the Father's will and in Jesus' total, glad response. Jesus' life was devoted to (it "fed" on, 4:34) doing the Father's will. There is (apart from the enigmatic touch in 12:27-30) no sense of struggle in the johannine portrait — no temptation account, no tension or resistance, no Gethsemane, and nothing of the emphasis found in the book of Hebrews that Jesus learned obedience through the things he suffered (Heb. 5:8). The moral character of Jesus' oneness with the Father binds him into the human condition. The Jesus of the Fourth Gospel consistently wills to do God's will. His union with the Father, J. A. T. Robinson observes, was "grounded in a moral affinity potentially open to anyone."[16] Moreover, his union with the Father was maintained in conditions of opposition and suffering — a connection that would doubtless come to the minds of the Evangelist's first readers, who were facing active hostility.

This small unit on the interrelation of loves ends as it began. The words *I abide in the Father's love* (of v. 10b) bring back *The Father has loved me* (of v. 9a). Jesus' requirement that the disciples love and obey (v. 10a) is enclosed by affirmations of the Father's love for Jesus and of Jesus' obedience to the Father (vv. 9 and 10b).

The coloration of the life of obedience is suggested as Jesus passes to speak of joy.

I have said these things to you,
so that my joy may be in you,
and that your joy may be complete. 15:11

15. W. H. Cadman, *The Open Heaven* (Oxford: Blackwell, 1967), 181.

16. J. A. T. Robinson, *The Human Face of God* (Philadelphia: Westminster, 1973), 172. Although Robinson said "open to any man," he no doubt would not if he were writing today.

I have said these things to you, so that . . . When a speaker begins to explain what he or she has been saying, it suggests that a unit of thought is ending. Since v. 11 is a turn in the inclusio of vv. 7-17, Jesus' "these things" may refer to what he has said since v. 7; he may, however, refer also to the discourse that began at 15:1. If so, it would suggest that the varied material on the vine, on abiding, on love and obedience — the whole of the life that is shared between Jesus and "his own" — is for the sake of joy, full joy. Existence in relation to Jesus is rewarding, satisfying, fulfilling — but always insofar as it remains in the relation.

The parts of this unit of thought can be examined singly:

- Jesus' words *my joy* present him as a fundamentally joyful person. The deep source of his joy, as this Gospel tells it, lay in his communion with the Father, his sureness in shared love and in the spending of life for the Father's will.
- But joy is unconfinable. Jesus says that he has spoken so that the joy which was his might be in his followers. The joy that Jesus imparts takes root within others. William Temple comments, "It is no alien gift."[17] It is not produced by favorable circumstances nor easily shaken by adverse conditions. Further, these words link *my joy* with *your joy.* The joy that is Jesus' own is at the same time lodged within his followers. It is his, but given; it is theirs, but received.
- Jesus speaks, finally, in behalf of "fulfilled" joy — joy that is *complete,* carried to its fullest (cf. 3:29; 1 John 1:4; 2 John 12). Jürgen Moltmann describes such joy as "the divine joy, the joy of eternal life, the overflowing joy that confers fellowship and gives joy to others. He has come, he suffers and dies for them out of the divine joy, not out of condescension, and for the joy of those who are his, not out of sympathy."[18]

Having in mind the entire discourse and the occasion of its writing, a reader will remember that this joy was not spoken of to a comfortable community, but to believers in Jesus who were being expelled from their ancient community of faith and worship. Their joy was acquired and maintained under adversity.

17. William Temple, *Readings in St. John's Gospel* (London: Macmillan, 1939), 266.

18. Jürgen Moltmann, *The Church in the Power of the Spirit* (New York: Harper and Row, 1977), 118.

The structure of the thought passes to the return half of the inclusio. Jesus has described the obedience and love that bind the Father and himself and the obedience and love that prevail between himself and his followers. But through v. 11 Jesus' terms have been general. Now in the "return" half of his verbal inclusio, saying "you," he describes this responsible sharing of life more particularly, explaining that the love of which he speaks is self-giving love that confers dignity on others, taking them into one's confidence, and establishing bonds of intimacy. Its supreme demonstration is in giving one's life for others.

Vv. 12-17 begin and end with Jesus' command that his followers love one another: *Love one another as I have loved you* (v. 12) and . . . *so that you may love one another* (v. 17). The branches which must live by their relation to the vine (vv. 1-6) are persons who also live in relation to one another.

> This is my commandment,
> that you love one another
> as I have loved you. 15:12

Only here and in the parallels of 13:34 and 15:17 Jesus gives an express command to his followers. (The language changes from the plural "commandments" of v. 10 to a singular term *commandment.*) The imperative *love one another* arises from the prior indicative *I have loved you.* The continuing obligation of Jesus' followers to one another is rooted in the supreme demonstration of Jesus' love which in the johannine narrative lies ahead (chapters 19 and 20), but which at the time of the author's writing (and the church's reading) stands as the foundational deed of faith and community.

> No one has greater love than this,
> to lay down one's life for one's friends. 15:13

Love is so complex a human characteristic and so open to self-deception that anyone who speaks of it seriously must identify the kind of love one has in mind. So Jesus explains: *No one has greater love than this, to lay down one's life for one's friends.* The love of which he speaks is self-giving. His community is not bound together as a group of people who enjoy one another's company. Rather, they are persons who have been overtaken by a great act of mercy. The love that Jesus commends is prodigal, un-self-regarding. He describes it by citing its fullest demonstration, the intentional forfeiture of one's own life in behalf of others. This general reference obviously has in mind Jesus himself — the Good Shepherd who lays down his life for his sheep (10:11, 17-18). The redemptive sacrifice of Jesus for others exemplifies the quality of the relation that should prevail among Jesus' followers. This text suggests the deep levels at which atonement and community are bound into one another.

The term "friends" which enters at v. 13 remains the theme of the next two verses. Jesus asks his listeners, as the Evangelist asks his readers, to use theologically the human capacity to have friends and to be a friend. He does not begin with suggestions about familiar, easy companionship and then build to a sense that there may be costs to being a friend. Rather the theme is introduced with abrupt realism — friendship may lead to the supreme expression of love, the giving of one's life for others. Friendship is a relation that is usually entered because of the satisfactions it brings. Jesus here reminds that it also contains the possibility of self-giving to the uttermost.

> You are my friends
>   if you do what I command you.
> I do not call you servants any longer,
>   because the servant does not know what the master is doing;
> but I have called you friends,
>   because I have made known to you
>   everything that I have heard from my Father. 15:14-15

Continuing to speak of his followers as friends, Jesus turns from general terms ("no one," "one's") to direct, first- and second-person terms ("you," "my," "I"). The disciples are friends of Jesus as they obey him (v. 14). However, Jesus does not ask for a servile following of arbitrarily imposed demands (v. 15). He shares his mind with his followers, making known to them what he has understood from the Father.

The actor in this passage is Jesus: *I have called you friends . . . , I have made known to you . . . , I chose you and appointed you.* Some of the deepest human communities — notably the family — are given in the very terms of human life; but friends are chosen. There is always in friendship an element of grace. One has no choice about one's parents or one's siblings; but no one who is a friend is so by necessity. The relationship described here is of Jesus' making. He has called his followers friends. Indeed, C. H. Dodd takes this passage to be more than description; it is part of the act of constituting the relation which it describes. Speaking of the performative force of these words (and to some extent of the entire Farewell passage), Dodd says that "Christ is not merely telling his disciples about life in union with Him and how to attain it; he is actually imparting it to them."[19] Jesus' sharing of deep insights in his long Farewell — his making known to his people everything he has heard from the Father — is verbal action, bringing other persons into a mature relation with himself through inviting them to respond freely and informedly.

When Jesus says, *You are my friends if you do what I command you,* he indicates that the designation "friends" does not raise anyone to a level of relationship in which obeying his commands is superseded. Jewish readers would understand that knowing and following God's commandments means being made sharers in divine counsel.

The term "friends" does not refer to an elite among Jesus' followers — select persons who are made party to privileged insight which is withheld from others. The word translated "friend" *(philos)* refers to "those Jesus loves." (Mary, Martha and Lazarus are Jesus' "friends" [*philoi*], 11:11, because Jesus loves them, 11:3, 5.) The reference of the word "friends" is as wide as those to whom Jesus says *so have I loved you* (vv. 9, 12). It includes all those for whom he lays down his life (v. 13). The Evangelist means for his readers to understand that believers as such are Jesus' friends with whom he shares himself.

> I do not call you servants any longer,
> because the servant does not know what his master is doing;
> but I have called you friends,
> because I have made known to you
> everything that I have heard from my Father. 15:15

Jesus drew on master-servant terms in 13:12-16, and he will use them again in v. 20. It is not demeaning to be a servant (or "slave" in Greek) of this Master. As Bishop Newbigin observes: "The master has done the work of a slave" for the disciples (in washing their feet, 13:1-20; and in giving his life, chs. 18–19). The master-slave relation is remade in the freeing, dignifying, informing, uniting act of the cross.[20]

Nevertheless, the term "servant" carries from human culture so many inadequate connotations that it cannot stand unmodified as a de-

19. Dodd, *Interpretation,* 418-19.

20. Lesslie Newbigin, *The Light Has Come: An Exposition of the Fourth Gospel* (Grand Rapids: Eerdmans, 1982), 202.

scription of the life that Jesus shares with others. Jesus says here that the term will not do *any longer.* A time, with its mode of relation, is passing over to another. As the disciples grow into informed intimacy, the term is superseded. *I do not call you servants any longer . . . but I have called you friends.* New relations require fresh designations.

Friendship is a free, egalitarian relation that stands outside the formal ordering of society. It is lived and enjoyed apart from necessity or from any calculation of means and ends, of advantage or of interest. A friend is not a friend *because of* something prior to the friendship or *in order to* achieve something beyond it. Jürgen Moltmann says, "Friendship is a human relationship which springs from freedom, exists in mutual freedom and preserves that freedom." He adds, "The more people begin to live with one another as friends, the more privileges and claims to domination become superfluous."[21]

C. S. Lewis, discussing friendship, speaks of "the exquisite arbitrariness and irresponsiblity of this love." He explains: "I have no duty to be anyone's Friend and no one in the world has a duty to be mine. . . . Friendship is unnecessary, like philosophy, like art, like the universe itself (for God did not need to create). It has no survival value; rather it is one of those things which give value to survival."[22]

Jesus explains that the difference between servants (or "slaves," *douloi*) and friends lies in the sharing among friends of understanding, meaning or intent. A slave is ordered and obeys; a slave has no right to request or expect explanation. Of course, in the ancient world, some slaves became trusted counselors; but Jesus keeps the image to essentials. Nothing in the role or status of a master requires that the reasons that may lie behind a direction be explained; and nothing in being a servant can demand that an explanation be given. The slave *does not know what the master is doing.* But between friends it is different. Friends confide and share, expressing their mind to one another freely. They bring one another into their hopes and plans, opening at the same time their fears and anxieties. One lets one's friends matter to oneself. Jesus uses this human bonding to speak of the relation of himself to his people. He seeks and asks an intelligent, consenting relation; and he shares his mind in a way that makes such informed intimacy possible: *I have made known to you everything I have heard from my Father.* The love and obedience that Jesus seeks are based in shared understanding.

21. Moltmann, *Church,* 202.

22. C. S. Lewis, *The Four Loves* (London: Geoffrey Bles, 1960), 84.

Jesus says further that he opens his mind to others as the Father confides in him. He describes himself as first a listener, one who has been made party to the Father's mind and purpose (cf. 5:19; 8:28). Then what he hears he makes known. Before he is a faithful speaker, he is an attentive hearer.

In this passage, spoken as by Jesus, the church declares its own experience. Throughout the Fourth Gospel, Jesus stands apart from others inasmuch as he *knows,* while others do not. There is a wide gap between what he knows and the ignorance of even those who are closest to him. But the community which produced the Farewell passages (and indeed the Fourth Gospel as a whole) can write about ignorance *then* because *now* that ignorance is transcended. In the light of Jesus' death and resurrection and in the ministry of the Paraclete, the church has come to know (see 1 John 2:20). The post-resurrection community of believers is beneficiary of new, powerful, reorienting insight which has come to it from the living Jesus, who shares himself, making believers intelligent participants in the divine purpose. Veils have been torn away. As Paul would say, *We have the mind of Christ* (1 Cor. 2:16).

The image of "friend" does not stand alone; no image can. It speaks of two parties, each committed to and receptive to the other. However, the church is constituted in a divine initiative enacted in Jesus, who says, *You did not choose me, but I chose you.* He sets the terms on which others are called into and sustained in his friendship (v. 14); he creates the new relation by imparting to his friends what he has heard (v. 15). Now the Discourse reaches into the ancient biblical faith and speaks of Jesus' people as chosen — a people whose reason for being, like that of Israel, lies in the sovereign divine, electing purpose.

> You did not choose me
>   but I chose you.
> And I appointed you. . . . 15:16a

Jesus' saying *I chose and appointed you* sounds directly applicable to the disciples, some of whom had been specifically called by Jesus (see 1:35-51; 6:70; 13:18). Yet one can overhear the late-first-century believers in Jesus (a community of second-generation Christians) speaking of themselves in these words. The church's situation at the time of the Second Discourse — a situation of threatenedness, persecution and defections — made it important that it keep a sense of its own divine calling. Although in the view of the synagogue and of Roman society, the small company of Christians may have been of little account, according to its own self-understanding, it was a people of God's own choosing. And if God were for it, who could be against it? Deep in the biblical faith and in the communities formed by it there lies the humbling recognition: "We did not choose, but we are chosen." In this Discourse, the words are spoken to the chosen by the chooser.

Jesus adds, . . . *and appointed you to go.* As in the election of Israel, being held in the favor of God makes one a participant in the redemptive divine purpose. Being chosen is an appointment to mission — to be "a light to the nations" (Isa. 49:6). Bishop Newbigin comments that when he offered his life, "Jesus made [his followers] his friends and made them also his missionaries."[23] The Greek verb for *appointed you (tithēmi)* is the same as that which in 15:13 speaks of laying down one's life — suggesting that the "going" may be costly. It may be an appointment to suffer.

If Jesus' followers are chosen to be missionaries, they are assured of being in some measure effective missionaries. If the "going" is costly, it will also achieve enduring results.

> . . . to go
> and bear fruit,
> fruit that will last, . . . 15:16b

The single word "fruit" returns from the vine image of vv. 1-6. The mission of the church is to *bear fruit that will last* (*menein* again; the fruit will abide). Although the language is not specific, the term "fruit" here would seem to have in mind converts that are won through the "going" of v. 16b. Jesus pledges that the additions to the fellowship of believers that are made through faithful mission work would be permanent. The words may provide some needed assurance, for 15:6 has referred to results that did not prove lasting. The mission which is rooted in a prior divine choosing holds promise also of an assured future.

Fruit that abides is a characteristically johannine expression. Neither here nor in the earlier passage about the vine is the fruit described as gradually ripening to harvest. Rather, the fruit appears fully formed and permanent — fruit that is always mature and that does not spoil.

The inclusio device that has organized the author's thought since v. 7 draws to its end by bringing back the theme of "asking" with which it began, as the previous verse brought back the "fruit" image from v. 8. Now,

23. Newbigin, *Light,* 202.

however, "asking" falls in a context created by the second half of the inclusio — a context of love, being chosen, going in mission; but, in the most developed of the themes, being friends. Among friends, one does not hesitate to ask. Friends listen to one another; they identify with one another's needs and hopes. They trust themselves to one another. They invest themselves in the well-being of one another.

> . . . so that the Father will give you
> whatever you ask him
> in my name. 15:16c

Jesus presents prayer as the dignifying of humanity. God invites Jesus' followers to speak as friends. God is pledged to hear as a friend. The link between friendship and prayer, which the Evangelist leaves implicit, was developed by Jürgen Moltmann:

> Jesus' friendship leads to certainty in prayer. . . . The prayer offered in the assurance that prayer will be heard therefore becomes the expression of life lived in friendship with God. God can be talked to. He listens to his friend. Thanks to this friendship there is room in the almighty liberty of God for the created liberty of man. In this friendship there is the opportunity for man to have an effect upon and with God's sole effectiveness.[24]

> I am giving you these commands
> so that you may love one another. 15:17

V. 17 repeats v. 12, as v. 16b repeated v. 7b. The writer is concluding a unit of thought. Jesus has been sharing himself deeply with his friends, speaking of the greatest love and of his appointment of his followers to bring forth enduring fruit. He brings the passage to an end with something concrete and close to everyday existence: *love one another.* A community of mutually loving persons is the actualization of the divine self-imparting in Jesus.

In the lectionary. The Revised Common Lectionary appoints 15:9-17 (roughly the second half of the first part of this Discourse) as the Gospel reading for the Sixth Sunday of Easter in Year B.

24. Moltmann, *Church,* 115-16.

Hardly anything in the Second Discourse depends on the "Farewell" situation of Jesus speaking on the night of his arrest. The "presentism" of this Second Discourse makes it pertinent to believing readers of any time or place. The "I" of this passage is the living Jesus, who declares his love for his people; who imparts to them his joy; who affirms that he has chosen them; who has made believers his friends and taken them into his confidence and appointed them sharers in his redemptive task. This present Christ asks his people to love him and to obey his commandments — which means to love each other. And all is for the sake of full joy, lasting fruit, and availing prayer.

Yet these are perilous themes for the preacher: Jesus as friend, joy, loving one another, praying confidently. These are features of the New Testament message that comfortable, friendly Christianity can turn into homiletic banalities. It is the task of the preacher, in the Easter weeks, to use these simple, evangelical terms: loving, obeying, remaining, asking, enjoying, and being friends — there are no real substitutes — but to keep them, in all their wonder and terror, from being domesticated.

A preacher may be helped in this difficult homiletic assignment by the pervasive christology of the passage — as of the post-Easter season. The central terms of this portion of the Second Discourse are the terms of human experience; yet they speak always of human life in transforming relation to Another. They belong to the secret, inner self-understanding of the church as a people whose life is not in itself but is Christ's life in it. The demanding, fulfilling experience depicted here cannot be reduced to techniques, formulas or programs. Fuller life is not a matter of being in touch with oneself. Rather, it belongs to the truth of the church's inner life that is brought to the fore in the Great Fifty Days. The Easter faith, as Jesus himself has said, is not publicly accessible. The living, present Christ is correlative of — he is, so to speak, enclosed by — the believing community. Jesus' Farewell (particularly in John 15:7-17) declares that the risen Christ is known in the loving, obeying, praying, witnessing, joyful church; for its life and his are one.

In looking at this portion of Jesus' farewell, a preacher might also have in mind the circumstances in which this presentation of life in Christ was written. On a quick reading, this passage can seem situationless — something like a devotional address for any occasion. A reader must keep in mind that the Second Discourse is organized so that all of the references to the circumstances of the church at the time of writing fall in its second part, 15:18–16:4a. Yet the situation spoken of there — a situation of being cast loose, of facing strong opposition — influenced the shaping of the entire composition. The reality of Christ and the church as described in 15:1-17 is the heritage of every Christian and can be heard, to one's godly comfort in any circumstances. However, these explorations into the divine-human life were occasioned by a search for inner moorings that could hold in a time of external stress.

Essay: Prayer in the Farewell Discourses

In his Farewell, Jesus says repeatedly that, although he will be gone, the Father remains within the reach of the voice and the desires of his praying followers. The disciples are invited to ask the Father in Jesus' name, assured that they will be heard.

In the Synoptic Gospels, Jesus — speaking sometimes in public, and sometimes privately to his disciples — says a great deal about prayer: It should be persistent (Luke 11:5-8, 18:1-8), without ostentation (Matt. 6:5-6; Luke 18:10-14) and confident in the readiness of the Father to hear (Matt. 6:32). He gives a model prayer in the Sermon on the Mount (Matt. 6:9-13, with another version in Luke 11:2-4).

All that Jesus says about prayer in the Fourth Gospel he says in his Farewell Discourses, always speaking to the disciples. What he says to them he says through them to his later followers, who comprise a continuing community of prayer. The theme of prayer is never developed at length, but it enters the Farewell five times, using similar terms, but with slight variations. Prayer is spoken of once in the First Discourse, 14:13-14, where the greater works are accomplished through prayer; twice in the Second Discourse, 15:7 and 16, where prayer arises from abiding in Jesus and from friendship with him; and in two closely associated places in the Third Discourse, 16:23b and 26, which present prayer as part of an open, loving relation with the Father.[25]

Jesus' remarks on prayer in his Farewell discourses exhibit some common themes and vocabulary:

Asking

Eight times in the five passages Jesus invites his people to "ask" (14:13, 14; 15:7, 16; 16:23, 24 twice, 26). The verb is *aiteō,* a common word for requesting or even begging (e.g., 4:9, 10; Mark 6:22-25; Luke 6:30; Acts 3:2). *Aiteō* is also used in Matthew and Luke when Jesus speaks about praying (e.g. Matt. 6:8; 7:7-11; 18:19; 21:22; Luke 11:9-13). However, in the Fourth Gospel, when the Evangelist says that Jesus prays, he uses another verb, *erōtaō* (14:16; 16:26; 17:9, 15, 20) as though to distinguish the relation from which Jesus spoke, even though there seems to be no sharp difference in meaning

25. There is a comparative analysis of these passages on prayer in Brown, *Gospel,* 633-36.

between the two Greek verbs. The most widely used terms for Christian prayer in the New Testament are the verb *proseuchomai* and the noun *proseuchē*, neither of which appears in the Fourth Gospel nor in the johannine epistles.

The life of faith is described as a life of asking. It is not silent, without speech, nor passionless, without desire. The johannine language virtually says that praying is asking (cf. 1 John 5:15). There are things that the believer and the community of believers need and earnestly seek from God. Petitionary prayer is not set on a lower level than other, more contemplative or disinterested kinds of prayer. Asking is spoken of as virtually constitutive of prayer. The invitation to ask uses "open," almost reckless terms, such as "whatever you ask" (14:13; 15:7, 16) and "anything" (14:14; 16:23). Nothing, it seems, is too great, and nothing too small.

Prayer so described arises out of human needs and is addressed to divine adequacy. Of course, we can be deceived about our needs. And much of modern culture is tooled to persuade us that we need things we do not. Yet we do have needs — needs that are specific and that are so bound into the human condition that they are without end. As needs persist, so prayer persists.

Asking Whom

Prayer, as the Discourses present it, is addressed to the Father (15:16 and 16:23). When the term "ask" stands alone (as in 14:14, according to one reading of the text, and in 15:7, 16:24, and 26), it evidently speaks of asking the Father. In 16:26-27, Jesus says, *I do not say to you that I will ask the Father on your behalf, for the Father himself loves you,* as though what the disciples ask does not need to be passed to the Father by Jesus, for the Father is directly accessible through his own love.

However, Jesus also shares with the Father in the divine hearing and responding. According to a well-attested reading, 14:14 says *if you ask me anything.*[26] E. K. Lee remarks that the Evangelist "would represent that prayers could be addressed either to the Son or the Father."[27] Prayer is di-

26. Verse 14 is omitted in some manuscripts, but editors generally regard it as a true text which some copyists dropped, thinking that it was a duplication of verse 13. Translations which do not accept the reading usually note it in the margin.

27. E. K. Lee, *The Religious Thought of St. John* (London: SPCK, 1962), 255.

rected to the Father and to the living Jesus, and both hear in love, for they are inseparable.

Conditions of Asking

Human needs are bewildering; they arrive unassorted and unsought. A believer's asking is both encouraged and regulated by certain conditions:

Human asking is to be in Jesus' name (14:13-14; 15:16; 16:24, 26). Prayer is mentioned in connection with the name; the name is mentioned in connection with prayer. Prayer is as old as the race. The disciples have all their lives stood in a great tradition of prayer. The new thing was not prayer, but the association of prayer with Jesus' name. In 16:24 Jesus says, *Until now you have not asked anything in my name. Ask. . . .* The use of the name marked a new age, a new relation. Moreover, Jesus' followers could not use his name casually. In Hebrew thought, the name carries the reality of the person named. To ask in Jesus' name means to ask in union with him.

The early Christians continued the spirit and forms of Jewish prayer. Yet a new name was a shaping factor in their prayer. Not just formally, at the end, but pervasively, informingly, Christians prayed as people in Christ. When they spoke to God, their knowledge of God and of their own good all owed everything to that mediatorial name.

Although Christians regularly pray in Christ's name, they seldom realize that virtually the only express New Testament basis for this practice (a practice as old and as widespread as Christian prayer) is this Farewell passage. (Matthew 18:19-20 speaks of prayer arising from people gathered in Jesus' name, which is close to but not identical with the johannine idea. Hebrews 13:15 speaks of offering praise in Jesus' name.) The departing one leaves his people the use of his name — a token that he is still with believers, still present, active and accessible.

Prayer in Jesus' name has become formulaic — the common way in which Christians bring their prayers to an end. Yet the formula arises from the very reality of Christian prayer. Ordinarily the formula and the reality are joined, but either can be present without the other. T. W. Jennings has remarked:

> The mere presence of the formula does not in any way assure us that the prayer is truly a Christian prayer. Our concern is whether public

> prayers are compatible with Christ's mission and ministry, whether our prayers are in keeping with what God has done and promised in and through Jesus.[28]

Praying, as the Second Discourse has it (15:7), depends on abiding: *If you abide in me, and my words abide in you, ask. . . .* Prayer arises out of a sustained relationship — abiding in Jesus, loving him, and keeping his commandments (15:7-9). The human word to God takes its rise from the words of Jesus living in a person who prays.

These two conditions, (1) that prayer be in Jesus' name and (2) that it arise out of abiding in Jesus and his words abiding in the person praying, are invitations or encouragements. Yet at the same time they are restraints. The name is not a talisman; abiding is not a superficial relation.

In this highly christological account of prayer, the use of Jesus' name identifies him with prayer and prayer with him. The prayer of a believer is given by the indwelling Word; it arises from union with Christ. Karl Rahner spoke to the point:

> Asking in Jesus' name means entering into him, living by him, being one with him in love and faith. If he is in us in faith, in love, in grace, in his Spirit, and then our petition arises from the centre of our being, which is himself, and if all our petition and desire is gathered up and fused in him and his Spirit, then the Father hears us. Then our petition becomes simple and straighforward, harmonious, sober, and unpretentious.[29]

Response

Prayer is assured of a hearing. The Father responds to human asking: *It shall be done for you* (15:7, which should be taken as a "divine passive"; God will do it); *the Father . . . may give it to you* (15:16; 16:23); *you will receive* (16:24). Believers do not pray uncertainly; the Father does not give reluctantly — *for the Father himself loves you, because you have loved me and have believed that I came from God* (16:27).

But Jesus is also spoken of as responding to prayer: *I will do it* (14:13-

28. T. W. Jennings, *Life as Worship: Prayer and Praise in Jesus' Name* (Grand Rapids: Eerdmans, 1982), 9.

29. Karl Rahner, *Biblical Homilies* (New York: Herder and Herder, 1956), 85.

14, twice). The divine giving as much as the human asking is in his name: *He will give it to you in my name* (16:24). In responding to believing prayer, the Son and the Father act as one.

Purpose

In two of the sayings about prayer Jesus declares the purpose of human asking and divine giving: *I will do whatever you ask in my name, so that the Father may be glorified in the Son* (14:13); *Ask and you will receive, so that your joy may be complete* (16:24). These final ends of human prayer — the glory of God and the full joy of humanity — it might be proposed, are not two, but are inseparable.

Discoveries and new encounters lie behind the prayer passages of chapters 13–16. In the intense experience of the early church, the new age was a release of the spirit of prayer.

The earliest Christians did not begin praying for the first time as a consequence of Jesus' life among them or his return to the Father, but they prayed as "until now" no one had (16:24). As believers in Jesus spoke with God, a new, shaping factor was present. Christ gives prayer; it is from and in him. Jesus' going to the Father created not distance and remoteness, but nearness and accessibility. The Christians could not think of God now without associating the reality of Jesus with the reality of the Father. Prayer — that activity which establishes an articulate, open bond between humanity and God — was now mediated by Christ. He who had been a person of time and history and who was now with the Father was yet living and present, carrier of the human voice of prayer. He was listener to the prayer that his words had prompted and granter of the asking that was done in his name.

3. In a Hostile World (15:18–16:4a)

At just about its midpoint, the focus of this Second Discourse shifts abruptly from the inner life of the believing community — its sharing in the very life of Jesus and its commitment to mutual love among its members — to its external situation. The lengthy verbal inclusion (15:7-17), ends as it began, saying *love one another,* and at once the theme passes to Jesus' followers' experience of social exclusion, *If the world hates you.*

The author is not analytic or descriptive. He provides no account of the community's circumstances nor does he trace its response to hostility. We can only gather by inference for what reasons the people of Christ were persecuted and by whom and for how long. This author does not give an account of Hellenistic society and of the social, political, intellectual and religious forces that opposed the church and its faith. He does not consider strategies — confrontational, persuasive, or accommodating — that might be used by believers.

The analysis put forward in chapter 3 of this study proposed that the two divisions — 15:1-17 and 15:18–16:4a — are parts of a single Discourse. They are addressed to one readership (or if they were developed first in spoken form, to one group of hearers). They deal with different but related aspects of the concrete experience of a community of believers in Jesus at a critical moment of its history.

The relation of the parts of this discourse can be thought of in two contexts:

Sociological. Modern readers — who are heirs of Troeltsch, Weber, and their followers — can see in the johannine church many of the marks of a "sectarian" community. A new religious group which cannot be assimilated by the society into which it is introduced will develop the duality reflected in the two parts of this author's discourse. The closeness of the members of an in-group and the intensity of their adherence to their defining story are the reverse side of the group's exclusion from the external society.

When the johannine Christians lost their identification with the synagogue, they were deprived of supportive social structures and of a community that might have been expected to provide them with a context of understanding. The people of Jesus held no status. Indeed, their existence within Roman society may have seemed somewhat subversive, for they, like the Jews of the synagogue, stood outside the religious accommodations that pervaded the Hellenistic world. A sign of their "outside" position was that they refused to offer incense to the Emperor as divine — an act of homage that was generally regarded in Roman society as little more than one's contribution to the perpetuation of the civic polity, but an act that was impossible for Jews, including those Jews who believed Jesus to be the Messiah.

Confessing Jesus differentiated one sharply from one's past social solidarities — at times breaking ties with family or occupation. The community of Jesus' followers had no nominal members, but was made up of convinced converts. The believers of the late first century exemplified "Christ against culture." They had no realistic expectation of gaining recognition by the Hellenistic world or of winning it over.

Theological. When the author considers the situation of Jesus' people, his mind goes to finalities. He sets the believers' experience within the overarching myth of his gospel — a myth in which the people of Jesus are a participant. The world's animosity derives from what the world is. Into this world of blindness and alienation — led by its "ruler" — Jesus came, sent from the Father. Jesus' mission — with its spiritual authority as well as its audacity and risks — was bequeathed to his people. The believers in Jesus saw themselves united with the light and life and truth of God. This bond was not of their creation, but traced to a gift of divine rebirth, which in turn traced ultimately to a calling which took its historical rise from the ministry of Jesus, the one sent from God. Jesus bound his people to himself and himself to them. He was present in them, imparting to them his very life. As the world could not assimilate or comprehend Jesus, so it rejected the people who were bound to him. Neither he nor they were "of the world." The world's treatment of the people of Jesus (vv. 18-21) replicated its treatment of him (vv. 21-25). But the world's rejection of those who confessed Jesus gave his people a mode of communion with the rejected Jesus. Fr. Lindars remarks that "the most impressive feature" of the passage that runs from 15:18 to 16:4a "is the debt it owes to the central themes of Johannine christology."[30]

As a marginalized group, the followers of Jesus had to depend on willing, mutual support and care from their fellow believers. Particularly the community needed to help those whose adherence to Jesus as Messiah brought them into hardship. Those who confessed Christ were upheld against the world's antagonism by the conviction that their faith linked them enduringly with a transcendent power and a victorious Redeemer.

The matter of "abiding" was urgent, for if it took courage to confess Jesus as the Christ, it also took courage to remain in that confession. Hellenistic society exerted a powerful appeal to abandon this new faith. Believers internalized deeply the church's truth-claims. Although the believing community might be of little account in the world's eyes, it saw itself as having been called into being by a divine summons and as being upheld by God.

Thus the two parts of this Second Discourse are related. The first (15:1-

30. Barnabas Lindars, "The Persecution of Christians in John 15:18–16:4a," in W. Horbury and B. McNeil, eds., *Suffering and Persecution in the New Testament* (Cambridge: Cambridge University Press, 1981), 62.

17), which is concerned with Jesus' people remaining in him is not reflective, meditative material about oneness with Christ, worked out in tranquil conditions. It was developed under the pressures that are spoken of in the second part (15:18–16:4a). This second part, when it speaks of life under opposition, does not just commend fortitude, but derives poise and confidence from the discoveries and inner resource that were set forth in the first part.

Who were the opponents of Jesus' people at the time of this Discourse? A modern reader wishes for information that the original readers knew and for kinds of analysis that would come easily to a present-day writer, but were absent from the thinking of the author of this first-century gospel.

As to the identity of the opposition, the terms "the world" or "it," referring to the world, are used nine times in 15:18 and 19. As the johannine community sees it, "the world" hates the believers in Jesus as it hated Jesus; it hates them because by Jesus' choosing them, they no longer belong to it, and it meets their strangeness with its exclusion. Then from 15:20 to 16:3 an undesignated *they* is referred to sixteen times. Clearly it is a Jewish *they. They* persecuted Jesus (v. 20); Jesus spoke to *them* (v. 22); he did *among them* works that no one else had done (v. 24); he cites *their law* against them (v. 25). Only Jews could put believers in Jesus out of the synagogues (16:2). Obviously the near-at-hand opponents were Jews, many of whom had been principal adversaries of Jesus and had now become adversaries of the church.

The author, writing for the late-first-century church, identifies the Jews of his situation with the Jews of Jesus' situation. As Raymond Brown has put it:

> John deliberately uses the same term for the Jewish authorities of Jesus' time and for the hostile inhabitants of the synagogue in his own time. During Jesus' lifetime the chief priests and some of the scribes in the Sanhedrin were hostile to Jesus and had a part in his death — I would judge that bedrock history. Those who have expelled the Johannine Christians and are putting them to death (16:2) are looked on as the heirs of the earlier group. Thus, on the double level on which the Gospel is to be read, "the Jews" refers to both.

The Evangelist's undiscriminating equation of these two groups seems to make all Jews responsible for an act in which some Jews had some part, and it identifies the Jews of the author's and the readers' late-first-century situation with the Jews of Jerusalem some half-century earlier. Brown refers to this habit of mind as "offensive and dangerous generalizing."[31]

Although the Jews are the only group that is clearly identified, antagonism to the revelation brought in Jesus and represented by his people is not depicted as

31. Brown, *Gospel According the John* (Anchor Bible; Garden City: Doubleday, 1966), lxxi-lxxii.

unique to them. They do not stand out as hostile in the midst of an otherwise friendly world. Rather, the smooth passage of the text from *the world* in 15:18-19 to the Jewish "they" of 15:21–16:4a suggests that in the Evangelist's mind the Jews seem to represent or bring to a focus the pervasive enmity of the world. The animosity between the synagogue Jews and the believers in Jesus was so bitter because their relation was so close. The Evangelist does not suggest that Christians were receiving better treatment from the pagan Empire. The forces that were at work in the Jewish opposition were at work also in the alienated *kosmos.*

Jesus begins his new theme by relating the world's response to his people to its response to him. There are five basic affirmations beginning at vv. 18, 20a, 21, 23, and 25. The first and last of these affirmations enclose the passage with the term *hate.* (The Evangelist always uses verbs, saying "to hate" or "to persecute," never the nouns "hatred" or "persecution.")

Jesus opens his new theme bluntly. The world hates his followers as it first hated him. The case of his followers is as his own — *As it is with you* (vv. 19-21), *So it was with me* (vv. 21-25). In the first part of the Discourse (15:1-17), Jesus described the unity between himself and his disciples in terms that gave support and confidence to his followers — terms such as abiding, love, and friendship. Now he makes it clear that their union with him also opens his disciples to the world's hostility.

> If the world hates you,
> be aware that it hated me before it hated you.
> If you belonged to the world,
> the world would love you as its own.
> Because you do not belong to the world,
> but I have chosen you out of the world
> — therefore the world hates you. 15:18-19

This unit begins and ends saying that the world hates both Jesus and his community (vv. 18, 19 and 25). This judgment is surely spoken from the church's experience. The rejection and exclusion of those who confessed Jesus are shared by Jesus himself. Speaking from his own encounter with opposition, suffering and death, Jesus identifies with his people, saying "as it is with you, so it was with me."

The world's hostility goes beyond incomprehension or indifference. The very grain of the world is so set against God that the appearance in the world of the true representative of God (whether Jesus or Jesus' people) comes as a rebuke to the world's self-understanding, which the world meets with passionate and determined rejection. When Jesus' followers approach the world in the name and spirit of Jesus, its response to them replicates its response to him. The world's alienation from God that was first demonstrated in its encounter with Jesus continues in its encounter with Jesus' people. (First John indicates that the later johannine community continued to see itself in the same way: *The reason the world does not know us is that it did not know him,* 1 John 3:1b.)

Jesus says that the world *hates* you (vv. 18, 19) and that it *hates* both himself and his Father (vv. 18, 23, 24). He adds that if his followers were not who they are the world would *love* them. The terms "hate" and "love" remove all middle ground. There is no modulated speech saying: "Some persons who do not share your faith may find no ready-made place for you in the worlds they have made for themselves." This author does not search for convictions that might be shared with pagan moralists nor with Jewish faith and ethics. His extreme circumstances have driven him to see as adversary all that does not arise from recognizing Jesus as the Messiah.

No doubt the background for this stark dualism is the polarization that follows when an eager new faith, with high claims, breaks upon a society. The new movement violates the pragmatic accommodations of thought and conduct by which the society coheres. The culture's existing religious voices satisfy its conscious religious needs. The presence of a strongly defined new group is provocative; it brings into question the very possibility of finding common ground; moderate voices seem unsatisfactory.

Hostility is not the only tone in which, even in the first Christian decades, believers in Jesus addressed the culture. Paul's speech at Athens (in Acts 17), whatever sources lie behind it, seeks a conciliatory tone. 1 Peter credits one's pagan neighbors or family members with ability to recognize the rightness or at least the innocence of law-abiding Christians (see 2:11–3:17). The second-century apologists, such as Justin Martyr, commended Christian faith to philosophers and sought fair treatment for Christians on the basis that they were honest and inoffensive citizens. However, the adversarial relation can be expected when a society (even one as tolerant and ecclectic as the Hellenistic world) has to deal with a faith that is convinced that it cannot be true to itself and at the same time accept assimilation on the terms set by the culture.

In addition to this situational factor, the extreme language of this Second Discourse reflects the Semitic habit of mind described by G. B.

Caird as "hyperbole and absoluteness . . . a tendency to think in extremes without qualification."[32] The Evangelist's style of thought runs to oppositions rather than to a measured, qualified way of seeing things. There are darkness and light, but no half-lit tones in between. Following such a habit of thought and expression, the Evangelist sees the world's hostility to the followers of Jesus as an expression of its hatred of God.

> If you belonged to the world,
> the world would love you as its own.
> Because you do not belong to the world,
> but I have chosen you out of the world,
> — therefore the world hates you. 15:19

Jesus explains more fully: if the community of believers had not been called into being by a transcendent summons, it would be loved, not hated. But as it is, Jesus' people form an alien, exotic presence. They cannot be accommodated, understood, or held in genial affection. They *do not belong* or fit in. As a second-century homily would say of Christians, "They live in their own countries, but only as aliens" (*Letter to Diognetus,* 5.5). The central, determining factor in the new people's life is that it has its origin in an initiative from beyond itself. It is not "of" the world. According to its own foundational story, it is not made by ethnic continuity nor by a contractual act of founding; it is born of God (1:13). It has been *chosen out of the world.* Such language is paradoxical. Those who confess Jesus are persons of and in history, subject to ordinary motives; they bring into their faith the common human material. They are deeply and necessarily involved in the world. A Josephus or a Tacitus could have described the origins of their movement in terms of traceable social forces. Yet, above the web of interrelations that bind believers into the human solidarities of ethnicity, language, discourse, kinship, cultural heritage, or socio-political order, their specialness lies in the deep summons of Jesus. Indeed, in responding to that call, the confessing community reproduces the dynamics of Jesus himself who, being "from above," could not be comprehended by those who were "from below" (8:23). The world, as the Fourth Gospel sees it, is coherent on its own terms. It listens to its own voices (1 John 4:5). It can take in all that shares the fundamental sense that humanity is its own mea-

32. G. B. Caird, *The Language and Imagery of the Bible* (London: Duckworth, 1981), 110.

sure — its own maker and redeemer. But it meets with hostility the implied rebuke of voices that challenge such assumptions. Not long after the Evangelist's time Ignatius of Antioch remarked that the genius of the Christian faith is best expressed when the world is seen as an adversary: "The greatness of Christianity lies in its being hated by the world, not in its being convincing to it" (*Romans* 3:3).[33]

Jesus' words *I chose you* touch deep currents of biblical faith. According to the prophets, Israel is what it is because, in freedom, divine choice was set upon it. In the earlier portion of this Second Discourse Jesus cited the motif of election in speaking of himself and his followers, encouraging them by recalling the strong link that his choosing had forged between himself and them (15:16). Here that same choosing is identified as the source of the conflict between Jesus' followers and the world. Jesus says "I chose you" to the immediate followers he called from everyday occupations to join him. However, the Evangelist no doubt intended that his readers — who were second-generation believers — would hear Jesus speaking to themselves as well. Indeed, over the centuries, Jesus' followers continue to express their conviction that, no matter when or how they come to stand within the community of belief, they did not choose; they were chosen.

> Remember the word that I said to you,
> 'Servants are not greater than their master.'
>   If they persecuted me,
>   they will persecute you;
>   if they kept my word,
>   they will keep yours also. 15:20

Jesus reminds his disciples of something he said earlier. After he had washed the disciples' feet, Jesus explained to them that they, his servants, could not be exempt from ministering roles such as he, their master, had assumed (see 13:16). Now in this Second Discourse, Jesus repeats the words, meaning this time that the disciples cannot expect from the world better treatment than it gave to him. They share with him a vocation which by its nature challenges the world's sense of itself. Jesus' followers may expect that the pattern of response that he provoked will be replicated in them.

33. The quotations from *Diognetus* and Ignatius are from the translation by Cyril Richardson in *Early Christian Fathers* (Library of Christian Classics; Philadelphia: Westminster, 1970), 217, 104.

The voice in the story is that of Jesus, reassuring his followers in advance. Yet in the "layered" character of this Gospel, the voice is also that of the early church trying to establish some meaning for its baffling experience. The Christians have come to a freeing, fulfilling faith. That faith, which, as they saw it, was rooted in the truth of things, was not only for themselves; it was for "whoever" would consent. The way of life and light should be welcomed by those who lived in darkness and death. Christians, moreover, commended their faith by a modest, inoffensive style of life, honorable in their relations with others, and compliant as citizens. Yet even by the first century, they were meeting such hostility that there was real risk in confessing Christ. Such a collective experience is certain to raise in the minds of devout people the anguished question "why?" "why us?" The Evangelist seeks to provide at least a measure of interpreting context.

Jesus repeats his point more insistently: *If they persecuted me, they will persecute you.* By these words, the first-century people of Jesus, in their experience of rejection and suffering, made a connection between themselves and the passion of Jesus. (The same association was being made at about the same time by the writer of 1 Peter, see 4:13-14.)

The word "persecute" *(diōkō)* is used in regard to both Jesus and those who believed in him. What was true of Jesus will also be true of his people. When Christians encounter the world's contempt, they identify with Jesus, by Jesus' invitation. Those seemingly bucolic terms of branches in a vine, with which this Second Discourse opened, speak of union with the Crucified. No "fruit" is borne without pain (12:24-25). The hated and suffering church is an extension in time of the passion of Jesus.

But this parallel between Jesus and the church can be deceptive. Even though the primal rejection of God's revealer is reproduced often, not every rejection of believers by non-believers can be accounted for by the offense of the cross. When a powerful image of a redemptive death is let loose in the world, some persons will *seek* what they take to be a crucifixion. Both wholeness and pathology can derive support from identifying with Jesus' passion, and there is no clear, general rule for distinguishing one from the other.

Yet, the response to Jesus' people is not universally negative. As in his own mission Jesus met with a measure of comprehension and acceptance, the disciples too will find some favorable reception. *If they kept my word* (as some of them did), *they* (or at least some of them) *will keep yours also.* Jesus' words assure his disciples that their witness, even in a sin-blinded world, will not be futile.[34]

The favorable response to both Jesus and the church is expressed in terms of "keeping" a word. It is *my word . . . your word* — Jesus' word and his witnesses' word. (Later, in his prayer, Jesus will describe his disciples as persons who have "kept" the Father's word, 17:6.) He was extended toward the world by his word in such a way that response to it was response to him. So also he speaks of his disciples as a people of the word (cf. 17:20). They engage their society through discourse. They venture themselves on the fragile, yet powerful filament of the spoken word.

With v. 21 the Discourse changes its emphasis. Vv. 18-20 have said that the persecuted followers reproduce in their experience the pattern of Jesus' challenge to the world, and its rejection of him is replicated as it rejects them. Vv. 22-24 speak more directly of Jesus — always, however, in such a way as to illustrate the experience of his followers. The affirmations of vv. 21 and 23 are both followed by "if" clauses, each of which is compound. In vv. 22 and 24, the condition *If I had not . . . they would not,* is answered by *but now they have.*

> But they will do all these things to you on account of my name,
> because they do not know him who sent me. 15:21

As Jesus puts it, the world's hostility to him arises from its fundamental alienation from God: *They do not know him who sent me.* The world perse-

34. Exegetes differ on how verse 20 should be taken. It might be read, as in this study, as "If they persecuted me (as they have) they will persecute you. However [changing tone], if they kept my word (as some of them have), they will keep yours also. Your witness will not be futile." Or it might say "If they persecuted me (as they have), they will persecute you; if they kept my word (and they have not), they will not keep yours either." Brown thinks that a shift from a negative meaning to a positive is "most unlikely." In favor of a shift to the positive, one might argue that the author does from time to time pass from a negative to a positive response to Jesus: see 1:11-13, where the statement of Jesus' rejection is at once qualified, and see the repeated note throughout the Book of Signs that "some refused, but some believed in him." The response to Jesus was not all negative. The existence of the church (the readers of this Gospel) is evidence that there was some positive response to the "word" of Jesus' people. But more conclusively, if there is not a shift to the positive here, Jesus seems, in effect, to be saying "I am sending you out with a 'word' (13:16, 20; 15:16, 27), but you can expect it to be rejected." That is not the tone of Jesus' pledge, and it does not reflect the experience of Jesus or the disciples.

cutes Jesus' followers because they bear his name. The johannine Prologue says of Jesus, the true light, *The world did not know him* (1:10). In the terminology of the Fourth Gospel, "knowing" divine revelation is inward and life-giving; similarly, "not-knowing" is a blinding, destructive condition — an ignorance which is death. Jesus has said that in knowing him one knows both him and the Father (8:19; 14:7; 16:3; 17:3), so in v. 21b he says that ignorance of him is ignorance of the Father also.

> If I had not come and spoken to them,
> they would not have sin;
> but now they have no excuse
> for their sin. 15:22

Jesus' presence exposes the world's enmity to God. "Sin" is not described as an intrinsic tragic flaw which can be understood through analysis of the human material. That way lies despair. Human self-contradiction is known as "sin" when it is seen in relation to divine self-manifestation — in relation to God's revelation in Jesus, the divine act which reveals the world's sin, even as it deals redemptively with it. Although Jesus is not "of" the world, he is yet a full participant in it, representing God to it. In this world which has shut itself off from God, Jesus speaks the true word, interpreting himself, and through interpreting himself, implicitly interpreting all else. The possibility that is opened in Jesus of either new human self-understanding or of deeper self-deception is not described hypothetically, but is spoken of as an actuality — *but now* Jesus has in fact come and spoken. The divine self-revelation intensifies the crisis of history. An innocence that was possible before is no longer possible. The coming of Jesus, which discloses the Father, in the same act discloses humanity's alienation. In a sinful world, the presence of a divine messenger is provocative (cf. 7:7).

When the reality of God is shown, nothing, not even sin, can remain as it had been before. The mystery of evil is brought to fuller actualization. Romano Guardini remarked, "Through the new Revelation the very passions are affected in a new way. Evil, for instance, will acquire, on the level of the new personality, a consciousness, an edge, a seriousness which were previously impossible." Guardini speaks of "the evil of wickedness which only awakens when the magnanimity of God reveals the glory of His kingdom." The divine demonstration of grace, Guardini says, intensifies evil:

> Only in the sphere of Christianity and in humanity's encounter with it does mature evil become possible, which is to earlier evil what the wrong-doing of an adult is to that of a youth or a child. As soon as God entered into history in the Incarnation, ready to take on a destiny from humanity, there appeared a possibility of evil which we can only speak of "in fear and trembling" and must define as the will to destroy God — and together with God — that which comes into humanity from him.[35]

> Whoever hates me
> hates my Father also.
> If I had not done among them the works that no one else did,
> they would not have sin;
> but now they have seen and hated both me and my Father. 15:23-24

Jesus is so united with the Father that his words are God's words and his deeds are God in action. God is the God who is shown in Jesus. The world's response to Jesus is at the same time its response to the Father. *Whoever hates me hates my Father also.* The attitude may be positive; to receive the Son is to receive the one who sent him (13:20); or it may be negative; failure to honor Jesus is failure to honor the one who sent him (5:23).

Divine activity cannot be regarded with indifference. Every prophetic, judging, redeeming initiative on the part of God leaves those to whom it comes either better or worse. *If I had not done among them the works that no one else did, they would not have sin.* What is said of Jesus' words in v. 22 is said of his works in v. 24. They are together the means of his impact on society and history — the words interpreting the acts, and the works actualizing the words; the words are performative, and the works are revelatory. After these works (these enacted words), nothing is as it has been. The unique demonstration of Jesus — the signs of the Messiah — confirmed the alienation of those who saw but did not comprehend or believe.

But now they have seen and hated both me and my Father: Jesus and the Father have been *seen* and *hated* (v. 24). To hate having never seen could be simple prejudgment made in ignorance; but to have seen and hated is a responsible determination, evidencing deep hostility.

To have "seen the Father" is a paradoxical expression. The Fourth

35. Romano Guardini, *The World and the Person* (Chicago: Regnery, 1965), 167-68.

Gospel, following the Hebrew scriptures, is clear that God cannot be seen (Exod. 33:20, and see John 1:18; 6:26). However, Jesus has so manifested God that whoever has seen the visible Jesus (even unbelievers) has through him seen the invisible Father (14:9 and 1:18). Yet, in the many-sided way in which this Gospel uses "see," the world has seen and not seen Jesus (cf. 9:39-41). Jesus has been present in the world, and the world has seen him. Yet it has not seen him insofar as it has not recognized the Father in him. It has reduced him to its own terms, and then not been impressed by what it has seen. With regard to observable evidence, Jesus' opponents have seen what his followers have also seen, but they have "seen and hated." The Fourth Gospel poses the opposition sharply, but it leaves unaddressed the mystery of why some of the human response goes one way and some the other.

> It was to fulfill the word that is written in their law,
> 'They have hated me without a cause.' 15:25

Jesus accounts for his rejection by his people by citing "their law" against them. (The Evangelist, speaking in his own voice, cited Isaiah to the same effect in 12:38-40.) In using the phrase "their law" the Jesus of the narrative puts a distance between himself and the Jewish people. He speaks as though he were not a Jew speaking to Jews. At this point, the Evangelist, as Raymond Brown puts it, is "speaking the language of the Johannine Christian for whom the law is no longer his own but is the hallmark of another religion."[36]

The quoted words (which are not cited exactly) may be from either Ps. 35:19 or Ps. 69:4. The latter may be in mind, for it depicts the suffering of an innocent person, and this Psalm (although not this verse) is cited of Jesus in other first-century Christian writings (see in this Gospel John 2:17; 19:28-30; elsewhere, see Acts 1:20; Rom. 11:9-10; 15:3), suggesting that it had become a common source among believers for biblical testimonies to Jesus. The quoted words are spoken by the "I" of the Psalm, who (by the typological reading of the early Christians) is Jesus — as Jesus' opponents are made the "they" of the quotation. As the writer of the Fourth Gospel sees it, these ancient words about the rejection of one who has given no cause for rejection are fulfilled in Jesus. The johannine church no doubt read itself into these words as well.

36. Raymond Brown, *The Community of the Beloved Disciple* (New York: Paulist, 1979), 41.

The terms in which the Evangelist speaks of persecution resemble the terms in which it is spoken of in the mission charge of Matthew 10:17-25 and in the Markan "Little Apocalypse," especially 13:9-13. Several ideas appear both in these Synoptic sources and in this Discourse:

Jesus predicts persecution.
His followers will be hated because of him.
Servants are not more important than their masters.
The Spirit will bear witness with the church.
Jesus' followers' faith may be "shaken."
They may be expelled from the synagogue and put to death.

Raymond Brown remarks that "no other long section of Johannine discourse resembles a section of Synoptic discourse so closely."[37] The resemblances are in words and phrases which may or may not indicate literary indebtedness. It may simply be that conditions of extremity brought together similar expressions of response in two first-century Christian traditions.

In the context of the world's rejection of both himself and his people, Jesus speaks again of the Paraclete. In the face of opposition, Christians will, through the Divine Spirit, find courage to bear testimony. Their testimony will be effective because the disciples will speak by *the Spirit of truth who comes from the Father.*

When the Advocate comes,
  whom I will send to you from the Father,
  the Spirit of truth
  who comes from the Father,
he will testify on my behalf.
You also are to testify
  because you have been with me from the beginning. 15:26-27

The Spirit *coming from the Father* introduces a new term. The Greek word used for "comes" is *ekporeuomai,* which has often been translated "proceeding." The term was to have a long, contention-ridden history in theological discussion, as the intra-trinitarian "procession" of the Spirit became a technical and a divisive term. The doctrinal controversies of the early church were conducted in terminology that was heavily johannine, and expres-

37. Brown, *John,* 695.

sions such as the "begetting" of the Son or the "proceeding" of the Spirit became the vocabulary of dogma. However in the Gospel itself, the term "proceeds" (which is used only here) is not describing the interior economy of the trinity (an impossible idea for a first-century writer), but the word is used to secure the reality and authority of the Spirit in the very life and activity of God. The Spirit is from the Father, as Jesus is from the Father.

The Fourth Gospel records no Pentecost fifty days after the resurrection. Jesus bestows the Spirit on the day of the Resurrection (20:22-23). But from the johannine point of view (no less than from the Lukan) the Spirit has a *coming*. Like Jesus and his "hour," the Spirit "comes" as a strange new power. Jesus describes an Advent of the Spirit.

The Discourse introduces here the idea that the Paraclete is witness: *He will testify on my behalf.* This function of the Spirit falls into a johannine context of persons and things that bear witness in behalf of God. The Greek verb is the strong word *martyrein.* Jesus' words and works are witness (vv. 22-24), Israel's law is witness (v. 25), the Paraclete is witness (v. 26), as are Jesus' followers (v. 27).

This Second Discourse says that the Paraclete will witness as Jesus has witnessed and will witness (18:37). Specifically, it is the Spirit's role to bear witness to Jesus. The work of Jesus is foundational; the Paraclete will have no independent or different thing to say. But what Jesus has done is made effective by the Spirit. In the Synoptic Gospels the Spirit is spoken of as prompting Jesus' followers when they face crisis: *When they bring you before the synagogues, the rulers, and the authorities, do not worry about how you are to defend yourselves or what you are to say; the Holy Spirit will teach you at that very hour what you ought to say* (Luke 12:11-12). Evidently Christians' awareness of the Spirit was drawn forth by the community's encounter with opposition. As the believers in Jesus met the enmity of the world, they found themselves supported and their words made effective by the nearness and power of God.

Speaking directly to his disciples, Jesus says: *You also are to testify because you have been with me from the beginning.* The Spirit and the believing people are coupled — perhaps suggesting the principle of Jewish law that two witnesses were required to establish the truth of a judgment. Testimony is given by the Spirit and by the community — the intangible, invisible, inaudible Spirit witnessing in and through the historical, societal, verbal and vocal church.

But priority belongs to the Spirit, as was remarked by the missionary statesman Bishop Newbigin:

> It is important to note what is not said. It is not said that the Spirit will help the disciples to bear witness. That would make the action of the disciples primary and that of the Spirit auxiliary.
>
> What is said is that the Spirit will bear witness and that — secondarily — the disciples are witnesses. . . . It is the Spirit who is sovereign. The promise to the community of the disciples is not that they will have the Spirit at their disposal to help them in their work. . . . The Spirit is not the church's auxiliary. The promise made here is not to the Church which is powerful and "successful" in a worldly sense. It is made to the Church which shares the tribulation and the humiliation of Jesus, the tribulation which arises from faithfulness to the truth in a world which is dominated by the lie. The promise is that, exactly in this tribulation and humiliation, the mighty Spirit of God will bear his own witness to the crucified Jesus as Lord and Giver of Life.[38]

The disciples, Jesus says, are qualified as witnesses because they have been with him *from the beginning* — that is, from the start of his public ministry. (See the criteria for one who might replace Judas in Acts 1:21-22.) Jesus and his community together form an identifiable event in history. The disciples, as part of the inaugural mission, are essential, foundational witness-figures. The church in every time and place is *built upon the foundation of the apostles and prophets* (Eph. 2:20). The struggling first-century community of believers, facing a hostile society, was called to do the thing which Jesus' people must do in every situation: to bear witness. Fundamentally, to give witness does not mean to speak words, nor show numerical growth, so much as to render a faithful manner of life. To cite Newbigin once more: "The primary reference of the word *martyria* in the history of the Church is not to proclamation but to suffering."[39] When the church can do nothing else, it can bear witness. When it ceases to bear witness, it forfeits the name of church.

The Discourse to this point has spoken in general terms, but at 16:1 it becomes particular and close-at-hand, saying "*you*." The author is seeking to bring insight and courage to a community in shock. This exhortation lets modern-day readers understand the threat under which those first-century Christians were living.

38. Newbigin, *Light,* 206-7.

39. Newbigin, *Light,* 206.

I have said these things to you
to keep you from stumbling. 16:1

Jesus explains why he has been speaking as he has. *I have said these things to you to keep you from stumbling:* "Stumbling" is the Greek verb *skandalizō,* which might be transliterated "to keep you from being 'scandalized'" — a metaphor which one commentator renders "tripped up" or "staggered."[40] The term has immediate reference to the disciples forsaking Jesus in the testing that is upon them (see 16:32). (In Matthew's account of Jesus and his disciples leaving the Mount of Olives prior to Jesus' arrest, Jesus uses this same verb: *You will all be made to stumble (skandalizō) because of me,* Matt. 26:31). Jesus seeks to give his followers a sure step in the events that are about to break.

The same words, however, may refer also to the first-century johannine community which is in danger of losing its footing and stumbling into unbelief. The *Didache,* a Christian document from the late first or early second century, warns its readers that in a coming conflict, "Many will fall away [be scandalized] and perish, but those who endure in their faith will be saved" (*Did.,* 16:5).[41] The counsel on the world's hostility in this second part of the Second Discourse was a tract for first-century Christians making their way on an uncertain and obstructed path.

The indefinite expression *I have said these things* doubtless refers at least to the Discourse since 15:18. But if the johannine Jesus speaks in order to keep Christians from staggering, such an intention makes a reader attach additional significance to the emphases of the first half of the Discourse, 15:1-17. The "abiding" that was spoken of in 15:4-10 is an urgent matter. The conditions under which the people of Jesus believe, love and obey are very difficult; remaining in the Messiah is not a passive, but a courageous and an intentional act. Those branches that did not abide in the vine (15:6) were not just careless. They were ordinary, believing persons, under great pressures. Being fools for Christ's sake simply, at some point, became more than they could bear. The entire Second Discourse should be read as an encouragement to constancy.

They will put you out of the synagogues. 16:2a

40. G. H. C. Macgregor, *The Gospel of John* (Garden City: Doubleday Doran, 1929), 295.

41. Richardson, ed., *Early Christian Fathers,* 179.

The Evangelist's "they" clearly refers to Jewish adversaries. The term *put you out of the synagogues (aposynagōgos)* appears in two other places in the Fourth Gospel, and nowhere else in the New Testament. (1) In 9:22, in the story of the man born blind, the author comments that *The Jews had already agreed that anyone who confessed Jesus to be the Messiah would be put out of the synagogue.* (2) In 12:42 the Evangelist refers to Jews who believed in Jesus secretly, but did not confess him *for fear that they would be put out of the synagogue.* In both of these incidents, the story of Jesus is told in a way that reflects the situation of the church a generation later. Jews who confess Jesus as Messiah risk expulsion from the synagogue.

Reading 16:2 against this background, it seems that by the time of writing, at least some persons who confessed Jesus as Messiah had in fact been expelled from certain synagogues. The circumstances seem to be told here by one who understands that the believers in Jesus were, for their part, willing to remain identified with the synagogue, but they were thrust out of it. But the events are shrouded in uncertainty. It may be sufficient for present purposes to say that over a period of years in the late first century the Jewish community increasingly found it impossible to contain this impulsive and unaccountably popular Jesus-movement.

Johannine scholarship, for some years, has said (to a great extent following J. Louis Martyn's work, *History and Theology in the Fourth Gospel*)[42] that this reference to the expulsion of the Christians from the ancient worship of God places this Second Discourse close in time to the Jewish community's addition (around 85 CE) to the Benedictions of the synagogue liturgy of a prayer against "deviators" — a prayer which is often taken to have been worded so as to exclude the Christians.

Martyn's work was one of the most productive recent contributions to johannine studies. It gave particularity and context to the break between the church and the synagogue. It urged persuasively that an argument with the synagogue shadows the polemic portions of the Book of Signs. Martyn's insights gathered consent and stirred discussion. However, some of his proposals have been found to contain more complexities than were apparent when his work first appeared. The issues are not simple. How large a factor the wording of the synagogue prayers played in excluding the Christians and how local or widespread such acts of exclu-

42. J. Louis Martyn, *History and Theology in the Fourth Gospel* (New York: Harper and Row, 1968; 3rd ed., 2003). The excluding prayer is found in C. K. Barrett, *The New Testament Background: Selected Documents* (rev. ed.; San Francisco: Harper and Row, 1987), 211. Brown, *The Gospel according to John*, 691-92, contains a summary of the evidence from the brief early period when there was some specifically Jewish persecution of Christians.

sion were are matters that continue to be discussed by informed scholars.[43] Methodological question is raised as to how important (or even how possible) it is to fix a reference in a literary document to a definite point in history. In the inquiry that continues to be made into the separation of the Christians from the Jewish community, Martyn's work remains a point of reference, but it does not carry the authority that it once did.

> Indeed, an hour is coming
> when those who kill you
> will think that by doing so
> they are offering worship to God. 16:2b

The phrase *the hour is coming* has the effect of associating Jesus' followers with Jesus himself. As there is an "hour" of severe opposition (or of glory in and beyond the opposition) which is climactic for Jesus' vocation under God (13:1), the followers of Jesus also have their *hour.* The knowledge that Jesus' *hour* was his redemptive death (12:24) may have upheld believers as conflict and even death became a possibility for them.

This passage speaks of a terrible thing: to kill one's opponents, thinking that doing so is an act of sacrificial worship *(latreia)* of God. Although there is evidence of early Jewish hostility to Christians, the Jewish authorities were not in a legal position to take life (18:31). An indirect action is probably referred to. Under the Empire all persons were required to take part in the worship of the Emperor or be liable to severe punishment. This participation in the cult of the Emperor could be carried out by a token act of homage, as much civic as religious, which was easily included alongside other casual allegiances by most members of eclectic Hellenistic society. The loyal citizen simply went to a Temple and offered a pinch of incense to the Emperor as divine. But Jews, with their exclusive faith in the one God, could not take part in such worship. They had gained for themselves a legal exemption from the cult of the Emperor. As long as those who believed Jesus to be the Messiah were within the synagogue, their conscientious refusal to engage in this unacceptable act was protected under the toleration that had been extended to Jews. But as the people of Jesus became sepa-

43. A recent statement on the historical and philosophical issues that have emerged since Martyn's work is in chapter 15, "The Expulsion from the Synagogue: The Tale of a Theory," of Robert Kysar, *Voyages with John: Charting the Fourth Gospel* (Waco: Baylor University Press, 2005), 237-46.

rated from the synagogue, they could no longer claim that legal protection, and they were exposed to real jeopardy. Very likely the two elements in v. 2 — *they will put you out of the synagogues* and *they will kill you* — are connected, and Jewish action was thought to be responsible for opening believers in Christ to this peril.

> And they will do this
> because they have not known the Father or me. 16:3

The Evangelist speaks of an ignorance on the part of his readers' opponents — an ignorance which is fatal. (The ignorance of both Jesus and the Father which is spoken of here echoes 8:19b in the Book of Signs, 14:7 in the First Discourse, and v. 21 above.) *They have not known* — and yet they act. When the author speaks of such actions, rooted in such unknowing, he opens his description, in principle, to the world. He began by speaking of "the world" as the opponent (15:18-19). Then his focus turned to the immediate antagonists who were the Jews of the synagogue. But now he concludes, identifying the problem as one of ignorance and unbelief — and hence as an issue for humanity, not in any exclusive way for one part of humanity. As D. Moody Smith has said, in the Evangelist's mind, "the Jews have become representatives of the world."[44]

Part of the terror of persecution is the ideological certainty without which it would falter. Persecutors must support their actions by a sense of reality which persuades them that the greater ends they serve justify bringing suffering and even death on others. The minds of persecutors reduce opponents to non-persons, and God is brought in as an ultimate sanction. *They have not known.* There are many things which a persecutor must determine not to know. This Evangelist writes out of a time when those who put Christians to death thought their actions to be the equivalent of making a sacrifice to God. A modern-day reader can legitimately extend the author's words to speak of morally distorted self-justification by persons who have taken part in ideologically supported persecution at any period and place.

> But I have said these things to you
> so that when their hour comes
> you may remember that I told you about them. 16:4a

44. D. Moody Smith, *John* (Proclamation Commentaries; Philadelphia: Fortress, 1976), 46.

At a surface level, this concluding remark of the Second Discourse says that Jesus speaks in advance so that his words can be recalled when future events bear them out. As future crises unfold, Jesus' followers will remember that he had spoken about them. However, this prediction by Jesus should be understood as, at the same time, an effort by the Evangelist to help first-century Christians to find courage in their extreme situation. The "then" of which Jesus speaks is the present time of the Evangelist and his readers. In the Gospel narrative, Jesus was about to be taken into custody and placed on trial and put to death. The forces that were at work in his critical moment were also at work in the crisis of the first-century community of faith.

If Jesus has his "hour," so does the opposition: *when their hour comes.* (Compare "your hour" in Luke 22:53.) But the first-century believers could meet the *hour* of their powerful adversaries, supported by their faith-informed memory of Jesus' passion. They could see those terrible events in a way in which they could not have been seen at the time they took place. As C. K. Barrett puts it: "The 'hour' of Jesus appears to mean his failure but is in fact his exaltation and glory; that of his enemies appears to mean their victory but is in fact their defeat."[45]

In the lectionary. The Revised Common Lectionary makes no use of this second half of the Second Discourse (15:18–16:4a). Perhaps the lectionary-makers were thinking of fairly comfortable Christian congregations, most of which would find this material about being persecuted for Christ's sake remote from their experience. The church in many places is not hated by the world, but is quite amiably accommodated to it.

Or it may be that the lectionary-makers feared that since among religious traditions, memories are long, preachers might make the text an occasion to speak about the very brief period during which some Jewish parties held power and did engage in some hostile acts towards some followers of Jesus. The Christian memory, when it thinks of persecution in connection with Jewish-Christian relations, should be haunted by the long and shameful period during which Christians were the persecutors.

Is the omission of these verses best for an ecumenical, widely used lectionary, created in a century which has been called "a century of martyrs"? There are in the present generation many persons of faith in many parts of the world who would quickly identify with this passage about enduring the world's hatred. They live where it lives.

Through the witness of this passage, which connects affliction and martyr-

45. Barrett, *Gospel,* 485.

dom with Jesus' passion and with the ministry of the Spirit, those Christian congregations which are not themselves oppressed and persecuted might be enabled to identify with those which are — or indeed, to identify in Christ's name with oppressed persons of any persuasion who are anywhere made to suffer for any reason.

While no part of 15:18–16:4a is appointed by the lectionary for regular reading at the Sunday eucharist, the passage stands as an integral part of the Farewell chapters, and it can be drawn on by preachers as circumstances make its content relevant. When hostility to the community of faith, of which this passage speaks, breaks out, as it can and does, these verses become a pertinent choice for reading, reflection and preaching. They will become relevant when Christians risk courageously to combat the injustices of their society and side with the poor, the hungry, the powerless and the oppressed.

For preachers who are guided by the ecumenical lectionary, this passage, even though it is not included among the appointed readings, can be important, for it comprises the second half of a literary unit whose first half is included among the liturgical readings. This second half of the Second Discourse supplies knowledge of the situation which gave rise to the content of the first half — the selection of its themes and the urgency and realism of their treatment. The theological themes of 15:1-17 are not quiet, contextless meditations about vines and branches or about abiding in the friendship of Jesus, and they are not treated with integrity if they are preached on as though they were. Rather they were themes forged in the conditions of extremity that are indicated by 15:18–16:4a. They offer a basis for courage to Christians who were facing life and death.

---

6. The Third Discourse: Joy Out of Sorrow (16:4b-33)

In this Discourse the Evangelist is clearly speaking to a community in distress. He mentions *sorrow* (16:6), *weeping and mourning* (16:20), *pain* (16:20, 22), and *persecution* (16:33). The text does not say what has occasioned the readers' trauma, who their adversaries were, what form the hostility took, or what tensions the encounter with opposition produced in the faith community. The writer does not need to describe what his readers all know.

The johannine community seems to have found its way through its separation from the synagogue. The crisis that was the preoccupying issue at the time of the Second Discourse is not mentioned again. The believers in Jesus now face a diffuse opposition from a world which takes pleasure when they are made to suffer (16:8-10, 20). This perverse world needs to be convinced of its wrongness — a transformation that divine power will enlist to bring about (16:8-11).

The church is facing adversity, but the Evangelist does not say that the believers' situation replicates Jesus' passion — the thought idiom by which he interpreted the community's distress in his Second Discourse (15:18–16:4a). Rather, the author assures the community of Jesus that in its conflict with the world it does not stand alone. The Paraclete will be sent from God to convince the world of its condition (16:8-11) and to inform the church's own life (16:12-15).

As the Discourse develops, the emotional tone changes. The Evangelist leads the community beyond its present conflicts, speaking of *your advantage* (16:7), your *joy* (16:20), indeed, your *complete joy* (16:24), and your *peace* (16:33). Jesus promises that *Your hearts will rejoice* (16:22), for in him the hostile world has already met its match (16:33).

This Third Discourse (like the First Discourse, and unlike the Second) is full of predictive terms. More than thirty main clauses speak of the future.

Jesus says of himself *I am going to the Father* (16:5). And of the Paraclete he says, *I will send the Paraclete* (16:7), who *will guide you into truth* (16:13). *She will glorify me* (16:14). *She will take what is mine and declare it to you* (16:13-14). Of his people he says *You will no longer see me, and you will see me* (16:16). *You will weep, but your pain will turn to joy* (16:20). *I will see you again* (16:22). And *You will ask in my name* (16:26). Jesus says that his followers, in the midst of what is, should live for what he declares will come to be.

In these words, which are presented as words of Jesus, a first-century writer is assuring his readers that although events in the present or the near future may test them severely, the adversity they face is penultimate. When Jesus tells his disciples that they live under the sign of his victory over the world (16:33), the Evangelist is at the same time calling the believers of his own day to be confident as they enter a new and bewildering life outside the synagogue and face-to-face with an inhospitable world.

The many parallels between the Third Discourse and the First suggest that when the author composed this third farewell speech, circumstances had brought the thought patterns of his first draft back to his mind. A reader may notice the twin motifs of Jesus' departure and the disciples' sorrow. Jesus again says often that he is leaving, and he implies that his followers are facing a new and unknown situation (as in vv. 12-13 and 16-24).

In addition to an overall similarity and intent, the two discourses have in common:[1]

- The disciples question Jesus about where he is going (13:36; 14:5 and 16:17).
- There are two Paraclete passages in each of these Discourses (14:15-17, 26 and 16:7-11, 13-15).
- There is a play between the disciples seeing Jesus after his resurrection and a future seeing (14:19 and 16:16-17).
- Jesus promises that the disciples can ask in his name, and they will be heard (14:13-14 and 16:23-24).
- Jesus bestows his gift of peace (14:27 and 16:33).
- Jesus assures the disciples of the direct love of the Father (14:21, 23 and 16:27).
- Jesus predicts that his followers will desert him (13:38 and 16:32).

---

1. Raymond Brown, *The Gospel according to John* (2 vols., Anchor Bible; Garden City: Doubleday, 1966-70), 589-93. In Chart I Brown shows the very extensive parallels between 16:4b-33 and 13:31–14:31. A simpler list is in Robert Kysar, *John, the Maverick Gospel* (rev. ed.; Louisville: Westminster/John Knox, 1993), 235.

This Discourse, like the others, is markedly christological. The situation of believers is interpreted under the overarching story of Jesus. Barrett remarks that the thought of the passage "is theologically rather than circumstantially motivated."[2] The going of Jesus is linked with his prior coming, holding together his origin and his destiny. He who came from the Father into the world is returning to the one who sent him (16:5, 27-28, 30). As in the First Discourse, when Jesus speaks of his going, he does not picture the place to which he goes nor use spatial images of descent and ascent. The departing Jesus speaks less of his own destination than he does of the disciples he leaves behind in an uneasy relation with the world.

The Discourse moves in thought episodes:

- *vv. 4b-11:* Jesus' departure brings the Paraclete, who has direct dealing with the uncomprehending world, which she will convince of its wrong-headedness.
- *vv. 12-15:* Although Jesus' teaching ends, the Paraclete succeeds him, guiding the church into its own truth.
- *vv. 16-24:* The disciples can expect testing, but in "a little while" they will again see Jesus, and they will rejoice.
- *vv. 25-28:* The indirect, obscure speech that Jesus has used will be replaced by plain speech.
- *vv. 29-33:* Jesus, at his hour of crisis, is cut off even from his disciples, but the Father is always near to him.

1. Jesus' Departure Brings the Paraclete (16:4b-7)

I did not say these things to you from the beginning,
  because I was with you.
But now I am going to him who sent me;
  yet none of you asks me, 'Where are you going?'
But because I have said these things to you,
  sorrow has filled your hearts. 16:4b-6

Jesus speaks of his own speaking as he had previously (in 13:19; 14:29; 15:11, 17; 16:1, 4), and as he will again (in 16:16-19, 25-26 and 17:13). He explains

2. C. K. Barrett, *The Gospel According to St. John* (2nd ed., Philadelphia: Westminster, 1978), 484.

why he has not said earlier what he is saying now: *I did not say these things to you from the beginning.*

Similar reference by a speaker to why he speaks as he does is frequent in the johannine epistles: *We are writing these things so that your joy may be complete* (1 John 1:4). *I write to you, little children, because . . .* (2:12-14, six times in three verses, and also 2:26; 5:13).

When a writer alerts his readers to what is being said and how they should hear it, he sounds like a teacher explaining himself. By the time this last discourse was composed, had the Evangelist taken on the manner of a Christian catechist — a manner which continues (whether by the same writer or by someone who has adopted the manner) in the First Epistle?

The *these things* of v. 4b refers to things the writer is about to tell his readers, as the *these things* of v. 4a *(I have said these things to you)* referred to what Jesus had just said. Thus, as we observed in chapter 3, a reader encounters here a "literary seam." V. 4a marks the conclusion of the Second Discourse, while v. 4b marks the opening of the Third Discourse.

Jesus says that he has not spoken to his followers from the start of his ministry as he would speak now *because I was with you.* While he was a public figure, Jesus spoke with principal reference to the situation that was created by his presence. His disciples attracted little attention (perhaps they were hardly noticed; see 18:8-9), while opposition was drawn principally to him. Jesus was his disciples' "advocate" — their encourager, teacher, guide, and protector. *But now. . . .*

But now I am going: Jesus' *going* which he has spoken of as future (see 7:33) has become *now.* One might paraphrase: "But now, since I am going, and know it, I must interpret my departure to you, lest the stark news that I am leaving bring you to despair."

Jesus' words *I am going* express his initiative; his going is in his own hands. Yet he always acts in relation to another; he is returning to *him who sent me.* He will be reassociated with the one from whom he has come and whose sending gave him his mission. The organizing "coming from/going to" motif of johannine christology is stated here, and it returns in 16:28. It begins and ends the Third Discourse.

Jesus' words *Yet none of you asks me, "Where are you going?"* raise a critical issue, for Peter asked this question in these very words in 13:36, and the question was also asked by Thomas in 14:5. This discrepancy is one piece of evidence that 13:31–16:33 was not originally a continuous passage, but its principal units (13:31–14:31; 15:1–16:4a; 16:4b-33) were composed independently. When the separately written drafts were put together, the text suffered from editorial inattention.[3]

Jesus' comment *none of you asks me* tells the disciples what they might have asked, but did not. Although only Jesus speaks, his words about the disciples' unasked question give the passage a feeling of dialogue.

The announcement by Jesus that he is leaving saddens his followers. *Because I have said these things to you, sorrow (lypē) has filled your heart.* The disciples' sorrow seems to create an emotional barrier so that they canot ask Jesus the obvious question as to where he is going (v. 5).

Rather than speaking of where he is going, Jesus tells the disciples of the Paraclete, who will come to them. The Paraclete is familiar to readers of the present text from both the First Discourse (14:15-17, 25-26) and the Second (15:26-27). (Nothing that is said in chapter 16 seems to assume that a reader would have encountered the Discourses that now stand earlier in the text.)

This passage forms the most extended and complex of the johannine Paraclete passages. It must be considered two passages — 16:7-11, which speaks about the Paraclete and the world, and 16:12-15, which speaks of the Paraclete and Jesus' people.

Jesus first emphasizes that the Paraclete will come because he himself is leaving.

> Nevertheless I tell you the truth:
> it is to your advantage that I go away,
>   for if I do not go away,
>   the Advocate will not come to you;
>   but if I go,
>   I will send her to you. 16:7

Jesus' opening words *Nevertheless I tell you the truth* are a claim to attention — more emphatic than the familiar johannine *Very truly I tell you.* If what Jesus is about to say is to overcome his followers' distress, heed must be paid. More profoundly, the expression *I tell you the truth* alerts Jesus'

3. See the discussion of these structural matters in chapter 3, "About the Discourses," pp. 64-71 above.

hearers to the revelatory character of the words he will speak about his departure and the Spirit's coming.[4]

Jesus tells his followers that it is to their advantage *(sympherō)* that he go away. When he is gone, they will live in a new age. (Recalling the two levels at which the Evangelist writes, the emphatic *to you* which concludes the last two clauses of 16:7 may be read to include both Jesus' disciples at the Supper and the later johannine church which has come through its own separation trauma and is living under new conditions.) The superiority of the new aeon lies in a new mode of divine presence and activity through the Advocate, whose coming to the disciples will follow from Jesus' departure to the Father.

Although the disciples say nothing, Jesus speaks as though they did not want him to leave. He speaks, first negatively and then positively, of his going and the Advocate's coming:

> For if I do not go away,
> the Advocate will not come to you;
> but if I go,
> I will send her to you. 16:7

The Fourth Evangelist does not usually describe redemptive acts as sequential. They are more likely to combine: the cross is the glory; the Spirit is given on Easter; Jesus' going is his coming; the Spirit is Jesus' other self; to see the Son is to see the Father. In this place, however, Jesus says that the Advocate's "coming" depends on his own "going" and his "sending." This dependence of the Spirit on the completion of Jesus' mission was anticipated in 7:39 in which the Evangelist spoke of a time when *as yet there was not Spirit (oupō gar ēn pneuma), because Jesus was not yet glorified.*[5]

This sequence no doubt reflects early Christian experience.[6] The

4. Rudolf Schnackenburg, *The Gospel According to St. John* (3 vols., New York: Crossroad, 1968, 1980, 1982), 3.127. Barnabas Lindars, *The Gospel of John* (New Century Bible Commentary; Grand Rapids: Eerdmans, 1972), 499, says that Jesus' introductory words imply that what he is about to tell his followers "is an imparting of the truth, an exposition of the plan of God, an instruction of the same order as the Spirit's future guidance."

5. 7:39 is an explanatory footnote by the Evangelist. One might translate the expression *oupō gar ēn pneuma* as "The Spirit was not yet" or "It was not yet Spirit."

6. Other forms of New Testament thought say in their different ways that the Spirit is subsequent to and dependent on Christ. Acts makes it sequential as it tells of the disciples' wait for the Spirit whose dramatic coming followed Jesus' departure (1:4-5, ch. 2). Paul de-

Spirit-informed and Spirit-supported life was only possible for the disciples in full awareness of Jesus' death and resurrection. Only after the shattering of old conceptions and after unprecedented and unexpected events had made their impact could new understandings be built around existence as reconstituted. (The writer may imply, somewhat secondarily, that only after the first-century believers had become independent of the synagogue could they discover the immediacy of the divine presence in which they lived.) The new understandings, when they come, are the gift of the new situation; Jesus when he is gone will send the Spirit.

Lancelot Andrewes (1555-1626), the Jacobean English bishop, scholar and preacher, in a sermon on John 16:7, dramatized this moment, saying in his characteristic, almost "telegraphic" style:

> This coming, or not coming, depends on Christ's going, or his stay. If Christ go not He cometh not. If Christ go, He cometh. Seeing then ye shall be losers by my stay, and gainers by my going, be not for my stay. My stay will deprive you of Him. Be not against my going, my absence will procure you Him. I love you not so evil as to stay with you for your hurt. Be not grieved, be not against that which is for your good.[7]

Jesus says in v. 7 that he will send the Spirit. In the First Discourse he said that the Spirit would be given by the Father in answer to his request (14:16) or in his name (14:26). In either way of putting the matter, the Paraclete is not generated by human initiative, but stands on God's side of things and engages human life out of divine freedom.

Vv. 8-15 set forth the mission of this new divine presence, first in relation to the world (vv. 8-11), and then in relation to the community of faith in Jesus (vv. 12-15).

---

scribes an order, but he makes no point of time. In Gal. 4:4-6 he speaks of God sending forth his Son and, because of the familial relation established in him, it is the Spirit of his Son.

7. Sermon IV in the Whitsunday series, preached in 1611, in Andrewes, *Ninety-six Sermons* (Library of Anglo-Catholic Theology; London: Parker, 1841-43), 3.165 (= http://anglicanhistory.org/lact/andrewes/v3/whitsunday1611.html). The passage that is quoted here contains 88 words, 71 of which contain only a single syllable, and none is longer than two syllables. Andrewes's staccato style (of which this passage is not an extreme example) gives evidence of a mind working at top speed and impatient with the connective tissue of more leisurely prose.

2. The Paraclete and the World (16:8-11)

When Jesus is gone, his disciples will be more exposed to the world, and he assures them that they will not face it alone. (The Evangelist, whose mind is working at two levels, implies that after the first-century believers in Jesus are no longer within the synagogue, but are face to face with the world, they will find divine support.) The Paraclete will present the case of God and of the believing community against the world. While the Advocate is teacher and guide of Jesus' people, she turns to the unbelieving world a face of severity. The Spirit will have dealings with the world concerning *sin, righteousness, and judgment* — three things about which the world needs to know and which it thinks it knows on its own. Each is mentioned in v. 8; then in vv. 9-11 each is connected with an aspect of the redemptive drama.

The encounter between the Spirit and the world is described in terms drawn from law and courts: *prove wrong, righteousness* (or *justice*), *judgment,* and *condemn* (so also *testify* in 15:26). The word "paraclete" *(paraklētos)* itself was associated with courts, where a "paraclete" was one who contended in behalf of another or who took the part of another in a proceeding of law.

Many devout readers over the generations (influenced no doubt by 1 John 2:1, *If anyone sin, we have a Paraclete with the Father,* and by their own felt inadequacies) have taken the Paraclete to be one who pleads the human case with God — something like a sinner's counsel for the defense. In this passage, however, the Paraclete is not a defender of believers, but a prosecutor carrying God's case against a world which is in the wrong. In this passage, as C. F. D. Moule put it, the Paraclete "is viewed as the Vindicator or Champion of the cause of God, as the Advocate, pleading God's cause against disobedience everywhere."[8] As Jesus has borne witness for God and against the world (8:45-46; 9:35-41; 18:37-38), so the Paraclete represents God, contending against a misguided world, acting as "a judge and prosecuting counsel in one."

The Evangelist may have had in mind a trial, such as had sometimes been portrayed by Jewish prophets and apocalyptists, with the nations arraigned before God, often in a cosmic setting. In Amos 1 and 2, the nations, including Israel and Judah, are judged by standards of natural justice. Perhaps the most vivid and extended law

8. C. F. D. Moule, "The Individualism of the Fourth Gospel," *NTS* 5 (1962), 182.

court scenario in the Bible is the opening of Isaiah, in which heaven and earth are asked to be witnesses as God, through the prophet, accuses the nations, his case coming to its climax as testimony is brought against Israel (Isa. 1:1-20). The apocalyptic *Book of Enoch* sets a scene in which the world is on trial, and Enoch acts as something like a court stenographer. In the Christian Scriptures, Matthew 24 depicts the nations assembled before the throne of judgment. In Romans 1, in a law-court setting, both Jews and Gentiles are found guilty before God.

This Discourse, although it uses the language of law, does not picture God's case against the world as though it were presented at a divine court nor a final assize. Rather, the condemnation of the world and the vindication of God are *now* — in the glorification of Jesus, in the ministry of the Paraclete, and in the witness of Jesus' people. In the world's encounter with the community which bears Christ's word, final things are met and ultimate determinations are rendered.

Legal terms are common in the Fourth Gospel — terms such as: accuse, condemn, confess, convict, deny, judge, judgment, lie, prove wrong, tell the truth, testify or bear witness. As Jesus' career builds, John the Baptist (1:6-7; 5:33; 10:41) and the scriptures (5:39-45) are cited as witnesses in behalf of divine revelation and against unbelief. Jesus is competent to testify on his own behalf (3:31-32; 8:14, 18). His works give witness to him (5:36), as do his words (12:48-49), and as does the Father (5:32, 37; 8:17-18). He has come to bear witness of the truth (18:37). The climax of this running legal contest comes in his trial and death, when, as George Caird says, "Satan, representing the world of which he is prince, loses his case because he has no hold over Jesus, and incidentally loses his hold over the world for which Jesus dies (12:31-32; 14:30)."[9] Theodor Preiss remarks that this legal terminology which is mingled with a highly interpersonal idiom of thought makes the Fourth Gospel "at once the most juridical and the most mystical of writings."[10]

And when she comes,
  she will prove the world wrong
    about sin and righteousness and judgment. 16:8

9. G. B. Caird, *The Language and Imagery of the Bible* (Philadelphia: Westminster, 1980), 159.

10. Theodor Preiss, "Justification in Johannine Thought," in *Life in Christ* (London: SCM, 1954), 29.

The world needs to be convinced of the truth about itself — something it cannot come to on its own. Yet without that truth, the world is forever self-deceived. The showing of the world to itself is the mission of the Paraclete, *when she comes.* The Spirit *comes* (as in 15:26); she engages actively with the world. As Jesus had been sent and came, so the Spirit.

In the expression *prove the world wrong,* the Greek verb is *elenchein,* which the NRSV translates "prove wrong." The Evangelist is going to use it to speak of the Paraclete's work with reference to sin, to righteousness, and to judgment.

Elenchein must be a flexible word, for what the Spirit might seek with reference to sin may not be what the Spirit would seek with reference to justice or judgment. The New English Bible uses four terms: ". . . *[the Advocate] will confute the world, and show where wrong and right and judgment lie. [The Advocate] will convict them . . . convince them,*" suggesting some of the varied meanings that can be carried by the Evangelist's single verb.

The writer's general thesis is clear: The world has gotten things wrong — things that it must get right if it is to understand itself and carry out its appointed work. But the self-enclosed world has no vantage from which to see itself; its efforts to gather the truth about itself from itself are futile. No observer, taking a point of view within the world, can be free of that darkening which pervades both the object of inquiry and the inquirer. That is the condition of the world — to find itself a continual object for its own investigation, to have the self-reflexive capacity for examining itself, but always to miss the truth about itself. Lacking self-understanding, the actions of the world easily become inhumane and unjust. When the world comes to a new understanding of itself, it will be through the revealing work of God's Spirit.

The Evangelist's nouns, *sin, righteousness, and judgment* — wrong, right, and discrimination — are obviously central terms for human self-understanding, and such understanding is necessary if the world is to act and judge truly. (The terms "sin, righteousness, and judgment" sound Pauline, yet the words here are not used in a Pauline way; they have no reference to the keeping of Jewish law.)

Setting these great realities in his distinctive context, the writer enlarges:

About sin,
  because they do not believe in me;
about righteousness,
  because I am going to the Father
    and you will see me no longer;
about judgment,
  because the ruler of this world has been judged. 16:9-11

In previous biblical depictions of the world brought to justice, prophetic accusers held the world to account for such things as oppression and injustice (Amos), or failure of compassion (Jesus in Matthew 24), or disobedience (Paul in the opening of Romans). This johannine identification of the world's fault centers specifically and concretely on its relation to Jesus. The world is not convicted against a naturally known standard of justice, nor against a revealed divine law; it is convicted for its rejection of Jesus. What the world does in relation to him demonstrates its basic alienation from God. Jesus and the world are correlatives; his coming is its light; its rejection of him is its judgment. The untruth of the world is shown in its relation to Jesus. The world fails to understand the deepest things of itself as it fails to understand him. The world is not truly known through data it supplies; it is known in relation to one person who, living in it and being part of it, was also God's action towards it and in behalf of it. The Spirit's indictment of the world is made against that measure.

About sin, because they do not believe in me (v. 9). As the Evangelist sees it, the criterion of the world's sin is Jesus as having come and shown himself and having been disbelieved. (Compare 3:19, *This is the judgment* [*Gr. the* krisis]. *That the light has come into the world, and people loved darkness rather than light.*) The wrongness of the world is not discovered by observing the human material and its flawedness, nor by tracing the effects of corrupting models and institutions. Such analyses are embedded in the material they seek to investigate. In the johannine view, the universal human missing the mark is exposed by Jesus Christ — the one sent from God to demonstrate and at the same time to remedy the world's alienation.

The writer's reference of the issue to the figure of Jesus gives a highly particularistic account of the world's sin. As Eduard Schweizer has put it, "Sin is not just any kind of wrongdoing; it is simply and solely the world's No to Jesus."[11] The world's sin, the sin that includes all other sins, is rejec-

11. Eduard Schweizer, *The Holy Spirit* (Philadelphia: Fortress, 1980), 106.

tion, blindness, unbelief in the face of God's emissary. An earlier passage said, *Those who believe in him are not condemned, but those who do not believe are condemned already, because they have not believed in the name of the only Son of God* (3:18, compare 8:24; 12:37-50). The rejection that took place in a court of a first-century Roman province is a demonstration of the human condition. As Rudolf Bultmann said, "The world understands sin as revolt against its own standards and ideals, the things which give it security. But to shut oneself off from the revelation that calls all worldly security in question and opens another security — that is real sin."[12] The Greek tense of the verb *they do not believe* indicates persistent rejection; unbelief is the world's settled habit of mind.

About righteousness, because I am going to the Father and you will see me no longer (v. 10). If the world is to understand itself, it is important that it rightly identify uprightness, justice or "righteousness" *(dikaiosynē)*. In the Fourth Gospel this word appears only in this passage. (The term *dikaiosynē* is used nine times in 1 John.) The term is, however, very important in Paul (especially in Romans, where it appears more that 35 times). *Dikaiosynē,* moreover, is a central theme of Plato's *Republic,* the principal dialogue in which this germinal Greek philosopher explores justice and civic virtue. The johannine term has ties with a perennial human quest for the right ordering of life.

However, when the Evangelist speaks of righteousness, he does not reach out to converse with any of these possible contexts, but again he speaks particularly of Jesus. The reality of righteousness is made apparent in the world's encounter with him. The Discourse does not, however, refer to Jesus' character, nor to his ethical teaching as a guide to conduct, nor (unlike Paul, see Romans 1:17; 3:25) to his death as setting forth God's righteousness. Rather, the Evangelist says that Jesus demonstrates righteousness in leaving his disciples and going to the Father — the event which is the climax, through and beyond his death, to which Jesus' work was always moving. Having carried out the saving commission he was given, Jesus' return to the Father validates his ministry and shows him as the Righteous One. Such a demonstration, although by its very nature it is unseen, overturns the judgment that has been rendered in history and demolishes the criteria by which it was made. As Bishop Newbigin put it, "According to the world's understanding of righteousness Jesus was found to be in the wrong by the highest judicial authorities of the Church and state. He and his disciples

12. Rudolf Bultmann, *The Gospel of John* (Philadelphia: Westminster, 1971), 563.

were discredited and scattered. The end of the story was 'the curse.' But in the higher tribunal of the Father he was found to be 'in the right.'"[13]

The standards by which the world rendered its judgment on Jesus are so embedded in its way of seeing things that it cannot on its own free itself of them and reverse its opinion. The inward, convicting work of the Spirit — the word from beyond the world — is required if the world is to come to recognize the vindicated Jesus. The divine Paraclete, and no lesser agency, must show the world how wrong it was about him who was in the right. From that revolutionary, divinely imparted insight, a new understanding of righteousness and an alternative ordering of human society can develop.

About judgment, because the ruler of this world has been condemned (16:11). In some of the later strata of the biblical writings, the forces that stand against the purpose of God and against the well-being of humanity are spoken of as coming to focus in a single figure, called by many names, but here called "*the ruler (the* archōn*) of this world.*" *Now is the judgment (the* krisis*) of this world, now the ruler of this world will be driven out* (12:31, compare 14:30; in the "school of Paul" writings, see 1 Cor. 4:4, Eph. 2:2). The ministry of Jesus brought the conflict between darkness and light to a critical moment. (The judgment theme runs through the Fourth Gospel, see 3:19; 5:22-23, 30; 8:16, 26, 45-46; 9:39. As the Spirit will put the world on trial, so the world has been on trial throughout Jesus' ministry; see 18:37.) If the world is under judgment, so too is the "ruler" by whom the world's rebellion is led.

The world supposes itself competent to judge; it has been writing law codes, enforcing taboos, approving some acts while disallowing others, and developing sanctions and theories of obligation throughout most of the history of the race. Applying its standards, it judged Jesus. But he was no ordinary criminal. In his condemnation, the judges themselves were judged; in his execution, the forces of Satan were dethroned. As Eduard Schweizer put it, "Judgment is not exactly what passes for judgment in the world with its moralistic censure; on the contrary, it consists in the fact that 'the ruler of this world' (that is, everything we otherwise regard as omnipotent and absolutely essential) can no longer prevail against the Jesus-event."[14] The power of the Spirit at work in the world is the actualization in history of the overthrow of Satan — an overthrow that is accomplished in

13. Lesslie Newbigin, *The Light Has Come: An Exposition of the Fourth Gospel* (Grand Rapids: Eerdmans, 1982), 212.

14. Schweizer, *Holy Spirit,* 106.

Jesus' "hour," a vindication that is pledged for the end, but that is operative now through the Spirit (cf. 1 John 2:13-14).

Nothing is said in vv. 8-11 about how the Paraclete convicts or judges. Modern minds want to know about methods and ways; but for the Evangelist it is important to know that God does a thing; how God does it is of no more than secondary interest. The ways of the Paraclete are mysterious and hidden. The Evangelist has previously said that the Spirit of truth has no direct, unmediated dealing with the world, which cannot receive or know her (14:17a). Thus, 16:8-11 speaks not only of the Spirit and the world, but, by inference, of the Spirit, the church, and the world. Although the world does not believe (v. 9), there is in the world a believing, witness-bearing community standing over against a world whose life is ordered in unbelief. Jesus has gone to the Father, but the correlative of the departed Jesus is the church, representing in history the Redeemer whom the world has rejected. The *archōn* of this world is judged (v. 11), and the church carries the knowledge of that sentence and lives in the certainty of Jesus' victory.

3. The Paraclete and the Church (16:12-15)

The Discourse turns from the Spirit v. the World to the Spirit-informed community of believers (the "you" of the text), which is the instrument by which God addresses the alienated world.

By the time of this Third Discourse the community of Jesus seems to be no longer a dissident group within the synagogue, but it is becoming a body with a growing sense of its own story, and with stronger internal development. It may have taken on enough independence that in these comments we may refer to it as "the church."

Bishop Newbigin remarked that it is not the church in itself, but the church in the Spirit which is the effective agent of God's purpose. He says, "the Spirit is not the domesticated auxiliary of the Church; [s]he is the powerful advocate who goes before the Church to bring the world under conviction."[15] The invisible, inaudible Spirit works through the visible, vocal church. The church, in, with, and under the Paraclete, engages in its mis-

15. Newbigin, *Light,* 211.

sion of persuading, convicting, challenging, and of actualizing in its own life an alternative to the world's way of seeing and acting.

> I still have many things to say to you,
> but you cannot bear them now. 16:12

Jesus moves from the Spirit and the world to the Spirit and the church by a transitional remark: *I still have many things to say to you, but you cannot bear them now.* There are things that Jesus' followers *cannot bear.* (The verb is *bastazein,* which means to carry a burden; there was truth which exceeded the disciples' capacity, and Jesus will say no more now than his hearers can hold.) The comment about the limitation of the disciples in a *now*-time is made from the advantage of the *then*-time, when Jesus' followers can sustain a greater weight of truth. It implies that the later church (the church of the Fourth Gospel) understood itself to have been led by the Spirit to an understanding of Jesus and of its own life in relation to God through Jesus which could not have been grasped during his life in history.

> When the Spirit of truth comes,
> she will guide you into all the truth. 16:13a

The Paraclete is referred to as *the Spirit of truth* (as in 14:17; 15:26 and 1 John 1:6 and 5:7). Again she *comes.* She will *guide* (*hodēgō,* a verb related to "the way," *hodos,* 14:6) the church *into all the truth.* (Psalm 25:5 asks, *Lead me into your truth,* which in the LXX uses much the same language as 16:13. On Wisdom leading, see Wisd. 9:11; 10:10, 17.) The Spirit, in a movement that is through truth and into truth, will lead Jesus' followers into the Truth that Jesus is. The claim that the church is led by the Spirit into its own truth seems to bear, as Schnackenburg notes, "the most powerful impress of Christian experience and points most clearly to the johannine school's understanding of itself."[16] The expression *all the truth (tē alētheia pasē)* refers not to speculative inquiry or a developed body of doctrine, but concretely to the truth which is Jesus, the word in which the church is constituted.

> For she will not speak on her own,
> But will speak whatever she hears,
> And she will declare to you things that are to come. 16:13b

16. Schnackenburg, *Gospel,* 3.133.

The Spirit, the Evangelist says, *will not speak on her own* (Gr. *aph' heautou, from herself*). The Spirit's message is not self-originated, but arises from a prior listening; she *will speak whatever she hears.* Earlier Jesus said of himself, *I have made known to you everything I have heard from my Father* (15:15; see also 5:30; 12:49; 14:10; 17:16-17). As Michael Ramsey wrote, "The Son utters no message of his own but what he has received from the Father. The Spirit utters no message of her own, but what she too receives."[17] (In his different idiom, Paul also describes the Spirit as dependent; the Spirit searches the depths of God, as the human spirit searches the inner things of the self, 1 Cor. 2:11.) However, the Spirit listens for the sake of speaking, as her speaking is informed by her listening. The indefinitely open expression *into all the truth* (13a) can be spoken confidently because the truth is rooted in God, who is always true — true in the divine character and in the divine self-imparting. The listening Spirit has access to the inexhaustible truth of God, and through the Spirit, the church is led into truth-unto-truth.

As to the Spirit *declaring things to come,* the early church evidently had some experience of gifted persons who could, by the Spirit, speak knowingly of coming events (Acts 21:11; Rev. 1:1; 22:6). The Spirit was *the power of the age to come* (Heb. 6:5) and was faith's present link with what would come to be. It was proposed in chapter 3 of this study that these Farewell Discourses originated in Spirit-prompted utterance. Yet when v. 13b says that the Spirit *will declare to you the things that are to come,* the Evangelist would not seem to be referring principally to predictive power. Rather, the words refer to the Paraclete guiding the church into its own future, making new things clear to it as they are called forth in the contingencies of history. The church does not move into the future holding a program of coming events; rather, it follows the living voice of the Spirit. The Paraclete's *announcing (anangelei)* of v. 13c is closely related to the Spirit's *leading (hodēgēsei),* spoken of in v. 13a, and the *speaking (lalēsei)* of 13b. The Spirit is the divine communicator; and the church is the first human listener.

The Advocate who *declares (anangelei)* the things to come (v. 13c) *declares* also the things that belong to Jesus (v. 14). The Spirit who is innovative in the newness of unfolding history is at the same time faithful to a given word.

17. A. M. Ramsey, *The Glory of God and the Transfiguration of Christ* (London: Longmans, 1949), 75.

She will glorify me,
because she will take what is mine
and will declare it to you. 16:14

The new teaching of the Spirit may lead the church to imagine and do things it has never thought or done before, yet the Spirit's revealing activity derives from and brings into the present the redemptive work accomplished in history by Jesus. As Bishop Newbigin put it, the Spirit's word "is the word of *Jesus,* it is not another word."[18] The expression *what is mine (tou emou)* seems deliberately unspecific; it speaks, as Barrett notes, "not simply of the teaching but of the mission and being of Christ."[19]

The Spirit glorifies Jesus, as Jesus has glorified the Father (13:31; 17:4). The Paraclete shares in the glory that is exchanged between Jesus and the Father, and through her that glory is imparted to Jesus' followers. The Spirit is faithful to the primary revelation which has been given in Jesus. Eduard Schillebeeckx says, "All that [the Spirit] does draws out of Christ's work of redemption."[20] The Spirit re-creates the Christ-event — making it contemporary with each generation of believers, with each unprecedented body of circumstance, and with each hearer of the word. By the Spirit the work of Jesus is made effective in the openness of history.

All that the Father has is mine.
for this reason I said that she will take what is mine
and declare it to you. 16:15

The Evangelist again uses the idiom of agency; the Father shares everything with the Son, his emissary, *All that the Father has is mine.* The Son, as "the agent of God for salvation,"[21] has made the Father known. Jesus will in the same way *send* the Paraclete (v. 7), who is his agent, as he is the Father's. The Spirit takes what is Christ's (and therefore also ultimately the Father's) and, as a faithful *shaliach,* declares it to Jesus' people. For the third time since v. 13, the term *declare (anangelō)* is used of the Spirit.[22] The Spirit

18. Newbigin, *Light,* 216.

19. Barrett, *Gospel,* 490.

20. E. Schillebeeckx, *Christ, the Sacrament of the Encounter with God* (New York: Sheed and Ward, 1963), 25.

21. J. C. Fenton, *The Gospel According to John* (Oxford: Oxford University Press, 1970), 167.

22. Schnackenburg, *Gospel,* 3.135, remarks that the word for "declare" here, *anangel-*

who is first a hearer (v. 13b), becomes articulate as a communicator, a preacher, a herald. All is finally from the Father; all is shared between the Father and the Son; but through the Spirit all is finally declared to *you.*

In the lectionary. The Revised Common Lectionary appoints 16:5-15 as the Gospel reading for Trinity Sunday in Year C.

The section, as we have seen, is of two parts, which together comprise the longest Paraclete unit in the Fourth Gospel. These verses say things about the Holy Spirit that are not said anywhere else in the Christian scriptures. The text asks to be preached.

The designation of this passage for Trinity Sunday throws emphasis on its witness to the complexity-in-unity of God in revealing-redeeming action. The passage centers on the Paraclete — but always on the Paraclete in relation to Jesus and to the Father, and on the three in relation to humanity. The triadic language of this johannine passage suggests in a functional idiom the richness of the divine life. Three named, distinguishable centers carry out a single work. None is independent of the others; none is reducible to another.

All is from the originating, outgoing activity of *the Father.* The redemptive divine work comes first to expression in the Father's sending of the Son (v. 5, also 3:16), who is the self-expression of God. The Father sends the Son for the sake of humanity.

The Son's engagement in human affairs is not that of one life separable from others, achieving or failing on its own. Rather, the Fourth Gospel envisions the race as a unity, and in his coming, the Son is made one with this solidary humanity — *the Word was made flesh.* Coming from the Father (vv. 27-30), with whose life he is bound up, the Son is God acting to save. In him God addresses the flawed human situation, bringing life and light. By his life of witness, Jesus brings into being a community of consent, with which he is united in love.

Through the *Paraclete,* the divine life engages persons authoritatively and inwardly. The Spirit of truth is sent by the living Jesus (v. 7) to rebuke the world, to demonstrate to it its alienated condition (vv. 8-11), and to inform the life of the church, clarifying in new situations what was accomplished in the saving work of Jesus (vv. 12-15; see chapter 7 below).

This passage speaks of important things that have happened in the world's behalf — Jesus goes to the Father, the Spirit is sent, the *archōn* of this world is condemned. But none of these actions was visible, public, or empirically verifiable.

---

lein, is "a term used in the vocabulary of revelation (cf. 4:25)." The Spirit, however, will not "proclaim anything with a new content," but will relate Christ's revelation to new situations. The prefix *ana-* is like the English "re-," and Brown (*Gospel,* 708) proposes "re-announce" or "re-proclaim."

The most important things that have been done for the world have been done, so to speak, while the world was attending to other things. These crucial but unseen redemptive acts will be made apprehensible through the church's style of life and through the grandeur and the folly of preaching.

The challenge for a preacher is to locate again the triadic nature of the church's basic message — not in traditional formularies or in cloudy vagueness, but in the depth of faith's grasp of God's creative, redemptive work — transcendent, historic, and immanent.

An observation on literary structure becomes pertinent here: The Third Discourse, from v. 16 to its end, forms a lengthy "inclusion." Subjects are introduced in vv. 16 through 22, and then after a turn at v. 23, they are repeated in reverse order in vv. 23 though 33, usually somewhat elaborated.[23] Such repetition gives the passage unity and emphasis, but at the same time the return of ideas in changed form gives variety and movement to the thought.

prediction of coming testing and subsequent consolation

remarks by disciples who do not understand

promise of blessing to be enjoyed by the disciples; opening with "very truly"

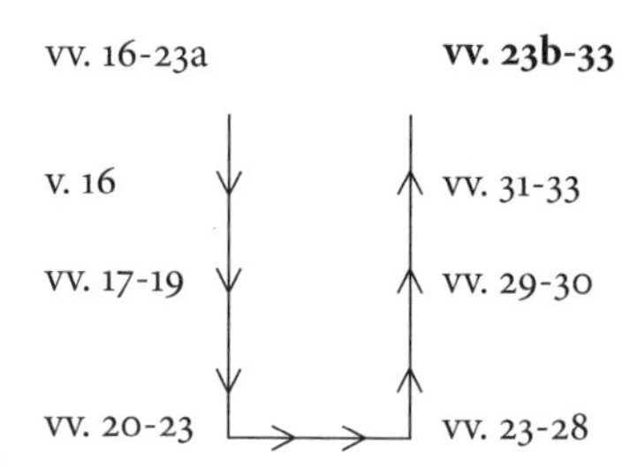

4. Joy Out of Testing (16:16-24)

The thought of vv. 16-23 (the first part of the inclusion) is expressed largely in paradoxical, unspecific terms. Abruptly in v. 16 Jesus poses something like a puzzle, saying that his disciples will not see him and they will see him. They cannot make out his meaning (vv. 17-18), and Jesus asks about their confusion (v. 19). When the dialogue of vv. 16-19 passes to explanation by Jesus in vv. 20-23, his words will still leave his hearers with questions.

The Third Discourse through v. 15 has been a monologue, but now in vv. 17-24 and 29-31 the disciples enter. (They spoke in the opening inci-

23. Brown remarks on this device.

dent, 13:6-11, 23-30, 36-38, and in the beginning of the First Discourse, 14:5-9. Their questions, which had come from named individuals in the First Discourse, are collective and anonymous in the Third Discourse.)

> A little while, and you will no longer see me,
> and again a little while, and you will see me." 16:16

Jesus' opening remark seems to be self-contradictory: *After a little while* his followers will not see him, and *again after a little while they will see him.* The cryptic statement arouses the disciples' attention and curiosity. (Two different Greek words for "see" are used, *theōrein* and *horaō;* but most exegetes do not think that in this Gospel these verbs denote different kinds of seeing or that the change in the verb carries the point of the remark.)[24] Subsequent statements by Jesus will clarify that he is speaking of breaking one mode of relationship and entering another; a seeing which is a not-seeing passes over into a seeing that sees. But Jesus' initial way of putting the matter is genuinely puzzling.

> Then some of his disciples said to one another,
> "What does he mean by saying to us,
> 'a little while, and you will no longer see me,'
> and 'because I am going to the Father'?"
> They said, "What does he mean by this 'a little while'?
> We do not know what he is talking about."
> Jesus knew that they wanted to ask him, so he said to them,
> "Are you discussing among yourselves what I meant when I said, 'A little while and you will no longer see me, and again a little while, and you will see me?' 16:17-19

Jesus' followers are mystified by his "oracular utterance."[25] Rather than questioning him directly, they ask among themselves in evident bafflement,

24. Many older commentators thought the different Greek verbs for "see" represent distinct, identifiable ways of seeing. Most modern exegetes find that such distinctions do not prove out. In the Fourth Gospel, as in common experience, there are different kinds of seeing, but they do not correlate with the Greek vocabulary of John. See Brown, *Gospel,* Appendix I (3), 501-3, and the essay "Believing Is Knowing Is Seeing Is Hearing Is Believing . . . ," pp. 142-49 above.

25. C. H. Dodd, *The Interpretation of the Fourth Gospel* (Cambridge: Cambridge University Press, 1953), 395.

what does he mean? And then they repeat Jesus' entire statement twice (vv. 17-18), adding (in v. 17b) *because I am going to the Father,* which was not part of Jesus' original puzzle, but which does echo his words in vv. 5, 7, and 10. (This addition by the disciples suggests, as Schnackenburg notes, "that the disciples have understood enough to know that Jesus is speaking of his departure.")[26] By this repetition the Evangelist seems to assure his readers that Jesus' riddle really is puzzling. Jesus, sensing his disciples' bafflement, asks them what they are discussing, and in the course of asking, he repeats his entire opening remark — which thus makes its fourth appearance in as many verses. The repetition (which can be tiresome when the passage is read aloud) creates emphasis and some suspense.[27]

The narrative then shifts from question and repetition of the question (vv. 16-19) to Jesus' explanation (vv. 20-24). However, his statement, except for the brief *I will see you again* (v. 22), does nothing with the motif of seeing him and not seeing him; it does not explain the phrase *a little while;* and it drops the reference to his going to the Father. At first glance, Jesus' statements in vv. 20-24 can seem like an answer to some question other than the one he was asked by the disciples in vv. 16-19. Godfrey Nicholson calls Jesus' words in 16:16-19 (along with 7:33-36, 8:21-22, and 13:33) "departure riddles," which are "a part of the larger johannine technique of misunderstanding." These riddles, Nicholson explains, are an element in the Evangelist's narrative strategy; he looks beyond the immediate story. "The solution to the riddle is not apparent to the people to whom it is spoken, but to the readers" of the Gospel, who have been informed about Jesus' origin and destiny.[28] Jesus seems to intend something para-

26. Schnackenburg, *Gospel,* 3.156.

27. Newbigin, *Light,* 219, notes that "Nowhere else in the whole discourse is such immense emphasis laid on a single phrase." Lindars remarks that "When this chapter is read aloud the repetitions become almost ludicrous" (*Gospel,* p. 508). Paul Duke notes this passage's "exasperating length, its interminable reiterative asking" (*Irony in the Fourth Gospel* [Atlanta: John Knox, 1985], 56). See Gail O'Day's remarks on vv. 25-33 in *Revelation in the Fourth Gospel* (Philadelphia: Fortress, 1986), 104-9. J. A. T. Robinson (*The Priority of John* [London: SCM, 1985], 341) suggests that "The laboured fourfold repetition in 16:16-19 of the saying about 'the little while' and 'because I go to the Father' seems extraordinary if the church had simply created these words. Why should it have invented them only to make such a meal of them? It looks much more as if it was wrestling with a remembered 'word of the Lord,' whose interpretation had been subject to debate and misunderstanding."

28. Godfrey Nicholson, *Death as Departure: The Johannine Descent-Ascent Schema* (Chico: Scholars, 1983), 58-60. Cf. Duke, *Irony,* 56, "The elongated 'we don't understand' of the disciples provides a dramatic irony to which informed readers can reply, 'But we do!'"

doxical, as though he were saying, "You will only 'see' me in the sense that matters most when I have left your sight."

The long, rather static holding back while toying with paradoxes seems to be coming to an end; Jesus says *Very truly,* as though he might be introducing an important pronouncement. Perhaps he is about to explain his almost teasing remarks about seeing and not seeing and about "a little while." However, further paradoxical and non-specific statements follow. Vv. 20-24 are Jesus' highly elusive answer to his own highly elusive riddle.

Jesus begins his reply with some sententious-sounding remarks:

> Very truly, I tell you
> you will weep and mourn,
> but the world will rejoice;
> you will have pain,
> but your pain will turn to joy. 16:20

Jesus' language changes from "seeing" and "not-seeing" to "weeping" and "rejoicing." His words take the form of two couplets; the second line of each contrasts with the first. Both couplets begin saying that Jesus' followers will be in deep sorrow. The second line of the first couplet says that the things that will bring sorrow to the disciples will call the world, for its part, to *rejoice.* The climax of the structured unit falls on the last line of the second couplet, which says that ultimately the disciples' pain will be transformed into joy. (The motif of joy is carried forward in vv. 21-24 and in the evangelical optimism of v. 33.)

The wording is vivid. The verb of the opening line, *You will weep (klaiein),* is also used to describe the reaction to the death of Lazarus (11:31, 33) and to the death of Jesus (20:11, 13, 15). The second verb in the first line, *and mourn (thrēnein),* is not used elsewhere in this Gospel, but see Luke 23:27. (The two verbs are joined in Luke 7:32, where children piping at a funeral complain that others do not respond with appropriate weeping and mourning.) In the final couplet, when Jesus says that his followers will have pain, he uses the word *lypeō,* anticipating the language of the strong illustration of childbirth which lies ahead in v. 21.

When Jesus' followers are made sorrowful, the hostile world *will rejoice.* The community for which the author writes has gone through specifically religious assault from persons who think that in bringing pain on them they are serving God (16:2). It is part of the human possibility that some persons can take satisfaction in bringing suffering on others. This is the world's condemnation: It can find joy in causing others to weep. The opponents of Jesus' people are depicted here as lacking in basic human empathy.

The last couplet promises a reversal: the experience of the disciples will pass from *pain* to *joy.* The Evangelist illustrates. The disciples' sorrow will turn to joy as a mother's pain and risk yield to delight and fulfillment when she gives birth to a child. A. M. Hunter calls v. 21 a "parable."[29]

> When a woman is in labor, she has pain,
> because her hour has come.
> But when her child is born
> she no longer remembers the anguish
> because of the joy of having brought
> a human being into the world. 16:21

In this illustration drawn from childbirth, Jesus uses the idiom of the *"hour"* which he earlier used for himself and the crisis of his work. The term "anguish" (*thlipsis,* translated "tribulation" in the KJV) is used in biblical talk of the end, where it speaks of the unendurable conflict which will bring the present era to its conclusion and will be followed by the time of the Messiah and the reign of God. (See Matt. 24:21, 29; Mark 13:19, 24; and Rev. 7:14.)

The eschatological use of the image of childbirth carries associations from the Jewish Scriptures. Some of the prophetic passages that use the image of a woman in travail to describe the Day of the Lord would include:

- Isaiah 13:8 describes the Day of the Lord, a time of divine anger, as *anguish like a woman in travail.*
- Isaiah 26:17-19 compares Israel in distress to a woman who cries out in pangs of childbirth, but she brings forth nothing. (Isaiah 26:20 contains the "little while" expression that has figured in 16:16-19.)
- Isaiah 66:7-9 portrays divine action that is so sudden that it is like a woman who gives birth before there were any labor pains. (There is an allusion to Isaiah 66:14 in John 16:22.)

29. A. M. Hunter, *The Gospel according to John* (Cambridge Bible Commentary; Cambridge: Cambridge University Press, 1965), 85.

- Micah 4:9-10 says that Israel's suffering, which led to captivity, is like the pangs of a woman in travail.
- Hosea 13:9-13 compares God's wrath on Ephraim to the pangs of childbearing from which no child is born.
- One of the hymns of the Qumran community (1QH 3.7, 9-10) reads:

> [L]ike a woman in travail with her first-born child. . . .
> [S]he labors in her pains who bears a man.
> For amid the throes of Death
> she shall bring forth a man-child,
> and amid the pangs of Hell
> there shall spring from her child-bearing crucible a Marvelous Mighty Counselor;
> and a man shall be delivered from out of the throes.[30]

Fr. Lindars notes that although this Qumran passage speaks of the birth of the Messiah, it is part of a poem of the emergence of the messianic people from the coming eschatological cataclysm.[31] The Evangelist may well have these or other scriptural passages in mind as he uses the image of childbirth to interpret Jesus and his passion.

In the coming Day of the Lord, as in a woman's giving birth, what is about to happen is not subject to human prediction or control, but is a time of human helplessness; events lie in the hands of God. The metaphoric setting indicates that the crisis of Jesus' mission is not just an individual going to his cruel and unjust death. The Messiah's affliction, as the Evangelist understands it (with the language of the prophets in his ears), is the Day of the Lord — an hour of judgment and suffering. Yet out of the anguish new life comes to birth.

Jesus' "parable" comes to its climax in the woman's *joy of having brought a human being into the world.* (The Greek word which the NRSV translates "a human being" is *anthrōpos,* which does not imply masculinity, although the Qumran hymn quoted above clearly does. The TEV translation of 16:21 says "a baby.") When the Evangelist connects echoes of Jewish Scripture with the eventual joy of Jesus' disciples, he is thinking of Jesus' passion as an epochal "Day of the Lord" out of which something new and living is born. The *human being* that is born into the world is, in the allu-

30. As translated in Geza Vermes, *The Dead Sea Scrolls in English* (3rd ed.; London: Penguin, 1987), 171-72.

31. Lindars, *Gospel,* 509.

sive language of the writer, the church, the new people. Macgregor comments, "John intends us to understand that the New Testament church is actually born at the Resurrection out of the travail of the Cross."[32]

> So you have pain now;
> but I will see you again,
> and your hearts will rejoice,
> and no one will take your joy from you. 16:22

Passing from his illustration back to his followers, Jesus says *you have pain now,* speaking of the "now" of the disciples on the eve of the crucifixion. But his words are also the Evangelist speaking to the "now" of the first-century community which is experiencing *pain (lypē).*

Jesus' promise *I will see you again* presumably refers, at short range, to his reunion with his followers in the resurrection appearances (chapters 20–21). After all that is about to happen that apparently separates him from his disciples forever, he does see them again, and when he does, they are *"glad"* (20:20). (The resurrection narrative in chapter 20 mentions "seeing" repeatedly.) The expression *I will see you again and your hearts will rejoice* alludes to a prophetic oracle of comfort, *You shall see, and your heart shall rejoice* (Isa. 66:14). Jesus' change from the prophet's "you shall see" to "I will see you" is probably intentional, emphasizing the initiative of Jesus. In the resurrection appearances, Jesus is not discovered by disciples who were looking for him; rather, he makes himself known unexpectedly. The disciples' passage from pain to joy is clearly the consequence of Jesus' passage from death to life.

Jesus' followers' movement from suffering to joy is the central theme of the Third Discourse. But the writing in vv. 20-22 is uncircumstantial. A reader does not know specifically what has occasioned the pain of Jesus' followers; and, other than his disciples "seeing" him (which is not a very specific reference), one is not told what turns their suffering into joy. What may a reader understand here? Will the adverse conditions in which the community is living now turn for the better, allowing happiness to replace anxiety? Or will the relation between the Christians and their opponents settle down into something that the people of Jesus can live with and in which they will find an inner resource that allows them to experience joy,

32. G. H. C. Macgregor, *The Gospel of John* (Garden City: Doubleday Doran, 1929), 301.

even in the absence of any apparent reason for joy? The writer does not inform or explain. The language of the passage does not seem to describe a situation in which the Christians are simply enduring or holding on, but rather the words *your hearts will rejoice* suggest the vital, unqualified joy of the Lord — satisfaction, fulfillment, trust, and hope. But the text gives no clue to the church's historical, social situation.

Jesus' words *no one will take your joy from you* suggests that hostile forces seek to deprive the disciples of their joy. Yet their sight of Jesus will inaugurate an inalienable joy — a joy that persists in spite of circumstance.

Vv. 16-22 exhibit a pattern. A series of contrasts describes a passage from loss to gain; absence and sorrow are replaced by presence and joy.

something painful will happen	**succeeded by something joyful**
vv. 16-19	
you will not see me	*you will see me* (or v. 22, *I will see you*)
v. 20	
you will weep and lament	*your sorrow will be turned to joy*
v. 21, an illustration	
a woman in travail has sorrow	*she rejoices that a child is born*
v. 22	
you have sorrow now	*on that day, you will rejoice*

This experience is all described from the point of view of Jesus' followers — their not-seeing and their seeing, their sorrow and their joy. The language is vivid, but through all of the repetitions of the pattern, the actions or events that bring about the sorrow or that will transform it remain unspecified.

Anticipating the transformation of his followers' situation, Jesus invites them, as a mark of their new condition, to pray confidently. Through his name, they will have access to the Father:

> On that day you will ask nothing of me.
> Very truly, I tell you,
> if you ask anything of the Father in my name,
> he will give it to you.
> Until now you have not asked for anything in my name.

Ask and you will receive,
so that your joy may be complete. 16:23-24

In these two verses, the word "ask" occurs four times, but two different Greek verbs are used. The difference in meaning between them seems to hold the significance of the passage.

In Jesus' first statement, when he says *on that day you will ask nothing of me* (v. 23a), his verb "ask" is *erōtaō,* which usually carries the sense of "inquire" or "ask questions of." (It is used in this sense in vv. 5, 19 and 30 in this chapter.) The disciples have often found Jesus' speech unclear, and they have asked him what he means. Jesus seems to be telling them that a coming day (which is the present day of the Evangelist and his readers) will be a time of clarity. The disciples' confused question-asking will come to an end.

But as Jesus continues, he speaks of prayer. When he again says "ask," his verb is *aiteō* (he uses the word three times in vv. 23b-24). This term, which usually means "petition," is a common verb for "pray" both in the Synoptic Gospels and in the Fourth Gospel. Jesus refers to a coming time when his followers will pray to the Father in his name, as *until now* they have not. The name of the living Jesus gives them access to the Father. *On that day* Jesus' followers will no longer be full of questions. Yet as they live with the mystery of God in their uncertain life in the world, their dependence and their need for articulated communion with the Father continue.

Jesus' words "ask and you will receive" closely parallel his counsel on prayer in the Sermon on the Mount, where he says *Ask and it will be given you* (Matthew 7:7). Hardly anything in the Fourth Gospel indicates that its author knew the Synoptic Gospels. But this verbal echo may indicate that this word of Jesus about prayer was known and exchanged among groups of first-century Christians apart from any familiarity they may have had with the written Gospels.

V. 24 contains a textual problem. The grammar in some manuscripts attaches the phrase *in my name* to the disciples' asking, while other manuscripts attach it to the divine giving. No doubt the Evangelist wrote one of these wordings, not both. Yet since the manuscript evidence on which interpretation depends gives no clear verdict, and since in johannine thought Jesus occupies a focal place in the divine-human relation, a present-day reader may not need to decide, but may think of both human asking and God's giving as acts done in Jesus' name.

The consequence of the access that Jesus offers is *so that your joy may be complete.* The joy that comes to displace the pain of Jesus' followers is the result of the divine/human bond which is established in him. The wise nineteenth-century American theologian William Porcher DuBose once remarked that joy is a worthy end, even though counterfeit joys attract, and enjoyment calls for discrimination.

> We cannot escape the conclusion that pleasure, happiness, blessedness, is not only an actual and universal, but is the proper and necessary end and determinant of life. Our freedom, our responsibility, our wisdom, and our salvation is in the choice of our pleasures, and in the quality and material of our happiness, in the truth and purity of our blessedness. In choosing God and the kingdom of Heaven we have made the wisest and best possible choice, but we have not chosen God because He is our duty alone, but because He is our highest pleasure or joy, our truest happiness, our essential life and blessedness.[33]

The passage of contrasts that runs from vv. 16 to 24 is the heart of the Third Discourse: *You have pain now, but your hearts will rejoice.* Now that the text is before a reader, one may ask what this enigmatic unit of thought is about. The language is highly allusive. What transforming events lie behind it? What time-frame is to be understood? Do these verses carry a single or a multiple reference?

The Evangelist has held to the narrative situation of Jesus taking leave of his disciples. He knows that in *a little while* his followers will not see him. But beyond the near-at-hand circumstances, Jesus says that he will return to his people — *a little while,* and they will see him. The Messianic reference in the illustration of the woman in childbirth indicates that the climactic events of Jesus' mission — his death and resurrection and the giving of the Spirit — stand between the "not seeing" and the "seeing." The sorrow "now" of the disciples will be turned to joy by Jesus' resurrection.

Clearly, this close-at-hand meaning is in mind. Yet the language looks beyond the resurrection and refers to life in the later church, as Jesus' reference to prayer indicates. The Evangelist sees the situation of the disciples between Jesus' death and his resurrection as a paradigm of the situation of the first-century church for which he writes. The passage implies the writer's subordinate, but not forgotten future eschatology. In the church's "now," Jesus is not seen, although in "a little while" he will be. The

33. W. P. DuBose, *The Reason of Life* (New York: Longmans, Green, 1911), 101.

Evangelist thinks of the life of the Christian community as played out between a seeing past and a seeing to come (compare 1 John 3:2). The not-seeing/seeing of the death and resurrection "anticipate and prefigure" the not-seeing/seeing of the parousia.[34]

However, the Evangelist's terms may imply another level of meaning. He counsels that believers can expect times of sorrow, pain and eclipse of vision. Such times belong to the very texture of life, and believers are not exempt from them. The johannine church has been through the crisis to which the Second Discourse was addressed, and it is now in another. But the writer assures it that such stressful times will be followed by occasions of relief. People of faith can expect harsh circumstances, and yet they can see beyond them.

The Evangelist writes for Christians who have gone through a traumatic conflict with the synagogue. The expulsion from the ancient worship of God, the interruption of social solidarities, and the loss of the legal protection that Jewishness gave them must have seemed calamitous to the believers in Jesus. They lost a life-supporting order and were exposed to grave threat. Yet that crisis has evidently been weathered, and on the far side of it the church is discovering a deeper sense of its own identity.

The Evangelist saw Jesus' death and his return in resurrection as decisive events of human redemption, but at the same time he saw them as events that were replicated in the crises of human existence. In knowing what he does about the one central crisis of Jesus' "hour," he has been given a clue to the perennial character of existence in faith. In the proximate crises of history, God, in unexpected ways, brings the covenant people through sorrow into joy. The Great Crisis of the death and life of the Redeemer is met also in the other crises that befall the Redeemer's people.

Andrew Greeley once described life in a world that is fallen and yet redeemed. He spoke of "the gaiety and joy that comes from Faith, hope, confidence and compassion. One laughs because one knows that no matter how desperate things are they are never serious in the ultimate sense. No matter how long things may go badly they will ultimately end well. No matter how tragic life might appear to be, it is, in the final analysis, a comedy.[35]

We observed earlier that, in the later half of the Second Discourse (15:18–16:4a), when the author wrote to interpret for his readers their en-

34. Barrett, *Gospel,* 491.

35. Andrew Greeley, "Humor and Ecclesiastical Ministry," *Concilium: Theology in the Age of Renewal* 5/10 (May, 1974), 139.

counter with bitter opposition, he developed a parallel between the rejected Jesus and the persecuted church. In effect, he saw Christian experience of pain and adversity through a *theologia crucis.* But a changed situation has brought forth a different theological emphasis. When this Third Discourse came to be written, the Evangelist's mind has moved on, and as he sees things now, the faith community, beyond its tears and pain, encounters the living, triumphant Jesus, and the Evangelist interprets its life through a *theologia gloriae.*

5. Speech, Obscure and Plain (16:25-28)

> I have said these things to you in figures of speech.
> The hour is coming
> when I will no longer speak to you in figures,
> but will tell you plainly of the Father. 16:25

Jesus speaks again of his own speaking. *I have said these things.... I will tell you* (cf. 16:4b, 12). He has spoken, he says, *in figures of speech (en paroimiais).* The term is translated "cryptic utterances" by Alan Richardson, "veiled speech, difficult of comprehension" by Barrett, "dark sayings" by Cadman, and J. A. T. Robinson says "in riddles."[36] But he promises a coming *hour* when, by contrast, he will speak *plainly (parrēsia) of the Father.*

Jesus may refer specifically to his immediately foregoing remarks, which have been unusually obscure; but more broadly the term may refer to the indirection by which the johannine Jesus customarily imparts his message.

Jesus promises that a time will come when he will communicate plainly. His use of the eschatological term "hour" suggests that the time of clarity is the age of the church and the Spirit — the age in which the readers of the Fourth Gospel are living. On the other side of the church's inaugural events, the barriers of misunderstanding which have marked the johannine narrative will be done away.

The Evangelist is not making a point about religious language or theological method — as though to say that speech about God could at

36. A. Richardson, *The Gospel according to Saint John* (Torch Biblical Commentary; New York: Harper and Row, 1959), 181; Barrett, *Gospel,* 495; W. H. Cadman, *The Open Heaven* (Oxford: Blackwell, 1967), 197; Robinson, *Priority,* 319, n. 73.

some time and under some conditions be univocal or non-metaphoric. Human speech about God is always to some extent *en paroimiais* — always in symbols and containing a measure of dimness and mystery. The author may, however, be suggesting something quite sophisticated about God-talk. The crisis of Jesus' death and resurrection and the emergence of the church's proclamation gave to Jesus' followers a concentrated experience of both the limitation and the power of language. This word-conscious Evangelist had been made aware that symbols, which are necessary to speech about God and to the human relation to God, can be a barrier to those who stand outside the reality that is symbolized — as most of Jesus' auditors find his image-laden talk baffling. However, those same symbolic terms can become clarifying and faith-imparting disclosures when consent is given to the things they represent. When by a shattering and remaking, the reality signified by the symbol comes to be known and trusted, the symbol-terms which previously impeded understanding become conveyors of meaning. Since they are symbols, they necessarily remain somewhat dim and unfocussed. Yet they communicate the puzzling but luminous reality of God.

A symbol is not "solved" as a puzzle may be solved and discarded. The direction-in-indirection by which the symbol presents itself is essential to communication concerning divine things. The Evangelist is saying that within the new age — the age informed by faith and the ministry of the Paraclete — the effort to communicate things that can only be spoken of indirectly (an effort largely frustrated during Jesus' ministry) will carry life-giving clarity. Believers will know because they are united with the thing they seek to know.

Jesus adds that the future time — the time of the Spirit and the church — in addition to being a time of clarity, will be a time of his followers' direct relation with the Father.

> On that day you will ask in my name.
> I do not say to you
>   that I will ask the Father on your behalf;
> for the Father himself loves you,
>   because you have loved me
>   and have believed that I came from God. 16:26-27

The subject of prayer returns. Jesus, still speaking of speech, says that love for him will open free communication between his people and the Father.

His followers, living in the new age, are a community of prayer. *On that day you will ask in my name.*

In his followers' new life of prayer, no one, not even Jesus, needs to ask on their behalf; they have direct access to the Father through the Father's own love: *The Father himself loves you.* The Father's love, however, is made accessible to the disciples through their identification with Jesus: *because you have loved me and have believed that I came from God.* Their love for Jesus and their faith in him as the one from God have enabled the relation with the Father. Although their relation with the Father is direct, the disciples ask in the name of Jesus, "as those whose life is his life, who can say 'Abba' with the same freedom as his, and who are beloved by the Father as he is."[37]

The less common New Testament verb for love, *phileō,* is used in this passage — both for the Father's love for Jesus' people and the disciples' love for Jesus. *Agapaō* is the more common and more developed New Testament word for love. Most modern scholarship judges that there is no significant distinction between the two words, both of which can be used for a wide range of the experience of loving and being loved. Yet the word carries echoes. *Phileō,* the verb that is used in 16:26, is related to the noun *philos* which was developed in the Second Discourse (in 15:13-15) as "friends" among whom understanding is shared. William Temple proposed that, to suggest the parallel between the verb and the noun, 16:27 be read, "The Father himself is friendly to you because you have been my friends."[38]

Jesus credits his disciples with believing that he came from God (v. 27). Then he expands his statement into a concise summary of the johannine christological claim. The one who has said that he would speak plainly now speaks of himself as plainly as he ever does.

> I came from the Father
>   and have come into the world;
>   again, I am leaving the world
> and am going to the Father."   16:28

This brief christological affirmation is shaped in paired clauses: Jesus has come from the Father and into the world, and he leaves the world and goes

37. Newbigin, *Light,* 221.
38. William Temple, *Readings in St. John's Gospel* (London: Macmillan, 1939), 299.

to the Father. In all four of the clauses there is movement — coming and going. (There is, however, no spatial imagery of "descent" and "ascent.") The statement is lean, containing only substantives and verbs. Although Jesus acts in relation to the Father and the world, his coming, his work, and his destiny are spoken of as in his own hands. Jesus is the actor, the "I" in all four clauses, the subject of all four verbs. The outer clauses identify the Father as the origin and the end; Jesus comes forth *from* the Father, and he goes *to* the Father. The middle two clauses speak of the world — his *coming into* it and his *leaving* it.

This summary (like the church's later creeds) emphasizes the mythic contour of christology. Although it speaks of Jesus' coming to the world and of his leaving it, this affirmation says nothing of Jesus' historic ministry, his teaching, healings, conflicts, his death and resurrection. This summary — which speaks of unseen, unverifiable movements — can almost seem like a frame without a picture. But, of course, other gospel passages supply the picture that fits the cosmic frame that the Evangelist sets out here.

This brief passage, coming near the end of the Farewell Discourses, echoes the words of the Evangelist that begin the Farewell, *Jesus, knowing . . . that he had come from God and was going to God,* 13:3b. Nothing indicates that the Farewell chapters were thought of as a literary unit. The present study regards the Farewell as comprising three separately written Discourses. Nonetheless, the long Farewell as we now have it opens and closes with these similar summaries of the contour of johannine christology.

These compact lines have the sound of a doctrinal statement; and Christians who know the classic creeds are likely to read this verse as though it described Christ, who is very God of very God, coming down from heaven and being made man. Then, his redemptive mission completed, he ascends to heaven, where he is seated at the right hand of the Father. Christians tend to read the New Testament through the spectacles of the highly formative Athanasian/Nicene tradition. However, much theological argument, clarification, and spiritual discovery fell between the spare christological affirmations of 16:28 and the developed incarnational theology of the creedal tradition. Interpreters need to attend to what these johannine affirmations say and to what they do not say.

I came from the Father: The expression *I came forth from the Father (exēlthon ek tou patros)* is used three times in the immediate context (vv. 27, 28 and 30). The repetition gives emphasis. The same wording appears in 8:42 and in 17:3, always speaking of Jesus; he is uniquely the one who has *come forth from the Father.* (The Greek tense speaks of his coming forth as a specific act.) The reason for the Jesus of the Fourth Gospel did not lie in himself, *I came from God and now am here. I did not come on my own* (8:42). The johannine church affirms in some sense the supra-historical rootage of the human figure of Jesus.

And am come into the world: Jesus was an active, responsible, vulnerable member of the human community. The Fourth Gospel says nothing about the manner of his coming. The words of the second clause are used of Jesus figuratively in 3:19, *Light had come into the world.* But in the Prologue, the same expression is universalized, speaking of *every person coming into the world* (1:9), meaning "every person who is born." Similarly, the words "to come into the world" mean "to be born" when Jesus in 18:37 says *for this I have been born, and for this I have come into the world.* The expression "come into the world" seems to refer to the common human entry into life. The words *I am come into the world* speak of Jesus entering the human lot as any person enters it.

I leave the world: In this terse summary, the cosmic christological drama is expressed from the standpoint of the world. "The world," the arena of human life, is the sphere in which Jesus has completed his work and which he now is leaving.

And go to the Father: All other human lives, insofar as they can be known, begin in this world and end in this world. Jesus leaves it to live. He leaves the world to be reassociated with the Father from whom he came forth. The christological narrative of Jesus' Farewell culminates in these significant, but strangely guarded affirmations: Jesus came into the world from the Father, and he leaves it to go to the Father.

The redemptive myth, stated here with great economy, concentrates the scandal and the glory of the johannine presentation of Jesus. Perhaps we would not press too much towards an Athanasian construction of the text if we were to say this much: The one who is from God comes into the world, where he acts in the name of God and in behalf of humanity. Through Jesus' *coming forth,* God is self-defined in human terms — the humanization of God. Whoever has seen Jesus has seen the Father. Then the one who bears the fullness of human living and dying *goes to the Father.* By the eternal Word being one of us, and by his going from us, while yet remaining one of us, the race is dignified — the divinization of humanity. This unifying work is accomplished, not by making God less godlike nor by slighting the creatureliness and sin of humanity, but by setting in the divine/human relation the unifying figure of Jesus Christ, the enfleshed divine Word.

6. Alone, but Not Alone (16:29-33)

> His disciples said,
> "Yes, now you are speaking plainly,
>   not in any figure of speech!
> Now we know that you know all things,
>   and do not need to have anyone question you;
>   by this we believe that you came from God." 16:29-30

Jesus said that a time of plain speech was coming but had not yet come. The disciples hurriedly conclude that in what Jesus has just said he is speaking plainly; they understand the time of clarity to be now. Their clauses tumble urgently upon one another with a sense of excitement and relief: *now you are speaking plainly (en parrēsia) . . . now we know . . . we believe.*

The disciples declare what they understand Jesus to have been telling them, *We believe that you came from God.* Yet in this confession of their belief, they seem to grasp no more than Nicodemus did when he recognized Jesus as *a teacher who has come from God* (3:2). The disciples use Jesus' own words, *I came forth from the Father* (27b, 28a). Yet Jesus, who knows, questions, *Do you now believe?* He uses the disciples' words *"now"* and *"believe,"* yet by his question, he seems to find their understanding of him inadequate. The disciples sought to turn the eschatological "hour" of which Jesus had spoken in v. 25 into a simple present *now we know.* However, they will not understand until the new age of the Spirit has dawned on the other side of the cross and resurrection.

The disciples' exchange with Jesus in vv. 29-32a repeats a pattern that appeared in 13:37-38, where Peter boasted that he would lay down his life for Jesus and Jesus foretold his unfaithfulness:

Jesus' follower(s)' confident overstatement:

13:37b	16:29-30

Jesus' questions, repeating the disciples(s)' statement:
13:38a 16:31
Jesus' prediction that his follower(s) will desert him:
13:38b 16:32

Despite their exhilaration, the disciples repeat only part of Jesus' account of himself (as he gave it in v. 28). They acknowledge that he is from God — a thing he has often claimed for himself. But Jesus has not only said that he is from God, but also that he is going to God. The disciples grasp the first part of the claim, and that is important. Jesus does not say that they have gotten wrong what they hold. His signs and his public presentation of himself, which have been widely rejected, have been accepted by his followers, who recognize that Jesus and his mission are from God (cf. 17:7-8). However, in the Farewell Discourses, Jesus has tried to tell his followers that he is going to the Father. As a community of consent, their own life and destiny are caught up in Jesus' going to the one who sent him. As they come to understand him and his going from them, they will understand themselves. Yet, the disciples' words indicate that they have not grasped a crucial part of what Jesus has labored to teach them.

Jesus answered them,
"Do you now believe?
The hour is coming, indeed it has come,
when you will be scattered,
each one to his own home,
and you will leave me alone.
Yet I am not alone because the Father is with me. 16:31-32

Jesus does not correct or rebuke the disciples, but he questions, *Do you now believe?* The inadequacy of their grasp of Jesus will become clear when they abandon him at the time of his arrest. He says, *The hour is coming, indeed has come, when you will . . . leave me alone.* Barrett comments, "The contrast with v. 25 is marked; the time of knowledge is future; the present is the time of offense and disaster."[39] There are in the Synoptic Gospels similar predictions that the disciples will desert Jesus (Matt. 26:31; Mark 14:27). They expressly cite Zechariah 13:7, *"Awake, O sword, against my shepherd,*

39. Barrett, *Gospel*, 497.

against the man who is my associate," says the Lord of hosts, "Strike the shepherd that the sheep may be scattered." Although the Fourth Evangelist does not call attention to this prophecy, it would seem to be the source of the weighted word "scattered" (*skorpisthēte;* in the Good Shepherd passage Jesus spoke of a flock "scattered" by a wolf, 10:12). Previously Jesus had foretold Judas's betrayal and Peter's denial (13:21-23, 38). Here he predicts a collective failure. The disciples, all of them, will desert him.

The Beloved Disciple is not mentioned in this passage, even indirectly. He was introduced after the foot-washing incident (13:21-30), but he does not figure in the Farewell Discourses and seems to be out of mind here. The johannine passion story places him, and only him, of all the disciples, at the cross (19:25-27). He did not desert. But he is not mentioned here as an exception to the general failure.

Jesus called his followers from their former places in life and their old social solidarities; they found new bonding with Jesus and his companions and a new reason for living. The threat of Jesus' "hour" relaxes his hold on them and isolates him. In this testing, the old roles and places will again attract them; their former ways of life were something to fall back on. The Greek simply says "each to his own" *(eis to idia).* Schnackenburg remarks, "Every disciple is concerned with his own safety and not at all with Jesus."[40] Jesus says, *You will leave me alone.* The one who has lived with and for others comes to the final events of his life deserted by all.

Isolation throws one upon one's inner resources. Is there a reservoir of confidence which belongs to the unshared depths of one's personhood and which will hold when external supports give way? Jesus, even when he was deserted by his friends, was supported by a relation with the Father which nothing could unsettle. *Yet I am not alone because the Father is with me.* At the end of the First Discourse (14:30-31), Jesus spoke of a hidden challenge of *the ruler (archōn) of this world.* Here, by contrast, he speaks of the hidden oneness with the Father which has all along been the substratum of his life. Earlier in his public self-presentation, Jesus has said, *The one who sent me is with me; he has not left me alone, for I always do what is pleasing to him* (8:29). Whatever cruelty might assault him, and whoever else might leave him, this bonding with the Father held, and that relation was what finally mattered.

40. Schnackenburg, *Gospel,* 3.165.

The cry of dereliction *My God, my God, why have you forsaken me?* which, according to Matthew 27:46 and Mark 15:34, Jesus called from the cross, cannot but come to mind contrasting with this expression of unbroken closeness to the Father to which, according to the Fourth Gospel, Jesus witnesses on the eve of his passion.

Jesus' interior life, as it is depicted in the Fourth Gospel, is not without complexity. In 12:27 he was overheard to say, *Now my soul is troubled. And what should I say — "Father, save me from this hour?" No, it is for this reason I have come to this hour.* This enigmatic passage, coming at the end of the Book of Signs, seems to be interior dialogue. Jesus asks the Father for relief from his destiny, yet he comes to terms with it. The words are often taken to be the johannine equivalent of Jesus' prayer in Gethsemane which is reported in two of the Synoptic Gospels.

The confident words in Jesus' Farewell in the Fourth Gospel, *I am not alone, for the Father is with me,* contrast markedly with the anguished lament *My God, my God, why have you forsaken me?* Very strikingly, in his cry of abandonment in Matthew and Mark, Jesus uses the opening words of Psalm 22. In the Psalm as well as in Jesus' use of it, the words are paradoxical. A person of faith cries out the loss of God *to God.* Although in extremity Jesus' relation to the Father has become deeply troubled, yet in his very abandonment, he calls out to God. These words from the tradition of Jewish spirituality witness that other persons of the covenant community before him had experienced God-forsakenness.

Does the Fourth Gospel represent a first-century tradition of Jesus' words and acts in which this unforgettable (and no doubt for Christians, shocking) cry had no place? Or, assuming that the writer of the Fourth Gospel knew the tradition of Jesus' cry of abandonment, is he quietly and deliberately setting it aside? Or is he interpreting it? For whatever reason, although two of the Synoptic accounts say that Jesus at the end was forsaken by all, and even to himself he seemed forsaken by God, the johannine account represents that Jesus in the crisis of his "hour" knew the Father to be with him.

I have said this to you,
  so that in me you may have peace.
In the world you face persecution,
  but take courage;
  I have conquered the world." 16:33

Again Jesus states his purpose in speaking, *I have said this to you so that. . . .* The *"this"* may refer to the immediately foregoing sayings, but it seems more likely that Jesus refers to the entire Third Discourse, in which he has always kept in mind the wrenching sorrow that filled his disciples' hearts (16:6). Jesus speaks to give his followers peace. What he says is, as D. Moody Smith puts it, "not so much an explanation they [the disciples] can immediately assimilate as a heritage upon which they shall draw."[41] Jesus himself taps a source of confidence even in the face of isolation and death. The disciples' peace comes from Jesus, and Jesus' peace is secured by his relation to the Father, who is always faithful. Walter Brueggemann commented, "Even though his 'friends' are scattered and even though he is abandoned, he is with God. Does this not suggest that shalom for the church as for Jesus is discerned in the assurance that God is abidingly present?"[42]

Using the idiom of place — where one is, where one dwells, whom one is with — Jesus says that his disciples are simultaneously in two locations: *in the world (en tō kosmō)* and *in me (en emoi),* in Jesus. In one location they find *persecution.* The Greek *thlipsis,* as was noted in v. 21, is an eschatological term that often refers to a terrible final time of testing. (See Mark 13:19, 24 and Rev. 7:14.) In johannine thought, this testing is *now,* as final things are now. In the other location, in Jesus, the disciples find *peace.* But peace is also an eschatological term, reaching beyond the conflicts of the present social order and seizing what is to be — God's original and final *shalom.* The ultimate reconciliation of all things, which is accomplished in Jesus and is pledged for the end, is accessible to Jesus' people now.

There is evangelical irony in the words *But take courage; I have conquered the world.* In the Gospel narrative, Jesus is going to his death at the hands of powerful opponents who want him out of the way. Yet he proclaims that his victory over the world is already accomplished.

"I have conquered the world," which appears only here in the Fourth Gospel, is used in 1 John 2:13-14; 4:4; and 5:4-5. Ragnar Lievestad, in his study *Christ the Conqueror* says, "Strictly speaking, the only warlike term in the [Fourth] gospel is *nenikēka* in 16:33."[43]

---

41. D. M. Smith, *Interpreting the Gospels for Preaching* (Philadelphia: Fortress, 1980), 91.

42. Walter Brueggemann, *Living toward a Vision: Biblical Reflections on Shalom* (New York: United Church Press, 1982), 120.

43. Ragnar Lievestad, *Christ the Conqueror: Ideas of Conflict and Victory in the New Testament* (London: SPCK, 1954), 192.

Jesus' words *I have conquered* speak as though his victorious death were already accomplished. Conflict will intensify in chapters 18–19 as Jesus is tried and put to death. But the ultimate outcome is assured. His death at the hands of the world is at the same time his conquest of the world.

The confident words *I have conquered the world* express the "Christus Victor" motif which the early Christians often used to express their understanding of Jesus' death. The imperative *take courage* indicates the difference it makes to live under the victorious Christ. The Fourth Gospel sees the world as human life ordered out of its own resources, determining its own purposes, and taking its own way, apart from God. This all-encompassing order of things — the darkened and destructive adversary of both Jesus and his people — opposes God and diminishes humanity. The world is very powerful, but Jesus has overcome it. Jesus by his coming into the world demonstrates the divine engagement with the cosmic opposition — an engagement in which Jesus, crucified and living, is the world's judgment and redemption. He holds fast in obedience and love where others give way. His victory, attested in the resurrection, was not, however, an individual achievement, but an event of universal significance. This first-century Galilean rabbi was divine grace and power — the very Word of God — engaged in behalf of humanity. At an earlier moment, poised between the completion of his public ministry and the opening of the passion events, Jesus had said *Now is the judgment of this world; now the ruler of this world will be driven out. And I, when I am lifted up from the earth, will draw all people to myself* (12:31-32). His solitary cross is a redemptive act in behalf of all.

In this closing counsel, on the night before his passion, Jesus speaks not simply of enduring, but of overcoming. Jesus' followers can live in an oppressive world, knowing that in Jesus the darkness, the negation has been met, and its power is broken. The disciples may suffer at the hands of the world. Yet they live in unity with the world's conqueror. They form a community of mutually self-giving persons who are led and taught by the Divine Paraclete, and who live an alternative style of life, informed by an alternative account of reality. In them *The light goes on shining in the darkness. It is not overcome by the darkness* (1:5).

The "Christus Victor" motif lay close to the heart of the religion of Martin Luther, who ended his series of sermons on John 14–16 saying:

> May God help us too, and may He dispose us to cling to Christ's victory in troubles and in death. Even though at present we are not able to

> grasp the meaning of these words fully and compellingly, yet may we think of them in the hour of need and say: this is what my Lord and Savior put into my heart. In Him I have a Victor over the world, death, and the devil, no matter how small and weak I am. Amen.[44]

In the lectionary. The Revised Common Lectionary makes no use of this Third Discourse, except for the opening Paraclete passage, 16:5-16, which is the Gospel reading for Trinity Sunday in Year C. (See the earlier comment on pp. 260-61.)

Perhaps the lectionary-makers thought that in 16:16-33 there is so much repetition of themes from chapter 14 that this second part of chapter 16 could be bypassed inasmuch as chapter 14 is used rather fully. Or they may have thought that at least some of the language of the last half of chapter 16 is so allusive and obscure that it would present preachers and congregations with more puzzles than immediate evangelical counsel.

For these or other reasons, the second half of his Third Discourse, although it contains valuable early Christian witness, is not read and preached in the churches that follow the ecumenical lectionary. The omission of this passage from the hearing/preaching cycle of readings can be dealt with in the more methodical coverage of daily Bible reading or in Bible study groups. One can encounter it for oneself by reading and by following the unusually good secondary literature on the Fourth Gospel. Of course, much of the material in the second half of this Discourse contains themes that have been introduced in the earlier discourses and that may therefore have been presented by the lectionary during the Easter season.

---

44. *Luther's Works,* vol. 24: *Sermons on the Gospel of St. John Chapters 14-16,* ed. Martin H. Berman (St. Louis: Concordia, 1961), 422.

7. The Paraclete

Although Jesus is departing to the Father, his disciples are not cast upon their own resources. They are not left to an anxious, effortful performance of the life of followers; they are not required by their own persuasiveness to win over a hostile world; and they do not have to recall in changing situations, events which were important, but which would recede in time. The divine investment toward them which they have known in Jesus — calling, leading, teaching, reminding, supporting, correcting, sharing — is not ended or diminished by Jesus' departure. Rather, it is extended, enlarged and made more lasting and inward through the presence among them of *"another Advocate."*

The Term and the Role

Jesus' term *"the Advocate"* (or *Paraclete;* the Greek word is *paraklētos*), enters the text at 14:16 with no preparation and no explanation. Even first-century readers might have been puzzled, for although they would have known the word, its common meanings might not have made clear what the Evangelist was saying by it. As he took over a word with a complex history and usage, he drew on some, but not all of its prior, largely secular meanings, and his way of using the term stretched it into new significance. He asked his readers to grasp his word on the terms set by his usage. Robert Kysar remarks that the Paraclete is one of the Evangelist's "innovative concepts."[1]

1. Robert Kysar, *The Fourth Evangelist and His Gospel* (Minneapolis: Augsburg, 1975), 234.

The Greek word combines *para* (alongside) and *kalein* (to call). It speaks of one who is called to the side of another. In Classical Greek it could mean an encourager, as when Xenophon speaks of exhorting men to the fairest deeds (*Anabasis* 31.24). The term also had a legal setting, speaking of one who enters a case as a friend of the accused or one who entreats or appeals in behalf of another. Philo spoke of the Jews in Alexandria, who were ill-treated, seeking a *paraklētos* to carry their cause to the Emperor Gaius.[2]

There is no Hebrew word behind this johannine term. Rather, a Greek word was put into Hebrew characters and taken into Aramaic as a loanword. In legal affairs a *paraklētos,* who took one's part, was contrasted with a *katēgoros,* who was an accuser. (The term *katēgorein* is used in John 5:45 as a verb, to accuse. Both the verb, to accuse, and the noun, accuser, occur in the textually spurious passage about the woman taken in adultery, John 8:6, 10. In Rev. 12:10, the devil is spoken of as the accuser of Christians.) Legal imagery was important as Jewish religion sought to picture humanity before God. A rabbinic text could say "In the heavenly judgment one's advocates *(paraklētoi)* are repentance and good works."[3]

Although one of the johannine Paraclete passages, 16:7-11, draws on the forensic background of the term *paraklētos,* the other passages suggest broader, more personal senses, referring to one who consoles another, befriends another, guides or teaches another, or to one who publicizes the truth of things. Translators have tried many equivalents for the Evangelist's term: Advocate (the choice of the NRSV), Comforter, Convincer, Counselor, Encourager, Friend, Helper, Teacher. Some have simply transliterated: "Paraclete." John Reumann judges that "No one English word catches all the nuances in the Paraclete passages."[4]

The translation of *paraklētos* as "comforter" was long familiar in the English-speaking world through the versions of Wycliffe and Tyndale which were taken up in the Authorized Version (1611), whence it came into hymns, sermons, and classic texts. In the LXX, the term *paraklētos* was used in Isaiah 40:1-12, where it was

2. The references in Xenophon and Philo are found in William Barclay, *More New Testament Words* (New York: Harper and Row, 1958), 128-35.

3. The rabbinic reference is also in Barclay, *More New Testament Words,* 128-35.

4. John Reumann, "Introduction" to Hans Windisch, *The Spirit-Paraclete in the Fourth Gospel,* trans. James Cox (Philadelphia: Fortress, 1968), xii-xiii. In the Fourth Gospel, "the Paraclete" is always a noun, a title, or a designation. The verb *parakaleō* is not used, and divine action is nowhere spoken of as *paraklēsis,* encouragement.

translated *comfort my people,* and in Job 16:2 it speaks of Job's *miserable comforters.* Through the first English translators, the term "comforter" became a name attached to the Holy Spirit. In one of his "terrible sonnets," the nineteenth-century Jesuit poet Gerard Manley Hopkins wrote the heart-wrenching lament, "Comforter, where is your comforting?"[5]

Even at its strongest, the translation of *paraklētos* by "comforter" would today seem to refer the work of the Spirit to occasions of weakness, sorrow or distress when sympathy is needed.

If "comforter" seems now to be a weak translation, its inadequacy traces not to bad judgment by the early English translators, but to developments in the language since the sixteenth century.

Tyndale would have understood "comforter" in the sense which came into English by way of Old French *(conforter),* from the Latin (*con,* an intensive + *fortis,* strong, brave). In Middle English (and later for those who heard the Latin or the Old French beneath the word) "comforter" meant something like "encourager," "inspiriter," or "strength-giver." It is later developments in the English language that weakened the term.

The Evangelist in 14:26 equates the Paraclete and "the Holy Spirit" — a term that was evidently already current among Christians in the late first century, but a term that is used only in this one place in the johannine writings. Perhaps the Evangelist sought to explain his unfamiliar word "paraclete" by setting alongside it the more familiar term "Holy Spirit," the breath of God.

In three places (14:17; 15:26; 16:13) the Evangelist describes the Paraclete as "the Spirit of truth," using a term that had some currency prior to the New Testament. *Testament of Judah* 20 contrasts "the spirit of truth and the spirit of error" (cf. 1 John 4:6): "the spirit of truth *testifies to all things and brings all accusations*" so that "he who has sinned is consumed in his heart and cannot raise his head to face the judge."[6] In the Qumran documents, *The Manual of Discipline* speaks of "the spirit of truth" as the helper or vindicator of the Children of Light, the accuser of the children of darkness, and the one who struggles against the spirit of darkness "in the hearts of men."[7]

5. "No worst, there is none," line 3.

6. As translated by H. C. Kee in James H. Charlesworth, ed., *Old Testament Pseudepigrapha* (Garden City: Doubleday, 1983), 1.800.

7. 1QS 3–4. The similarity of such ideas to the johannine Paraclete theme is unmistak-

The Paraclete — who stands on the divine side of things, but at the same time is effective in the lives of men and women — suggests other powers, more or less personal in character, which, in Jewish thought, were divine teachers, witnesses, or intermediaries. *Angels* were sent to make God's will known and to guard the interests of people (Daniel 10:13; Mt. 1:20-22; Luke 1:11-20, 26-38; Acts 5:19; 8:26; 12:7-10). *Wisdom,* who was eternally related to God, "takes root" within godly persons, giving them understanding (Sir. 24:12, 26f). God's *Spirit* ("breath") came upon certain persons, giving them special skills, prophetic words, and inner gifts for demanding tasks. Pre-Christian Judaism understood there to be powers lodged within God, but sent from God to minister to and give support and guidance to the covenant people.

The Evangelist describes the Paraclete as filling a social, relational role; the Advocate stands with or between people. Unlike a "kategoros," an accuser, a "parakletos" is supportive — assisting someone who is disadvantaged, strengthening those who are overtaxed, supporting those who are engaged in a struggle, speaking in behalf of someone who is accused. At the point where "paraclesis" is needed, one party is inadequate and another lends support. At times one may be taking a wrong direction or may be deceived, and one's truest helper is one who judges and corrects. Moreover, the term implies commitment and passion. A paraclete allies herself or himself with another, caringly and perhaps costingly. An Advocate is self-invested in the well-being of another. A paraclete is partisan — always *for* another.

The Evangelist developed the possibilities of his term with considerable originality. To cite Robert Kysar again, "With the word Paraclete he catches the imagination of a wide range of readers and opens numerous avenues of meaning for the Spirit."[8] In this johannine coinage the Evangelist did not let the pre-existing term restrict his meaning; the church's experience of the divine Spirit governed. The legal sense of Jesus' term "paraclete" is drawn on only to a limited extent. The term is stretched to accommodate and disclose; it does not confine the reality that the Evangelist seeks to present.

---

able, but scholars cannot establish a direct literary debt of the Fourth Gospel to the community of the Scrolls. See A. R. C. Leaney's summary essay, "The Johannine Paraclete and the Qumran Scrolls," in James H. Charlesworth, ed., *John and the Dead Sea Scrolls* (New York: Crossroad, 1990), 38-61.

8. Kysar, *Fourth Evangelist,* 94.

The Paraclete Passages in Summary

The five *Paraclete* passages in Jesus' Farewell have been noted in the consecutive comments earlier in this study; each has an emphasis suitable for its context. A few summary observations here will bring them into a single view:

(1) The First Discourse (13:31–14:31) is concerned with the discontinuity occasioned by Jesus leaving his disciples. In **14:16-17** the Paraclete is described as an enduring presence which takes the place of the departing Jesus. Nothing is said as to what the Paraclete will do, only that the Spirit will be Jesus' "new presence" with and in his people.

Jesus is leaving. Who can fill his role? Can the community adjust its life to its changed situation? The concern for continuity in 14:16-17 may have suggested occasions of delegation or succession in the Jewish histories. In Num. 11:4-25, seventy elders are designated to share the responsibility which has become too much for Moses alone, and God puts on them some of the spirit that has been on Moses (11:25). Later, as leadership passes from Moses to Joshua (Deut. 31:7-8, 23; 32:44; 34:9; Josh. 1:1-9), the people are exhorted to do according to the law of Moses (Josh. 1:7-8), and Joshua is given "the spirit" (Deut. 34:9); God's presence and strength are pledged to him (Deut. 31:7-8, 23; Josh. 1:1-9). Similarly as Elisha succeeds Elijah (2 Kings 2), a double share of Elijah's "spirit" is asked, and "the spirit of Elijah" rests on Elisha (2:15). In these instances, the breath or vitality of a great figure passes to a successor. In John 14:16-17, the Spirit does not rest on an individual designated successor nor on an appointed eldership. Rather, the Spirit is herself the successor who dwells persistingly in the community of Jesus' followers. Such biblical instances of succession must have been present in the Bible-saturated minds of the Evangelist's first readers (who were themselves losing the leaders they had depended on).

(2) Later in the same discourse, in **14:26**, Jesus equates the Paraclete with the Holy Spirit and mentions for the first time that the Paraclete will teach, reminding his followers of all that he has said to them. The Spirit answers the concern of the disciples: without Jesus present to speak for himself, were they cut off from his living voice and authoritative instruction?

The assurance of the continued presence of the Paraclete and the confidence that she would remind the "orphaned" followers of what Jesus had said (14:26) were emphases that were relevant, at a second level of significance, to the first-century johannine community which through the loss of its principal witnesses (who traced to the Beloved Disciple) feared that it was losing its primary links with the figure of Jesus.

(3) The Second Discourse (15:1–16:4a) introduces the Paraclete in **15:26-27**, where Jesus, speaking of persecution, says that the Paraclete will "testify in my behalf." The Synoptic Gospels similarly link the early church's discovery of the Holy Spirit with its experience of persecution (Matt. 10:16-25 and parallels, see pp. 232-36, above). When the church needed one to stand alongside it, the Spirit could be counted on. If the Paraclete will be effective outside the community of believers, it will be so through the collective actions of believers: *She will witness . . . you will witness.*

In the Third Discourse, the long passage on the Paraclete, 16:7-15, is, as we have seen, two units: 16:8-11 concerns the Paraclete and the world, which the Paraclete corrects and judges; while 16:12-15 speaks of the Spirit's supportive ministry to the community of Jesus.

(4) Using forensic terms, **16:8-11** says that the Paraclete exposes the world's alienated condition. The world orders its life in such a way as to identify right and wrong, rewarding one and punishing the other. Yet lacking the central clue provided by Jesus and belief in him, it gets them wrong, as its treatment of him demonstrated. If the world is to come to a new mind about the central issues of civil polity, it will do so through the witness of the Paraclete whereby it can reassess Jesus and through him learn the truth about itself.

(5) In **16:12-15** the Paraclete guides Jesus' community into *all the truth,* but it does so in a complex way: The Paraclete will move the church towards the future, declaring things to come, while at the same time the Spirit will speak only what the Spirit has heard — the things of Jesus, and hence things that are the Father's. The Spirit's instruction turns in two directions, speaking of originality, newness and the future, and at the same time of dependence, givenness, and the continuing authority of what has been disclosed.

The supreme purpose of the Spirit's work is the glorification of Jesus (16:14). By the Paraclete, the fullness of the divine life that is brought in Jesus is made known and accessible to redeemed humanity.

The question has been raised as to whether or not these Paraclete passages are integral to johannine thought and whether they fit their context. They enter only in the Farewell Discourses, where they may seem to stand somewhat apart from their immediate contexts as well as from the terminology and thought of the rest of the Gospel. Some critics have thought them to be a separable body of material, which may have had an origin outside the Gospel.[9] It is possible, of course, that these passages had some prior identity, and they may have been entered into the text of the Fourth Gospel as it grew into its present form. However, in whatever way this small body of material came to be, the original writer (or a later editor) seems to have made it his own, and it fills a convincing place in Jesus' Farewell.

The Divine Self-Imparting

The Paraclete, Jesus' successor, is described in personal terms. (The noun and associated pronouns are masculine gender, which does not denote maleness. In fact, there is an old tradition in Christian theological and spiritual writing of referring to the Holy Spirit as feminine. The present study uses feminine pronouns for the Holy Spirit.) Jesus and his closeness are not to be replaced by a vague sort of something. The Spirit is described in these johannine passages in terms of the relational life of persons; she will continue to do many of the things that Jesus has done. The Paraclete represents direct, intimate divine involvement, supporting and teaching believers and challenging the world, as Jesus did.

In speaking of the Paraclete, the Evangelist often uses triadic terms. He sets the Spirit in relation to the Father and the Son; the Paraclete holds a place in the complex divine life. The writer puts the matter in different ways: The Spirit is given to the disciples by the Father on the request of Jesus (14:16), or she is sent from the Father in Jesus' name (14:26). The Paraclete is sent by the Son from the Father, or she comes from the Father (15:26). Trinitarian questions and the categories for discussing them would, of course, only develop in later Christian thought, and when they did, the active, personal terms of the johannine Paraclete sayings provided the early theologians with rich (although not unambiguous) material.

The Farewell does not describe the divine *pneuma* as an all-pervading *Geist,* but as specific revelatory act and presence. The Paraclete will be *sent,* as Jesus was sent (14:26). She will *come,* as Jesus came and as Jesus and the Father will come (14:23). To the world, disordered as it is, the Spirit is an alien presence which it cannot receive or know (14:17). The

9. The thesis that the Paraclete passages form a somewhat separable part of the Fourth Gospel is associated with the German exegete Hans Windisch. His principal essays on the matter were translated and edited in *The Spirit-Paraclete in the Fourth Gospel,* noted above. The booklet contains a valuable introduction by John Reumann.

Evangelist describes an advent of the Spirit. The Spirit will *witness to* the world (15:26), showing it to be in the wrong (16:8-11) — as Jesus witnessed to the truth and against the world's mistaken self-understanding (18:37). The Paraclete who will witness against the world will *teach* the church. As believers make their uncertain way in the world, the Spirit will impart to them things they need to know but that they cannot come to know by self-initiated inquiry (14:26; 16:13-15).

Such expressions locate the Spirit with the transcendence and free initiative of the divine. The johannine idiom does not present the Paraclete as an immanent, latent force which is progressively brought to articulateness and power by an inner drive of all things towards their fulfillment. The Spirit is not depicted in the Fourth Gospel as a diffused power that does everything in general. The divine Helper is not a symbol for the intrinsic relatedness of the creation to God. Rather, the Farewell Discourses describe the Paraclete as a speaker and an actor, a partisan, engaged for specific things and against others. The Spirit is the Spirit of God, the Spirit of Jesus, acting within the followers of Jesus and through them upon the refractory world.

While the Paraclete is related to the divine life, she is at the same time related to humanity — an intimate strengthener, correcter, reminder, instructor. The Spirit is God *in you* (14:17), and the author of 1 John says, *The anointing that you received from him abides in you* (1 John 2:27). The Spirit is a participation of the transcendent God in redeemed humanity and of redeemed humanity in God.

In the johannine description of the Spirit, these two things are held together. The one who is inward becomes inward from beyond. The one who is God-in-ourselves is not-ourselves. The Spirit is, in John V. Taylor's fine phrase, "the beyond in the midst."[10]

The Paraclete and Christ

Jesus' Farewell depicts the Paraclete as dependent on Christ. The Evangelist makes the point in several ways: The Paraclete comes because Jesus leaves (14:16, 26; 16:7); or Jesus, having gone, sends the Spirit (15:26; 16:7); or the Spirit is sent by the Father in Jesus' name (14:26), or at Jesus' request

10. John V. Taylor, *The Go-Between God: The Holy Spirit and the Christian Mission* (Philadelphia: Fortress, 1973), 5.

(14:16). The Paraclete does not inaugurate some original line of acting or teaching, but reminds the church of Jesus' words (14:26); she shows it the things of Christ (16:14-15). As J. E. Fison said: "There is to be no possibility of driving a wedge between the Spirit and Christ any more than there is to be any possibility of absorbing the Spirit in Christ."[11]

When the Spirit is introduced as *another paraclete* (14:16), the expression suggests that the Spirit is Jesus' alter ego — that Jesus has been a "paraclete" and that the Spirit will be to Jesus' followers as he has been. The Paraclete is caught up in the profound exchanges that Jesus has spoken of as part of the spiritual commerce between himself and the Father. The Paraclete will glorify Jesus (16:14a), as Jesus has glorified the Father (7:18; 13:31; 14:13; 17:4) and the Father has glorified Jesus (8:50, 54; 13:32; 17:1). The Spirit stands in relation to God and to humanity as Jesus has. The Spirit's presence re-creates the situation of "God with us" that prevailed in Jesus' historic ministry, *The Word . . . lived among us* (1:14).

Parallels between Jesus and the Paraclete have been identified by Raymond Brown, who concludes that "virtually everything that has been said about the Paraclete has been said somewhere else in the Gospel about Jesus."[12] To summarize his findings:

The Paraclete will *come* (15:26; 16:7, 8, 13) as Jesus has come into the world (5:43; 16:28; 18:37). The Paraclete *comes forth* from the Father (15:26) as Jesus came forth from the Father (8:42; 13:3; 16:27-28; 17:8). The Father who will *give* the Paraclete (14:16) also gave the Son (3:16). Both the Paraclete and Jesus are *sent* by the Father (said of the Paraclete in 14:26; 15:26; 16:7, and of Jesus many times).

The Paraclete is the Spirit of Truth (14:17; 15:26; 16:13), and Jesus is the truth (14:6). The Spirit which came on Jesus at his baptism and remained (1:32-33) is the Spirit which Jesus breathes into his disciples after the resurrection (20:22) and who will remain with them and in them forever (14:17), binding them into Truth.

The disciples who knew Jesus (14:7, 9) will also know the Paraclete (14:17). The Paraclete will be in the disciples (14:17), but Jesus and the Father make their dwelling in them as well (14:23). Both the Paraclete and Jesus teach (6:59; 7:14, 28; 8:20). Both bear witness (said of the Spirit, 15:26, and 1 John 5:7-8; said of Jesus, 3:11, 32-33; 5:31; 7:7; 8:14, 18; 18:37).

The Paraclete cannot be received by the world (14:17), as Jesus himself was rejected (5:43; 12:48; 15:18-20). The world which does not know the Paraclete (14:17) did not know Jesus (16:3).

11. J. E. Fison, *The Blessing of the Holy Spirit* (London: Longmans, 1950), 137.

12. Raymond Brown, *The Gospel according to John* (2 vols., Anchor Bible; Garden City: Doubleday, 1966-70), 1140.

Brown summarizes his detailed analysis, saying that the Evangelist presents the Paraclete as "another Jesus."[13] In the Spirit's presence, Jesus is present. He does not so much depart as in the Paraclete he comes freshly and stays on.

The emphasis in the Farewell chapters is on the indwelling Paraclete, who is the life of God in the church. The johannine church thought of itself as an anointed community (1 John 2:20, 27). Yet the Evangelist's insistence that the Spirit is dependent on Jesus may imply a cautionary note. Perhaps an emphasis on the Sprit was taking independent directions in the johannine community, and the writer had to make it clear that nothing can be considered a work of the Spirit which does not derive from and is not answerable to the revelation concretely given in Jesus Christ.

The Spirit in the church, the author says, *will not speak from herself (aph' heautou),* but is first a listener (16:13). The Paraclete will take the things of Christ *(the things that are mine, ek tou emou)* and declare them (16:14-15). Bishop Fison describes the humility of the Spirit, "The true Holy Spirit of God does not advertise Herself: She effaces Herself and advertises Jesus."[14] The Spirit is dependent on the Son. Yet it is through the Spirit, whose inward working makes the events of Jesus' ministry into a believed and preached kerygma, that Jesus' work becomes creative of a church and a new life. All that is accomplished in the One for the many is made effective in the many by the Spirit.

A reader observes an *order* in johannine thought: The Spirit is not spoken of as an immanent, diffused divine presence which comes to concentrated focus in Jesus the Christ. Some theologians have developed such an understanding of the Spirit, thinking of the Spirit as divine immanence, active in nature, in human gifts, and in the development of universal history, as well as stirring in the redemptive story and inspiring individual courage and holiness. Such an understanding of the Spirit has a place in some systematic theologies, particularly in some of the immanentist theologies of the late nineteenth and early twentieth centuries. But that is not the way in which the Paraclete is presented in the Farewell Discourses. The Presbyterian theologian George Hendry expressed the johannine pneumatology when he said, "The Spirit is presented [in the New Testa-

13. Brown's appendix, "The Paraclete," *Gospel,* 1136-44, is a superb summary of the johannine material.

14. Fison, *Blessing,* 138. Quotation altered.

ment] in a purely christocentric reference. There is no reference in the New Testament to any work of the Spirit apart from Christ. The Spirit is, in an exclusive sense, the Spirit of Christ."[15] In johannine thought, the activity of the Spirit is bound to the particularity of Jesus and the believing response to him. The Spirit's ministry is distinctively from Jesus and for the community that believes in Jesus. The Evangelist says that the world cannot see or know the Paraclete (14:17). Insofar as the Paraclete ministers to the world, it is as a witness to Christ (16:7-11) and a sharer in the witness of the church: *She will testify on my behalf. You also are to testify* (15:26-27). Just as Jesus is a hearer (5:30) who says what has been given him from the Father (7:17; 8:26, 28, 38, 40; 12:49-50), so the Spirit speaks only what she has heard (16:13). The vital divine self-imparting, which begins in the Father, moves to Jesus, and from him to the Paraclete, and to the church, through which it reaches the world. The Spirit depends on Christ; Christ is apprehended through the Spirit.

The Paraclete Communicating

By the Paraclete, God imparts God. It is by the outgoing activity of the Spirit that the divine life communicates itself in and to the creation. The Spirit is God-in-relations. The Paraclete is the divine self-expression which will *be and abide with you,* and *be in you* (14:16-17). The Spirit's work is described in terms of utterance: *teach you, didaskō* (14:26), *remind you, hypomimnēskō* (14:26), *testify, martyrō* (15:26), *prove wrong, elenchō* (16:8), *guide into truth, hodēgō* (16:13), *speak, laleō* (16:13, twice), *declare, anangellō* (16:13, 14, 15). The johannine terms describe verbal actions which intend a response in others who will *receive (lambanō), see (theōreō),* or *know (ginōskō)* the Spirit. Such speech-terms link the Spirit with the divine Word. The Spirit's initiatives imply God's personal engagement with humanity: The Spirit comes to *be with* others; the *teaching* Spirit implies a community of learners; forgetful persons need a prompter to *remind* them; one *testifies* expecting heed to be paid; one *speaks* and *declares* in order to be heard. The articulate Spirit is the correlative of the listening, Spirit-informed community.

The final Paraclete passage closes with a threefold repetition of the verb *she will declare (anangellō),* 16:13-15. The Spirit will *declare the things that are to come* (v. 13), and she will *declare* what is Christ's (vv. 14, 15). The

15. George Hendry, *The Holy Spirit in Christian Theology* (Philadelphia: Westminster, 1956), 26.

things of Christ are a message that must be heralded. The Spirit is a proclaimer, an evangelist to the church.

The God who speaks is heard as the depths of receptive persons are met and transformed by an initiative from the divine. As Bishop Fison put it, "Religion is established in its full reality, not as any substance or thing, objective or subjective, but in the living between-ness of all real relationship."[16]

The Ministry of Truth

The Paraclete's expressive teaching, declaring, witness-bearing, and judging actions exhibit the Paraclete's role as the Spirit of Truth. This title, as we have noted, antedated the Fourth Gospel and had some currency among the covenanters of Qumran. A member coming into the desert community would be cleansed "by the spirit of holiness uniting him to His [God's] truth." The counsels of the Spirit yield a character of humility, patience, charity, goodness, mighty wisdom, and discernment.[17]

To speak of "the Spirit of truth" connects the Paraclete with a johannine structure of reality that might be formulated along these lines:

- God is true, truth is of God. God speaks and acts in truth. God is what God reveals and does. God will be what God pledges. God cannot deny God.
- Jesus is truth. He is God's reliable witness, declaring what is true. His words arise out of an inner truth derived from his rootedness in God. He is God's truth shown forth in human flesh.
- The Paraclete is the Spirit of truth. The Spirit listens to God, and she speaks the truth that she has heard. The truth of God is imparted to and is reproduced in humanity by the truth-bearing Spirit.
- God's truth is truth for humanity. It exposes and heals an inner untruth and opens a free relation with God. God's truth indwelling is the joy and fulfillment of humanity.

One comes to this truth by an inner about-face. This strange new truth is grasped in a personal venture of commitment in which one comes to new life (3:3-8). Truth is not facts one knows nor concepts one grasps, but

16. Fison, *Blessing*, 144.
17. 1QS 3–4.

it is a self-imparting divine initiative by which one is grasped. In consenting to it, one passes from death to life (5:24; 1 John 3:14). Encounter with the reality of things reorders the self so that the truth is not external to oneself, but belongs to the rootage of oneself in oneself and in God. The intention of the Spirit of truth is the restoration of an alienated, deceived humanity.

The Paraclete and the World

The Spirit of truth engages with the world, albeit, according to the First Discourse, not directly (14:17), but through the believing and very human community of faith. On its own, the alienated world cannot "receive" or "see" or "know" the Spirit. Augustine once said, "Worldly love possesseth not those invisible eyes, whereby, in an invisible way, the Holy Spirit can be seen."[18]

In relation to the church, the Spirit is counselor, teacher and guide; but in relation to the world, which is carried away in untruth, the Spirit goes on the offensive: *She will prove the world wrong* (16:8). Christians who hear the Spirit described as "Advocate" tend to think of the divine Paraclete as one who stands with them, taking their part before God. They have an image of a court in which God is judge, and weak, erring persons are in need of a partisan, forceful representative if their case is to carry. But such an understanding of the Spirit's advocacy should not be read into this Paraclete passage. The Evangelist might think that such a construction of his terms represented, to say the best for it, a half-converted understanding. When he uses the legal aspect of his Paraclete terminology most fully (in 16:7-11), he depicts the Paraclete as a prosecutor, a power that is effective on the world, contending against it and in behalf of God. A verdict for God is sought from humanity. The urgent need, with respect to God and the world, as the Evangelist describes it, is not that humanity be represented before God, but that God's truth and judgment be set before a world that is largely closed against them. The Paraclete gives the case for God her potent advocacy.

The Teaching Spirit

The teaching role of the Paraclete tends to be remembered as a major emphasis of the Farewell Discourses, yet only 14:26 says *She will teach you all*

18. Augustine, *Tractates on John* 74.4.

things. (Teaching is, however, implied when 16:13-15 says that the Spirit will *guide you into all the truth,* and will *speak* and *declare.*) Franz Mussner remarks that the word used in 14:26, *didaskein,* "means literally 'teach, instruct,' but in John it nearly always means to reveal."[19]

The church is taught by God, as Israel was instructed by Yahweh. In John 6:45 Jesus cited Isa. 54:13, *They shall all be taught by God.* Jesus' followers have his words, as Israel had the Torah, and through those words they have the divine presence. The Paraclete is the agent of divine instruction, leading the church into truth. Her teaching is an interior teaching (14:17). God's truth is imparted through an informing shared life.

Thus it is of God that humanity comes to know God. God is self-interpreted. (The point that God makes God known was familiar in the Jewish tradition, even though there was no developed understanding of the Holy Spirit in Judaism. See Pss. 25:5; 143:10; Wis. 9:11; 10:10, 17.) Only God knows God; only God makes God known.

What the biblical writers say about the human apprehension of God has analogues in cultural movements. Any powerful innovation in art or ideas that sets thought or perception in new directions cannot be contained by old frames of understanding. It will, out of its own vitality, refashion the observers or the hearers, opening new regions of perception and providing the categories by which the new forms will come to be appreciated. In order to grasp anything new — whether it is the first viewing of the paintings of Mondrian, or the abstract expressionists, or the sound of Renaissance music or the minimalist compositions of Arvo Pärt on ears accustomed to Richard Strauss — anything that strikes one, on first encounter, as new and unassimilable — something must happen within one. The innovative composer gives new notes for performers to play or sing, but the composer also fashions new ears and minds with which to listen.

The new reality draws on much that has gone before, even as it refashions the hearing, seeing, apprehending self. Yet it pushes into interior regions untouched by any previous experience. A vital initiative in art or thought will not communicate to us if it remains outside us; rather, it enters us and begins to make us anew. The new is self-revealing, self-imparting. In some sense, as we come to appreciate it, in its newness and unexpectedness, it makes us sharers in itself. Similarly the Spirit who makes God known does so by making persons capable of knowing God.

19. Franz Mussner, *The Historical Jesus in the Gospel of St. John* (London: Burns and Oates, 1967), 59.

The divine teaching is inward and subtle, carrying no unmistakable insignia of its source and authority. Can the Spirit's teaching be mistaken for something else? Can deceptive spirits be mistaken for the Spirit? Yes, demonstrably yes. The Paraclete's instruction is accommodated to the fallible ways of human knowing, not overwhelming human learners, but winning by persuasion. The powerful divine witness is at the same time vulnerable — capable of being diverted by willful rejection or even by conscientious, well-meant, but misdirected efforts to understand. One follows what one takes to be the Spirit's teaching with fear and trembling.

The Teacher's Tools

The instrumentalities that may have been used in the Spirit's teaching and reminding work in the first century are barely hinted at in the Fourth Gospel. Apostolic witness is at least suggested, almost in passing (15:27; 17:20; 20:21). Nothing is said of units of narrative or of ethical counsel passed on orally, of written testimonies, of biblical interpretation, ecstatic experiences, charismatic prophets or authoritative teachers, collective deliberation, or of an accepted rule of faith. No doubt some of these things existed in some form or other in the johannine church as they did in other parts of the Jewish-Christian movement, but the Evangelist shows little interest in *how* the Spirit teaches. He assumes both the competence of the Spirit to teach and the capacity of believers to receive her instruction. (In 1 John 2:20 the writer says that the capacity to know comes through a divine anointing — which also goes unexplained.) Setting aside the means that are in fact required, the Evangelist goes to final agency, saying, in effect: "It is of God that you know God and that your grasp of divine things holds on course. To know that is enough."

How and by what means may the Spirit have taught in the johannine community is not beyond responsible conjecture. To cite a central locus: at the beginning of the Christian era the synagogue was the principal center for teaching in the Jewish community. It was a "house of study." The scriptures were read, the Psalms were sung, and gifted persons would relate the Law and the Prophets to the life of the day. Children (male children) were taught. The followers of Jesus began their communal life in the synagogue. When later the Christian movement stood on its own, it used and adapted the synagogue model for a portion of its worship (see 1 Cor. 11–14 and Justin Martyr's *Apology,* ch. 67). Commenting on given texts or traditions, but responding to the Spirit, prophetic persons, speaking at the pneumatically charged assembly of the Word, brought the revelation in Jesus into vital contact with contemporary experience. In the gathered community on the Lord's Day, new truth spoke creatively with old truth.[20]

Soon, however, Christian prophets, speaking in the assembly, were not in themselves sufficient to maintain the tradition of Jesus. The church was faced with contesting voices claiming to represent the true Christian teaching. The right tradition had to be identified and transmitted, credentials had to be established, and criteria for what was truly of Christ had to be made explicit.

A reader of 1 John can observe the later johannine community struggling to discern true teaching. *Beloved, do not believe every spirit, but test the spirits* (1 John 4:1). To be sure, the author speaks of a general illumination: *The anointing teaches you all* (1 John 2:27). Yet at the same time this "epistle" from the johannine community (usually taken to have been written somewhat later than the Gospel) speaks urgently of objective determinants, doctrinal touchstones for the discrimination between false teachers and true (1 John 2:4-6, 9-11, 18-27; 3:4–4:6; 5:6-12; also 2 John 7-11). However, at the time when the Fourth Gospel was being written, the criteria were evidently less firmly established. The Evangelist simply affirms the reality in the church of the Paraclete who interprets Jesus and his words. As it became necessary for Christians to know the truth of Jesus, the Paraclete would make it known — largely at first through Spirit-led prophets and teachers, working in an oral tradition. The community held gifts of imparting the Spirit's truth, but also gifts for recognizing the Spirit's truth. The Evangelist would no doubt have considered his own written Gospel to be one of the Spirit-given instrumentalities for formulating the tradition of Jesus, but also for launching it into creative engagement with the faith of believers — *But these are written so that you may come to believe* (20:31).

The Spirit's Subject-Matter

Jesus says that the Spirit's task is to receive *"what is mine" (ek tou emou)* and declare it to his followers. The Spirit, like Jesus, teaches according to the capacity of her pupils (16:12-13). The Paraclete does not override the incapaci-

20. The point is developed in Eskil Franck, *Revelation Taught: The Paraclete in the Gospel of John* (Lund: Gleerup, 1985), 42-45, 99-124.

ties that belong to the time-space-and culture-boundedness of every generation. This proposition may clarify what the Spirit does not teach. As bearer of the divine redemptive life to the race, the Spirit did not and does not impart new and reliable information, or right history, anthropology, cosmology or psychology. The Spirit's witness-bearing and teaching are carried out under the terms of the information and the concepts that are available at any given time to the culture, the church and the believer. The Spirit accommodates to the prevailing world-view, and she works through the cultural forms and the ways of learning that are at hand. H. Wheeler Robinson, two generations ago, spoke of "the *kenosis* of the Spirit."[21] Whatever the Spirit teaches is imparted in such a way as to respect and affirm rather than to set aside the time-and-space-and-society-bound human condition. In the mystery of learning from the Spirit, one learns through the ordinary human modes and draws from the accessible sources. To be sure, there may be heightened consciousness and moments of dazzling insight. (There may also be weeks of careful analysis, mental struggle, and searching discussion — and perhaps also periods of misdirected enthusiasms and dissipated effort.) Even though moments of heightened consciousness are unusual, they lie within the common human possibility. It needs to be said that no exalted experience or states of mind are of themselves authentications of the Spirit. In fact, they may be self-deluding. The Spirit teaches, but the ways of the Spirit are held within her own counsel. In every age, through the modest ways of divine leading, and through the church's own insights and despite its blind spots, the redemptive word is spoken and heard. The criterion as to the authenticity of the Spirit's tutoring is whether or not through what is imparted the things that have been given in the long creative/redemptive saga that culminates in Jesus Christ are more truly understood and followed.

The Spirit and Christian Memory

The Paraclete is presented in the Farewell speeches as a prompter, recalling Jesus and his words in relation to the new situations which make such remembering crucial and which may well require a creative, interpretive remembering. *She will teach you everything, and remind you of all that I have said to you* (14:26b; see also 16:14-15). In considering the ways of Christian

21. H. Wheeler Robinson, *Redemption and Revelation: In the Actuality of History* (New York: Harper and Row, 1942), 290-97.

memory, it would seem useful to note that any particular Spirit-prompted recalling, if it is to be effective, must assume a background of a more or less continuous and pervasive shared memory of Jesus, without which the moments of intense recall would be unintelligible. One can only cite Jesus authoritatively in a community in which he is generally remembered and believed in. Thus, the Spirit's reminding work is not sporadic, but it goes on regularly in such ordinary ways as the ritual acts and the more or less formalized words of worship, regular preaching, the maintenance of tradition, and patient teaching and study. If the Spirit's revelatory work has its occasions of blazing intensity, these occasions have their ground in structured, routinized forms which hold Jesus in the attention of his people. The two need each other, and both are of the Spirit.

The johannine presentation of the Paraclete shows a remarkable tensiveness. On the one hand, the divine Spirit supports a confident moving into the future, declaring *the things that are to come, ta erchomena* (16:13b). Yet on the other hand, the Spirit keeps the community faithful to what has been given in Jesus; *The Holy Spirit . . . will remind you of all that I have said to you* (14:26). The Christian community lives in history and hence is impacted by newness as creativity stirs in thought and culture. Yet at the same time, the church and its faith derive from determinative past persons and acts. How can the faith and its perception of Jesus change, as any living thing must change, while yet it remains itself?

The Fourth Gospel does not answer the issue directly, but it points to the Spirit as the source of such satisfactory answers as there will be. The Holy Spirit bears witness to Christ, never claiming to surpass him. One may think of Gabriel Marcel's phrase "creative fidelity." This issue may have arisen rather sharply in the johannine church not long after this Gospel was circulated. Evidently some persons in the johannine community thought they were in advance of the apostolic tradition, for the author of 2 John had to warn: *Everyone who does not abide (menein) in the teaching (didachē) of Christ, but goes beyond (proagō) it, does not have God.* The Spirit sometimes calls forward, and sometimes she must call back.

Jesus' place in the saga of God's self-communication to the race is determinative. God will not say more than he has said in Jesus Christ, the eternal Word made flesh. Yet what has been given in Jesus is revelatory mystery, requiring perennial exploration and interpretation. What was given in time-and-space-specific terms in the past must be repossessed and restated in an open succession of new situations. It is characteristic of history, as part of divine creativity, that it introduces new conditions and casts up new circumstances — new events, new understandings of the natural world and of the constitution of humanness, new pictures in the mind, unprecedented social patterns. In each new situation, as J. E. Fison put it, "The Jesus of history, who lived in the first century has to be reproduced not with the slavish echo of a literal imitation but with the authentic voice of an original in every generation."[22]

One cannot hold to past formulations, attitudes, responses, or forms of action, as though doing so demonstrated one's loyalty to a once-for-all divine disclosure. Anything that is taken to be authoritative was originally done, said or given in relation to a past situation. Jesus thought and spoke as a first-century Palestinian Jew. He knew nothing of constitutional democracy, romantic love, technological society, or nuclear fission. For later believers, in changed situations, to repeat literally what any past authority said in an earlier situation risks divinizing the finite. Knowing as much as we do about what Jesus or Paul or Amos did and said in their time, and seeking fidelity to them, we ask what they might do or say in our quite different conditions. And it seems certain that they would not do or say now exactly what they did in their past situations. In the strange movement that Christians must adopt in the era of historicism, we may demonstrate faithfulness to the past by entertaining change. As we turn to the past with new questions, the past may deliver new answers.

In the clarity, the subtlety, the certainty and the obscurity of the Church's encounter with Christ, the Paraclete is the assurance that the divine activity which was present in a plenary way in Jesus is present also in the church's ever-renewed effort to grasp him freshly in each new situation. The past event and the contemporary apprehension of it are both God-given. Although Jesus of Nazareth lived under the time-and-place-specific, culture-bound terms of human life, yet as the enfleshment of the divine Word, he never recedes into a distant past. His life is a moment accessible to and contemporaneous with every moment — a moment which through the Spirit is always redefining and re-creating itself.

The Inner Witness

The johannine writings do not psychologize; they undertake no analysis of the self, and they do not describe the Spirit's ways of working. Many Chris-

22. Fison, *Blessing,* 138.

tian traditions, restless with the Spirit's subtlety and elusiveness, have sought to find marks of the Spirit in certain emotional or behavioral or verbal manifestations. But the New Testament shows no interest in identifying such criteria. Such a search might, indeed, have seemed to most of the earliest Christians to be a way of seeking to confine or control the endlessly innovative ways of the divine Paraclete. The only criteria of the Spirit the New Testament offers are love, joy, peace, patience, kindness and humility.

The Divine Counselor, who is rooted in the interiority of God, is also effective in the interiority of believers. The actions of the self in thinking, responding, desiring, feeling, intending, yearning, and knowing, are, in a mysterious but powerful and self-authenticating way, shared. A divine Other thinks, responds, desires, feels, intends, yearns, and knows in and with a human self. As the Spirit works, the human self is not diminished or qualified. Its powers are drawn on and enlarged, while its fallibility and capacity for self-deception remain in working order. But the reflective believer is never alone.

Martin Buber, speaking out of his Jewish tradition, described the way in which this interior communication of God engages the self's converse with itself:

> God's speech to men penetrates what happens in the life of each one of us, and all that happens in the world around us, biographical and historical, and makes it for you and me into instruction, message, demand. Happening upon happening, situation upon situation are enabled and empowered by the personal speech of God to demand of the human person that he take his stand and make his decision.[23]

In all knowing, but most clearly in the coming-to-know that takes place between persons, one knows through a self-disclosure which comes, as it were, from the other side. An other makes her/himself known. But as one encounters that other, in all of her or his distinct, luminous otherness, one is altered. The encounter makes demands and opens opportunities. If one is to know the other, one must in the same act come to know oneself freshly. The knowing of the other becomes, as it were, an interior factor in one's continual discovery of oneself.

23. Martin Buber, *I and Thou* (2nd ed.; New York: Scribner's, 1958), 136.

The Spirit and the Community

The inwardness of the Spirit requires persons to consult their own unique experience. Yet one's self — one's "I" — can be shared, and in the relation of human persons with God, it necessarily is shared in the community of faith.

The pledge of the Spirit in the Farewell Discourses and the bestowal of the Spirit in the resurrection account (20:22) are made to the gathered disciples. The promise is spoken in the plural. The giving is into the common life, on which each individual is borne. There is a fulness of knowing which belongs not to any individual Christian, nor to any single generation, but to the collective, perennial life of the church. Jesus' promise that the Paraclete *will be with you forever* (14:16) obviously has in mind not only an individual, nor a single generation, but the continuing body of the faithful.

God, through the Spirit, relates to persons as the distinct centers of selfhood they are. Significant and authoritative personal relations are, in the long run, not with collectivities, but between persons. A group is not fully personal, as each of its members is. Yet personhood is not an individual attainment. The humanity of each person is acquired, tested, fulfilled, and limited in the relationships within which one is born and comes to maturity. The johannine presentation of the Paraclete sets the believer's relation with the Spirit within the common life. One encounters the Spirit as one encounters the Spirit-bearing community. No one can come to a fuller engagement with the Spirit by oneself. One shares in the Spirit's life — her leading and her teaching — as one shares in the living, learning, ever-changing, ever-constant community of the Spirit.

Essay: "Not Now, But Afterward"

The Fourth Gospel contains a figure of ideas which will be called here the "not now, but afterward" motif. It does not always show the same form or vocabulary, but it is evidenced by a three-stage movement of thought (expressed or implied): (1) something is remarked as not grasped, but (2) after critical events take place, (3) understanding will come.

This recurrent figure suggests that in the deep structure of the Evangelist's thought he makes a distinction of times; and this distinction creates part of the tension or interest in his Gospel. The story he tells is set in the former time, the time of Jesus' ministry; but he speaks (or has Jesus speak) of the incompleteness of that time. The Gospel narrative thus contains a forward thrust into a time in which the incompleteness will be done away. That time of believing, recognition, knowing and understanding will not be developed in the Gospel itself, but it is the time to which the Gospel story points forward, and it is the time in which the Evangelist writes and his readers live.

The motif appears in the Fourth Gospel nine times in fairly complete form and at least four times in more fragmentary form. It is sometimes expressed by the Evangelist, and sometimes by Jesus. It occurs three times in the Book of Signs, five times in the Farewell chapters, and once in the narrative of the resurrection.

To cite the more complete expressions:

1. 2:21-22: The Evangelist observes that Jesus' disciples did not understand his action at the cleansing of the Temple, but that after the resurrection, they remembered the act and the interpreting scriptures, and they believed.
2. 8:28: Jesus, speaking to a general public, says that there will be a recognition of who he is after he has been "lifted up."
3. 12:16: The disciples did not understand Jesus' entry into Jerusalem, but when he was "glorified," they remembered the act and the associated scriptures.
4. 13:7: The full meaning of Jesus washing his disciples' feet was not grasped at the time it took place, but Jesus says that "later" *(meta tauta)* his followers will understand.
5. 13:19: Jesus speaks of his betrayal in advance so that when future events develop as he has foreseen, his disciples will believe.
6. 14:25-26: Jesus says that during the time of his ministry he was limited in what he could say to his followers, but in the "after-age" of the Spirit, they will remember and understand.
7. 14:29: Jesus tells his disciples that he has spoken so that after the "coming" of the *archōn* of this world and the crisis which is to follow — that is to say, after his departure to the Father — they may believe.
8. 16:4: A critical time is coming. The forces that are set against Jesus and his people have their "hour" as he has his. When the opposition's moment of apparent victory comes, Jesus' followers will remember *(mnēmoneute)* that he foretold it.
9. 20:9: The Evangelist makes an editorial interruption in his account

of the resurrection appearances. "As yet" *(oudepō)* the disciples had no knowledge from the Scriptures that Jesus would rise from the dead. The text implies that in the light of the event, they came to know.

Some fragmentary or variant instances of the motif may be noted:

- In the exchange with Nathanael in 1:50-51 Jesus says that although Nathanael believes because of what he has seen, he will see greater things. This exchange has at least some of the characteristics of the motif. It promises an "after" time, which will be greater.
- In telling about the cleansing of the Temple (2:17), the Evangelist reports that the disciples later remembered the interpreting scriptures.
- The "afterward" usually has the form of a promise to Jesus' followers — a pledge that at a later time they will understand. But 8:21-22 seems to invert the motif. Speaking with unsympathetic listeners, Jesus says *I am going away.* Then he says *afterward you will seek me* — futility. *You will die in your sin* — despair. The new age will come, but it will be darkness and not light.
- The now/later structure of 13:36 at least suggests the motif. In Jesus' exchange with Peter, he says that Peter cannot follow now, but he will follow "later." Jesus speaks here of "following," rather than of "believing" or "knowing." The "then-time" will be a time of understanding, but also a time of following.

This group of passages depicts the two ages as separated by the crucial events of Jesus' ministry — his death, his going to the Father, and the coming of the Paraclete. These events brought about the reconstruction of the disciples' sense of things. "Afterward" they knew, they remembered, they understood and believed.

Two things are mentioned as belonging to the new age:

(1) In several instances of this motif (2:17, 12:15-16, 13:19) a new grasp of the Scriptures is spoken of — suggesting that the new age brought with it a new understanding of the scriptures of Israel. This aspect of the motif may hint that the Christians were aware of their growing christological understanding of the Jewish Scriptures, and they thought of it as in some sense God-given.

(2) Several instances indicate that in the new age, events in the life of Jesus were remembered and understood as they were not earlier. The "afterward" part of the motif suggests the church's recalling, with significantly

altered insight, the acts and words of Jesus. Perhaps the Evangelist implies the basis for his radically distinct interpretation of Jesus.

This handful of johannine passages can provide a clue to the character of this Gospel — its audacity and its freedom with its sources. Doubtless for the author, the crucial events in the history of the race were those he recounts in his story of Jesus. Yet in his narrative the Evangelist never implies, "The *then*-time was better; we can only reproduce it dimly now." He never romanticizes the time of Jesus, as though to yearn, "If only Jesus could be with us now as he was then," or "If only we could be with him now as his first followers were." In the Fourth Gospel's theology, it is not the beginning time that is the primal reality, all the times that follow being derivative or shadowy. Rather, the author believes that his own *now* — the age of the church and the Spirit — is the time to which previous times looked forward. It is a time of knowing, remembering, understanding, and following beyond that which was possible for Jesus' disciples when he was with them. The "greater works" are being done. Now an abundant life that was not accessible before is open to "whomsoever." That life depends, to be sure, on the previous crucial events of the "*then*-era" — Jesus' ministry and his glorification. But *that* was instrumental to *this*. The author is realistic. If this is the time of life and understanding, it is also the time of rejection and persecution (16:4a). But no such realism will hold back the Evangelist's vision of the age of the Spirit in which he and his readers live. The vitality of the Fourth Gospel derives, in considerable measure, from the author's conviction that as he tells the story of Jesus, he is not saying "The days of perceived truth, of knowledge, and divine communication were the days of Jesus' earthly ministry." Rather, he is saying, "They are the days in which we are living."

8. Jesus' Prayer: Recalling and Requesting (17:1-26)

The discourses are ended. Jesus will soon go to the garden where he will pass from the company of his friends to the custody of his enemies (18:1). At this point in the story, with no note of circumstance or change of setting, Jesus turns from speaking with his disciples to a lengthy prayer, which voices the very interior of the Jesus of the Fourth Gospel. He speaks out of his unique relation to the Father, citing his accomplishment of his appointed work, but speaking also of his departure, his people who remain in the world, their struggle, and their eventual sharing in his glory. Three parties share the focus: Jesus, the Father, and Jesus' followers.

In the Gospels, although Jesus prays and commends prayer, he does not pray with others. His prayer in Gethsemane, in the Synoptic Gospels, is overheard by others, although it is unshared. In Matthew and Luke he gives his followers a model prayer, which speaks in the plural, saying "we" and "our." But when he prays, he is alone and he says "I." The Gospels suggest that something in Jesus' relation to God set him apart; his prayer was in some way uniquely his. The prayer of chapter 17 arises from his singular vocation. It is neither a prayer that anyone else could say nor a model for others to use.

Throughout the Fourth Gospel Jesus' acts and his words are rooted in the unity and mutuality that persists between himself and the Father. He mentions depths of hearing and being heard, teaching and learning, giving and receiving, loving and being loved, initiating and imitating, that constitute the hidden ground of his life and mission. He has come from God; he is one with God; the Father is always with him; he does the work given him by God, and he returns to God. The johannine Jesus holds the central place in the divine economy of redemption, and he is aware that he does.

In the Book of Signs Jesus based his claim for himself on this unique relation with the Father. Those who failed to recognize the relation evidenced that they were blind, both to Jesus and to God. Yet the relation itself seldom came to expression. At the grave of Lazarus, Jesus gave public voice to the intimacy with the Father in which he always lived, *I knew that you always hear me* (11:41-42); but his words at that moment are too isolated and brief to be very self-revealing. Later, in a cryptic exchange (12:27-30), Jesus, troubled in soul, appealed to the Father, *Save me from this hour,* and a voice from heaven (which bystanders could not understand) replied.

In the discourses of chapters 13–16 Jesus speaks extensively of his relation with the Father, and his words catch believers up into that relation. However, he is telling of the relation, not giving expression to it in direct address.

Thus the prayer of chapter 17 seems like a window on an interior life whose existence has previously been intimated. The johannine Jesus, who stands in an unshared relation with the Father and whose character and work are explained by it or not explained at all, now gives voice to that relationship. The one who has spoken often and audaciously of himself and the Father is now overheard speaking with the Father. Here he does not talk to his followers about himself and the Father, but to the Father about himself and them. Jesus, who has told the disciples that he is going to the Father, now says to the Father *I am coming to you* (v. 13).

This chapter is usually referred to as Jesus' "prayer." No other term commends itself. Yet it is not a prayer as the word is commonly understood, and it is not called a prayer in the Gospel itself. It does not arise from helplessness or need, and Jesus does not speak from a stance that would be described as faith. Some commentators have proposed the term "communion." Although only one party speaks, the language suggests an exchange. This Gospel has depicted the union between Jesus and the Father. They are two; yet their understandings and wills are one. Jesus lives always in the presence of the Father (8:16, 29; 16:32). When Jesus at the grave of Lazarus spoke aloud (the word "pray" was not used), he indicated that he did so for the sake of those who crowded around. For himself, he knows that he is always heard (11:41-42). It is as though the constant interior discourse of the self with itself that is a mark of human consciousness is, in the case of Jesus, always also a discourse shared with the Father. This prayer of John 17 lets others overhear a portion of the continuing, articulate but hitherto unvoiced communion that persists between Jesus and the Father.

One supposes that there must be models for this unusual passage. Yet few of the texts which the Evangelist might have followed for his Farewell contain a prayer. (In any case, there are no really "farewell" touches in this chapter, and, as Christopher Evans asks, "How could one pray a farewell?")[1] The ties that this chapter has are all with earlier johannine material and especially with the Farewell Discourses. Chapter 17 must have grown out of long reflection by the Evangelist. Evans proposes, "It is possible that the prayer as a whole had no model, and that it is to be approached as *sui generis*."[2]

The title "high priestly prayer" remains attached to John 17. Some special designation seems called for, and this one has lodged itself in tradition.

This title is usually traced to the Lutheran theologian David Chytraeus (1531-1600) who spoke of this prayer as a *precatio summi sacerdotio.* The designation was, however, anticipated in Clement of Alexandria.[3] The title suggests the book of Hebrews which presents the redemptive work of Christ on the model of the actions of the high priest at the Day of Atonement. To some readers this prayer has seemed to be Jesus' priestly preparation for his coming sacrifice. The prayer, however, makes no forward reference to the cross.

The only priestly characteristics of the prayer fall in vv. 17 and 19 when Jesus asks that his followers be sanctified *(hagiason autous),* and he says *for their sakes (hyper autōn) I sanctify myself (egō hagiazō emauton).* These cultic terms suggest the self-consecration of a priest before offering sacrifice. They may put a reader in mind of the returned Jewish exiles keeping the Passover: *For both the priests and Levites had purified themselves; all of them were clean. So they killed the Passover lamb for all of the returned exiles, for all their fellow priests, and for themselves. It was eaten by the people.* (Ezra 6:20-21). Based on the suggestion of this portion of the prayer, some commentators (perhaps following the influential nineteenth-century commentator B. F. Westcott) have preferred to speak of chapter 17 as Jesus' "Prayer of Consecration."

Terms such as *hagiazō* and *hyper autōn* do carry sacrificial and atonement meanings elsewhere in the New Testament (as in 1 Cor. 1:30 and Heb. 2:11), but they are peripheral and undeveloped in the thought of the Fourth Gospel, and they do not stand at the heart of this prayer which nowhere speaks of sin, sin-bearing, or sacrifice. The widely used title seems inadequate for a prayer which takes account

1. Christopher Evans, "Christ at Prayer in St. John's Gospel," *Lumen Vitae* 24 (1969), 585.

2. Evans, "Christ at Prayer," 584.

3. On this history, see Edwyn Clement Hoskyns, *The Fourth Gospel,* ed. F. N. Davey (London: Faber and Faber, 1947), 494; Raymond Brown, *The Gospel according to John* (2 vols., Anchor Bible; Garden City: Doubleday, 1966-70), 747.

of the range of thought that John 17 does. Appold thinks that the designation "high priestly prayer" is "clearly a misnomer."[4]

However, the prayer does contain a strong element of intercession, and the high priest was a representative of the people. Exodus 28:1-4, 9-10, 29-30 (which is given in the Revised Common Lectionary as a supportive reading during the week of the Seventh Sunday of Easter in Year B) describes the garb that was to be worn by Aaron when he made sacrifice in the holy place. His breastplate was to carry two onyx stones inscribed with the names of the sons of Jacob, six names on each stone, *So Aaron shall bear the names of the sons of Israel in the breastplate of judgment upon his heart, when he goes into the holy place, to bring a continual remembrance before the Lord.* In the sense that the high priest was an intercessor who carried his people before God, the prayer of John 17 might be thought to carry some priestly characteristics.

The Prayer's Setting in the Gospel Narrative and Myth

The prayer of chapter 17 fills an important place in the structure of the Fourth Gospel. It is filled with "echoes."[5] It draws on much that has gone before — so much so that it is difficult to suppose that chapter 17 would be memorable or even fully intelligible to a reader who lacked familiarity and sympathy with the preceding sixteen chapters. Readers who have found this Gospel opaque to this point will probably find that chapter 17 intensifies their bafflement, but readers who have found the book persuasive will think that this section commands particular interest and authority.

Jesus expresses in prayer, as he has said earlier, that the fundamental stratum of his life is his relation to the Father. All derives from, and all is rendered to the Father. His relation to his followers, important though it is, is governed by the prior receiving and owing that persist between himself and the Father. Hence, before the passion events begin, and before he returns to the one who sent him, this final accounting to the Father gives voice to his life's ultimate bonding.

Jesus' words concerning himself look back, *I glorified you on earth by finishing the work you gave me to do* (v. 4); and they look forward, *I am coming to you* (v. 13). He speaks of his followers who stay on in the world,

4. Mark L. Appold, *The Oneness Motif in the Fourth Gospel: Motif Analysis and Exegetical Probe into the Theology of John* (Tübingen: Mohr, 1976), 194.

5. C. H. Dodd, *The Interpretation of the Fourth Gospel* (Cambridge: Cambridge University Press, 1953), 417, says that "almost every verse contains echoes."

but by their link with him are no longer defined by it. He prays that they may be protected (vv. 11-12) and sanctified (vv. 17-19), that they may remain united (vv. 20-21, 23), and may be effective witnesses in the world in which they are located, but as an alien presence (vv. 18, 20-23). And he prays finally that, after their conflict and their work of witness are concluded, they may be with him where he is (v. 24). The prayer has no single theme, but it moves subtly between the foci of Jesus, the Father, Jesus' people in the world and beyond the world.

A prayer in close association with the passion events suggests the accounts in the Synoptic Gospels of Jesus' prayer in Gethsemane (Matt. 26:36-46; Mark 14:32-42; Luke 22:39-46). In both the Synoptic and the johannine traditions, Jesus, in a prayer on the night of his betrayal, interprets his coming passion from his own point of view.

- *In the Synoptic Gospels,* Jesus, with his disciples, leaves the Upper Room and goes to the Garden of Gethsemane, where he takes three disciples apart with him and then goes on alone to pray. *In the Fourth Gospel,* the prayer comes without leaving the place where the meal has been eaten; no note is taken of others who may be present; when the prayer is concluded, Jesus and his disciples go across the Kidron valley to a garden, which is unnamed.
- *The Synoptic Gospels* emphasize Jesus' anguish, *I am deeply grieved, even to death.* He falls prostrate on the ground, sweats drops of blood, and asks repeatedly that the "cup" of suffering might be removed (Matt. 26:38-39; Mark 14:36; Luke 22:42). In the Synoptic Gospels Jesus is a vulnerable figure, uttering, as Brown puts it, "a human prayer occupied with the present time." *In the Fourth Gospel,* by contrast, the lengthy, complex and urgent prayer is spoken without sorrow or inner distress or shrinking from what is to come; it is confident and is spoken in a manner marked, as Brown says, by "divinity and timelessness."[6] A cryptic, brief expression of Jesus' desire to be saved from his "hour" and of his willingness nevertheless to undergo it comes in the Fourth Gospel, not in the passion events, but at the end of the Book of Signs, in 12:27-30.
- *The prayer in Gethsemane* voices Jesus' struggle with the apparent will of the Father: *If it is possible . . . yet, . . . what I want . . . what you want.* In *the prayer in John 17* Jesus expresses untroubled identification with the Father's purpose.
- *In the Synoptic accounts,* Jesus shrinks from the next step, the cross: *Let this cup pass from me. In the prayer of John 17,* Jesus moves forward confidently to

6. Brown, *Gospel,* 748.

his return to the Father — the climax of his mission, which includes the cross, but which goes beyond it.

- *In the Synoptic accounts,* although the disciples were nearby, they slept through Jesus' agony, and Jesus rebuked them, *Could you not watch? In the johannine account,* the prayer has no setting, no circumstance. If readers are to understand that it was spoken aloud in the midst of the disciples, the narrative makes no point of there being others near to Jesus who listen in. The readers of the Evangelist's Gospel are, at first hand, the overhearers.

In the large scheme of the Fourth Gospel events show a contraction: Jesus leaves the public forum (12:9, 12, 29, 34) to speak with his close followers (12:36b; chs. 13–16). After he has spoken at length of his relation to the Father and to his people, he retires to a further level of privacy in which he prays out of the unshared relation between himself and the Father (ch. 17). Then abruptly the context expands: Jesus passes to the tumultuous public events of his arrest, trial, and crucifixion (chs. 18–19). In literary terms, as Paul Minear remarks, the prayer "forms a major turning point in the narrative."[7]

The Prayer's Character and Structure

The explicit transitions from the immediately foregoing context to Jesus' prayer, and from it to what follows, are minimal, only *After Jesus had spoken these words* (17:1 and 18:1). The prayer seems to be a self-contained unit, having a distinctive tone, characteristic phrases, and an identifiable shape. Finding in it a subtle rhythm of ideas, some commentators remark that it is more like poetry or a hymn than like discursive prose. But poems and hymns have structure. How is this passage organized?

The Large Outline

Jesus' prayer passes among a number of short themes which interweave, giving it a more associational flow and more interior reference than a de-

7. Paul Minear, *To Die and to Live: Christ's Resurrection and Christian Vocation* (New York: Seabury, 1977), 107.

fined outline would show. As Appold put it, "The prayer is not marked by an evolving progression of thought or dominated by a singular theme. It is rather circular in nature, touching in summary fashion on key themes."[8]

A common analysis suggests that the prayer is in three major sections of widening perspective. Jesus begins by speaking of himself and his mission from the Father (17:1-5). The opening *glorify your Son* (of v. 1) and the *glorify me* (of v. 5) enclose the first five verses as a unit in which Jesus speaks of his own relation to the Father. He then moves on to speak in vv. 6-19 of his followers, referring repeatedly to the believing community.

It is not certain, however, that a major break in the text should be located between vv. 5 and 6. While Jesus begins to speak of his followers in vv. 6-8, he speaks of them first in terms of what has been done; he connects his followers with the account he has given in vv. 1-5 of his own work. Only in v. 9 the thought turns to the difficult relation in which Jesus' people stand to the world. It seems preferable to think that the first large unit of the prayer runs from v. 1 to v. 8. It speaks of Jesus' work as rendered to the Father and creative of a people.

In the second major unit of the prayer, which begins at v. 9 and continues through v. 19, Jesus turns to the future and speaks more fully of the followers he is leaving. They are hated by the world (v. 14) as he has been rejected, and Jesus asks the Father to protect them (vv. 11, 15).

From v. 20 to the end of the prayer, attention widens again to include a more extended community of faith — *not only these, but also those who will believe in me through their word.* A "second generation" of the faith community is in view.

However, to make this widening of focus the principal organizing feature of the prayer suggests a more linear pattern than the text exhibits. The prayer does not read as though it were composed of three defined blocks of text. W. H. Cadman remarked:

> Already in the opening section Jesus prays not as an individual, but as the inclusive representative of all who through his Passion are to be drawn into that love relationship with Himself and the Father which is eternal life; so that the second and third sections should be regarded as the unfolding of ideas already implicit in the first five verses.[9]

8. Appold, *Oneness Motif,* 224, n. 3.

9. W. H. Cadman, *The Open Heaven* (Oxford: Blackwell, 1967), 203. Evans, "Christ at Prayer," 585, says "The Church is already in view in 1-6, while references to the Lord's own commission are found frequently in later verses."

Alongside this widening focus, the prayer is threaded by unifying themes:

Continuing Vocabulary

The prayer does not develop a topic and then close it to go on to the next. Several running terms unify the composition:

- The term "give" is used in all parts of the prayer. It occurs in vv. 2 (three times), 4, 6 (twice), 7, 8 (twice), 9, 11, 12, 14, 22 (twice), 24 (twice) — 17 times in all; only between vv. 15 and 21 is the theme missing. Jesus' prayer expresses a virtual theology of giving. The Father, the original giver, gives power (v. 2), glory (vv. 22, 24), his name (v. 12), a mission (v. 4), and a people (vv. 2, 6, 9, 11, 24) to the Son. Jesus gives life (v. 2), the Father's word (v. 14), and glory (v. 22) to believers.
- The term "know" appears nine times, five of them in the final two verses (vv. 3, 7, 8, 23, 25 three times, and 26 twice). The disciples know (vv. 7, 8, 25); knowing God and Jesus is eternal life (v. 3); the world must come to know (v. 23), although at present it does not (v. 25); Jesus knows the Father (v. 25), and has made him known (v. 26).
- *"In"* or *"into"* phrases occur twenty-one times in twenty-six verses, appearing more frequently towards the end of the prayer: see vv. 5, 8, 10, 11 (three times), 12, 13 (twice), 17, 18 (twice), 20, 21 (three times), 23 (twice), 24 and 26 (twice). Things or persons are described in terms of relation — what or whom they are "in." Jesus and the Father are *in* one another, and believers are *in* them (vv. 10, 21, 23, 26). But *"in"* can also speak of the spiritual environment of things. Events take place *in the world* (vv. 11, 13, 18); actions are *in truth* (v. 8, 17) or *in love* (v. 24).
- *The world* is mentioned throughout the prayer, 18 times in all, concentrating in the later verses. Jesus has come to the world (vv. 13, 18); the disciples were given to Jesus out of the world (v. 6), although they continue in it (vv. 11, 15, 18). The judgments on the world that are made in the prayer are generally negative; the world does not know Jesus (v. 25); indeed, it hates him and his disciples (vv. 14, 16). Yet the disciples are sent into the world as Jesus was sent into it (v. 18), so

that it may come to believe (vv. 21, 23). The mission of Jesus and of his followers is for the world's sake.

- *Glory* and *glorify* occur eight times, the occasions clustering early in the prayer and again at the end. Jesus has glorified the Father (v. 1), and he asks to be glorified (vv. 1, 4, 5); the glory Jesus has received from the Father he has given to his followers (v. 22), and he is glorified in them (v. 10). Jesus' work begins in a solitary glory (v. 5) and ends in a shared glory (v. 24). The fabric of relationships that is described in the prayer is bound up in giving glory and receiving glory.
- *Send* occurs seven times, six of them falling in paired expressions in which the Father sends, and Jesus is sent (vv. 3, 8, 18, 21, 23, 25). Jesus in turn is sender of his followers (v. 18).
- *"Your [the Father's] name"* is mentioned in vv. 6, 11, 12, and 26.
- The Father's *"word"* is mentioned five times. Jesus has given the disciples the Father's word (vv. 8, 14) which they have received (v. 8) and kept (v. 6). The Father's word is the truth in which the disciples identity is constituted (v. 17). V. 20 speaks of the disciples' word through which others have come to believe. The prayer depicts a fabric of relationships that is constituted in speaking and hearing.

As suits a prayer of summing-up, inclusive terms such as *all* (vv. 2 twice, 10) and *everything* (v. 7) and *none* (v. 12) are used.

Thus, a few repeated expressions give unity and consistency to this prayer. The expressions are not unusual, yet ordinary words are made to suggest depths of meaning, and their repetition gives the prayer its distinctive sound.

Marks of Structure

Certain features suggest the organization of the prayer:

- Jesus makes six express requests: two for his own glorification (vv. 1b, 5); and four for his followers: *keep them* (v. 11); *sanctify them* (v. 17); *I pray* (v. 20); *I desire* (v. 24). The first four are imperative; the last two are indicative. Two requests fall in each of the three large sections of the prayer which have been identified.
- There are six direct addresses to the Father: *Father* (vv. 1b, 5, 21b, 24);

Holy Father (v. 11b); and *O righteous Father* (v. 25). The requests and the addresses coincide at vv. 1b, 5, 11, 20, and 24.
- Alongside these petitionary expressions, there are nine affirmations of what Jesus has done: vv. 4 (two), 6, 8, 12 (two), 14, 22, and 26. Christopher Evans notes that the chapter contains two kinds of material, "Prayer in the form of petition for the disciples is interlaced throughout with doctrinal statements about the Lord and about the disciples."[10]

Appold carries this observation further, noting an alternation between petition and affirmation: "If any literary principle at all is apparent in the construction of ch. 17, then it is the constant exchange between retrospect or review on the one hand and petition on the other."[11]

Jewish prayer and praise often reprise events that demonstrate what God has done in the past and provide the basis for present requests. Jesus' prayer in John 17, however, does not draw on a salvation-history panorama. Rather, its "retrospect" identifies Jesus' own work. Appold puts the point:

> In constantly revolving themes Jesus points to the accomplished work which he has done. . . . The form of the retrospect is entirely personalized. It deals not with the works of another but with the person of the one who is praying . . . [with] the cumulative work of the Son. Significantly, however, the Son's work is the work of the Father.[12]

As to *petition,* in Jesus' six requests he asks twice for himself that he may be glorified (vv. 1, 5). When he turns to pray for those who have been given him, he asks that they may be kept in unity (vv. 9, 11), be kept from the evil one, and be consecrated in the truth (vv. 15, 17). And he asks that those who are yet to believe may also be one with those who already believe (vv. 20-21) and that all may finally be with him where he is (v. 24).

The prayer can be analyzed, showing the alternation between units of petition and units of *review* (see p. 318).

This analysis, however, can be too schematic. The principal rhythm of ideas stirs counter-rhythms.

10. Evans, "Christ at Prayer," 585.
11. Appold, *Oneness Motif,* 224.
12. Appold, *Oneness Motif,* 224.

1	vv. 1-2b	*petition,* glorify your Son.
	v. 4	*review,* I finished your work.
	v. 5	*petition,* glorify me.
	vv. 6-8	*review,* I made your name known.
2	vv. 9-11	*petition,* keep them.
	vv. 12-14	*review,* I guarded them.
	vv. 15-17	*petition,* protect them/consecrate them.
	vv. 18-19	*review,* you sent me into the world.
3	vv. 20-21	*petition,* that they may be one.
	vv. 22-23	*review,* I have given them your glory.
	v. 24	*petition,* may they may be with me.
	vv. 25-26	*review,* I made your name known.

Some irregularities and complexities are apparent:

Vv. 4 and 5 form an obvious parallel, even though v. 4 belongs to a unit of review and v. 5 belongs to the petition which follows; the division between the two should not obscure the continuity between them.

Similarly there is verbal connection from v. 14 (review) to v. 16 (petition). In this instance a petition is prompted by and linked to a previous unit of review.

There are reasons for thinking of vv. 6-8 as review associated with the previous petition of v. 5. Yet these verses introduce the subject of Jesus' followers, a theme which will continue through v. 19, and some analysts regard v. 6 as the start of a new large unit of the prayer.

V. 11 (petition) shows verbal ties with vv. 12 and 13 (review). Vv. 12-14 contain some echoes of vv. 6-8.

Vv. 14-16 for a brief inclusion which lies partly in a unit of review and partly in a unit of petition.

Vv. 17-19 have internal connections and continuities that bridge the break between 17 (petition) and 18 (review).

The tight connections within vv. 20-21 and 22-23 form an unusual passage that is more complex and closely unified than would be indicated by describing it only as petition followed by review.

In sum, although the prayer is constructed in identifiable sections, important ideas run through it, and the play of thought often disregards the apparent organization. The prayer, as M. Appold has said, is "loose and flexible, totally in keeping with the Fourth Gospel's characteristically fluid style determined more by theological concern than by structural form."[13]

The Prayer's Setting in the First-Century Church

The prayer, no less than other parts of the Fourth Gospel, was written from and for the first-century church. "Petitions," Paul Minear comments, "usually reflect a need on the part of the praying community."[14] The passage may seem situationless; no circumstances are expressly mentioned. Yet, as Fr. Lindars notes, "It is shot through with a sense of urgency, which betrays John's concern for the state of the church in his own day."[15] Can the text suggest conditions in the first-century church that would have given rise to a prayer like this?

The situation of the Community of the Beloved Disciple may have remained much as it had been when the Third Discourse (16:4b-33) was written. (Nothing in chapter 17 suggests that the active conflict between Christian believers and the Jewish community is still the church's principal concern.) Since the break with the synagogue, the followers of Jesus have been face to face with an unfriendly world — a world from which their faith does not remove them (v. 15; cf. 15:18-19; 16:20). Believers have the obligation to bear witness in the world, as Jesus had (v. 18; cf. 15:27). They are hated as an alien presence (vv. 14, 16; cf. 15:18–16:4a; 16:33). Behind the hostile world is the power of the evil one (v. 15; cf. 14:30); hence Jesus' people need to be guarded (vv. 11-12; cf. 16:1, 33b). They need to hold to the name (v. 12), to the Father's word (v. 14), and to the truth (vv. 17, 19). The prayer is for a beleaguered community.

Jesus' prayer that believers may be one (vv. 21, 23) suggests that their unity was imperiled. The johannine community had grown beyond an initial group of adherents (vv. 20-21a). Some of those who had formed the early core of the johannine church were still present, but a later group had grown up alongside them. Evidently in the late first century some tension had developed between two generations in the faith. The earlier group and the later group needed to live, worship, and serve together, even though they had different experiences of life in the church.

13. Appold, *Oneness Motif,* 204.

14. Paul S. Minear, *John: The Martyr's Gospel* (New York: Pilgrim, 1984), 140.

15. Barnabas Lindars, *The Gospel of John* (New Century Bible Commentary; Grand Rapids: Eerdmans, 1972), 516.

The prayer says little about the church's outward circumstances. However, it sets Jesus' people in the context of the redemptive story. They are a people given to Christ by the Father (vv. 2, 6-7, 9, 24); they are sharers in the divine name (vv. 6, 11, 26); they believe and know (vv. 3, 7, 8, 25). The church is a holy people (v. 19), sent as an alien presence (v. 16) into a world dominated by the evil one (v. 18). Jesus prays for it to be kept (vv. 11, 15) for its ultimate destiny with him (v. 24). The church's context in the redemptive narrative is set forth clearly, while its social and historical circumstances may only be gathered by inference.

This prayer reads like a semi-independent set piece, having internal consistency and standing slightly apart from the surrounding text. One can only conjecture how this unusual composition might have come into being.

In developing this extended passage, a creative early Christian may have stood in the tradition of prophetic prayer. Bringing his reverent imagination into play, and putting himself in the place of the departing Jesus, he spoke according to his ability — as Justin Martyr says bishops continued to do in the extempore prayers of the early Christian generations (*Apology*, 67). When one asks where in the life of the first-century church a passage such as the prayer of John 17 might have originated, one must consider a liturgical setting. The authority of the prayer which is expressed as Jesus' own speech should perhaps be taken as rooted in the depth with which a Christian prophet, speaking at a gathering for prayer, has been grasped by divine reality. He speaks from within himself, but what he articulates is not his own. Lindars says:

> John writes from within the Christian experience, perhaps two generations after the events he describes. In the meantime that experience has not lost its vitality. John has a vivid sense of the union with Christ which his words describe. He feels that he has the aid of the Paraclete (16:12-15). He can say with Paul "we have the mind of Christ" (1 Cor. 2:16).[16]

Few passages in the Fourth Gospel seem more likely than this to have originated from a Christian prophet speaking in the church gathered for Word and Supper.

The narrator may have intended his readers to understand that the prayer was said aloud with the disciples present. However, nothing is said

16. Lindars, *Gospel*, 517.

about them. As part of the written gospel the prayer is "also intended to be heard by later believers."[17] The overhearers the Evangelist is most interested in are his readers.

The Prayer's "Voice"

Jesus' prayer in John 17 raises acute hermeneutical issues. It expresses the distinctive Christ-myth of the Fourth Gospel in compact form, as though it were spoken at a significant moment by Jesus himself. A naive reading takes the prayer to give a reader the christology of Christ. Yet any critical account of this Gospel must consider this chapter to be a composition arising (through some now irrecoverable process) from the first-century johannine church.

How bold, how confident of anyone to write so! Or else, how audacious and presumptuous! The difficulty and the scandal of the johannine Jesus concentrate here. But so, of course, do the redemptive offer and claim.

It is often said that modern christology begins with the human Jesus — a person who was one of us and who represented God working in genuinely human terms. Once we have that starting point, we can deal with the interpreting names, metaphors, and categories that present the redemptive significance and universality that the earliest Christians understood Jesus Christ to carry. Christological construction must begin with Jesus of Nazareth.

In John 17, however, the interpreting myth has so taken over that a historical, recognizably human figure has been made problematic. The self-knowledge expressed by Jesus in this prayer is more the self-knowledge of a heavenly Redeemer-figure than it is a self-knowledge which fits historical, social, psychological experience. Could a Jesus who understood himself as the praying figure of John 17 does really be one of us?[18]

Perhaps one can begin to answer by asking an essentially literary question.

What "voice" speaks in this prayer? Clearly it is, at least in part, the

17. Rudolf Schnackenburg, *The Gospel According to St. John* (3 vols., New York: Crossroad, 1968, 1980, 1982), 3.168.

18. "What other utterer of a prayer has asked for an exchange of glory with God as if on equal terms with him (vv. 1, 5) or claimed authority over all humanity and power to give the life of the final age (v. 2)? Who else described himself as having 'come from God' (v. 8c)?" Gerard Stephen Sloyan, *John* (Interpretation; Atlanta: John Knox, 1988), 196.

voice of the Evangelist, whose credentials are not "an auditor's notebook, but an interpreter's perception."[19] The Evangelist, however, lives and believes in a community. The shifting tenses in the prayer (*while still in the world, I say this,* v. 13, and *I am no longer in the world,* v. 11) carry one away from a setting at the Last Supper and towards the living Jesus of the first-century church from and for which this Evangelist wrote.

However, beyond the first-century historical situation (which intrudes quite subtly), the depth of suggestion in the text itself prompts a further possible answer: The voice that was heard and reproduced in that first-century church (perhaps at a Lord's Day assembly) may have been that of the risen, living Intercessor.

It seems to have been an article of faith in the early church that the living Christ intercedes for his people (see Rom. 8:34 and Heb. 7:25). Christians were convinced that the ascended Lord prays for the church and that he does so because he cared for and he continues to care for his people.

The prayer in chapter 17 may have been, at least in part, a johannine development of the theme of Jesus as intercessor. The living Christ prays through the voice of the departing Jesus as the departing Jesus speaks through the voice of the Fourth Evangelist. In his unique idiom, the writer articulates the first-century Christian spiritual certitude, *We have an advocate* (1 John 2:1). Moreover, like the compassionate priest of Hebrews (2:18), this Eternal Intercessor is bound by shared human experience to the believers for whom he prays.

Through an inspired first-century prophet, the risen, living Jesus interprets to the church both its rootage in himself and its situation in the world. Believers listen in as the living Christ, having reclaimed his primal glory with the Father, prays for his own.

Even though in the idiom of John 17 the Son prays to the Father, saying "I seek . . . for the church," a reader discerns that through this prayer one Christian has presumed to say, "I know what the living Christ wants and seeks for the church" (or, by implication, "what Christ does not want"). Such a device can seem heavy-handed. When a person (often it is a preacher) says "I know what Christ would want for the church . . ." or "If Christ were here, he would say . . . ," an element of cheapness seems to intrude. The voice of Jesus sounds too much like the voice of the preacher. Reverence and mystery are slighted. The chastenedness required for claim-

19. Kenneth Cragg, "According to the Scriptures: Literacy and Revelation," in M. Wadsworth, ed., *Ways of Reading the Bible* (Brighton: Harvester, 1981), 30.

ing the ultimate sanction of Christ is ignored. One's own agenda (the usual human mixture of grandeur and small-mindedness) prevails, and Jesus is brought in to support it. Listeners or readers may feel manipulated.

Yet somehow the subtlety and modesty of presentation and the seriousness of thought in the prayer of John 17 raise it to the level of revelatory authority. The prayer comes to expression through the Evangelist who is caught up in the holy reality of which he writes. While his idiom is audacious, ultimately the Christian community has found it believable.

1. Part One (17:1-8)

> After Jesus had spoken these words, he looked up to heaven and said. . . . 17:1a

Only a brief transition introduces the prayer. There is no change of location, and the disciples are not mentioned. At the grave of Lazarus (11:41) Jesus' attitude in prayer was described as *lifting up his eyes.* Here Jesus turns his address from the disciples to the Father, with only "one silent gesture."[20]

This terse, minimal transition suggests that no shift of attention was called for when Jesus spoke with the Father. Heaven was never far away. The "preparedness" that busy people find useful or even necessary when they pray today was not something that Jesus required. Schnackenburg remarks, "'Heaven' here symbolizes the transcendent space of God, to which Jesus belongs and with which he is closely associated. When he uses the form of address 'Father,' Jesus enters, praying, the familiar space that is close to God — the space from which he had never been released."[21]

No doubt we may suppose that the disciples were present as overhearers of this prayer, even though they go unmentioned. The author will let us suppose what we will. For him, the disciples, present or absent, are unimportant. This Evangelist has no interest in scene-setting; there is no tableau, with the disciples attentive at the table where the meal has ended, or with Jesus separating himself from the group in some way while his followers listen, stirred, but only vaguely comprehending. Readers go to this prayer directly. A present-day reader's encounter with this prayer is not mediated by (or perhaps distracted by) persons who are mentioned as

20. H. B. Swete, *Jesus' Last Discourse and Prayer* (London: Macmillan, 1920), 160.
21. Schnackenburg, *Gospel,* 3.170.

present at the time. The words come through the voice of the speaker alone. The readers of the Fourth Gospel are the persons present. We are, at first hand, the listeners-in.

As the prayer develops, units of petition are followed by units of review. Jesus asks, looking to the future; then he gives account, speaking largely of his own mission:

The prayer opens with the briefest of addresses to God (v. 1b), followed by a petition (vv. 1b-2) which mentions eternal life, a term which leads to a somewhat parenthetic explanation (v. 3). A short review section follows (v. 4).

> "Father, the hour has come:
> Glorify your Son
> so that the Son may glorify you, 17:1b

Jesus turns his speech from his disciples to God by a simple address, only the word *Father* (as in 11:41 and 12:27).

In the Synoptic Gospels, Jesus speaks to his hearers of *your Father in heaven,* and he teaches them to pray to *our Father* and to seek to be like their Father. In the Fourth Gospel, by contrast, throughout his discourses and his controversies, Jesus has used the word "Father" to speak of a relationship that was uniquely his. The term "Father," designating God, is in a primary sense Jesus' term (which he only opens to his followers when after the resurrection he says *I am ascending to my Father and your Father,* 20:17). When others come to know God as Father, they know him as God and Father of Jesus Christ. When, in this prayer, Jesus gives account of his mission, his address to God articulates the unique filial relationship in which that mission has been rooted.

The prayer takes its occasion and its tone from Jesus' *hour (hōra)* of which it is part, *the hour has come.* For biblical thought, time is not featureless, objective, non-significant "clock-time," nor is it unreal or illusory. Rather, as part of the creation, time is the medium in which God acts and in which God is met in judgment and redemption. Momentous determinations are made and divine purposes are set in motion and brought to completion in time. In biblical vocabulary, common designations such as "hour," "year," "season," "day," "night," "time," or "times," carry this understanding of meaning-laden moments — time under pressure. As the Synoptic Gospels express it, *the time* (*kairos,* the appointed moment in history) *is fulfilled* (e.g., Mark 1:14-15).

The Fourth Gospel speaks of times of anticipation and of fulfillment, of preparation and accomplishment, of intensity followed by retirement. At past moments, Jesus' hour *had not yet come* (2:4; 7:6, 8, 30; 8:20), then it approached (12:23, 27), and now it *has come*. The term *hour* appears in Mark's account of Jesus in Gethsemane where he prays *that if it were possible, the hour might pass from him* (Mark 14:35; *that the crisis might pass him by,* TEV). In the prayer of John 17, Jesus does not shrink from his "hour," but meets it confidently. He speaks of glory: *The hour has come, glorify your Son*. His *hour* was described earlier as *his hour to depart from this world and go to the Father* (13:1). His *hour* brings to completion his own work and it inaugurates for his people the new age, the new relation to God, the new possibility.

Jesus, speaking of himself in the third person, asks glory for himself, *glorify your Son*. Earlier he said, *If I glorify myself, my glory is nothing. It is my Father who glorifies me* (8:54). However, glory is given and returned: *Glorify your Son so that the Son may glorify you*. Jesus stands within an exchange of glory. (The theme was articulated earlier, in the prologue to the Farewell, 13:31.) The glory of the Father is the final reality; the Son is the Father's appointed agent; his glory is for the sake of the glory of the Father (cf. 8:50, *I do not seek my own glory*). Yet glory-giving between the Father and the Son is mutual; each receives and each gives. The act which most fully reveals the glory of one reveals the glory of both.

On the night of his arrest, at the start of the terrible sequence of events which will lead to the cross, Jesus speaks of "glorifying." This Gospel speaks paradoxically of glory in the abandonment of glory, a glory which is shown in self-giving (cf. 12:23-25). Jesus' cross is his "glorification," and his "glorification" is at the same time God's glorification. This mutual glorifying of Father and Son catches up human redemption into itself.

The Son's glorifying of the Father is a revealing, life-giving action — a showing-forth of the divine splendor. Christopher Evans put it, "For the Son to glorify the Father is for him so to speak, to act and to be . . . that God may be fully apprehended as God." Yet if the "glorifying" which Jesus asks here has reference to his bringing eternal life to humanity and to his revealing of the Father, it has reference also to himself and to his vindication in the completion of his work. "The prayer for glorification is the prayer for his removal into the mutuality of heavenly existence."[22]

22. Evans, "Christ at Prayer," 588.

since you have given him authority over all people,
to give eternal life to all whom you have given him. 17:2

The connective *since* (Greek *kathōs*) implies that the glorification which Jesus requests in v. 1 is linked to his mission to bring eternal life to humanity, which is the subject of v. 2. Jesus' authorization is for his mission; his mission is grounded in divine authorization. Jesus has been given *authority over all people.*[23] Some other strands of New Testament thought describe the risen Jesus holding universal, cosmic place and authority (see Mt. 28:18; Phil. 2:9-11; Eph. 1:20-23; Rev. 1:12-18). However, in the Fourth Gospel, the term *authority (exousia)* does not have cosmic Lordship in mind. Christ's supremacy over all things is a matter of little interest to this Evangelist. Jesus' plenary authority is specifically authority to bring eternal life to all people; it is the divine sender's authorization of his agent to be the Redeemer.

Jesus is given *authority* (Gr. *exousia*) in order that he might *give eternal life. Exousia* is held in an exchange of givings: authority is given to Christ (5:27; 17:2), to be exercised by him (5:27; 10:18), and ultimately to be given by him to others (1:12). The final aim of the conferral of right on Jesus is for his redemptive work which is an outflow of generosity, a divine bestowal. In our sin-structured world, authority often seems oppressive — authority over others. Jesus, however, receives authority so that he may give life. The presentation of authority in the Fourth Gospel reclaims the very idea of authority.

The word "give" appears three times in this one clause: The authority for Jesus' redemptive mission is *given* to him; he *gives* life to humanity; but those who receive life from him are themselves spoken of as the Father's *gift* to him. The proposition that persons are given to the Son by the Father turns aside the emphasis that persons become related to Jesus by their own decision, choice, or a deliberate act of commitment. Nothing is said here about hearing Jesus, or believing in him, or about "come and see." The open "whoever will" of the invitations of the Book of Signs goes unmentioned. Believers are spoken of here as a gift from the Father to the Son. This first-century writer shows no interest in how divine choosing and free human response may be reconciled. In speaking of the divine/human relation he describes at one moment the willing, choosing, giving God and

23. More literally "authority over all flesh" — a Semitism which speaks of authority over human life and destiny.

at another moment the responding, believing, or rejecting person. Each aspect of the matter makes religious sense. He does not ask whether and how they may be compatible or brought into a systematic statement.

Jesus prays for his followers as "given" to him by the Father five times in this prayer: vv. 2, 6 twice, 9, 24. (The expression appeared in the Bread of Life discourse: 6:37, 39, 44, 65.)

The idiom places exclusive stress on divine initiative. The fact that persons have believed is not traced to their insight or consent, but to an act of God. They are the Father's gift to the Son of that which was and remains the Father's. Readers of this prayer are, in effect, overhearing human salvation being spoken of between the Father and the Son. In intimate discourse, the johannine Son identifies believers as a gift to himself from the Father. Persons are given to Jesus, much as the Father's words, name, and glory were given to him. Human redemption is spoken of as a matter of divine ownership and gifting. A Christian writer is not saying to fellow believers: "You are elect in Christ." Rather, the Son says to the Father, "These persons are your gift to me."

The point is made through affirmations about Jesus, the Father, and the church. Yet this way of putting the matter was arrived at as an imaginative construction by human minds who were seeking to interpret their own existence in faith. Self-understanding of an intuitive sort is presupposed. Some of the earliest Christians, in their inquiry into themselves, realized that their being in Christ was not finally by their own determination, but was an act of God for them and in them.

Christopher Evans suggests how Christians may have thought of themselves in relation to the initiative of God:

> The Church does not exist by human volition, nor does it exist by any independent volition of Christ, as though he had conducted a self-appointed enterprise with success, and was about to leave the results behind him in the form of his personal disciples. The Church is here a heavenly entity, which is first the possession of the Father, and then becomes his gift to the Son.[24]

Eternal life having been mentioned, is given a parenthetic description: The Evangelist speaks for a moment in his own voice. Jesus would hardly have spoken of himself in third person as "Jesus Christ." Barrett calls v. 3 "a footnote."[25]

24. Evans, "Christ at Prayer," 591.

25. C. K. Barrett, *The Gospel According to St. John* (2nd ed., Philadelphia: Westminster, 1978), 503.

And this is eternal life,
that they may know you, the only God,
and Jesus Christ whom you have sent. 17:3

Eternal life is spoken of often in chapters 1–12, but this verse and the previous one mark its only appearances in chapters 13–17. Knowing Jesus and the Father confers the supreme gift, the life of the final age.

Some features of 17:3 suggest that it (or components of it) may have had some prior identity as a christological formula.

The wording of 17:3 has marked similarities with the next to last verse in the epistle (or homily) from the later johannine church which we know as 1 John: *And we know that the Son of God has come and has given us understanding so that we may know him who is true, and we are in him who is true, in his Son Jesus Christ. He is the true God and eternal life* (1 Jn. 5:20).

Observing the common terms *"eternal life," "knowing," "the true God,"* and *"Jesus Christ,"* Schnackenburg suggests that this explanatory parenthesis which is entered at 17:3 may have been a gloss coming "from the same circle that was responsible for the first epistle."[26] Appold proposes that 17:3 "most likely had its roots in the confessional tradition of the Johannine church" and is a "definitional sentence . . . a piece of pre-formed Johannine confessional or prayer tradition which the evangelist incorporated."[27]

This confession was presumably intended to affirm the uniqueness of God and the saviorhood of Jesus.

The concluding element of v. 3, *and Jesus Christ whom you have sent,* introduces a christological theme, "Jesus was sent from the Father," which was frequent in the Book of Signs and will appear five more times in this prayer: vv. 8, 18, 21, 23 and 25. Appold proposes that the repeated description suggests "a confessional formulation such as 'Jesus is sent from God' which in Johannine circles had the same thrust and weight as did e.g. the confession 'Jesus is Lord' in other circles."[28]

Eternal life is not described as natural immortality, but as a gift of the Son — it is grace, not metaphysics. *Eternal life* is to *know.* This Christian "gnosticism" was spoken of earlier in the Fourth Gospel, where, especially

26. Schnackenburg, *Gospel,* 3.172.
27. Appold, *Oneness Motif,* 224, n. 2.
28. Appold, *Oneness Motif,* 160.

in chapters 14–16, "coming to know" was a virtual equivalent of "believing," "receiving," "seeing," or "obeying." "Knowing" is a dwelling in the truth, a sharing in life.

Eternal life consists in knowing the only true God. The early readers of this Gospel, who came to faith in Jesus from Judaism, brought a conviction of the oneness, the singularity of God and the falseness, nothingness of the gods of the nations. The emphasis of the prayer on *the one God* would have been familiar. But converts from casually syncretistic first-century Hellenistic society needed to understand that in identifying with the followers of Jesus, they were engaging with the one true God. With respect to other things, knowing or not knowing may have been more or less important. With respect to this ultimate reality, coming to know is to begin to live. One must know *the only God,* not one among many, *the true God,* not counterfeit, insubstantial, delusional.

The expression *that they may know* uses a present tense *(ginōskōsin),* which implies continuing action — "that they may come to know and go on knowing." In interpersonal knowing, while one may know the other truly, one never knows completely. Although what one knows may be sufficient to establish a stable relationship, one realizes that there is always more to be known. Close and prolonged knowing does not diminish the mystery of the other. In personal relationships, when new knowing stops, the relationship is at risk of termination.

This knowing has a dual object: *that they may know you, the only true God, and Jesus Christ whom you have sent.* Here, as elsewhere in the Fourth Gospel (see 14:1, also 5:22; 8:16; 12:44-45; 14:9; 15:23-24; 16:3) the name of Jesus is brought into association with God. Life-giving knowledge is to know the only true God and at the same time to know Jesus Christ, his sent one. As the johannine Christians saw it, Jesus and God are known together, or else neither is rightly known.

The Father and Christ are similarly linked in what is usually taken to be a pre-Pauline formula which appears in 1 Corinthians 8:6:

> For us there is one God, the Father,
> from whom are all things,
> and for whom we exist,
> and one Lord Jesus Christ,
> through whom are all things
> and through whom we exist.

Schnackenburg proposes that 17:3 is the johannine equivalent of Paul's "twofold confession of the one God, the Father, and the one Lord Jesus Christ as the mediator of salvation."[29]

Jesus' request for glorification, *now glorify me,* is followed by a brief passage of review.

> I glorified you on earth
> by finishing the work
> that you gave me to do. 17:4

Jesus, having asked the Father to glorify himself (17:1, words of petition), says now that he has glorified the Father by carrying out his appointed work (17:4, words of review). Glory is given and glory is received in mutual, free exchange.

Jesus reports an action completed; *I glorified you.* He has carried his work to fulfillment, and in the discharge of this ministry given to him, the Father has been glorified. Jesus speaks in the past, even though, in the terms of the Fourth Gospel narrative, the climax of his work in his passion and resurrection lies ahead. He anticipates a completion future and certain. The original readers of this Gospel, for their part, would, of course, look back on Jesus' finished work.

In his account of his work, Jesus reintroduces the understanding of himself as God's agent. In the Jewish idea of agency, an agent upon completing his commission reports to the sender.[30] In this brief review section of Jesus' prayer — as in the review passages taken together — God's *shaliach,* who has been true to his appointed task, gives account to the one who sent him, speaking of *the work that you gave me to do.*

When Jesus speaks of *finishing* his work, he uses the same term *(teleō)* that he will speak from the cross when he says *It is finished* (19:30). The use of the term in these two places suggests that the cross accomplishes the work which Jesus speaks of in his prayer and that his prayer anticipates the work that will be completed on the cross. He speaks here of his mission as a unity, his *work* (cf. 4:34). His task was single: to bring eternal life, and it was discharged faithfully.

29. Schnackenburg, *Gospel,* 3.172.

30. Peder Borgen, "God's Agent in the Fourth Gospel," in J. Neusner, ed., *Religions in Antiquity: Essays in Memory of Erwin Ramsdell Goodenough* (Leiden: Brill, 1968), 142-43.

Vv. 4 and 5 are closely linked. While v. 4 is the "review" associated with the petition of vv. 1b-2, and v. 5 begins a new section of petition, unlike the usual sequence of the prayer, the petition of v. 5 grows from the wording and idea of the immediately foregoing review:

17:4 [review]	17:5 [petition]
I glorified you [2]	*So now, glorify me* [3]
on the earth	*in your own presence*
by finishing the work that you gave me to do.	*with the glory that I had in your presence before the world existed.* [1]

The parallel expressions in vv. 4 and 5 summarize the three-stage johannine christological myth: The last words in this unit reach farthest back. The redemptive action begins in a primal glory that Jesus had in the Father's presence before the world existed [1]. The redemptive saga passed to earth, where Jesus glorified the Father by accomplishing his appointed work [2]. It culminates in glory resumed in the Father's presence [3]. Jesus' redemptive work is from glory, through glory, and to glory. The glorifying of the Father in an earthly mission has been Jesus' act, *I glorified you;* the subsequent glorifying which Jesus asks is the Father's act, *Now glorify me.* Jesus acts and is acted upon. It is not his task to glorify himself, but to glorify the Father. As he does so, the Father glorifies him. A new petition breaks out:

So now, Father, glorify me
in your own presence
with the glory that I had in your presence
before the world existed. 17:5

The Son, by carrying out his appointed mission, has given glory (v. 4), *so now* he asks that glory be given to him.

The pronouns are juxtaposed and are set first and last in the Greek text of vv. 4 and 5, which puts them in places of emphasis. The word order makes unacceptable English, but it may suggest the vigor of the thought: *I you glorified . . . and now glorify me you.*

This mutual glorifying is an engagement between the Father and the Son which has eternal life for humanity as its purpose. The Father glorifies the Son, giving him authority to bring eternal life. The Son glorifies the Father by carrying out his saving commission. Lindars notes that the connective *so now (kai nun)* can be "a technical expression to introduce the plea after the relevant facts have been stated, both in judicial (eg. Isa. 5:3, 5) and liturgical (eg. Dan. 9:15, 17) compositions."[31] The emphatic *now* seems to have in mind the passion events which have begun and which in johannine understanding are Jesus' glorification.

The glory that Jesus requests is a glory *in your presence* (contrasting with *on the earth,* in v. 4). The Greek *para* (*para seautō:* with, near yourself) speaks of persons who are, to use a modern expression, "present to" one another. (NAB translates *"at your side."*) Jesus' destination is again described in relational terms rather than in terms of place, status or splendor. He will be with the Father as the Logos was from the beginning with God, as Jesus has been with his people (7:33; 12:8, 35), and as his people will ultimately be with him (14:3; 17:24).

The glory to which Jesus goes reclaims a prior glory (v. 24b, cf. 6:62). In biblical idiom, "glory" speaks of ultimacies — often of a future ultimacy, the life of the age to come. However, in the "protology" that appears in the johannine christological myth, glory refers also to a deep past. The glory that Jesus prays for is not a new condition freshly granted, but a condition that has always belonged to him — *the glory that I had in your presence before the world existed.*

The expression *before the world existed* (like *before the foundation of the world,* in v. 24) speaks of a time before there was anything. The mind cannot escape from time terms, even when they can only be used paradoxically, as here when they speak of a time before creation — a time before there was time. Before there was a cosmos, Jesus says, there was a loving, glory-filled relation between the Father and the Son.

"Transcendence" is probably most often thought of as a metaphor of space — "up" or "above." But space and time are correlatives. To speak of God *before* the world is another way of speaking of God *above* or *beyond* the world. Hebrew idiom spoke of God who antedated everything, whose time span indefinitely exceeds our own. A God who is beyond time and sequence, as a story-teller is beyond his or her story, is only spoken of by persons who live within time — by persons inside

31. Lindars, *Gospel,* 250.

the story-teller's story, so to speak. Divine beyondness is suggested by the time-metaphor of before the world (as the Sabbath suggests God after the world).

In a now rather old exploratory study, Edwyn Bevan proposed, "The inconceivable life of God, though not durative to God Himself, can be apprehended by any finite mind only as duration, the changeless contemplated from the standpoint of someone who is changing."[32]

Here that life of God beyond (beyond in the metaphor of time) is described as a life shared in glory between the Father and the Son. In terms of the johannine myth, the earthly life of Jesus began from and was continuous with that relation-in-glory to which, having completed his redeeming work — a work suffused with glory — he now returns.

Jesus, having spoken of his discharge of his appointed task and of the glory that has been exchanged between himself and the Father (vv. 1-5), now introduces the apostolic others, the community of faith, in a complex passage of review (vv. 6-8). ("They" or "them" referring to the disciples is mentioned in every main clause in vv. 6-8 and is the subject of the clause six times.) The Father's name and his words have been made known to them; believers themselves have been given to Jesus; and five of their significant response actions are cited: they have kept the Father's word; they know Jesus' derivation from the Father (mentioned twice); they have received the Father's words; and they believe Jesus to be sent from God. The community of believers is the Father's people, through the ministry of the Son.

In this study, the opening section of the prayer is thought of as extending through v. 8. Vv. 6-8 are taken to be Jesus' review associated with his petition of v. 5. Jesus' community is introduced in the review in vv. 6-8 to complete the thought of the foregoing petition. Jesus' work, which was given to him by the Father and was rendered to the Father, was creative of a people. The community of Jesus, which is introduced in v. 6, remains the central subject of the next section which runs from v. 9 to v. 19.

In this review, Jesus cites his community-forming acts. He has shown the Father's name (6a) and given the Father's words (8a, and 20) to the com-

32. Edwyn Bevan, *Symbolism and Belief* (London: Allen and Unwin, 1938), 122.

munity of consent which his work brings into being. The disciples, for their part, have received and kept Jesus' words (6b, 8b). They have believed and recognized his divine origin (8c). All three verses (6, 7 and 8) say that what Jesus has and speaks comes from the Father. However, Jesus cannot state the link between himself and the Father without including believers, nor can he speak of himself and believers without stressing that the unit is the Father in himself in believers:

> The Father's name and words
> were manifested by Jesus and given
> to the disciples.
> The disciples
> received and kept them
> and believe and know the rootage of Jesus in the Father.

Jesus' credentials before believers are the Father's name and words, which he has manifested. Believers are constituted such because they have recognized that what Jesus says and gives originates in the Father.

Jesus' review opens describing divine self-imparting and human response. He speaks in short, simple words (30 monosyllables in NRSV).

> I have made your name known
> to those whom you gave me from the world.
> They were yours,
> and you gave them to me,
> and they have kept your word. 17:6

Jesus has *made known (ephanerōsa)* the Father's name. Jesus' mission was revelatory. The Greek tense wraps his whole showing forth of the Father into a single act. In Hebrew thought, one's name is as oneself. In making the Father's name known, Jesus has made the Father known. The TEV translates *I have made you known.* In telling another person one's name, one is, at least in a germinal way, self-communicated. In making the Father's name known, Jesus made God near and apprehensible. A. T. Hanson remarked, "What the Father's name means is God's nature as mercy and faithfulness."[33]

Jesus says that he has made the name known to those who were given

33. A. T. Hanson, *Grace and Truth: A Study in the Doctrine of the Incarnation* (London: SPCK, 1975), 31.

to him by the Father from *the world.* Jesus' revelatory mission was polarizing. Some persons who heard him could not hear. Jesus prays for those who, by the Father's gift, have heard and believed and known. A community of response makes possible an exchange of sympathies and understanding — conditions required for a significant manifestation (cf. 1:12). Jesus' people, by their response to him, are taken *out of the world.* He came to the world and was rejected; those who believe in him are, by their identification with the rejected one, separated from the world. They live on in the world, but by God's call, they live as strangers in it.

Jesus says, as he said in v. 2, that his followers were given him by the Father, but he enlarges the thought: *They were yours, and you gave them to me* (6b). They were the Father's before they were the Son's; they became the Son's by the Father's gift. Again Jesus draws on the Jewish principle that an owner's property might be transferred to his agent. The community of redemption is comprised of persons who belong to the Father, but are given to Jesus.

Having put the matter in terms of divine act, the Evangelist turns, without transition, to say *and they have kept your word (your* logos*).* The divine *logos* required a reordering of life. Keeping the divine word implies responsible, intentional human actions. Believers show themselves to be God's own people, given to the Son. As such they are the focus of Jesus' prayer and objects of the Father's care and blessing.

Only in this place in the Fourth Gospel are persons spoken of as answerable to God's *word* — generally, God's word is given to and kept by Jesus (as 8:55; 15:10), while the disciples are to keep Jesus' word (8:51-52; 14:23). Here it is said that since Jesus' word is the Father's word, his disciples, by responding to his teaching and his works, have kept God's word, for Jesus' word is the word of the one who sent him (14:24).

The review concludes:

Now they know that
    everything you have given me is from you;
for the words that you gave to me I have given to them,
    and they have received them
    and know in truth that I came from you;
    and they have believed that you sent me. 17:7-8

The people who have believed in Jesus form a community of recognition. (The recognition is affirmed four times in five clauses, using three different verbs: they *know,* they *have received,* and they *have believed.*) It was the principal thrust of the Book of Signs that Jesus' acts and words — indeed Jesus himself — are from God. The disciples are those who, despite some incomprehension, recognize the divine source of what they have seen. They encountered Jesus, associated with him, heard him, watched him, and, where many had failed to grasp or had rejected, these *knew* that everything that the Son had — his authority, his words of life — had come from the Father. They knew that Jesus' mission was transparent to God, the very expression of God, the living God acting in their midst.

This perception on the part of the disciples is emphasized in v. 7; *Now they know that everything you have given me is from you.* The disciples know a gift to be a gift; they recognize God's work as God's. They know to be true what is true — a recognition not to be taken for granted.

Jesus has borne witness through words. The term *everything (panta)* with which this verse opens is narrowed to *words* (*rhēmata,* translated "message" in TEV). Meaning, or the connectedness and interior sense of things — one's account of reality — is conveyed by words. Jesus has been a faithful steward of the world of meaning he received from the Father.

Jesus turns to speak of the disciples' reception of the words he has given. (Again we may note that the principal form of the word in the time of the New Testament was the oral/aural form.) Words, spoken and heard, that arise from the depths of the self, can become formative within the self of another. When speaking of words, one expects a term such as "hear," a term common enough in the Fourth Gospel; but in this place Jesus uses three terms, none of them auditory. The disciples (1) have *received* Jesus' words. In a study, now a few years old, the German pastor Walter Lüthi commented, "They open the door to the words which are seeking to dwell in them."[34] On the basis of Jesus' words, they (2) *know in truth* that he is from God; and they (3) *have believed* that the Father has sent him. (This description of the disciples' reception of the revelation in Jesus might include also "they have kept your word" from v. 6b.) This rich vocabulary of reception suggests that the disciples have taken in the witness of Jesus profoundly. "The Word has found its way into their hearts, their minds, their feelings and their wills, and has taken possession of their whole being."[35] *Knowing* and *believing* are not contrasted here, but are "almost interchangeable."[36]

34. Walter Lüthi, *St. John's Gospel: An Exposition* (Richmond: John Knox, 1960), 247.
35. Lüthi, *St. John's Gospel,* 247.
36. Brown, *Gospel,* 744.

Lüthi remarks that receiving precedes knowing: "The sequence is significant. We always try to do it the other way around; first of all we want to know, and only then are we willing to receive. But the Word of God will remain a mystery to you, as long as your willingness to receive is conditional upon your knowing."[37] (These verbs of response all designate free, willed acceptance, an emphasis which, as Robert Kysar observes, "stands in tension with the predeterministic emphasis" of v. 6.)[38]

Receiving Jesus' words yields a knowledge of his identity. The disciples *know in truth;* they grasp reality. They know *that I came from you, and they have believed that you sent me.* In the christological expression *I came (came forth) from you (exēlthon,* from *exerchomai)* the historic reality of Jesus is represented as his "coming-forth from the Father." (This expression is also used in 8:42; 13:3; and 16:27, 28, 30). The disciples recognized that the origin of the Jesus they had known lay with God.

When Jesus says "they have kept your *logos*" (v. 6c), "they know" (v. 7), and "they have believed" (v. 8c), he may seem to claim more for the disciples than is due them. (He spoke of them in a more qualified way in 16:31-32). Here, however, Jesus is speaking as though from the other side of the cross, the resurrection, and the coming of the Paraclete. He knows of the faithfulness and certainty the disciples will display beyond the lapses and desertions of the passion events. The judgment that Jesus' followers *have kept your logos* is open to the inclusion of the later church.

Here, as at the end of the Third Discourse, 16:30, even though Jesus credits the disciples with recognizing that he has come from God, he does not say that they know he is going to God — this despite the emphasis he has given in the Farewell speeches to his departure to the Father and to the significance that his going held for him and for them. Since Jesus credits his followers with knowing what they do, it seems significant that, knowing what a reader does about the structure of johannine christology, Jesus says this much and no more.

The unity and flow of the ideas of 17:6-8 was summarized by Franz Mussner:

> Here we have a connected group of terms (*phaneroun,* make known — *ton logon,* the word — *tērein,* keep — *ginōskein,* know — *ta rhēmata*

37. Lüthi, *St. John's Gospel,* 247.

38. Robert Kysar, *John, the Maverick Gospel* (rev. ed., Louisville: Westminster/John Knox, 1993), 257.

> *didomai,* give the words — *lambanein,* receive — *pisteuein,* believe) which denote definite steps in the process of revelation. As origin the Father is named ("The words you gave me"); his envoy Jesus Christ "makes known his name" and hands on the words of the Father to the disciples; these in their turn keep the word of the Father entrusted to them which they have received from God's envoy and so come to "know" and "believe." This knowledge of Jesus' divine mission is not something held for the disciples in the future, but it is theirs "now," and it is not pious guesswork, but knowing "in truth."[39]

In the lectionary. The Revised Common Lectionary uses the prayer of John 17 as the Gospel reading on the Seventh Sunday of Easter — the concluding Sunday of the Easter season — in all three years, dividing it so that vv. 1-11 are read in Year A, vv. 12-19 in Year B, and vv. 20-26 in Year C. Thus, the opening verses, which have been considered in the foregoing pages, are the Gospel in Year A.

In some respects this reading may seem too little, and in other respects too much.

This lection, 17:1-11, is the first part of a large, important, structured, unified portion of the johannine text. In congregations that follow the Common Lectionary, churchgoers will hear and preachers will consider this prayer in thirds, rather than as a whole. Preachers who by temperament are teachers and expositors may feel that they are dealing with a fragment. They would surely not want to consider the whole prayer on one Sunday, for the chapter is large and complex; any homiletic treatment of the whole would necessarily be quite summary. But they may find it frustrating to preach on one part of a unit, knowing that it will be a year before the liturgy will introduce the next section and three years before all of the prayer will all have come around in the lectionary.

Yet the passage set for Year A presents rich content in compressed style. This prayer sums up much that has been established about Jesus and his mission in earlier portions of the Gospel. Although its words sound simple, they require a reader to bring to them some prior understanding. A preacher who wants to present this text must, to some extent, be an explainer. Although the language of the prayer has little color, any portion of John 17 is embedded in a narrative context and in a dense body of thought and cannot well be grasped just by being read out. The situation, the relational thought, and the vocabulary of this prayer are so important in the johannine presentation of Jesus that it would seem desirable for the preaching on Easter VII to locate itself to some extent in the thought idiom of the biblical text.

39. Franz Mussner, *The Historical Jesus in the Gospel of St. John* (London: Burns and Oates, 1967), 31-32.

The opening section of this prayer establishes the rootage of the church and of Christian existence in Jesus himself and the rootage of Jesus and his redemptive mission in the purpose of God. It assumes that theology is serious business for the preacher, for the church, and for the individual Christian. The appointed lection may seem too full of profound ideas — ideas which come in quick succession, the ideas often taking for granted things that were said earlier. A preacher must select and narrow without oversimplifying. A preacher will need to isolate prayerfully, not John 17 as a whole, nor even 17:1-11, but a single manageable phrase or theme which engages the imagination. And then one begins to reflect.

---

2. Part Two (17:9-19)

The Redeemer's work, which he has carried out in obedience to the Father's commission, has brought forth a community of believing, receptive persons. Jesus has included in his prayer the people who have been given to him and who have known and kept his word. Now in two sections of petition (vv. 9-11 and 15-17) and two of review (vv. 12-14 and 18-19) his community claims his attention more fully and circumstantially. The divisions between these sections are not sharp, and important terms often carry over from petition into review, the connections producing subordinate units of thought.

As Jesus prays, he sets the believing community alongside its hostile context. "The world" is mentioned repeatedly in vv. 9-19. It is mentioned more frequently in John 17 than in any other chapter in the Bible. Clearly the world is an unfriendly setting for believers; it hates them as an alien presence (vv. 14, 16). Jesus' followers are a people given to him by the Father (v. 9), and in them he is glorified (v. 10). His people share his detachment from the world; they *do not belong* to it (v. 16). Yet they are sent into it (v. 18), entrusted with the Father's word (v. 14). Jesus' people remain an object of his care. He prays that in their situation of peril the Father will maintain them in truth (vv. 17, 19) and in unity (v. 11) and protect them from the Evil One (vv. 11, 12, 15). Jesus seeks for them the fullness of his own joy (v. 13), even as they experience the world's rejection.

I am asking on their behalf;
  I am not asking on behalf of the world,
  but on behalf of those whom you gave me,
    because they are yours. 17:9

Jesus clarifies who is being prayed for and who is not. He prays for his immediate followers, describing them, as he did in v. 6, as *those whom you gave me.* Jesus does not refer exclusively to the eleven; however, the Farewell situation does focus attention on the crucial first generation, whose missionary witness brought into being the community for which the Evangelist writes. Walter Lüthi commented that Jesus' specific intercession for his immediate disciples is like a farmer's interest in a handful of seed which carries the promise of a harvest. The field would remain desolate and barren without that small fresh start. Jesus' particular focus, he observes, does not dismiss the world. "Far from failing the world, when Christ prays for the disciples, He does so in the world's own interest."[40]

Those for whom Jesus is concerned are the concern of the Father also; *they are yours.* Jesus' followers have been given to him by the Father (the theme appeared in v. 6), but at the same time they remain the Father's. (In the Jewish understanding of agency, an owner's goods, even when they are entrusted to an agent, remain the possession of the original owner.) As John Fenton says, "There is" in the matter of possession "no separation between the Father and the Son."[41]

Jesus' prayer introduces a clarifying distinction. He cares about the world, as does the Father (3:16). He sends his disciples into it (v. 18); his "word" is intended for it; he seeks that it may believe (v. 21). Ultimately God's purpose has the world in view. Walter Lüthi explains that Jesus' focus on his followers is "a matter of concentration rather than exclusion." Jesus' intercession is released where a responding community exists, but the world, as "human life in rebellion against God,"[42] can turn aside even the prayer of Jesus.

Jesus' description of believers as given to him by the Father while yet they remain the Father's (v. 9) leads to a parenthetic explanation of the closeness with which he is bound to his people, and both he and they are bound to the Father.

> (All mine are yours,
> and yours are mine;
> and I have been glorified in them.) 17:10

40. Lüthi, *St. John's Gospel,* 251.

41. J. C. Fenton, *The Gospel According to John* (Oxford: Oxford University Press, 1970), 174.

42. J. A. T. Robinson, *The Priority of John* (London: SCM, 1985), 334.

Jesus has said that believers who had been given to him were and remained the Father's. Here his reciprocal terms, *All mine are yours, and yours are mine,* say that all that belongs to either the Father or the Son belongs also to the other. In possessive, competitive modern Western society, "mine" and "yours" would often be taken to be distinct and exclusive. Even things that are held jointly ("community property") often lead to antagonism and broken relations. Ordinarily, I define myself by what is "mine," and what is "mine" cannot in any significant way at the same time be "yours." But between the Father and the Son it is not so. What either has, the other has. Possessions are not occasions of contest, but of mutual fulfillment and joy.

The community of faith belongs to the Father and the Son. It is possessed by the divine life which is unitary, but which is at the same time knowable and addressable under two names. When believers are given to Jesus they are not thereby alienated from the Father. These two possessors are so united that the church is jointly owned.

As the Father and the Son are glorified in one another (vv. 4-5), so Jesus is glorified in those who are his — that is, who are both his and the Father's. *And I have been glorified in them.* As Jesus' historic work glorified the Father (v. 4), so the believing, obeying church is the glory of Jesus — by it his mission is extended, his name is made known. Jesus is glorified in the church as the Father is glorified in him.

The words give pause. During Jesus' ministry as it has been told in this Gospel he has not been glorified in any significant way by his disciples. The narrative has portrayed them as somewhat slow and lacking imagination. Yet they stand out as having made a positive response to Jesus, and Jesus' words here suggest faith and obedience that are to come. When Jesus says *I have been glorified in them,* his prayer seems to step into a post-resurrection perspective, and it credits his followers with a loyalty and courage that will be.

> And now I am no longer in the world,
> but they are in the world,
> and I am coming to you. 17:11a

And now signals a dramatic anticipation. Jesus passes over the events that are to come in chapters 18–19 and says *I am no longer in the world . . .* but *I am coming to you.* The events that will carry him from the world and to the

Father have begun. For the first readers of this Gospel the words expressed the *now* of an existing condition. Even though Jesus is no longer in the world, his followers stay on as witnesses (ultimately the only witnesses) to who Jesus was and what he did.

The sent one returns to his association with the sender. In the unique first person idiom of this prayer, Jesus says *I am coming to you.*

After much holding back, Jesus' prayer comes to his actual petition:

Holy Father,
protect them in your name that you have given me,
so that they may be one,
as we are one. 17:11b

Jesus opens his petition with a renewed address which is full of tensiveness. Only in this place Jesus says *Holy Father.* His familiar term "Father," which speaks of intimacy and nearness, is modified by "holy," speaking of beyondness, awesomeness. The term "Holy Father" is used in the prayer at the eucharist in *Didache* 10:2. The church is protected by the transcendent Holy One, who is also the close-at-hand Father; or by the intimately known Father, who is unapproachable in holiness.

The petitionary verb *protect* them (*tēreō,* a military term) seems not so much to ask that Jesus' people may be guarded from external enemies (although the hostility of the world will be mentioned in v. 14) as that they may be maintained in faithfulness (cf. 1 John 2:18-25). When Jesus' speech passes from God's "keeping" of the group in v. 11 to the loss of one, *the one destined to be lost,* in v. 12, it suggests that when he prays for his followers' keeping, his principal meaning is "Hold them together. Preserve them from losses and defections."

In biblical usage, the name represents the person, The unusual expression *Protect them in your name* [*that you have given me*] means, in effect, "keep them united with yourself." The name had been entrusted to Jesus (see v. 12); his mission had made known the divine character.

Jesus asks the Father to guard the community so that it will remain united. *Protect them . . . so that they may be one, as we are one.* The petition suggests that the unity of the church was precarious. The church of the second and third centuries became preoccupied with problems of schism and of the lapsed. Some persons who had been a part — to all appearances, a well-established part — of the Christian community had left it or had been expelled. Could such persons return? If they could, on what terms? The

Fourth Gospel was written some years before these disciplinary issues arose urgently and specifically. Yet Jesus' concern for unity and his reference to Judas (v. 12) suggest that the problem was already looming (and see 1 John 2:18-19). The community feels keenly the defections it has experienced. Jesus asks the Father to protect the people of faith from disintegrative tendencies. The integrity of the community's life and witness would be deeply qualified if it were to become divided. Jesus cites his relation to the Father as the basis for his people's oneness. Each believer is one with every other believer. (The subject of the unity of believers returns in vv. 21-23 with a somewhat different emphasis.)

Jesus asks the Father to "keep" his followers, as he himself has kept them while he was with them (v. 12). The retention of believers in the divine-human life was spoken of as the disciples' responsibility when Jesus encouraged them to "remain" (15:4-5). But it is now referred to the "keeping" role of the Father. The protecting of Jesus' followers so that they are not lost or do not fall to the Evil One is here spoken of as the Father's responsibility, prompted by Jesus' prayer. Johannine thought affirms both divine initiative and human responsibility. Neither is qualified by the other; the two are sometimes juxtaposed; but the Evangelist makes no effort to reconcile them or to bring them into an internally consistent doctrinal construction.

> While I was with them, I protected them
> in your name that you have given me. 17:12a

The thought passes from petition to review, with the theme of *protection* providing a connection. Jesus called his followers, and while he was with them he continued to guard them (10:27-30: *No one will snatch them out of my hand*). He asks that when he is departed the Father will hold his followers in the divine life, as he has held them. Jesus' words *While I was with them* step out of the time frame of the passion events and the prayer and into the time of the church. While he was with his followers, Jesus protected them in the Father's name. The expression "protecting in the name" suggests the Hebrew idiom in which God's name is a secure bastion, a tower of refuge (see for example Prov. 18:10). Here, Schnackenburg remarks, Jesus is sharing with his disciples "an inner revelation of the reality of God, an introduction into the sphere of God and a communion of the love and joy of God from which Jesus himself lived."[43]

43. Schnackenburg, *Gospel*, 3.181.

> I guarded them, and not one of them was lost
> except the one destined to be lost,
> so that the Scripture might be fulfilled. 17:12b

Jesus says that he has *guarded* all who were given to him, *and not one of them was lost.* (He said earlier, *And this is the will of him who sent me, that I should lose nothing* [*mē apolesō*] *of all that he has given me, but raise it up on the last day,* 6:39. His guarding holds for the last day.) Jesus has guarded them successfully — all but one. *Not one of them was lost except the one destined to be lost.* Karl Barth says, "Among the elect of Jesus Judas is the one for whom the presence and protection and vigilance of Jesus were in vain."[44] The NRSV wording, *the one destined to be lost,* interprets the strong idiom of the original which says: "none is lost *(apōleto)* but the son of loss *(huios tēs apōleias).*" Schnackenburg notes that *apōleia* is "an extremely harsh word" meaning destruction or ruin, and it can mean "condemnation or exclusion from salvation."[45] Judas is spoken of as "son" of the discreative forces that rebel against God; he is the very offspring of the adversary. The image speaks of Judas as one born of the negation which finally claimed him.

This attribution of Judas' loss to destiny, to kinship in a spiritual family, suggests a largely undeveloped image of a counter-family. The devil is a father whose children demonstrate family traits (cf. 8:44-45). Judas is not self-explanatory; he is the "son of perdition." The image offers an explanation of the treachery of one so close to Jesus; yet the explanation only drives the problem back a stage. If, in pursuing causes, the Evangelist offers the fatherhood of Satan, the Evil One, to account for Judas, the next question is surely, what accounts for Satan? If Judas yields to "loss," why does anyone yield to "loss"? The thought stops because it has run to the limit of the author's mythic world. Judas represented concretely, historically the forces that work against God; the moral enigma of Judas is a specific, concentrated instance of the moral enigma of the world.

Jesus goes on to say that in the defection of Judas, scripture is fulfilled. Although no specific biblical reference is cited, Ps. 41:9 is probably in mind, *Even my bosom friend in whom I trusted, who ate my bread, has lifted the heel against me.* This text was cited expressly in 13:18 in connec-

44. Karl Barth, *Church Dogmatics* 2/2 (Edinburgh: Clark, 1957), 461.

45. Schnackenburg, *Gospel,* 3.182.

tion with Judas, and there, as here, the Evangelist comments *It is that the Scripture might be fulfilled.*[46]

Pointing to fulfilled Scripture serves in some measure to explain Judas, the unexplainable. The fulfillment of Scripture attests that the adversary, the discreative, however terrible its opposition may be, stands within the foreknowing and final purpose of God. If the forces of perdition were at work in the passion events, the reference to the Scriptures witnesses that the long-laid saving intention of God was at work as well and would prevail.

Jesus continues:

> But now I am coming to you,
> and I speak these things in the world
> so that they may have my joy
> made complete in themselves. 17:13

Jesus' prayer is within his final passage to the Father. *But now I am coming to you.* While he is still *in the world* it is important that *these things* be said. His departure is not just his leaving; it is an act filled with meaning, particularly for his followers. This prayer is a final disclosure to them (and to the readers of the Gospel) of that redemptive meaning.

One who encounters this prayer, aware of its location in the plot of this Gospel or having in mind the Gethsemane prayer of the Synoptics, would hardly expect Jesus at this time to speak of joy — of fortitude, or acceptance, perhaps, but not of joy. Yet Jesus says that he speaks *so that they may have my joy made complete in themselves* (cf. 15:11; 16:24; 1 John 1:4; 2 John 12). His own life, rooted in his relation with the Father, yielded a joy that was his to have, and his to give — a joy that existed to be communicated. There are persons around whom others lose their preoccupation with themselves and are lifted out of sadness or depression. Encountering them, others can reshape the personal reality in which they live — they see freshly, remember freshly, and forget freshly. This joy that comes to one from another becomes genuinely one's own. It is not a part being played; it is not superficial excitement nor de-

46. The Evangelist leaves his reference indefinite. There are several possibilities. Acts 1:20 cites Ps. 109:8 of Judas. A. T. Hanson thinks that text speaks to the "perdition" of Judas better than does Ps. 41:9 (*The Living Utterances of God* [London: Darton, Longman and Todd, 1983], 115-16). Matt. 27:3-10, speaking of Judas, cites Zech. 11:12-13 (and possibly Jer. 32:6-15).

A reader may wonder whether this last portion of v. 12 is to be thought of as Jesus' words or as an explanatory insertion by the narrator — which would resemble his practice in 12:14-15.

lusion. Jesus' joy is given to others; it is rooted in each recipient, where it can come to its own completion — *my joy is made complete* (Gr. *plēroō*) *in themselves.* Genuine joy is an expression of fullness of being. Joy is active; it is given intending its own increase and maturation.

However, the term *made complete* suggests that more is implied in this text than joy as socially transmitted well-being. The Jewish scriptures speak of eschatological joy — a God-given, inalienable joy belonging to the fullness of salvation (see, among other places, Isa. 12:3; 35:9-10; 51:11; 61:7, 10; 65:18-20; Psa. 126, and note in this Gospel the passage about Abraham rejoicing to see Jesus' day, 8:56; and we may observe the eschatological overtones in John 16:22). This request of Jesus for full joy for his followers says that, in the midst of troubled proximate things, believers in him are touched by final things. Again, the Fourth Gospel says that now, in the life of the church, the ultimate future is encountered.

> I have given them your word,
> and the world has hated them
> because they do not belong to the world,
> just as I do not belong to the world. 17:14

Still speaking in the mode of review, Jesus says *I have given them your word.* The word of the Father, given to the church by Jesus, is a word for the world. But since the world is set against God, the divine word is divisive, polarizing. Because Jesus' followers carry the word from the Father which Jesus has given them, the world hates them.

The community that Jesus leaves is constituted in the divine word. A word is a fragile thing to transmit. In the cultures of the Bible, the common form of the word was the spoken form, a form that is gone as soon as it is uttered. Yet in an oral culture, the spoken word is bound up with the speaker in a way that written, objectified and stored words are not in a print culture. A spoken word can call from the depths of one person to the depths of another. As it lodges in a hearer, it may be a creative, life-shaping, community-binding force; but it may also be an alienating, hurtful force. The word which Jesus has faithfully given, which is the Father's word, is a vital force in history — building up and casting down (cf. Jer. 1:9-10).

In Jesus' petition *protect them* in v. 11b, he said, in effect, "I protected them, but I am leaving. Now, Father, keep them, for their peril in the world is brought about by the word which they received from me. And that word is yours."

The uttering of the divine word creates crisis. A "yes" or a "no" is required from hearers. Indifference is not possible. The disciples, by their consent to the strange, new word of God, are alienated from the world — they no longer *belong to* it; they are not "of" it; they are not defined by it. As johannine usage has it, the world becomes world as it turns away from the Divine Word. The world is provoked by divine utterance into declaring itself. It is not a tolerant system which can make a comfortable place for Jesus and his community; rather, what it cannot define or control, it rejects. It *has hated them because they do not belong to* it ("hated" echoes the Second Discourse, where it was used of the world's response to Jesus, his people, and the Father, 15:18-23). In johannine terms, an aggressive new presence which the world cannot receive on its own terms, it "hates."

The divine word, which separates the believing community from the world, at the same time creates a link between believers and the rejected Jesus; the world hates Jesus' followers as it hated him, for *they do not belong to the world, just as I do not belong to the world.* The Evangelist is giving the first-century church a christologically informed account of its own experience. (This self-understanding appears in the Second Discourse, see 15:18-21, and it is echoed in 1 John 3:1b, *The reason the world does not know us is that it did not know him.*)

The power of the world, ordered on its own and making sense to itself on its own terms, is so great that Jesus' followers, who are necessarily persons in the world and sympathetic to portions of what it gives and requires, are always in danger of internalizing the world's judgment and consenting to its demand that they "belong" to it. Small accommodations seem harmless — it is still God's world, and the habit of going along makes believers lose the sense that their final "belonging" is not to the world, but to Another.

But the divine calling to separateness creates uneasy tensions and is not easily carried out. Problems do not arise only from giving in to the pressures of the world. Scrupulosity as to what may be regarded as "worldly" can lead to a sterile and inhuman sort of unworldliness. Some believers may tend to see the world as harmless and benign; others may see it as relentlessly hostile. Neither party can see what the other sees.

Extreme conflicts between the demands of Christ and what the world asks have at times marked the church's past. Tension is uncomfortable, and there is a common tendency to moderate the church/world opposition. However, in critical situations (which have sometimes come to be called *chairos* situations) Christians cannot remain indecisive. Many earnest believers have discovered in such situations that, as in Jesus' case, the place outside — the place to which they are driven by faith — is the place of power. Dietrich Bonhoeffer, speaking in one of the most extreme instances of conflict between the claims of faith and the power of the world, put it:

> The crucified Christ has become the refuge and the justification, the protection and the claim for the higher values and their defenders that have fallen victim to suffering. It is with the Christ who is persecuted and who suffers in His Church that justice, truth, humanity and freedom now seek refuge; it is with the Christ who found no shelter in the world, the Christ who was cast out of the world, the Christ of the crib and the cross under whose protection they now seek sanctuary, and who thereby for the first time displays the full extent of his power.[47]

> I have given them your word,
> and the world has hated them
> because they do not belong to the world,
> just as I do not belong to the world. 17:14

V. 14 forms a transition. It concludes the section of review that has run from v. 12 to v. 14, but it also anticipates the vocabulary of the petition which begins with v. 15. The world, whose hostility is emphasized in v. 14 remains in focus through v. 19. The clause *they do not belong to the world just as I do not belong to the world* of the second half of v. 14 is repeated as v. 16. (This portion of v. 14 is omitted in some manuscripts, and some text critics think it was brought into v. 14 from v. 16 by an early copyist. The manuscript evidence, however, seems to favor its retention in both places.) Thus (if the words are allowed to stand) vv. 14-16 form a brief *inclusio* within which a section of review ends and a section of petition begins.

> I am not asking that you take them out of the world,
> but I ask you to protect them from the evil one.
> They do not belong to the world
> just as I do not belong to the world.
> Sanctify them in truth;
> your word is truth. 17:15-17

Jesus clarifies his petition stating what is not prayed for. (He spoke similarly in v. 9.) He is *not asking* the Father *to take* his followers *out of the world.*

47. Dietrich Bonhoeffer, *Ethics* (New York: Macmillan, 1965), 181.

Even though Jesus is leaving the world, and although his followers' ultimate destiny is to be with him where he is going (v. 24 and 14:3), their present identification with him does not remove them from the world. Were there some first-century Christians who thought that their faith and Jesus' deliverance should release them at once from the Christ-rejecting world?

Yet belief in Jesus does set his followers in an uneasy relationship with the world. They live in history; they are required to be faithful in social compacts, to respect cultural continuities, to accept responsibilities in the communities of work and justice, in the tasks of family and child-rearing and caring for one's elders, of serving the poor and the disadvantaged. The sustaining orders of life which comprise the workable human world are aspects of God's creation and are not to be renounced, generally or selectively, in the name of faith.

Jesus' followers live in an order of things which they must in a great measure affirm. The human city and the city of God interpenetrate. Yet the world overreaches, and Jesus' people find themselves engaged, as he has been, in a contest of cosmic scope, and they are opposed by a power that is too much for them. Throughout his ministry, Jesus has guarded his people (12a); now, however, their keeping passes to the Father. *But I ask you to protect (tēreō) them.* The disciples' adversary is *the evil one.* (The term that is used here, *ponēros,* appears nowhere else in the Fourth Gospel, but it is used in 1 John 2:13-14; 3:12; 5:18-19, in *Didache* 10:5, and in the Lord's Prayer, Matt. 6:13.)[48] Jesus' old opponent, *the prince of this world* (14:30), opposes his people. Jesus asks the Father to protect them.

The complex relation in which Jesus' followers stand with the world is brought about, as the johannine view sees it, because those who are united with him are born with a birth that is from God; they live by a life that does not trace to *the world,* and they have a destiny that lies beyond *the world. They do not belong to the world, just as I do not belong to the world* (cf. 1 John 3:1b).

48. The term "the evil one" is used both in John 17 and in Matthew's version of the Lord's Prayer (Matt. 6:13b). Other parallels with the Lord's Prayer can be observed, such as the address "Father" and the emphasis on the name. Some exegetes have gone to some lengths to establish further parallels. But the two prayers are surely very different. The Lord's Prayer is a model which Jesus gives for others, and it is quite general in character, whereas John 17 could be prayed by no one but the johannine Jesus; it arises from his unique mission. A great deal of what is in each is not in the other. The thought forms of the Lord's Prayer are eschatological, while Jesus' prayer in John 17 belongs only in the distinctive theology of this Gospel.

In Jesus' prayer, this alien role of the faith community is stated with no explanation other than that the community is to the world as he himself has been. It is given no qualification or nuance. Individual believers and Christian societies struggle perennially with the conflict between the due claims of the world and the ultimate claim of Jesus Christ, and there is no easy formula for determining a faithful course of action.

Extremes can be identified. Some groups have so emphasized the opposition between Christ and the world as virtually to set the community of redemption against what are known in some theological traditions as the orders of creation. Other groups have so accommodated the church to the spirit of the world that church and world have become all but indistinguishable. Of course, there are careful and selective choices in between such extremes. There are complexities in every community and in every concrete situation, and there are many ways of making, in good conscience, poor decisions. Christians must work out some resolution of the church/world tension in their historic, always complex situations.

Account should be taken of the legitimate vocational asceticism which some Christians have practiced. A specific calling, such as to poverty, or celibacy, or pacifism is an intentional "signing off" at crucial points from the received order of things. But such determinations (whether made by individuals or by groups) do not imply wholesale rejection of the world — which is an impossibility. Such callings can witness against absolutizing the claims that goods, or sex and marriage, or a nation at war may make. Such creative disaffiliation can actualize, at crucial points, an alternative moral and social order. And out of this critique, historic change can arise. Discipleship must be pursued, courageously and discriminatingly, amid the relativities and contingencies of life in the world. It may take different forms for different persons or different faith communities.

The simply stated emphasis of Jesus' prayer — "*in,* but not *of*" the world — holds before the church in every time and circumstance the church/world tension itself and the reason for it. Bishop Newbigin remarks the essentiality of a considered otherworldliness: "When the Church is kept in the holy name of God it has a final commitment which is outside the comprehension of the world. Without this radical otherworldliness the Church has no serious business with the world."[49]

Persons who live in this dialectical relation to the world must have a

49. Lesslie Newbigin, *The Light Has Come: An Exposition of the Fourth Gospel* (Grand Rapids: Eerdmans, 1982), 231.

firm hold on that which sets them apart from the world. The church must know what constitutes it as church. Hence Jesus prays: *Sanctify them in the truth.*

> Sanctify them in the truth;
> your word is truth.
> As you have sent me into the world,
> so I have sent them into the world.
> And for their sake I sanctify myself,
> so that they also may be sanctified in truth. 17:17-19

Vv. 17-19 form a short unit of thought with internal connections:

- Again an identifiable, closely knit passage lies partly in a section of petition (vv. 15-17) and partly in a section of review (vv. 18-19).
- The term "sanctify" is used three times: *sanctify them . . . , I sanctify myself . . . , that they may be sanctified.*
- "Truth" is used three times: *Sanctify them in the truth. Your word is truth. That they also may be sanctified in truth.*
- Each clause is compound and contains a repetition of an important idea:

a *Sanctify them in the truth;*
a¹ *your word is truth.*
b *As you have sent me into the world,*
b¹ *so I have sent them into the world.*
c *For their sakes I sanctify myself,*
c¹ *so that they also may be sanctified in truth.*

a and c¹ which open and close the unit, echo one another. The theme of the church's mission (b) is enclosed by the theme of the church's sanctification (a and c).

"Sanctify," which is used by NRSV to translate *hagiazein* (and which appears three times in these verses) is a difficult term to translate in a culture which has all but lost a sense of the holy. "Make them holy" (J. B. Phillips) shows how the word would have been understood by persons who heard the Greek *hagios* behind the verb *hagiazō* or the Latin *sanctus,* "holy," behind "sanctify." TEV paraphrases "Make them your own in truth."

Jesus' term *sanctify them* identifies his followers as a people set apart for God. The language suggests God's ancient call to Israel to be a "holy nation." (Cf. Deut 7:6; 26:19; 28:9; Isa. 62:12. See especially Lev. 20:26, *You shall be holy to me; for I the Lord am holy, and I have separated you from other peoples to be mine.* The summons of Israel to be holy in Exod. 19:6 is adopted for the church in 1 Pet. 2:9.) God alone is the Holy One. Holiness speaks of the otherness and mystery of godhood (see, among other references, Isa. 6:1-5; 10:20; Amos 4:2; Ps. 99:3-5). Yet in a derivative sense, holiness can be ascribed to places, times, persons and things which are "holy to the Lord" — things which are set apart from other associations and belong distinctively to God. *Remember the Sabbath, and keep it holy* (Exod. 20:8). The holiness of God can be acknowledged by human beings in praise (e.g., Ps. 99:3-5; Isa. 8:13) and obedience (Lev. 19:2, *You shall be holy, for I the Lord your God am holy*). Israel's religion combined the people's sacral calling with ethical requirements. The "Holiness Code" (Leviticus 17–26) which sought to distinguish Israel from other peoples is the place which said *You shall love your neighbor as yourself.* Thus Jesus' petition that the Father "sanctify" his people asks, in effect, "Take your people apart from other claims, and separate them to yourself. Gather them to yourself; impart yourself to them; make them like you. Draw them as a dedicated and compassionate people into your own holiness and justice."

Jesus asks that his people be sanctified *in the truth* — a word which, as we have seen, speaks of the reality and trustworthiness of God, the faithfulness of Jesus, and the requirement that his followers be reliable as God is reliable. Human pledges are often not made good, but Jesus prays that his people may remain committed to the sovereign, gracious purposes to which God has called them.

Jesus adds *Your word is truth.* God's "word," divine self-expression, is always reliable. God's word is an address conveying the reality of the divine speaker. It is a living and potent thing, judging and making holy. Bultmann says that believers are set apart in the truth as "the reality of God, manifesting itself in the Word, takes them, though still in the world, out of the world's sphere of power."[50] God's word, as it binds believers to the one who speaks, alienates them from the world (v. 14). "Truth" speaks here of the saving truth, the redemptive word, for to be set apart in such truth implies mission — to which the thought of the prayer passes.

Jesus spoke earlier of himself as one whom *the Father has sanctified and sent into the world* (10:36). Now he says that his followers too are to be *sanctified* (vv. 17, 19) and *sent into the world* by him *as* he was *sent into the*

50. R. Bultmann, *Theology of the New Testament* (New York: Scribners, 1955), 2.19.

world by the Father (v. 18). The holy people is an apostolic people. The "setting apart" of Jesus' followers implies a godly detachment: "they do not belong." They cannot bring to the world anything that world does not already have on its own unless they have been made in some respects distinct from the world. Yet these people, who do not belong to the world, are to take responsibility in it. Their being in the world is not an inevitable, somewhat regrettable condition. The world (even in its alienation from God) is the setting in which believers participate through Jesus, the Sent One, in God's saving, freeing, uniting purpose.

As the thought passes to v. 19, the christology of this Gospel is again illuminated by the motif of agency, which provided that "an agent can appoint an agent."[51] Jesus has said repeatedly that he has been sent by the Father (see in the Prayer, vv. 3, 8, 18, 21, 23, 25). Here he says that as he has been sent, he sends his followers. As part of his leave-taking (which he will enact in 20:21), he commissions his community. As he was sent *into the world* — which he engaged judgingly, redemptively, sacrificially — so the church is sent *into the world.* As he carried the authority of the divine sender, so it will.

The Fourth Gospel, unlike the Synoptic Gospels, reports no sending of the disciples in association with the preaching and healing mission of Jesus. (There is, however, the isolated, unexplained *I sent you* of 4:38.) It is only as Jesus is departing that he sends his disciples (13:16, 20; 15:16; 17:18); they are specifically commissioned by the risen Jesus in 20:21. The sending of the church into the world is the correlative of Jesus' going to the Father. The post-Easter church is a community which knows itself to have been sent into the world by the living Jesus.

Jesus' words *The world has hated them* in v. 14 provide realism; the church is sent into an unreceptive world. The world does not welcome the word of its own salvation. The church's sending, like the sending of Jesus, provokes opposition.

The term "sanctify" returns in v. 19, this time referring to Jesus, who says *I sanctify myself.* He sets himself apart for the sake of his people, that they too *may be set apart in truth.* Hoskyns comments, "They are consecrated, He consecrates Himself and His consecration must precede theirs."[52]

51. Borgen, "God's Agent," 143.
52. Hoskyns, *Fourth Gospel,* 504.

The cultic terms "sanctify" *(hagiazō)* and "for their sakes" *(hyper autōn)* are the principal evidence that might support referring to John 17 as Jesus' "high priestly prayer." The phrases can suggest a priest consecrating himself before he offers sacrifice. Jesus' consecration of himself can seem to be his dedicatory act as he approaches the cross. Yet the prayer does not call attention to such sacrificial hints. John 17 makes no clear reference either to Jesus' death or to him as offerer or as sin-bearer. When Jesus asks that his people be sanctified he prays that they may be separated from the world (vv. 14-16) by God's word (v. 17), drawn into union with himself, and thrust into mission in the world (v. 18), where they are to seek those who will believe (v. 20). Their mission is made credible by their oneness (v. 23). Jesus prays, as Christopher Evans put it, for "their preservation from temptation to deny the truth of their heavenly existence and to fall back into the sphere of the unsanctified or profane."[53] This touch of priestly language in Jesus' prayer speaks of a prophetic mission.

This section of Jesus' prayer (v. 9-19), has spoken urgently of the church in its complex, ambiguous, painful, necessary, yet splendid situation — a people of Christ and his word, taking its identity and life from him, having a destiny beyond history, yet located in the alienated world, there to be Jesus' people, a sign and a witness.

3. Part Three (17:20-26)

Jesus' prayer passes beyond his immediate disciples to include those who will believe through their witness. The prayer has been leading up to this emphasis, for most of the original readers of this Gospel were believers of a second generation, and here Jesus' prayer expressly widens to include them.

The words give indirect evidence of the historical situation from which the prayer was written. The mission of original evangelists, whose tradition traced to the Beloved Disciple, had brought into being (at an unknown place, far from Judea and Galilee) a community of believers in Jesus. As the group of converts persisted, there had come to be in it a substantial number of believers who lacked firsthand familiarity with the roots of the Jesus-tradition that traced to the original evangelists and through them to the Beloved Disciple. They did not know firsthand the

53. Evans, "Christ at Prayer," 594.

foundational tradition of the johannine community. Yet, even though they were latecomers, the *word* of the original witnesses, which they had received, had made these believers-at-second-hand contemporaries of the events to which that formative word witnessed. They should not think of themselves as in matters of faith at some disadvantage. Jesus' prayer names and includes them specifically, *I ask not only on behalf of these* (the immediate disciples), *but also on behalf of those who will believe in me through their word.* He prays for unity between the first and the subsequent generations of the people of faith: *that they may all be one.*

The newer believers owed everything to the original witnesses. Yet the original witnesses could not be continued, and their role could not be replaced. Their passing was a critical event in the life of the Community of the Beloved Disciple. As the believers in Jesus took on a history, the original evangelists and the first believers had come to represent an honored past, while the newer believers held the future. Should the older group, however great the debt that was owed to it, be allowed to determine the character of the community? Yet the older group no doubt felt that it was owed some deference as the bearer of the Jesus tradition. Could newer believers be trusted to know what had been given in Jesus? Would they have the necessary depth of familiarity with the tradition? Could they ever really step into the informed roles that would be needed to hold the growing church on course?

Such a crisis can be expected in any new group which comes into being with a comprehensive vision or sense of purpose. Such a group necessarily has a specific point of beginning. It has an initial vision of itself and its purpose which is articulated in a particular time and place and usually among a small body of people. This group, if it is to serve its vision, must perpetuate itself.

As it does so, it faces a critical moment: Can such a group break beyond its founders and the particularity of its origin? Can it spread geographically, incorporate new perceptions and new human variety, and remain itself even while it changes? When history creates generational rifts, can groups that were separated by the passage of time discover interior resources for maintaining their identity and the continuity of their witness?

If a new group can surmount the crisis of the second generation, perhaps any number of later crises can be overcome. Success at this critical point can seem a pledge of its ability to offer a space-time-and-people-embracing unity.

The first-century people of faith in Jesus was not an ethnic identity which passed from generation to generation. Rather, it was shaped as persons came to believe in response to witness. How does such a people define itself, retain its identity, and remain united even as it continues, grows, and changes?

Differing ideas were no doubt articulated on many sides, while, in the stress of conflict, unifying convictions were obscured. As the generations tended to polarize, unity no doubt often seemed fragile.

The prayer of Jesus addresses this urgent subject, opening the theme with a tightly structured passage (vv. 20-23). Two successive sentences parallel one another closely. There is no other rhetorical unit like it in this Gospel. Paul Minear's diagram of the organization of this passage (which is reproduced here) indicates its grammatical parallelism:[54]

Sentence One, vv. 20-21 [petition]	**Sentence Two, vv. 22-23** [review]
a^1 *I ask not only on behalf of these, but on behalf of those who will believe in me through their word,*	a^2 *The glory that you have given me I have given them,*
b^1 *that (hina) they may all be one.*	b^2 *so that (hina) they may be one*
c^1 *As (kathōs) you, Father, are in me and I am in you,*	c^2 *as (kathōs) we are one, I in them and you in me,*
d^1 *may (hina) they also be in us*	d^2 *that (hina) they may become completely one,*
e^1 *so that (hina) the world may know*	e^2 *so that (hina) the world may know*
f^1 *that (hoti) you have sent me.*	f^2 *that (hoti) you have sent me and that you have loved them even as you have loved me.*

Vv. 20-23 shape a complex unit, some of whose structural and grammatical characteristics may be identified:

Vv. 20-21 are petition; Jesus prays that there may be unity between the Christians of the first and the second generations. Vv. 22-23 are review; the church is constituted by Jesus, who gives it the glory that he himself has been given.

54. Minear, *John: The Martyr's Gospel*, 132-33. There are similar analyses in Brown, *Gospel*, 769, and J. F. Randall, "The Theme of Unity in John 17:20-23," *Ephemerides Theologicae Lovanienses* 41 (1965), 373-94. Appold, *Oneness Motif*, 157, observes "this remarkable parallelism and unique structural form."

But close interior connections of structure and wording unite the petition and the review:

In the main clause a^1, Jesus begins to ask; and he introduces the second generation of believers. These persons believe because of a word passed from earlier believers. In the main clause a^2, Jesus ascribes the existence of the faith community to the glory that he has been given and has given to his people.

There are six purpose clauses *(b, d, e)*. They speak of the oneness of believers *(b, d);* and they propose that the measure of this unity *(kathōs, c)* is the oneness between Jesus and the Father.

The concluding clauses *(e* and *f)* speak of the world — what it must come to believe and know (f).

The two *"as" (kathōs)* clauses (c^1, c^2) contain the johannine "reciprocity formula" — *x* is in *y*, as *y* is in *x*. Jesus and the Father are "in" one another. The second of them (c^2) includes Jesus' people in whom he lives as he and the Father live in each other.

The two final *"that" (hoti)* clauses *(f)* state characteristic christological affirmations: The Father has sent Jesus (f^1 and f^2) and has loved both Jesus and Jesus' people (f^2).

This carefully crafted language (moving in parallelism which repeats, but expands ideas, all parts being complementary) suggests that this unit may have begun as a piece of pre-formed tradition, which was worked out for an earlier purpose and was found to be usable in this prayer. Appold judges that "What we are dealing with here are typically Johannine dogmas or confessional statements that had acquired normative character for the Johannine church."[55]

To look at this unit of the prayer in the sequence presented by the text:

> I ask not only on behalf of these,
> but also on behalf of those who will believe in me
> through their word,
> that they may all be one.
> As you, Father, are in me,
> and I am in you,
> may they also be in us,
> so that the world may believe that you have sent me. 17:20-21

The continuance of the faith community depends on the perpetuation of the church's "word," *logou autōn*. The term is used here as it is nowhere else

55. Appold, *Oneness Motif*, 160.

in the Fourth Gospel. Elsewhere, when it is theologically significant, "word" refers either to Jesus as God's Word or else to the word of the Father as it is made known in Jesus. Here it speaks of the church's effective word of witness. (The Samaritan woman's "word," 4:39-42, gives a partial parallel.) The disciples received Jesus' *logos* (vv. 8, 14). Now they too are bearers of a faith-eliciting *logos.* The church carries the divine word, passing it from one generation in the faith to the next. The church lives through the word it bears; the word lives in the church it creates.

This passage is written from and with reference to a time when most of the readers of this Gospel were Christians of a second generation in faith. Evidently the johannine community contained two groups, who might be called "disciples at first hand and disciples at second hand."[56] Although the contribution of the original witnesses (who represented the tradition of the Beloved Disciple) was essential, such witnesses would become fewer with time and would eventually pass from the scene. Evidently as this Gospel was being written, these original bearers of the word were becoming reduced in number. The express inclusion in this prayer of the disciples at second hand — who may have constituted a vigorous and growing group — suggests that they may have thought of themselves as having been admitted only into somewhat disadvantaged positions in the community.

The naming of the two generations and the prayer for their unity suggest that some tension had grown between them. As Paul Minear says, "A generation gap is recognized in the very effort to overcome it."[57] The two identifiable groups in the johannine church were both followers of Jesus. But they had different histories, and their different experience of the church had led them to somewhat dissimilar perceptions and priorities. (There is an undeveloped reference in *1 Clem.* 3:3 to a rivalry of "the young against their elders." Does it evidence a similar generational conflict in second-century Rome?)

In this conflict of generations in the first-century church, Jesus prays *that they may all be one.* This passage in Jesus' prayer has become an ecumenical watchword by which to criticize the divided churches of modern

56. Paul S. Minear, "The Audience of the Fourth Evangelist," *Interpretation* 31 (1977), 344.

57. Minear, "Audience," 344. The proposal that the plea for Jesus' followers to be one is specifically directed to a rift between two generations in the johannine community has been developed effectively by Minear. Other interpreters have taken the appeal to refer to other kinds of threats to unity. I find Minear's analysis convincing, and I follow it here.

Christendom and to hold before them the vision of oneness in Christ. Yet the words seem to refer in the first instance to the need to reconcile the old and the new factions in the johannine church. In speaking to this first-century local division, Jesus' prayer does not analyze the church's internal stresses nor suggest action to bring about unity. It does, however, direct attention to Jesus as the central determining figure to whom the faith of both generations had final reference (*believe in me,* v. 20) and to the *word* (vv. 14, 17) that had been carried initially by one group, but was owned by none. Jesus' prayer holds before the church the unifying realities that are more powerful than the division-making irritants that have claimed the community's attention in this early time of communal fragility. The church is united in the *name* that came from God and that thus sustains the community (vv. 11b, 12); it held a common *glory,* given now (v. 22) and pledged for the future (v. 24); and it is bound by the *love* which came from God and was bestowed first on the Son and through him on the church where it was lodged in each believer (vv. 23, 26b).

The church's unity, as this prayer describes it, has its source and model in the mutual indwelling of the Father and the Son: *as you, Father, are in me, and I am in you.* And the goal of the church's oneness, rooted in this indwelling, is that the world may recognize that Jesus is from the Father. Jesus prays, *May they also be in us, so that the world may believe that you have sent me.* The relation between the Father and the Son is the basis of the unity of Jesus' people. Jesus offers a kerygmatically rooted vision of a community in which persons are bound to one another, loving and being loved, trusting and being trustworthy. In this community each member is fulfilled in and through the relation to the others.

Jesus expresses as prayer the reciprocity theme that appeared in the First Discourse: *You in me . . . I in you . . . they in us.* The Father is in the Son and the Son is in the Father (see 14:11), and the Father and the Son dwell in believers (see 14:23). In his prayer, he describes believers as received into the mutual coinherence of the Father and the Son (17:21). In the profoundest sense, the unity of the church, as it is set forth in this prayer, is not an achievement; it is a gift. It is not to be created, but received, recognized and exhibited. It exists primally in the mutual indwelling of the Father and the Son. That indwelling is shown forth in believers who are drawn into it.

The oneness of the church exhibits to the world that Jesus and his mission are of God — *that you* (the Father) have sent me. Jesus' own public self-presentation in the Book of Signs bore witness that he was from God. But his message, which was largely about himself, was disregarded. Now that Jesus is departing, his continuing presentation through the church has the same intent. Jesus is shown to be the one from God.

Thus the church's mission is, in effect, a continuation of Jesus' own mission, meant to lead the world to believe in his divine origin. Paul Minear notes that, surprisingly, "The world comes to believe not that I (Jesus) have sent them (the messengers) but that you (the Father) have sent me (the Son). The world is to believe in the Father's love in sending the Son whom the world hated. . . . The [believers'] message is not about themselves but about the Father and his Son."[58] Jesus has credited the disciples with believing truly that he came from God (vv. 8, 25, and 16:30-31). Here and in v. 23 Jesus prays that the world will come to believe what the disciples now believe — that Jesus and his mission are God's self-revealing action. If the world comes to believe that, it can come to understand more. But lacking that belief, it remains in darkness.

It might be asked: Does the church's actual dividedness qualify the gospel's believability in the eyes of the world? Perhaps the world has become so accustomed to Christian disunity that it interprets it in its own terms and expects nothing else.

The Scottish theologian Elizabeth Templeton provided a touch of realism when she remarked a few years ago that the idea that division among Christians is an occasion of scandal is more a part of the way the church sees itself than it is the perception of the general society:

> To me the most signal failure of the Church is not our divisions, but the fact that, though we *talk* of "scandal," most people outside do not find it at all a scandal. It is to them a predictable, to-be-expected manifestation, in one more social context, of the normal human capacity for separatedness. . . . Our denominations and our ideological divides really shock very few people outside. If they merit attention at all, it is likely to be a rather bored shrug of the shoulder, a half raised eyebrow. . . . The secular world pays no more attention to our broken eucharist than it would to the fact that golfers eat their Sunday lunch in different golf clubs.[59]

Jesus has prayed for unity among his people — a unity rooted in divine being and action. Now, within this tightly woven unit, petition passes to review. In

58. Minear, *John: The Martyr's Gospel*, 136.

59. Elizabeth Templeton, "The Church's Task in Reconciliation," *Theology* 94 (1991), 329.

his review, Jesus speaks of what he has given to his people, a giving of glory which provides the theological basis for the unity he requested in v. 21.

> The glory that you have given me
> I have given them,
> so that they may become one
> as we are one.
> I in them and you in me,
> that they may become completely one. . . . 17:22-23a

A single, pervasive *glory,* primally the Father's, has been given to the Son, and imparted by him to the believing community. The glory is given for the sake of unity; the unity is rooted in the shared radiance. The prayer speaks of a glory already given — given in the completed work of Christ which the prayer presupposes. Unity among believers — specifically unity between the diverging generations in the johannine church — exhibits the unity between the Father and the Son. The language holds together the duality and the oneness of the Father and the Son, which is to be demonstrated in the plurality and unity of the Messiah's people.

The unity of believers is not something they strive to bring about in response to their perception of the oneness of the Father and the Son; rather, it is their participation in that very oneness. A. M. Ramsey said, "Herein lies the meaning of the Church. It is the mystery of the participation of men and women in the glory which is Christ's."[60] *I in them and you in me.* John Fenton puts it in third person terms, "Jesus in the faithful, and the Father in Jesus."[61]

The "in" phrases of the prayer, particularly those which speak of persons being "in" one another, concentrate in this final section:

Eight such phrases occur within seven verses: Jesus prays for those who "*believe in*" him, v. 20b, and he asks that his love (which is the Father's love) may be "in" his people (v. 26b). The relationships which are spoken of are: the Father "in" Jesus (vv. 21, 23), Jesus "in" the Father (v. 21), Jesus "in" his people (vv. 23, 26), and Jesus' people "in" himself and the Father (v. 21).

In the terms of the Fourth Gospel, the Father and the Son are intimately and

60. A. M. Ramsey, *The Glory of God and the Transfiguration of Christ* (London: Longmans, 1949), 87. The quoted text is altered.

61. John Fenton, *John* (Oxford: Oxford University Press, 1976), 127.

deeply bonded. Yet they remain themselves. The relation does not diminish or qualify, but fulfills the parties to it. They are sharers in life, love, listening and speaking, in willing, in glory, and in joy.

This johannine idiom says nothing about the followers of Jesus being "in" one another. (The point is made, however, in Ephesians 4:25.) Believers who stand in relation to Jesus and the Father, are also related to one another. But this author's relational thinking is dominated by the divine life that is lodged within believers and by believers who are themselves brought within the divine life.

Implications for life together are latent in the johannine proposition that persons can, on the model of divine life, indwell one another. These implications have been explored over the Christian centuries through venturesome theology and spirituality and in intentional, self-disciplined communities. And they will certainly continue to be explored.

Jesus says that what believers are in relation to him traces to the relation that persists between himself and the Father. Unity among Jesus' followers makes a christological statement — as does their disunity. The Intercessor prays *that they may become completely one.* As long as unity among believers is incomplete, Jesus' prayer must make them restless with its incompleteness.

The glory given (v. 22a) is for the sake of oneness (v. 22b, 23a), and the glory and the oneness are for the sake of the world (v. 23b).[62]

. . . so that the world may know
  that you have sent me
    and have loved them
even as you have loved me. 17:23b

In the parallel structure of vv. 20-23, both units (the petition, vv. 20-21, and the review, vv. 22-23) describe the church as a sign for the world. V. 21 said *that the world may believe.* When the thought returns in v. 23, Jesus prays *that the world may know.* Here again, believing is a kind of knowing, and knowledge is given as one consents in faith. The work of Jesus and the mission of the church intend that the un-knowing and disbelieving world may come to know and believe.

V. 21 said that the world must know *that you have sent me.* The parallel thought in v. 23b adds *and have loved them even as you have loved me.*

62. Brown, *Gospel,* 776, notes that a unity among believers which is to have an effect on the world must be a unity belonging to this life.

The world must come to know essential things — that God has sent Jesus, and that the church is loved as Jesus is loved. These are not bits of recognition which the world acquires casually, but they represent a miraculous reversal of awareness on the part of the world. The Jesus who was rejected comes to be known as God's own emissary and a bearer of divine love; the church, which is marginalized and whose members are at risk of being put to death in God's name (16:2) comes to be known as a special object of God's love. Paul Minear summarizes:

> The world that kills believers in presumed loyalty to God, ignorant that God has sent Jesus, will have its deepest convictions vetoed. God is in fact the Father who has sent Jesus, Jesus is the Son whom the Father has sent. The world is summoned to believe by the very witness whom it has murdered.[63]

Jesus' prayer moves out of the tight, compressed unit of vv. 20-23 and passes beyond the present world in a final passage of petition and review (vv. 24-26).

The conclusion of Jesus' prayer repeats some themes that were entered earlier. To identify some of the reiterated motifs:

those whom you have given me, v. 24a
  repeats vv. 2b and 6b.
my glory, v. 24a
  repeats vv. 1b and 5.
my glory which you have given me before the foundation of the world,

v. 24b
  repeats v. 5b.
these know that you have sent me, v. 25b
  repeats v. 3.
I made your name known to them, v. 26a
  repeats v. 6a.
The indwelling theme, v. 26b
  repeats v. 10.

Informally, the prayer, towards the end, circles back to earlier thought.

---

63. Paul Minear, "Evangelism, Ecumenism, and John Seventeeen," *Theology Today* 35, no. 1 (1978), 11.

Jesus' final petition for his people moves beyond the conflicts and ambiguities of their present life and speaks of their ultimate destiny:

> Father, I desire that those also,
> whom you have given me,
> may be with me where I am,
> to see my glory,
> which you have given me
> because you loved me
> before the foundation of the world. 17:24

The church is located firmly in the world, where it carries the truth the world needs to know (vv. 21, 23), and where, even though it is hated (v. 14), it lives in union with the Father and the Son (vv. 21-23), holding the gift of glory (v. 22). However, the community of Jesus' followers is not defined by the world. Rather, it is called by a divine summons to a destiny beyond the world. Jesus, as the Farewell Discourses have emphasized, leaves the world and goes to the Father. His people are, in God's final purpose, to be with him where he goes. The glory and the unity with the Father to which Jesus returns, having accomplished the Father's will, are to include the others whom he has been given. In the redemptive saga of the Fourth Gospel, although the coming was of the one, the return is of the one in union with the many.

The petition begins with a renewed address, *Father,* and with the request, *I desire (thelō), I will* or *I wish.* Jesus, as Raymond Brown comments, "majestically expresses his will. . . . In Johannine theology this 'I wish' is not presumptive, for Jesus' will is really that of the Father (4:34; 5:30; 6:38)."[64]

Jesus asks that his followers, who are the Father's gift to him, *may be with* him where he is. (Jesus' *where I am* is spoken as though he were already there — another mingling of tenses and times.) *With me where I am* uses again the johannine metaphor of location — where persons are from, where they are, and where they are going. Paul Minear remarks, "To be where the Father and the Son are is to become one with them."[65]

64. Brown, *Gospel,* 772.
65. Minear, *John: The Martyr's Gospel,* 130.

The phrase "be with me where I am" may suggest to some modern readers the category *Mitsein,* "being-with," which was developed in the philosophy of the eminent German philosopher, Martin Heidegger. Human life, as Heidegger sees it, is not so much a matter of being as of being-with. We are not alone when we are born; our being is received in being-with. Our life is always opened, limited, supported, thwarted, and defined by our being-with. The theologian Douglas Hall observes that this idea did not originate with Heidegger, but has roots in biblical anthropology. "To *be* in the Hebraic meaning is to be *with;* its antithesis is not non-being, but being-against or being-alone. It is not incidental that the New Testament names the incarnate God 'Emmanuel' ('God with us')."[66]

The term "with" has been theologically significant throughout the Fourth Gospel: *The Word was with God. . . . He was in the beginning with God* (1:1-2). *No one can do these signs unless God is with him* (3:2). *I shall be with you a little longer, and then . . .* (7:33). *He who sent me is with me* (8:29). *I speak of what I have seen with my Father* (8:38). *. . . that we may die with him* (11:16). *The poor you always have with you, but you do not always have me* (12:8). *The light is with you a little longer* (12:35).

The expression has been met in the Farewell events and discourses: *You have no part with me* (13:8). *Yet a little while I am with you* (13:33). *Have I been so long with you, and yet . . . ?* (14:9). *Another Counselor to be with you forever* (14:16). *He dwells with you, and will be in you* (14:17). *We will come to them and make our home with them* (14:23). *You also are to testify because you have been with me from the beginning* (15:27). *For the Father is with me* (16:32).

Being-with has already figured in Jesus' prayer: *With the glory which I had with you before the world was made* (17:5). *While I was with them, I kept them* (17:12). V. 24 of Jesus' prayer is the supreme instance of the *being-with* theme in the Fourth Gospel. Throughout the story, Jesus has been with others where they are. He has gone to a wedding of friends of his mother, healed the ruler's son and the lame man at the pool and the man born blind; he stood at the grave of Lazarus and wept. He loved his friends and washed their feet. Now Jesus is going to a glory that has been his and will be his again, and he prays that those he has loved may be with him.

In this verse Jesus asks that his followers may *see his glory.* Seeing is sometimes presented in the Fourth Gospel as a prelude to believing; here,

66. Douglas Hall, *Lighten Our Darkness* (Philadelphia: Westminster, 1976), 233, n. 36.

however, it is spoken of as virtually the supreme human good. The words anticipate a completeness of seeing beyond that which is possible under the conditions of existence in history. The Prologue to the Gospel reports that Jesus' people *have seen his glory* (1:14). Now 17:24 speaks of a fullness of seeing, the *visio dei,* which will be known when believers are with him in the place to which he has gone.

The glory is Jesus' glory, given to him in a love that was his *before the foundation of the world.* The primal relation of God to the Word was spoken of in the Prologue (1:1-3), and glory that is shared between Jesus and the Father was mentioned in 17:5. Here the relation is described in terms of love. Before there was a world, there was love in the interiority of God. As Helmut Thielicke put it:

> The New Testament expresses the fact that God is in himself the one who loves by saying that he loved the Son before the foundation of the world. This means that God's love is not a particular event which is triggered by the world. He does not love only from the time there is a world. He is love from all eternity in himself.[67]

In this passage, which envisions final things, Jesus returns to the idiom of the opening of the First Discourse (14:1-3); he anticipates others being with him where he is going. The church's present knowing, seeing and loving are pledge of an ultimate knowing, seeing and loving.

In the review passage with which the prayer ends, following the visionary themes that culminate in v. 24, Jesus returns to the situation of the disciples in stubborn, resistant historical reality. In the midst of an unknowing world, Jesus knows the Father; and his knowledge has been imparted to others; and the knowing is for the sake of love — the final reality.

Righteous Father, the world does not know you,
  but I know you;
  and these know that you have sent me.
I made your name known to them,
  and I will make it known,
    so that the love with which you have loved me
    may be in them,
      and I in them."

17:25-26

67. Helmut Thielicke, *The Evangelical Faith* (Grand Rapids: Eerdmans, 1974-82), 2.165.

After a new direct address, *Righteous Father,* the prayer changes from the idiom of *seeing* to terms of *knowing.* The verb *know (ginōskō)* is used in five consecutive clauses. Jesus declares first a negative, *The world does not know you* (cf. 8:19, 55; 15:21; 16:3). The world's ignorance is not a trifling unawareness. Although the world knows much, it is ignorant in a matter in which ignorance is fatal. Then the next two propositions speak positively about things that Jesus knows. In the midst of the unknowing world, Jesus has primary, direct knowledge of the Father, *But I know you.* He knows the Father as no other does. Then, speaking of his followers, Jesus says, *And these know that you have sent me.* Jesus' followers recognize the sentness of the sent one — a powerful, arresting knowledge. The next two clauses speak of Jesus as a bearer of knowledge. *I made your name known to them:* The thrust of Jesus' work was to make the Father apprehensible. To make the name known to his followers is to bring them within the shared divine life (see 1 John 3:1). He says *And I will make it known:* In his ministry on earth he has made the Father's name known (vv. 6, 26); he will make it known in the passion and resurrection (12:28); and he will continue to make it known in the church (14:20-24). What Jesus has done in bringing about a vital relation between the Father and his followers he will continue to do.

Jesus here credits the disciples with knowing that he was sent by the Father (cf. v. 8 and 16:30). His speech again implies that the disciples have not yet learned what he has tried to teach them of himself — that he has come from God and is going to God. They will come to know the full contour of Jesus' work when after his departure they themselves are united with the life of the Way who has gone to the Father. Meanwhile, knowing what they do, they have understood the heart of the matter. To put it so: God is not commonly accessible, but is known by self-manifestation — a self-manifestation that has been made in Jesus. To know that Jesus is sent by the Father, represents the Father, speaks for the Father, is the Father insofar as the Father is accessible to human apprehension, is to know the central thing. Knowing that, more can become known.

The knowing of Jesus' sentness leads to love, and love leads to indwelling: *so that the love with which you have loved me may be in them, and I in them.* Love is vital, self-imparting, self-communicating. Jesus' work comes to focus on a specific people; the name is communicated to *them.* The divine love, which has been in Jesus, is in them; Jesus himself is in them.

The prayer which began by speaking of an exchange of glory between Jesus and the Father (17:1b, cf. 13:31-32) ends by speaking of a love that is first shared between Jesus and the Father and which then includes those who are Jesus' own. Jesus is loved by the Father, reveals the Father, and makes known the divine name. He makes the name known so that believers may share in the very love by which he is loved. *The love with which you have loved me* — that love, and not another, secondary or derivative love — is in them. And Jesus himself — as the plenary expression in human terms, of the boundless divine love — dwells in them: *and I in them.*

In the lectionary. The Revised Common Lectionary appoints John 17:11b-19 for the last Sunday of Easter in Year B and John 17:20-26 for the same Sunday in Year C. These passages, like the prayer as a whole, are thought-filled, inward, non-narrative, and not easy to read aloud effectively. Nevertheless, there is much in both of these portions that is central to the New Testament presentation of Jesus and the church and that virtually asks to be preached.

A leading theme of the Year B passage is the difficult vocation of the church — a people which takes its rise from the mission of Jesus and which is destined to be with him beyond history, but which is now firmly located in the world, where its tasks are to worship, to witness and to minister. When it is about its appointed tasks, it stands in uneasy relation with the general society which lives in ignorance of the true God and sets its priorities accordingly. The church's situation, which is described as "in, but not of," can create uncertainty and painful tension.

The world, its life ordered apart from God, can be powerful and attractive. Moreover, the world, since it is God's world, can make just demands. Most Christians serve God in considerable measure through their contribution to the life of the commonweal. The world's social, cultural and intellectual achievements are God's gifts which can draw out the best in conscientious persons. And yet the world — taking its own way and asking its own loyalties — has little check against its tendency to make total claims that only God can justly make. Can believers find the discrimination and the courage to hold the *in the world* up against the *but not of the world* — or perhaps the courage to be more truly "in" by being somewhat less "of"? The theme calls for discernment and for pastoral preaching.

The passage appointed for Year C contains the strongest statement in the New Testament in behalf of unity among Christians. Probably no text is more often quoted in support of ecumenicity. Many persons who over the years have cared deeply about church unity, if they were asked why they identified so passionately with this cause, would have replied "obedience."

John 17 speaks in behalf of Christian oneness theologically, not sociologically or strategically. Christ seems to say that a church that is not one is a self-contradiction. No Christian who takes the New Testament seriously can acquiesce in a divided church. Jesus' prayer says that the church's unity arises from its participation in the oneness-in-love that persists between himself and the Father. Its unity comes to it from beyond itself and is to be discovered and maintained. The church's dividedness traces in part to a history of idealism and a quest for doctrinal integrity, but it traces also to arrogance, ideology, and collective self-deception. Time in itself did not make things as they are; history was turned in the directions it took by ideas, intentions, and a grasp for power and dominance. Time in itself will not undo the past. Yet in the midst of stubborn human folly, the church's redemptive message should give it an interior resource for addressing the sin of its own dividedness. Perversely, however, the Christian message itself can be made a theological support for division. History can move toward the healing of old divisions, while history can at the same time solidify existing divisions and even create new separations.

The prayer of John 17 does not go far towards solving the difficult issues that divide the Body of Christ. Despite Jesus' prayer and the generations of devoted efforts towards church unity, it remains the case that most churches are able to live, to a great extent, as though no other church existed or needed to exist. Jesus' plea "that they may be one" does not in itself help a congregation be cordial to another down the street which may travel under a different name. Nor does Jesus' prayer guide the wide-ranging conversations that now go on between denominations or confessional groups. And it gives no guidance in the even more complex matter of Christian relation with other faiths. But, coming on the authority it does, Jesus' prayer that all may be one holds Christians to the issue.

Essay: Glory and Glorifying

Glory, the word and the idea: "Glory" (Gr. *doxa*) is an organizing term of biblical literature; the word "glory" carries an unusual history; and the term is used in distinctive ways in the Fourth Gospel. In Greek, outside the writings that were influenced by Jewish thought, *doxa* meant "opinion" (whence "orthodoxy," or "right opinion"). It could also mean the opinion others have of one, one's reputation. But in the Greek translation of the Jewish Scriptures, *doxa* was used for the Hebrew *kabod*, which originally meant "weight," but was often used, as Rabbi Heschel remarked, in the metaphoric sense of "the weight a person carries, one's status, importance, worth, impressiveness, majesty."[68] Rabbi Heschel spoke of persons who "have presence," whose outwardness communicates something of their indwelling power or greatness. Hence *kabod* came to mean the honor or the esteem which was one's due and in which one was held.

68. Abraham J. Heschel, *God in Search of Man: A Philosophy of Judaism* (New York: Farrar, Strauss and Giroux, 1951), 82.

In Jewish thought, glory belongs primally to God alone, as Isaiah 42:8 says, *My glory I give to no other.* This glory refers, in G. B. Caird's words, to "God's own essential worth, greatness, power, majesty, everything in him which calls forth man's adoring reverence."[69] However, the divine glory is outgoing, expressing itself in active power. In Psalm 29 it is compared to a violent storm which uproots trees and strips the bark from them. *The God of glory thunders* (v. 3). In a distinctive development of Jewish thought, *doxa* came to speak of the divine presence as light or unapproachable brightness. A visible radiance was associated with the giving of the law (Exod. 16:10; 24:16; 40:34-35) and with the visions of some of the prophets (Isa. 6:3; Ezek. 8:4 and others). Dodd says that the term denotes "the manifestation of God's being, nature and presence, in a manner accessible to human experience . . . conceived in the form of radiance, splendor, or dazzling light."[70] In the imagination of Israel, light enclosed the very mystery of God. Christopher Evans remarks that God's glory (together with God's name) is "the nearest that the Old Testament had come to an ontological way of speaking. It denotes, without further specification, the being or life of God."[71]

The early Christians were heirs of these terms and meanings, which, to their minds, readily spoke of Christ and redemption in him. Light suffuses the nativity story in Luke (2:9-14), the Transfiguration incident in the Synoptic Gospels (Matt. 17:1-8; Mark 9:2-8; Luke 9:28-36), the conversion of Paul (Acts 9:1-9; 22:6-11; 26:13), and the visions of heaven (Rev. 1:12-16). Paul speaks of the primal light of creation which shines in the face of Jesus Christ (2 Cor. 4:6). Indeed, the biblical message could be put in terms of *doxa:* A glory in God, eternal and irrepressible, creates and creates anew. It flashes out in the history of Israel. It is made apprehensible in the Incarnate Word (John 1:14). An intended human glory is lost, but is restored and is now held in pledge. Glory is lodged in mystery, yet makes itself known. The glory which is dimly apprehended now will be shown in the end and celebrated in heaven and earth. Bishop Newbigin once said, "To interpret the word 'glory' is to interpret the whole Gospel."[72]

69. G. B. Caird, "The Glory of God in the Fourth Gospel: An Exercise in Biblical Semantics,"*NTS* 15 (1969), 267.

70. Dodd, *Interpretation of the Fourth Gospel,* 206.

71. Evans, "Christ at Prayer," 588.

72. Newbigin, *The Light Has Come,* 224.

Distribution in the Fourth Gospel

The noun "glory" *(doxa)* and the verb "glorify" *(doxazein)* are together used more than forty times in the Fourth Gospel, more frequently than in any other book in the New Testament. Sixteen instances fall in chapters 13–17 (eight more fall in the transitional chapter 12).

In view of the frequency with which the word appears and the importance of the imagery of light in the Fourth Gospel (at least in the first half of the book in which Jesus is often spoken of as light and as one who gives light), it is striking that the Fourth Gospel tells the story of Jesus without any visible manifestations of light. There is no glory-filled nativity story (as there is in Luke) and no Transfiguration. (Imagery of brightness is at least suggested when in 12:41 the Evangelist speaks of Jesus' glory which Isaiah saw in the Temple. He refers to the radiant vision in Isaiah 6:1-5.) The glory which is said to suffuse Jesus' entire life is consistently veiled in the flesh of the Incarnate Word and is discernible only to faith (1:14). The Fourth Gospel presents the story paradoxically; Jesus' glory is chiefly demonstrated in his self-giving in the cross — glory in the absence of apparent glory.

In the Farewell Discourses, the uses of the term *glory* cluster at the beginning of the passage and at the end: five fall in the closely worded "prologue" to the Book of Glory (13:31-32), and eight in the prayer in chapter 17. In addition, the verb "glorify" appears in 14:13; 15:8 and 16:14. In the first twelve chapters of the Gospel, of the 19 instances of the term, 13 are the noun, *doxa,* while in chapters 13–17, thirteen of the 16 instances are the verb (*doxazein,* glorify). (This distribution might suggest that in johannine thought "glory" and "glorification" are words of the church, so it is unexpected that neither the noun nor the verb appears in the johannine epistles.)

Glorifying and Receiving Glory

Jesus has spoken of persons who seek to gather honor to themselves (5:41, 44; cf. 7:18). "Glory," so understood, refers to the power one holds, the goods one possesses, or the recognition one has gathered. The word carries the ambiguities of *doxa* in a sin-structured world. The pursuit of glory for oneself suggests self-aggrandizement and the diminishment of others.

But when Jesus speaks of his own glory, he describes an exchange between himself and the Father; glory is not sought or claimed except in the mutuality of the Father and the Son in which glory is given and glory is received:

> Now the Son of Man has been glorified,
> and God has been glorified in him. 13:31
>
> Glorify your Son
> that your Son may glorify you. 17:1
>
> I glorified you . . .
> And now, Father, glorify me. 17:4-5

Jesus as the Father's agent receives glory. But the glory he receives is the glory he shares with the one by whom he is sent. (The passive voice, *The Child of Humanity has been glorified,* 13:31a, indicates that he has been glorified by God.) Commenting on this passage, Calvin said, "The Father did not seek His glory from the death of the Son without making the Son a partaker of that same glory."[73] Yet in the story of Jesus, God is glorified (13:31b); by discharging his commission to bring eternal life, Jesus has glorified the Father (17:4).

The two are not rival glories. What is given to one is not taken from the other. The glories stand within a free, un-self-regarding exchange. As G. B. Caird puts it, "The glory of Jesus is the glory of God himself. Where Jesus is active, God is also at work, and where Jesus manifests his glory, the glory of God is also to be seen."[74]

This equal and generous giving and receiving of glory offers an implicit critique of an individualistic, competitive society in which glory is likely to be thought of in quantifiable terms. Glory must be acquired at someone else's cost; winners are covered with glory, but losers with disappointment or even shame.

In present-day society, we most often attach the idea of "glory" to things like competitions in which a successful group or individual reaps glory. Others can share vicariously in that glory, as whole schools or cities, parties, or nations can identify with a victory and say "We won." However,

73. John Calvin, *The Gospel According to St. John, 11–21* (Calvin's Commentaries 5; Grand Rapids: Eerdmans, 1979), 68.

74. Caird, "Glory of God," 270.

such victories are usually accompanied by disappointment and diminishment on the part of those who lose out and those who may be made to feel that they let others down. In our flawed world and our skeptical age can one think of glory in ways that illustrate mutuality of interest between two active parties?

Partial analogues for exchanged glory come to mind. As a troubled person works though an emotional problem with a sensitive counselor, both persons give, and both receive. In scholarly or research teamwork or in artistic collaboration, all take personal satisfaction in a result, knowing that no one could have been effective without the others. Or one may think of a memorable performance by a choral group. Or perhaps one should simply think of companions enjoying mountains or the sea together. Such things may illustrate touches of splendor in which there are no losers, but in giving, each participant receives.

Glorifying in Jesus' Redemptive Work

In the Farewell chapters, divine glory is not described as abstract or static, but (as the preponderance of verbs over nouns might suggest), it is active. As Christopher Evans says, it "always includes the element of effective power by which God shows himself to be God."[75]

The prophet Isaiah described divine deliverance as a burst of light. Israel's return from captivity was as the rising of the sun, *Then shall your light break forth like the dawn* (Isa. 58:8), and *Arise, shine, for your light has come, and the glory of the Lord has risen upon you* (Isaiah 60:1). It is the way of light to be unconfined, to enter wherever it is admitted.

Such imagery from the prophets was at hand to describe Jesus' redemptive work as divine glory in action: *I glorified you on earth by finishing the work you gave me to do* (17:4). Although Jesus' whole mission was a demonstration of glory (1:14), the Evangelist sees his glory concentrating in the passion events, as when 13:31 speaks of glorifying *now* and 17:1 speaks of Jesus' *hour* to be glorified. To cite Calvin's comments again, "The glory of God shines, indeed, in all creatures on high and below, but never more brightly than in the cross."[76]

Whether glory is given by the Father, or is received by the Son, or is

75. Evans, "Christ at Prayer," 588.
76. Calvin, *Gospel,* 68.

given to Jesus by the Paraclete, or is shared with believers, one observes, following Caird, "the dominant christological sense which *doxa* has throughout this Gospel."[77] The whole work of the Redeemer is from glory, through glory and to glory. Appold summarizes:

> Jesus prays that he be glorified with his preexistent glory (17:5). That glory has already been singularly manifested in the incarnation so that those who have seen the Incarnate One can respond that they have seen the glory of the only begotten Son of the Father (1:14). That same glory was made known in demonstrative epiphanies of power through Jesus' ministry. Now in the impending hour of the cross, it received further expression. Not even Jesus' death disrupts his oneness with the Father. His death is rather the hour of glorification and return to the Father. For Jesus there is no abdication of preexistent glory which is then resumed at a later point. Jesus' glorification on the cross is with the same glory that had always been his. There is no qualitative difference, no change in essence. The Incarnate One, the Crucified One, is the Glorified One because Jesus was and always is one with the Father. Clearly here is a *theologia crucis* that is a *theologia gloriae*.[78]

Glory in the Church

Jesus' whole work is for the sake of human redemption, and redemption is an imparting of glory. Michael Ramsey was quoted earlier describing the mystery of the church as "the mystery of the participation of men and women in the glory which is Christ's."[79] Jesus is glorified in bringing into being a people who share his life (17:10) and to whom he gives his glory (17:22). The Father is glorified in a "fruitful" church (15:8).

Glory, in biblical imagery, commonly has an eschatological reference. It speaks of final things, of things to be revealed, or of that which is true of God, but hidden — hidden, yet apprehensible in the midst of the prevailing darkness and declarable in anticipation of a splendor that will be fully manifest at the end. Thus it is a striking instance of johannine presentism to find the claim that glory is manifested in Jesus, in Jesus'

77. Caird, "Glory of God," 270.

78. Appold, *Oneness Motif,* 229-30.

79. Ramsey, *Glory of God,* 87. The quoted text is altered.

death, and *now,* and that his glory is given to the church and is encountered as the community bears fruit, lives in unity, and finds its prayers answered.

Yet this present sharing in glory between Jesus and his people is a pledge of the ultimate destiny of "his own" who Jesus says will live with him and behold his glory (17:24).

AFTERWORD:
The Farewell Chapters and the Life of the Church

One thinks of urgent human issues — many of them perennial, and most of them, ancient or modern, given intensity by today's world. Then, with the pain and trauma, the psychic waste, the moral and spiritual conflicts of the twenty-first century in mind, one turns to the Fourth Gospel and in it to Jesus' final counsel to his followers. And when one does so, Jesus' words can seem isolated and self-enclosed. What does he have to say about suffering? He does not mention the word. He does not anatomize the conflict of the human heart with itself as Jeremiah and Paul do. The Fourth Gospel presents belief and unbelief as simple moral alternatives, or if the writer recognizes complexities in faith and doubt, he does not speak about them here. This Gospel does not describe the stir of God in judgment and redemption in the affairs of people and nations; the prophets' passion for justice is missing. The Fourth Gospel lacks the intellectual rigor of Romans or the cosmic sweep of Ephesians. Its language, while effective for its purpose, is oddly limited — almost an anti-language. It is hard to think of an important writing that seems less concerned to commend its own relevance.

Although there are many things about which modern-day readers seek counsel that are of no concern to this Evangelist, he did not write for our peculiarly tormented cultural moment. If we can imagine him in dialogue with modern readers, he will not invite us to set questions and then give him high marks if he answers them well and low marks if he does not. Even though (as earlier chapters of this study have indicated) he wrote in his own day for conditions of extremity, he left the connections between his writing and the circumstances which gave rise to it largely unexpressed. His agenda as he writes is his, not ours, and he might justly ask to be taken on his terms.

Even if it is granted that things we might legitimately seek we will not find in the Fourth Gospel, it is fair to guess that over the centuries few sympathetic readers have thought of the Fourth Gospel in terms of its limitations. Rather, they have recognized this book as one of the supreme expressions of the Christian message and a central account of Christian existence. It opens the world that Christians inhabit. If we may think of things we might well seek which these pages do not supply, it is also fair to ask what faith and life would be like if we did not have this Gospel and in it Jesus' Farewell.

These final Discourses do not commend themselves by meeting opposing ideas or arguing a case for Jesus and for faith. Their author, if he could know our modern questions or our hunger for relevance, might think we have set our requirements too narrowly. The life-giving "word" to which he bears witness is not an answer to a body of human questions. It is an affirmation, rooted in divine disclosure, by which human questions themselves can be judged, deepened and extended. This Evangelist insists that humanity on its own — in his term, "the world" — misjudges its own needs; it is a stranger to its own heart and hence to its own most urgent questions. The Evangelist's work sets our human living and dying, our clarity and confusion, our suffering and joy, our ultimate meaning and destiny in the context of an overarching redemptive myth.

That divine saga, which begins in glory and ends in glory (17:5, 24), centers in one, space-time-specific person, Jesus, son of Joseph and Mary. This Jesus moved among his friends and among the ordinary people of his nation. His father and mother were locally known (6:42). People turned to him for counsel and for healing. He claimed that his life and his mission were rooted transparently in God. He offered light and life. He invited trust in himself. He was accepted, and he was rejected. He was a figure of history, but, as the Fourth Gospel has it, he was not confined to the account that history could give of him. Believers (not at the time, to be sure, "but afterward") saw him as the one in whom God was working under the conditions of human history to do for humanity what only the Word made flesh could do. He was the central figure in God's long-laid purpose to bring flawed humanity into union with the Creator. He was God's challenge to the alien forces that held the world in darkness. This central figure, even though he was from God, was unwelcome among "his own people" (1:11). The darkness resisted the presence of the light. He was occasion of offense, but occasion of life as well. His presence posed deep alternatives. One had to come to terms with him.

This rejected Jesus created a new people. Through his love to the uttermost he brought those who believed in him out of alienation into union with himself and through him into union with God. Entering this union was a turn-about so radical that it could be described as being born in the midst of life — in the midst of a life so separated from its own truth as to be a life-which-is-death. This Jesus was the one in whom the darkened, sin-structured world, although it remained powerful, had been overcome, and Jesus' people lived on in it, but under the sign of his victory.

Jesus has departed to the Father, and the world no longer encounters him, but it finds in its midst a unique society — a people under the Word, taught by the divine Spirit, representing an alternative reality, the sign of the myth which is true, the witness to Jesus and the offense and the salvation that center in him. The community of faith lives from ultimate things which are present and apprehensible here and now. In encountering this community of Jesus, the world encounters Jesus; and in encountering Jesus, it encounters God (13:20).

This faith community has a distinctive interior life. It lives in communion with the risen Jesus — loving and being loved, knowing and being known, listening and speaking, bonded in lasting friendship, holding to truth and being held by it, rejoicing when there is no apparent cause to rejoice, dwelling in God and being indwelt by God. The community's life is not exempt from ambiguity and from pain, but it is touched with splendor, for Jesus' people have been given the glory that the Father gave to Jesus. Without these richly developed, highly personalized Farewell chapters, how much less the church would understand than it does of its own hidden interior life!

As the believers in Jesus saw it, the world was darkened, diminished, alienated — unable to remedy or even to recognize its own condition. Indeed, heedless of Jesus, of Jesus' people, or of God, it plunged ahead confident of its own rightness. In first-century Hellenistic society, a small struggling group loyal to Jesus and committed to love for one another, walked to the beat of a different drummer; and through an original, faithful prophetic spokesman it left this somewhat isolated, yet deeply faith-informing record — a record which invites its readers into the life it presents.

The strange, new, exotic community and the audacious faith it claimed were, despite all appearances, the judgment and the redemption of its own age and every age. That peculiar, generally unstructured, "sectarian," ingrown community of the Beloved Disciple did not seek by argument to make itself understood by its own age — let alone by ours. Yet it held and bore witness to the truth which was God's word to every age — a word which opened the final dimensions of existence, which separated and united, which brought light where there had been darkness. It asked "whoever would" to come to terms with that truth — a thing that no age could do if the truth of God as it had been shown in Jesus were not held faithfully, in life and in death, by those who knew themselves called by it.

Index of Modern Authors

Index of Scripture and Other Ancient Sources

NON-CANONICAL WRITINGS